The selected papers of
Wolfgang Köhler

WOLFGANG KÖHLER IN 1957

The selected papers of
Wolfgang Köhler

EDITED BY MARY HENLE
The Graduate Faculty
New School for Social Research

LIVERIGHT
New York

WITH TRANSLATIONS BY HELMUT E. ADLER, ERICH GOLDMEIER,
AND MARY HENLE

*"Human perception": translation of La perception
humaine,* Journal de psychologie normale et
pathologique, *1930, 27, 5-30. Translation copyright ©
1971 by Mary Henle*

*"Methods of psychological research with apes":
translation of Die Methoden der psychologischen
Forschung an Affen. In Emil Abderhalden (Hrsg.),*
Handbuch der biologischen Arbeitsmethoden, *1921
(Abt. 6, Teil D). Translation copyright © 1971 by
Mary Henle*

*"Psychology and natural science": translation of
Psychologie und Naturwissenschaft.* Proceedings of the
15th International Congress of Psychology, Brussels,
1957, 37-50. Translation copyright © 1971 by Mary Henle

*"On the problem of regulation": translation of Zum
Problem der Regulation.* Wilhelm Roux' Archiv fur
Entwicklungsmechanik der Organismen, *1927, 112,
315-332. Translation copyright © 1971 by Mary Henle
and Erich Goldmeier*

*Standard Book Number: 87140–505–9
Library of Congress Catalog Card Number: 79–113054
1.987654321*
DESIGNED BY BETTY BINNS

Manufactured in the United States of America

Wissen Sie eine Antwort, meine Freunde?
Nein, auch Sie nicht. Aber heute ist mehr Glauben
in inständigen Fragen als in irgend einer Antwort.

WOLFGANG KÖHLER

Contents

Preface

THIS collection covers the time span from 1913 to 1967—almost the span of Wolfgang Köhler's professional life. It starts with the earliest formulation of the point of departure of Gestalt psychology, the rejection of the constancy hypothesis ("On unnoticed sensations and errors of judgment") and extends to his latest overview of this approach to psychology ("Gestalt psychology"). Several criteria have been used in the selection of papers from Professor Köhler's voluminous writings. In addition to general papers on Gestalt theory, this book contains articles in many of the fields to which he has made contributions: perception, thinking, values, brain physiology, animal psychology, anthropology, and others. His more technical experimental papers have not been included, to make the collection more accessible to the general reader in psychology and related disciplines; but the results of many of the investigations are summarized in the more general articles. In the selection, material was favored that is not easily available to the psychologist. The German papers included here have not heretofore been translated into English. Of the articles originally written in English, two are previously unpublished and a number of others appear in places which psychologists could easily miss. For the same reason, with one exception, papers have been excluded that have appeared in other collections (*Source Book of Gestalt Psychology*, edited by W. D. Ellis, *Documents of Gestalt Psychology*, edited by M. Henle, etc.). Limitations of space have made it necessary to exclude certain papers I would have liked to include. In particular, the article "Zur Boltzmannschen Theorie des zweiten Hauptsatzes" is perhaps the most impressive illustration of Professor Köhler's contributions to natural science. It was omitted from a book whose content is largely taken from psychology and its immediate neighbors; it is to be hoped that it will be reprinted in another publication. While the reader may criticize the omission of certain papers, I cannot imagine that he will regret any of the selections.

This book was originally planned as an eightieth birthday present for Professor Köhler. Although he himself made several suggestions for its contents, he did not live to see it completed. I only hope that he would have liked it.

A number of people have generously helped with this book. I am grateful to Professor Solomon E. Asch of the Institute for Cognitive Studies, Rutgers University, with whom I had the privilege of discussing the choice of papers at the outset of this project, and who made valuable suggestions; he also very kindly undertook the preparation of figures. To Professor Paul Weiss of Rockefeller University and Professor Richard Held of the Massachusetts Institute of Technology I am grateful for assistance in the selection of papers in their fields. My warm thanks go to Dr. Erich Goldmeier and to Mrs. Lili Köhler for many hours of careful work and very many helpful suggestions that have improved several of the translations. I am grateful to Professor Edwin B. Newman of Harvard University, who compiled the bibliography of Professor Köhler's writings that appears in this book, and to Miss Annelise Katz for her invaluable help in preparing the bibliography. Finally, the unfailing patience and good will of my publisher, Mr. Arthur Pell, have helped to bring this volume to completion.

MARY HENLE

Ridgefield, Connecticut
January 21, 1971

*The selected papers of
Wolfgang Köhler*

Wolfgang Köhler

IN one direction after another, Wolfgang Köhler broke new ground in psychology. With Max Wertheimer and Kurt Koffka, he was a founder of Gestalt psychology. The thinking of this group, and particularly of Köhler, its foremost experimentalist, has strongly affected psychology for more than half a century.

Köhler was born in Reval, Estonia, on January 21, 1887, the child of German parents. When he was six, the family returned to Germany, settling in Wolfenbüttel. He attended the universities of Tübingen, Bonn, and then Berlin, receiving the Ph.D. there in 1909. His early studies in audition marked the beginning of an extraordinarily productive scientific career. In 1909 he became an assistant in the Psychological Institute at Frankfurt a/M, where began the collaboration with Wertheimer and Koffka. Among the contributions of this period was a paper, "Über unbemerkte Empfindungen und Urteilstäuschungen" (1913) which constituted an examination and rejection—on logical and empirical grounds—of the then prevailing elemen-

With minor changes, from *Year Book of the American Philosophical Society*, 1968, 139–145. Reprinted by permission of the author and publisher.

taristic psychology. Köhler's frequent reviews in the *Zeitschrift für Psychologie*, written during these same years, likewise contain lively criticisms of traditional conceptions.

The collaboration with Wertheimer and Koffka was temporarily interrupted when, in 1913, Köhler became director of the anthropoid station that the Prussian Academy of Sciences had established on the island of Tenerife. World War I kept him there until 1920. In the isolation of this period—an isolation which made it a considerable undertaking even to obtain current scientific books—he developed his thinking in significant and original directions. His work *The Mentality of Apes* is the best-known product of this period; it has correctly been described as a turning point in the psychology of thinking. It combines a freshness of observation with a gift for simple and elegant experimentation. A student of Max Planck in Berlin, Köhler also began to reflect on the relations between field theory in physics and the findings and theories of Gestalt psychology. Out of these reflections came *Die physischen Gestalten in Ruhe und im stationären Zustand.*

On his return to Germany in 1920, Köhler became acting director of the Psychological Institute at the University of Berlin. He was professor of psychology at Göttingen for a year, and in 1922 he was called to Berlin as professor of philosophy and director of the Institute. The period from 1922 to 1935 was one of lively development of Gestalt psychology. An unusually able and eager group of students came to study with Köhler; also with Wertheimer (who remained in Berlin until 1929, when he returned to Frankfurt) and Kurt Lewin. The *Psychologische Forschung* was founded by Köhler and his friends; it contains much of the record of Gestalt psychology during these years. In the pages of this journal one can watch the penetration of Gestalt theory into one problem area after another. In addition to experimental studies, Köhler's own contributions to the *Forschung* continue the polemics with the traditional psychology. His criticisms were directed, in particular, against atomistic conceptions and against attempts to explain away puzzling psychological phenomena by means of empiristic hypotheses, themselves never subject to test.

Köhler twice interrupted his work in Germany with periods of teaching in the United States. He was a visiting professor at Clark University in 1925–1926, William James Lecturer at Harvard in 1934–1935, and a visiting professor at the University of Chicago in 1935. He became well acquainted with American psychology; his *Gestalt Psychology*, first published in 1929, was written in English, "for America."

In 1935, when the Nazi regime had become unbearable, Köhler emigrated to the United States, where he became professor of psychology, then research professor of philosophy and psychology, at Swarthmore College. During this period, he published his William James lectures as *The Place of Value in a World of Facts* (1938). *Dynamics in Psychology* (1940) followed, again making explicit the relation between field theory in physics and Gestalt psychology. This volume contains the first description of a line of investigation that again broke new ground: figural aftereffects. A monograph on figural aftereffects, written in collaboration with Hans Wallach, was published in 1944 in the *Proceedings of the American Philosophical Society*. This investigation, starting from a simple perceptual observation, arrives at a specific hypothesis about the cortical processes corresponding to form perception and tests this hypothesis in psychological experimentation. Such moving back and forth from psychological observation to physiological consequences and back to psychological test is basic to Köhler's thinking. The work on figural aftereffects stimulated a great deal of research both in this country and abroad; it led Köhler himself to the direct investigation of the cortical currents he had earlier hypothesized as corresponding to perception. One by-product of this work was a new theory of attention.

In 1958 Köhler retired from Swarthmore to continue his scientific writing and research. Moving to New Hampshire, he continued his experimental work at Dartmouth College. He delivered the Gifford Lectures in Edinburgh in 1958. Another notable series of lectures, the Herbert Langfeld Lectures, was given in Princeton in 1966; they have been published as *The Task of Gestalt Psychology* (1969). In between, he lectured widely. He made almost yearly visits to the Free University of

Berlin, acted as adviser to the faculty there, kept the psychologists in touch with American psychology, collaborated with them in research, and engaged in lively discussions with them. He continued to develop the theory of figural aftereffects. He conducted new investigations in memory, in depth perception, and in other fields. He died on June 11, 1967.

During his distinguished career, many honors came to Köhler. He was a member of the American Philosophical Society, the National Academy of Sciences, and the American Academy of Arts and Sciences. He received honorary degrees from the Universities of Pennsylvania, Chicago, Freiburg, Münster, and Uppsala, Sweden, and from Swarthmore and Kenyon colleges. He was an Ehrenbürger of the Free University of Berlin, an honor bestowed on very few others—the only Americans being John F. Kennedy and Paul Hindemith. He received the Distinguished Scientific Contributions Award of the American Psychological Association in 1956, and was to have been awarded its gold medal in 1967; he was president of the Association in 1959. He received the Warren Medal from the Society of Experimental Psychologists and the Wundt Medal from the Deutsche Gesellschaft für Psychologie. The latter organization made him its honorary president on the occasion of his eightieth birthday.

Psychology, at the time of the emergence of Gestalt psychology, was deeply involved in what, in Germany, was called the crisis of science. Science seemed unable to deal with—seemed even to lack interest in—significant human problems. One popular solution had been the abandonment of natural science altogether, the adoption of the approach of *Geisteswissenschaft,* of understanding (as opposed to explaining) psychology. Wertheimer and Köhler proposed that the difficulty was not with science itself, but with the current conception of natural science among psychologists, an elementaristic conception. The Gestalt psychologists began to build a psychology along nonatomistic lines. Köhler, in particular, saw Gestalt psychology as an application of field theory, as developed in physics, to problems of psychology. He was impressed by the similarities he saw between the behavior of perceptual organizations and of physical systems: the tendency of both, for example, to reach as simple an organization as possible, the dependence of part processes on the system as a whole, and so on. From an examination of such physical *Gestalten*, it was but a step to consider the physical processes that might take place in that most complex and interesting physical system, the brain. Isomorphism, the hypothesis that there are structural similarities between phenomenal events and the corresponding brain processes, had already been adumbrated by Wertheimer in the paper on apparent movement that had launched Gestalt psychology. In Köhler's hands, this hypothesis took on more specific meaning, first in *Die physischen Gestalten*; and he successively clarified it until it became a powerful research tool—leading finally to his recording of cortical currents during organized perception.

Köhler's work stands at the meeting place of physics, biology, and psychology. In physics itself, in addition to *Die physischen Gestalten,* he wrote a remarkable paper on the Boltzmann theory of the second law of thermodynamics. In biology, he entered the then current controversy as to the nature of regulation. His examination of the theory of evolution clarified for psychologists the relation between its principle of invariance and that of change. Here he broke out of the dichotomy of nativism-empiricism, calling attention to a third category of factors, those concerned with action, that organisms share with all of nature. Neglect of these factors has, as he said, adapting an old quotation, long led us to try to play *Hamlet* without the Prince of Denmark.

Köhler's work, in addition, clarifies relations of psychology to philosophy. He constantly tried to bring to bear on the mind-body problem issues that could be handled empirically. His searching analysis of values led him to reject the position that values are "merely subjective" and to discuss them in terms of requiredness, as this term was used in natural science. His work thus offers an alternative to the relativism that long dominated discussions of value.

His relation to phenomenology is everywhere apparent. "There seems to be a single starting point for psychology, exactly as for all the other sciences," he wrote, "the world as we find it, naïvely and uncritically." A corrective was here offered for the neglect of direct experience by behaviorists and the distrust of it that was one effect of psychoanalytic theory.

Köhler had a lively interest in anthropology. His relation to the arts, particularly to music, was strong. In both fields his work contributes to a clarification of problems. His informal lectures dealt with such topics as education, impartial empiricism, the naturalistic interpretation of man, phenomenalistic and causal representative theories, humanism and scientism. Thus he pushed his thinking into disciplines related to psychology and enriched his psychological thought from these neighboring fields.

He was widely recognized as one of the most outstanding experimenters psychology has ever had. His experiments—like his writing—possess the elegance of simplicity. One after another of his students and younger colleagues (this writer included) report that they have learned from him the importance of simplifying. If you want a clear answer from nature, you must ask a clear question, he would say. And if you want to measure, be clear first of all what it is you are measuring. He had no patience with measurement in psychology for the sake of measurement; premature quantification would never give psychology the scientific stature of physics. But to reject premature measurement was not to condone laziness either in research methodology or in thinking. When, for example, his own research carried him to problems of brain physiology, he acquired the necessary skills—though his early electrodes, as he once remarked, were as temperamental as adolescent girls. And he never gave up experimental work. At the time of his death, he was just preparing a new set of experiments on the nature of associations.

Wolfgang Köhler once wrote that it is the obligation of each scientific generation to make explicit the implicit assumptions of its predecessors. His own work shows a truly remarkable ability to make explicit his own implicit assumptions. The seeds of his later work are to be found in his earlier writings. Reading *Gestalt Psychology* now, for example, one has the impression that he knew things he could not possibly have known, since the work had not yet been done. There is thus an unusual consistency in the development of his thinking, a productive consistency. From his theory of perception, for example, he was led to a theory of memory processes and of associations.

"All his life," wrote Hans-Lukas Teuber, "Wolfgang Köhler saw things that all of us could have seen but did not see." Each problem he touched seemed to come to life—even the time error in psychophysical procedures, which had been no more than a nuisance to earlier psychologists, acquired significance and theoretical interest when Köhler began to think about it. It is impossible to estimate the amount of psychological research that was done around the issues raised by Gestalt psychology, and especially by Köhler, the great experimenter in this remarkable group.

Köhler was a man of quiet courage. In April, 1933, he wrote an article for *Die Deutsche Allgemeine Zeitung* which was to be the last anti-Nazi article published openly in Germany under National Socialism. Speaking of his friends who had not joined the Nazi movement, he said: "Never have I seen finer patriotism than theirs." He continued:

> During our conversation, one of my friends reached for the Psalms and read: "The Lord is my shepherd, I shall not want. . . ." He read the 90th Psalm and said, "It is hard to think of a German who has been able to move human hearts more deeply and so to console those who suffer. And these words we have received from the Jews."
>
> Another reminded me that never had a man struggled more nobly for a clarification of his vision of the world than the Jew Spinoza, whose wisdom Goethe admired. . . .
>
> It seems that nobody can think of the great work of Heinrich Hertz without an almost affectionate admiration for him. And Hertz had Jewish blood.
>
> One of my friends told me: The greatest German experimental physicist of the present time is Franck; many believe that he is the greatest experimental physicist of our age. Franck is a Jew, an unusually kind human being. . . .

When the article appeared, it was expected that Köhler would be arrested by the Nazis. The Köhlers and a group from the Psychologische Institut—Duncker, von Lauenstein, von Restorff, and others—spent the night playing chamber music. (The Gestapo always appeared at 4:00 A.M.) But no one came.

As a man, Wolfgang Köhler possessed the same simplicity —the elegant and sophisticated simplicity—the same directness, the same dignity that his thinking did. He had a quality that gave every human contact a special character: everyone with a Köhler story to tell—colleague, friend, laboratory technician, student— cherished it as a treasured possession. Despite his many honors, he remained modest. He enjoyed life—and he enriched it by his work and by his personality. Hans Hörmann speaks for both sides of the Atlantic when he writes:

> Honors come to anyone who, like Wolfgang Köhler, has deci-sively influenced the history of science. We had much more reason to honor him. He showed us the potentialities of the human being, combining modesty with dignity, sensitivity with perseverance, reserve in personal relations with zest in scien-tific work, goodness in relation to men with hardness against what he recognized was not right, as he showed in his un-compromising rejection of the national socialist regime, which so blatantly contradicted his conception of the dignity of man and the freedom of inquiry.
>
> For his work, all of psychology is grateful to him. We who were privileged to know him are still more grateful to him for showing us what a man could be.[1]

MARY HENLE

[1] H. Hörmann. Wolfgang Köhler zum Gedenken. *Psychologische Forschung*, 1967, 31, xvii.

one

GESTALT THEORY: FOUNDATIONS AND CURRENT PROBLEMS

1: *On unnoticed sensations*
and errors of judgment

EVERY young science, confronted by a tremendous richness of material, tries to find points of view that will bring some order into the first unintelligible mass of data. Certain principles of ordering—the first laws, the first solid facts, the first constants —begin to appear.

Once a number of such relatively solid laws have been discovered, there is a very natural and altogether justified tendency to regard them as valid, even under circumstances where their validity is not yet established or where it may be difficult to

Über unbemerkte Empfindungen und Urteilstäuschungen. *Zeitschrift für Psychologie,* 1913, 66, 51–80. Reprinted by permission of Johann Ambrosius Barth and translated by Helmut E. Adler.

[The rejection of the constancy hypothesis is the point of departure of Gestalt psychology. This paper is the first general and explicit statement of the case against this hypothesis; thus it occupies a special place in the history of Gestalt psychology. Since the constancy hypothesis itself is tenable only if bolstered up by certain auxiliary assumptions, the method of the paper consists in showing that these bolstering assumptions must themselves be rejected. If the contemporary reader is not familiar with some of the specific theories discussed here, this is because these theories have not survived; and their failure to survive, in turn, is doubtless largely a result of this paper.—Ed.]

prove. Indeed, where difficulties stand in the way of such a generalization, a further hypothesis will be made, with the help of which the old ordering principle can be maintained, rather than seek an entirely fresh point of view for the ordering of the phenomena. It is well known how the help of the ether had to be invoked in order to explain by mechanical principles the passage of light rays through empty space; and hypothesis upon hypothesis followed in order to preserve at least the general foundations of the old mechanical point of view.

This procedure may be useful, but I do not believe that it is called for in the case of the material which will be discussed here. Correlations between stimuli and sensations were first found under specific conditions and within certain limits; here they seemed to hold without exception. A large number of psychologists are still inclined to accept these relations even where we have no evidence for them (and perhaps cannot produce any). This desire for constancy of these relations appears even in cases where direct observation speaks definitely against it.

If such a discrepancy between observation and expectation should appear, then the following auxiliary assumptions generally still permit the retention of the constancy hypothesis.[1]

1. Consciousness, for example a sensory content, may occur in two different forms: as noticed and as unnoticed. While it eludes direct observation in the latter case, it does not forfeit its psychological reality because it can only be inferred.[2]

This assumption finds its application particularly where a mass of stimuli of the same sense modality occurs, and it is not possible to find everywhere in direct experience those sensations that would be expected from the previously established relation between *single* stimulus and *single* sensation. In many such cases, under specific conditions of attention, sensations may still appear that correspond to the constancy hypothesis; therefore it is assumed that these sensations have psychological reality in the

[1] This term will be used repeatedly in what follows to designate the basic assumption that the correlations in question have a general validity beyond observations.

[2] The term "unnoticed" is used in a different sense by Cornelius. The following remarks are directed only to the unnoticed in the above sense.

same way, except that they are unnoticed, even when the conditions of attention do not permit them to be observed directly. Accordingly, it is no more than an application of assumption 1, or one consequence of it, particularly for cases of stimulus complexes, if it is said, in favor of the constancy hypothesis: Attention changes nothing in the sensory contents.[3]

2. Judgments, which follow a sensation or perception, are in theory to be distinguished sharply from these. But they often deceive us so badly about the sensations actually present that we believe we have experienced different ones.

3. The application of assumption 2 leads immediately to a special addition to assumption 1, which must be taken into account in many examples. Since in these cases, as it turns out, the judgments which are supposed to have caused these errors could not at all be confirmed in experience, or at least do not at all need to be experienced, assumption 2 can only be applied if assumption 1 holds for these judgments—i.e., if in addition to noticed judgments, there are also unnoticed ones, and if in these cases judgments of the latter kind are at work. Furthermore, since in such examples there is often nothing in the sensory content to observe which would correspond to the constancy hypothesis, but rather only the "error" can be observed, it is a necessary conclusion also that the judgment is based on an unnoticed sensation and that it gives false testimony about this.[4] Thus Schumann, for example, believes, ". . . attempts cannot be considered unpromising which trace to errors of judgment the difference in apparent size which is seen when retinal images of the same size are projected at different distances."[5] It would be impossible to avoid the above-mentioned conclusion in such an

[3] Exceptions, as for example those allowed by Stumpf, will be discussed below.

[4] Cf. F. Hillebrand, Die Stabilität der Raumwerte auf der Netzhaut. *Zeitschrift für Psychologie*, 1893, 5, 4. This author has used the strange sensory character of the "result of the illusion," as well as the fact that it is a compelling conscious content, in a penetrating argument against several such judgmental explanations.

[5] F. Schumann, Über einige Hauptprobleme der Lehre von den Gesichtswahrnehmungen. *Bericht über den 5. Kongress für experimentelle Psychologie*. Leipzig: Johann Ambrosius Barth, 1912, 181.

attempt. For a perceptual image of the "true" size, whose existence such a theory surely assumes, cannot be substantiated by even the most careful observation.[6]

Krueger has several times argued against the kind of psychological thinking described here and has raised a number of objections to it, primarily that it physicalizes the field of psychology, so to speak, that it represents a "false atomism." In his reply, Stumpf emphasizes that ". . . there is indeed a kind of atomism with regard to sensory phenomena. It cannot so simply be branded as 'false atomism', but must be admitted as one possible general point of view for relating observed facts—one need not be dogmatic about it."[7] Stumpf thus states explicitly that this is meant to be a theory, and he rejects with great clarity the dogmatic assertion, "That's the way it is." Accordingly, he writes in specific defense of the hypothesis of unnoticed sensations:

> . . . but in any case, the psychologist who distinguishes between perception and apperception has as much right as the atomistic chemist to know that his statements will not be regarded as the product of absurd, childish thinking, but as a *theory*, constructed with full awareness of the rules of scientific investigation, and one which must be tested in accordance with the same rules.[8]

These words have brought a most welcome clarity to the whole discussion: If the constancy hypothesis is not to be regarded as something rigorously proven, but as a theory, as a possible point of view for the connecting of data, then it is, of course, not possible simply to criticize this theory as an absurdity. But—and this

[6] Professor Schumann tells me that he has been aware of the consequences of such a theory from the start. He believes that he does not need to draw the conclusion, and would in any case not want to draw the conclusion, that what is called judgment (comparison process) would itself normally be unnoticed with the appearance of the perceived size (which does not correspond to the retinal image). But I still cannot accept this conclusion and must hope, therefore, that Professor Schumann will soon find the opportunity to present his view in more detail.

[7] C. Stumpf, Differenztöne und Konsonanz. *Zeitschrift für Psychologie,* 1911, 59, 175.

[8] C. Stumpf, Erscheinungen und psychische Funktionen, *Abhandlungen Königliche Akademie der Wissenschaften,* Berlin, 1906, 20.

is my point—it is possible, and one must be permitted, *not* to choose this theory, but to let one's own inquiry be guided by other points of view.

In order to avoid misunderstanding, let me say explicitly that for me too the task, the goal of scientific investigation, seems to be the finding of constants, the discovery of constant properties and their consistent ordering in a theoretical structure, or the discovery of unchanging laws governing the variation of characteristics and of their relations. Nobody doubts this; and, of course, I am also far from denying that the sense data which are here under discussion are strictly lawful and follow a lawful course, so that constant laws hold for them too. I will add that, of all objects of psychological investigation, one class in particular, that of peripherally aroused sensations, stands out for this reason: Under conditions of the most far-reaching isolation[9] and investigation of individual examples, it shows "constancy" in a special sense, namely, dependence on a smaller number of factors than appears to be the case elsewhere in psychology. Given this isolation and given a healthy individual, we must in fact say that such sensations (or attributes of sensations) seem to depend primarily on the stimuli and their peripheral reception. We already know quite well many relations that hold between stimulus and sensation in these simple cases. Finally, I also willingly acknowledge a part of one of the special assumptions mentioned above, although it leads to a trivial result. It can certainly not be doubted that *reports* of perceptions may be made that are determined by anything but these perceptions and that if—because of the attitude during judgment—the reports in question say anything about these perceptions, there results a kind of error of judgment. Anyone who has ever been a subject when overtired will have caught himself in such errors. The same holds true for anyone who, after a long, drawn out experimental session, was supposed to give further reports, again and again, about already

[9] It does not detract from the value of the thing in itself that this isolation is often remote from everyday life and has to be artificially produced, both externally and internally: simple stimuli (such as sinusoidal waves) and preparation of the individual as observer in investigations of the usual kind in sensory psychology.

half-forgotten experiences.[10] But even this concession must later be given a limiting condition.

If, now, on the whole, I do not accept the above view and the related auxiliary assumptions, I do not want to base my position on an attack on the arguments of Stumpf, for example. I believe that I may proceed in a different manner after Stumpf has so clearly represented his point of view as a possibility, thus not as something that has been strictly proven.[11] If he had taken the latter position, then anyone who does not agree would have the task of first refuting these arguments. Still another reason prevents me from undertaking a refutation of that theory: Logically, there is surely no objection to the entire point of view; it may be worked out without inner contradictions. Epistemological arguments of the usual type that might be advanced do not change the mind of anyone who is firmly convinced of his position, as we well know. Thus there remains only the refutation by observations and experimentation, and this too must be considered hopeless, since it is precisely one of the basic assumptions of this view that there is unnoticed, indeed unnoticeable, psychological content, and thus, it can be seen, the relevance of observation is excluded once and for all. Any experiment that might be cited against this view could be used in support of it by reference to unnoticed errors of judgment.

I prefer, therefore, to base my opposition on the fact that, for a number of reasons, I consider the auxiliary assumptions—without which the constancy hypothesis cannot be maintained—as unsuitable from the scientific point of view.

I

Even those psychologists who make the above assumptions in order to maintain the desired constancy of the relations between

[10] It is, of course, not to be denied that, for the most part, we immediately and forever forget a good deal, if not most, of what we experience. It seems to me to be one of the main tasks of an introspective observer to prevent this forgetting in a particular case in the interest of science. Besides, we must be careful not to pass off as "unnoticed," contents that are ordinarily quickly forgotten.

[11] I do not know whether there are still psychologists today who take another point of view and believe that they have strict proof. Most will probably hold the same opinion as Stumpf in this matter.

stimulus and sensation, are quite clear that there are departures from this constancy. Nobody denies exceptions, distortions of sensation where pathological processes or congenital defects are to be observed in the peripheral sense organs, and also where there are normal physiological conditions for the absence of sensation or its change. In such cases, of course, no attempt is made to satisfy the desire for constancy by means of the auxiliary assumptions. Likewise, assumption 1, for example, will generally not be used when aggregates of stimuli do not give rise to the aggregates of sensations that would correspond to the simplest constancy hypothesis, but where, nevertheless, the resulting sensations are connected to the stimuli by sufficiently simple and very general laws. Thus we do not dispute the fact that stimuli which correspond individually to red and green, acting together under certain circumstances, produce gray. Nor is it said that this gray contains unnoticed red and green, because it was easy to find a law of color mixture which makes the relation between the mass of stimuli and the sensory result appear just as constant as the still simpler relation between individual stimulus and individual sensation. But still other departures from the constancy principle must be admitted. Stumpf considers the lowering of pitch of loud, low tones to be a change in sensation. It seems to him also that

> the sensory process . . . is not quite immune to central influences, particularly those which depend on the aftereffect of previous experiences. To this category belong Hering's "memory colors," as well as related phenomena in the area of space perception (for example, the apparent size of objects as it is affected by apparent distance), and likewise touch sensations insofar as they are of central origin.[12]

[12] C. Stumpf, Beobachtungen über Kombinationstöne. *Zeitschrift für Psychologie*, 1910, 55, 79. On these questions, of course, not all advocates of the constancy hypothesis pay due respect to observable phenomena, as Stumpf does. Külpe (*Die Realisierung: eine Beitrag zur Grundlegung der Realwissenschaften*, Leipzig: S. Hirzel, 1912–1920, Band I, 166f.) holds, if I understand him correctly, that "memory color" is the mere appearance of a color in contrast to the psychologically "real" color, which would actually be given in accordance with the sensation, but which remains unnoticed. Thus he adheres strictly to the constancy hypothesis; but the further development of psychology should decide for Stumpf in this matter.

Once such exceptions are admitted, the question arises of what criteria we have to decide whether or not, in a concrete case, the constancy hypothesis is to be upheld by unnoticed sensations, etc.

a) In the presence of a stimulus without perception of the sensation "that belongs to it," in many cases the criterion for unnoticed sensations consists in the fact that suitable behavior allows the missing sensation to appear. This cannot be considered sufficient, for it amounts to no more than a repetition of the basic hypothesis itself. It simply says that in all cases where the usual sensation does not appear regularly with a stimulus, the expedient of "unnoticed conscious content" is available. In the especially important cases in which a change of the observer's behavior supplies the desired sensation, although the stimulus is unchanged (attention), this circumstance alone may naturally not be offered as criterion for previously existing sensations; for the dispute turns precisely on whether or not the corresponding sensation was present but unnoticed. This conclusion becomes obvious since the constancy hypothesis has maintained that the sensation depends only, or almost only, on the stimulus and its peripheral reception, even under these conditions; thus the sensation is little or not at all susceptible to central factors. On the other hand, we may not hold the basic hypothesis but rather, in accordance with observation, assume that just in such cases (usually cases of great numbers of stimuli, or "complexes"), the momentary direction of attention, set, and other central factors exert a powerful influence on the sensory processes themselves. Then again, only this hypothesis—of as absolute a constancy as possible—stands against trust in direct observation, which sees the appearance of sensations in such cases as determined by important factors other than the stimulus. Only a possibility of decision that would be independent of the basic hypothesis could serve as criterion in the individual case. I cannot imagine that such a possibility exists or even could exist, since observations cannot serve as a basis for decision. And thus the position taken with regard to each case is rather arbitrary. When, for example, Stumpf might wish to relate the masking of weak tones by the simultaneous presentation of other tones "not simply, as Krueger

does, to more or less difficulty in observation, but to a real influence on the strength of sensations"[13]—it is not quite clear
why. My guess is that, in this case, he foresees a simple law of
sensation, a simple relation between stimulus and sensation, as
in the case of color mixture, where particularly simple laws have
also been found for the case of great numbers of stimuli. I too
hope that we shall soon discover such a law. But it depends on
the state of the science at a given time, on the level of its
methodology, whether approximate or exact laws can be found in
particular cases. I see no essential difference between this case
and others where, for the moment, no simple law is yet in sight.
Even in the present example, the constancy of the relations between stimulus and sensation is provisionally greater if I make
Krueger's, and not Stumpf's, assumption. Another example shows
even more clearly the unavoidable arbitrariness if an advocate
of unnoticed conscious contents has to make a decision in an
individual case. According to Stumpf, it is possible by suitable
direction of attention to strengthen weak tones that are sounded
together with others.[14] "It may be observed quite clearly that in
certain cases there is an actual intensification through attention."
I am afraid that no decision can be reached on this question as
long as the assumption of the unnoticed is retained, and as long
as degrees of noticing are explicitly utilized as an explanation in
a hundred other cases where observation, as in this case, points
to changes in the sensory material. Observation, then, by hypothesis, cannot decide. To be consistent, I must assume here too
—the stimuli and their peripheral effects, of course, remaining
constant—that the sensation was just as strong before attention
was directed to it as after, and that the difference lies solely "in
the function of noticing."[15] But if observation is to decide in this
case, then what is reasonable here is right for the other cases,
and I could say, for example (as I really want to say), that in the
so-called hearing out of an overtone I can accurately observe the
occurrence of a pitch (corresponding to the appropriate fre-

[13] C. Stumpf, Beobachtungen, op. cit., 142.
[14] C. Stumpf, Tonpsychologie. Leipzig: S. Hirzel, 1883–1890, Band II,
290f.
[15] C. Stumpf, Erscheinungen, op. cit., 20.

quency) which previously did not exist (before the hearing out), so that pitches can actually be brought into existence by hearing them out. If it is objected that a plausible neurophysiological hypothesis also supports the sensory change through attention claimed by Stumpf,[16] I will acknowledge this and only reply that an equally simple and plausible explanation may be devised for my statement about the pitch of overtones. In fact, this explanation is, in part, very similar to the one that Stumpf accepted for one case.

b) If observations are made that, if correct, would involve a departure from the usual relations between stimulus and sensation, and if the reports vary widely without stimulus change, it is assumed that this is a matter of errors of judgment. This explanation is believed to be particularly justified if suitable procedures, particularly continued practice, reduce these departures from the usual laws or possibly abolish them altogether. I repeat that I do not take every report at face value. Extreme and unsystematic variability of a subject's reports, which cannot be eliminated by making the instructions more precise, certainly indicates that the report is influenced by all kinds of factors, and only to a lesser extent by whatever it is that I really want to investigate. Then the suspicion arises either that the question has not yet been well stated by the experimenter, so that the sensations and perceptions obtained do not permit a conclusive answer to the question posed, or that the particular subject is unsuited to answer the question at the time of the experiment (or always). For example, if a tone were presented binaurally and the subject asked to compare the intensities "of the two simultaneous tone sensations to the left and right," then a timid subject might perhaps try to fulfill the task and come up with a strange mixture of judgments[17]—assuming that he could get away from the localization of one tone sensation that is normal under these conditions. These reports would, of course, have no basis in perceptual fact at all, and should thus be subject to every chance influence. The example of a tired subject, or of one who

---

[16] *Tonpsychologie*, II, 305ff.
[17] I believe that anyone who knows how to observe would strictly refuse the task where the question is so obviously impossible.

no longer remembers his perceptions but still makes reports, has already been mentioned. Here, too, extreme variability would be expected. Whether or not such cases should be called errors of judgment is only a question of terminology. But it is worth mentioning that certainly not every report may simply be related to the objects of the investigation, and that extreme variability without recognizable pattern naturally indicates that something is not quite right with the experiments. Only the fault here is usually the experimenter's, and the subject will not long remain in doubt about the value of his reports and will express himself accordingly on his own.

But such extreme cases by no means make up the bulk, or even the important part, of the famous errors of judgment that have been so frequently mentioned in the psychological litera- ture. Here it is rather a matter of cases where the variability of reports is not at all very great, where even naïve subjects make definite statements with the greatest confidence, statements that do not fit the stimulus determination of sensations and where, therefore, only the other criterion can lead to the verdict of "error of judgment." In other words, with identical stimuli, there is the possibility of a certain (but not random) change of observa- tions through suitable behavior, and sometimes a reduction of the whole phenomenon through continued practice in a certain direction, so that finally observations correspond to the usual relation between stimulus and sensation. Thus Schumann, for example, states:

> The fundamental fact is that most geometric optical illusions are considerably reduced, or disappear altogether, as soon as we inspect the figures in question more often and try always to compare them as exactly as possible. This definitely supports the assumption that, at least with many of the illusions, we are dealing with pure errors of judgment.[18]

And likewise Stumpf writes, "It is characteristic of mere errors of judgment that they are reduced and eventually disappear en- tirely with appropriate practice and by turning consciousness

[18] F. Schumann, Beiträge zur Analyse der Gesichtswahrnehmungen, III. *Psychologische Studien*, Abt. 1, 1904.

away from secondary influences toward the objects to be compared."[19]

It is obvious that this criterion is based entirely on the fundamental assumption. The criterion can be used only if it is taken for granted that sensations are strictly stimulus bound,[20] only if practice in a given direction can therefore change nothing in the sensory material itself. The fact that practice, that isolation in consciousness of what is to be judged, can finally provide the desired perceptions, may not properly be regarded as an *independent* indication of errors of judgment,[21] and thus a proper criterion is again lacking. As for the rest, the situation here is exactly the same as in the case of unnoticed sensations. Since, according to the third auxiliary assumption, observations and statements about the presence or absence of the necessary judgments cannot be decisive (unnoticed judgments are always possible), it is again somewhat arbitrary whether or not errors of judgment are assumed in a particular case. For certainly no psychologist still argues that stimuli alone completely determine sensations in all cases.[22] But once other influences are admitted, once certain departures from the basic assumption have been accepted because of the impressiveness of the observations, then the question can naturally not be completely avoided in individual cases: How am I to decide for one or the other assumption? This question becomes still more urgent when Stumpf, for example, can write that even the central changes in sensation, which he grants, can be reduced by practice and attention, just

[19] C. Stumpf, Beobachtungen, *op. cit.,* 77.

[20] I hope that I will not be misunderstood here. I am, of course, not suggesting that sensations are somehow independent of physical stimuli and physiological processes. I object only to the idea that stimuli and their peripheral reception are, so to speak, the only independent variables in the determination of the sensation. I regard the other variables also as physiological in nature.

[21] Cf. also V. Benussi, Zur Psychologie des Gestalterfassens. In A. Meinong (Hrsg.), *Untersuchungen zur Gegenstandstheorie und Psychologie,* Leipzig: Johann Ambrosius Barth, 1904, 403f.

[22] The reduction of the phenomena under discussion can be made theoretically comprehensible without the assumptions in question. As soon as we grant that other (central) factors besides the stimuli influence sensations, we can also understand very well the effect of "isolation" or of practice in a certain direction.

as is the case with mere errors of judgment: ". . . they are not so easy to eliminate, but finally one always succeeds."[23] But now errors of judgment are robbed of their only distinguishing characteristic; they must share it with things that in proper psychological perspective should be entirely different from them. And so the following comment of Stumpf's no longer seems quite conclusive to me.

> It should be remembered that there are very convincing errors of judgment, which occur regularly in many observers, and yet are mere errors of judgment. The Poggendorff illusion, the Müller-Lyer illusion, and innumerable others in the field of space perception offer proof. . . . The fact that the space sensation itself is nevertheless unchanged follows from the possibility of overcoming the illusion by sufficient concentration of attention on the lines to be compared and by abstraction from the inducing lines which disturb the judgment (isolation in consciousness, according to F. Schumann).[24]

If the central changes of sensation (i.e., departures from the pure stimulus relation), which Stumpf grants, show the same characteristic, why should such things not figure in this case too? The fact that the well-defined Müller-Lyer illusion is easier to reduce than, say, color constancy is, however, by no means proved. In any case, a small difference in the difficulty of reduction would not be conclusive for our question, where a very fundamental conflict of hypotheses exists.[25] Accordingly, the "reduction criterion" no longer seems to be applicable.

[23] C. Stumpf, Beobachtungen, *op. cit.*, 80.

[24] *Ibid.*, 112f.

[25] Stumpf (Beobachtungen, 80) seems to see a sufficient difference here. But if this is really the only difference, then it is astonishing that two things which, in reality, must be separated so emphatically because they are supposedly quite different, are capable of producing at most a small, gradual difference in the observed data. But if "memory colors" and "apparent size" should therefore be considered modifications of sensation because we already have a positive theory in this case, according to which effects of experience (traces) are able to modify the sensations, while this theory does not work for the Müller-Lyer illusion, for example, then I must confess that this theory of "memory colors" and of "apparent size" does not seem very satisfactory to me; individual experience might not have had so very much to do with their origin. And if a positive theory is the only thing that is missing, this lack could, after all, be remedied.

Meantime, there is at least one criterion that is useful, but it can only be employed, if at all, to decide *against* the hypothesis of errors of judgment in the individual case. Where it can be shown that judgments which could produce the "illusion" are impossible under the circumstances, and that even the most noticed judgments could not achieve what is observed as "illusion," there is naturally no longer any place for errors of judgment. On the basis of such considerations, I believe, Stumpf has decided to consider size and color constancies as *perceived* and not merely the results of errors of judgment. It is absurd to ask of children the judgments that could result in size constancy and color constancy, while it is most probable, and in part demonstrated, that they show both phenomena. The systematic working out of the consequences of "errors of judgment" might have a similar result in many other cases.[26] But let it be emphasized once more that where the hypothesis of relevant judgments is not in itself absurd, it does not therefore by any means have to correspond with the facts. For such cases we are again without a criterion. Unfortunately, even in cases where the criterion is appropriate, we are beginning only very gradually to make use of it.

The review of criteria, therefore, does not give us a cheerful picture. Even the last mentioned means of making a decision is only of limited applicability. Once errors of judgment of the kind under discussion, and unnoticed sensations, are admitted, we have in most cases no possibility of reaching a decision between an explanation in these terms and trust in observation. We might try to eliminate these explanations by all kinds of arguments and experiments in one case or another, but we cannot even hope to achieve much with the advocates of these assumptions. Again and again, systematic interests come into conflict with those of research in the true sense. The system is, in any case, already quite simple if the auxiliary assumptions are retained at any

[26] The same is true in some cases of the thinking out of explanations which use unnoticed sensations. I have once used this criterion (W. Köhler, Akustische Untersuchungen, II. *Zeitschrift für Psychologie,* 1910, 58, 86).

price. How can any arguments and observations help? The latter, as we have seen, are by hypothesis inconclusive.

On the other hand, the consequence of the uncertainty of the criteria (natural with such assumptions) should also be stressed: Somewhat reluctantly, cases have been admitted where the basic assumption cannot be maintained. Even though the principle has thus been violated, the interests of a conservative system can be overwhelming in the absence of independent criteria: [27] Every time experience provides observations that depart from the usual laws, the danger can be averted by appeal to unnoticed contents of consciousness, to errors of judgment, and particularly to unnoticed judgments. The vagueness of the criteria, then, acts in fact like a bonus to maintain artificially, and by very convenient means, the absolute rule of the stimulus, as these laws assume. This is the case despite the fact that, because of the admitted exceptions, that rule seems generally doubtful by its very nature. We need not investigate here the extent to which the origin of modern psychology and the ideals of exactness borrowed from physics play a part in this development.

II

Further consequences that affect the practical work of science may readily be observed. They are a direct result of the fact that, while the basic assumption is indeed a hypothesis, it is not effective only as such. In reality, by way of a very intensive attitude, the stimuli and perhaps also the peripheral physiological conditions of stimulation, so far as we know them, determine our whole approach to sensory psychology.

a) We may recall how often we have heard the words "error of judgment," "unnoticed idea," etc., and how quickly they are brought up when something really new has been observed anywhere, and it is a question of taking a stand. Wherever observation does not conform to one of the rigorous stimulus-sensation laws, then the assumption, e.g., of an error of judgment—for it is just an assumption—suffices to override the observation. We

---

[27] I.e., decision principles independent of the basic hypothesis.

easily do this instead of at least attempting to give the assumption a definite form, as would be absolutely necessary. Whether or not the actual conditions suggest any errors of judgment is never first investigated, and besides, if it somehow proves possible to make the observation turn out "in accordance with the stimulus," then the first observation is surely soon forgotten although, as we have seen, this circumstance need not at all be conclusive. The mere term "error of judgment" thus sometimes carries more weight than the most careful observations—just the phrase alone! For as long as it is not stated which judgment, a judgment about what, the expression has hardly any scientific value by itself; and it is actually supposed to invalidate a perfectly good observation, just because this was unexpected, to finish it off with empty words.

How this error can be avoided by seeking out as completely as possible the relevant sources of an observation that does not conform to the stimulus, Stumpf has shown, for example in the previously quoted work on combination tones.[28] There, at least, one knows the where and the how. And where errors of judgment are discussed elsewhere in the literature, it is at least usually stated about what, and in what way, false judgments are supposedly made. But the cases that concern us here are those that, by their very nature, do not generally come into the open. They belong to the everyday psychological work in our laboratories. Who knows what fraction of new facts that our science will find in the next decades could actually have already been discovered today. But instead they are occasionally observed and forgotten again, because the stimulus determination, the familiar laws, do not lead us to expect such facts and make us distrustful of our own observations! I know of two such recent cases in psychology, and I will not hesitate to report them. In one laboratory, the similarity of vowel sounds of many tones on the tuning fork had been observed occasionally, long before I called attention to it; but it was not followed up, since it was obvious that unnoticed associations resulted in errors of judgment! Likewise, the so-

[28] C. Stumpf, Beobachtungen, *op. cit.,* 114f.

called covariance phenomenon discovered by Jaensch had been known in one psychological laboratory as a curious error of judgment (the observers did not yet have the necessary practice in spatial experimentation!), even before the author published his research.

Each science has a sort of attic into which things are almost automatically pushed that cannot be used at the moment, that do not quite fit, or that no one wants to investigate "at the moment." Not by intention, but in fact, it seems to me, the assumptions with which we are concerned here have precisely this effect: We are constantly putting aside, unused, a wealth of the most valuable materials. To put it bluntly, the practical use of such explanations may be very helpful in maintaining the constancy of stimulus-sensation laws, and thus in making possible an early systematization of the young science. But, on the other hand, the actual effect of these expedients which guarantee the system is often enough mainly to discredit our one way of moving forward—observations and the pleasure in them—and thus to paralyze the will to advance. Fortunate are those who consider these words exaggerated!

In addition, a related consideration may be mentioned which is directed particularly against the treatment of the famous "errors of judgment" in the visual field. The Müller-Lyer illusion, for example, is called an error of judgment by some investigators, and we are told that sizes quite different from those actually to be compared play a role in the reports. That supposedly settles the matter. And yet the question should immediately suggest itself: How does it happen, then, that it is so very difficult in the Müller-Lyer figure to compare just those lines in isolation which the task requires us to compare? How does it happen that these lines do not allow themselves to be separated from the added lines? How is it that this difficulty in separation persists even when the observer is quite clear about the facts of the "illusion"? This is an astonishing fact and can only be a matter of the characteristics of the perception itself. Ultimately the whole "illusion" must thus be rooted in these properties. Present-day psychology of space perception does not have a satisfactory answer.[29] Once we think in terms of the basic assumption, and if we have gone no farther in the solution than the term "error of judgment," we are far from admitting that we lack an answer and, of course, far from the search for the actual perceptual basis of the "illusion." It may therefore be asserted that the dragging in of the hypothesis about judgments in this case (and also in others) brings about an unfortunate obscuring of the problem insofar as, at most, only the beginning of an explanation has been given. One is satisfied as soon as the blame for the "illusion," so to speak, is shifted from the sensations, and a resolute investigation of the primary causes of the illusion is usually not undertaken. Such an investigation would, of course, lead also to a phenomenological description and theoretical treatment of the visual field which would contradict the basic assumption of the psychology in question. The explanation in terms of judgments thus seems to miss just the essential point of these phenomena, from which we could make progress.[30]

b) A second consequence follows directly from the same causes: If an observation does not quite fit what we expect in terms of the stimuli, then we attend again and again to all the processes accompanying pure sensations, processes that are difficult to observe, and unnoticed, until finally the report is made. And, if one has accepted this suggestion, the judgment given seems to be a kind of blind, natural effect that is always subject to the strangest influences. If the situation is really as bad as all that, if the judgment about our own sense data is really such a blind, deceptive affair, then we should expect *always* to regard this judgment with a certain skepticism, even when it agrees completely with what is to be expected in terms of the stimulus. It is widely held that there are complicating effects of the "pro-

[29] Pointing out that the figures "are perceived as a unit" or the like does not provide a solution. We cannot stop there; for these words merely repeat the problem, though without recognizing this.
[30] Cf. V. Benussi, Zur Psychologie des Gestalterfassens. In A. Meinong (Hrsg.), *Untersuchungen zur Gegenstandstheorie und Psychologie*, Leipzig: Johann Ambrosius Barth, 1904, 383, note 2. It seems to me that the Graz psychologist has done very significant work on these questions so far as the research itself is concerned, asking questions that lead to experimentation. I am afraid that it is his theory, under Meinong's influence, that is to blame for the indifference with which his work has been received.

cesses between sensation and judgment." The same complications, and therefore the danger of "illusion," are likewise present
here. But in such cases we hear nothing of errors of judgment,
not even when the specific conditions of perception themselves
invite "illusions" exactly as in those other cases. Now, suddenly,
the observation is considered correct without question, and the
complicated events between sensation and report seem to be
forgotten. Why? Because the observation corresponds to the
stimuli! And yet this should not be granted, at least not by those
researchers who have generally admitted that the stimuli alone
do not determine sensations. If, for example, in the investigation
of the well-known optical illusions, an observation seems to show
that the actual space perceptions are not changed, why should
we so simply trust this observation?[31] In particular, it cannot be
denied that the conviction that the spatial sensation really agrees
with the stimulus, and that optical illusions are to be explained
as errors of judgment, may covertly influence reports of this
observation just as much as secondary lines do. It is similar
where subjective changes are reported in the pitch of one component of a chord that is slightly out of tune. We now ask
whether the pitch has really changed or whether there is only
an error of judgment. Now we either adjust a second tuning fork
to the tone in question by a successive comparison technique,
while isolating it as much as possible through attention, or we
observe whether the tone really changes when the other components, which alone can be the causes of the phenomenon, are
alternately sounded simultaneously with it and omitted. In such
cases Stumpf and his co-workers (myself included) have always
finally found that the tone was only apparently shifted, thus that
there had been an error of judgment.[32] If errors of judgment are
supposed to occur so readily, I cannot suppress the thought that

[31] Incidentally, the observation must be such that it can contribute something. If one draws the two parts of the Müller-Lyer figure, geometrically
one exactly under the other, and now observes that subjective verticals at
the end points of the lower line precisely meet the end points of the upper
line, "then the conscious contents corresponding to the two lines must
have the same extent." But this would be the case only if Euclidian geometry holds for two-dimensional visual space. Neither Wundt nor Schumann
has proved this. Cf. Schumann, Beiträge, *op. cit.*, 114f.

[32] C. Stumpf, Beobachtungen, *op. cit.*, 117f.

such errors are in principle just as possible in the validating experiments, particularly in the second case, where the original pitch of the critical tone, when it is sounded by itself, is continually present for purposes of comparison. Is it not possible that the tone heard in isolation, which sounds much stronger than the tone in the chord that is out of tune, falsely "determines the judgment of pitch" by assimilating the tone heard in the chord? I do not by any means wish to claim that things are really this way in this example, but I miss the mention of such a possibility and want to point out that somebody might well get the idea of turning the tables and using errors of judgment *against* the basic assumption, for which it normally serves as support. This much seems certain: When we use the interpretation in terms of judgments, we are in danger of unintentionally applying different standards. We tend to think of errors of judgment only when observations do not fulfill our secret wish to find the dependence of sensations on stimuli as constant as possible.

c) But we must go still farther with respect to errors of judgment. It is not only that we freely use the words "error of judgment," etc., for an observation, without developing a definite idea of how the error is to be explained by means of judgments, and that such assumptions are made somewhat one-sidedly only when an observation threatens the absolute rule of the stimulus over the sensation. The judgments are accepted unhesitatingly even where no observation can establish them. They must also be capable of remaining unnoticed (at least I would otherwise be unable to understand the whole theory in many cases). But once they have arrived in this somewhat obscure region in which no observation can decide anything with certainty, they display great ability to adapt to all kinds of changing conditions. The deceptive processes were originally introduced as judgments; thus the word "judgment," even when the process was regarded as unnoticed, should mean nothing different from what we all know from experience by this name. If objections are raised today against an interpretation in terms of judgment, which show a contradiction between the alleged judgmental nature of these processes and the properties of the illusion to be explained, then we can sometimes hear that "no true judgments" are meant, but that a term like "apperception" [*Auffassung*] is preferable. Yet no clear and definite statement is made about it, by which we can experience by way of an example whatever is called "apperception," so that the new theory would at least have an intelligible meaning.[33] And why should it? Once we have decided more or less to disregard observation and to construct theories in the obscurity of the unnoticed, there is no more point in definiteness of theories and auxiliary assumptions. And if unnoticed judgments are difficult to refute, the unnoticed X is impossible. This is a great advantage. I am well aware that there are those who prefer the term "apperception" to "judgment" in this connection, because they do not believe, as Brentano does, in the specifically unitary nature of judgment experiences. They are, rather, of the opinion that these experiences involve a good deal of heterogeneity that should first be analyzed. But whether these investigators are right or wrong in relation to Brentano, they cannot conceal from themselves the fact that, in this way, their view of illusions becomes increasingly vague. The word "judgment" at least pointed out an approximate direction in the realm of experience in which we could look for what was meant. On the other hand, the sharp antithesis of sensory change and error of judgment loses all meaning if apperception may be substituted for judgment, and almost anything may be substituted for apperception. Does the statement "This observation depends on error of apperception" still have any positive meaning? Obviously not; for apperception may mean an associated idea, as well as the addition of "traces," or, finally, associated sensations anywhere in the body. Does the statement mean anything negative? Perhaps "This is no sensory change"? Not in the least! For the kind of explanation of direct observations with which we are here concerned has completely obscured the boundaries of what should be called sensation. We are therefore also unable to distinguish sensations from other things, for example, from apperception, and so finally, considering the indefiniteness of the meaning

[33] This criticism does not apply to Stumpf's use of this term, insofar as in *Tonpsychologie*, I, 5, apperception is defined as "elementary judgment."

of the term "apperception," the so-called errors of apperception could simply mean a sensory change.[34] The whole controversy thus turns only about a word.

Why is it, then, that the investigators whom we are discussing still put so much emphasis on this distinction? I know of no other explanation than the following, an explanation that they will certainly not admit to themselves or to us: The stimulus determines the sense data! An attitude of this kind is what is actually decisive, but the word "apperception," or something like it, gives the appearance of a positive theory of observations which do not fit the basic assumption. What it means for the advancement of science if these remarks are even partially correct is clear: A blind alley. Fortunate again are those who consider these words exaggerated!

III

I expressed the fear above that the theory of errors of judgment and of unnoticed sensations may inadvertently lead to the neglect of valuable material and the blocking of scientific progress. Not long ago Stumpf explicitly advanced as an argument for the theory of unnoticed sensations "the impossibility or extraordinary difficulty of any descriptive theory of the phenomena on the opposite assumption."[35] In the field of audition, for example, he has pointed out the abundance of new and remarkable phenomena that must be recognized and investigated: "The complexity so arising is scarcely conceivable."[36] Yet this kind of thing becomes theoretically so simple if we decide, for example, to treat the changes that continued analysis causes in a chord as merely in the function of noticing. From this argument of Stumpf's it must be inferred that a detailed descriptive theory

[34] This would be the case, for example, if the error of apperception were to be more precisely defined as "addition of traces." The meaning here could only be physiological, and so would that of the primary correlate of consciousness, in this case the "error." If we do not want to call such a case a change in sensation, then I would like to know what in the world could be so designated.

[35] C. Stumpf, Erscheinungen, *op. cit.*, 19.

[36] *Ibid.*

should, in general, not include those changes as such which are so striking in immediate observation and which, indeed, are of the greatest variety. But if these changes hold only for noticing, then we may either show that these most varied processes can in principle be described in terms of noticing, or we must carefully investigate just these changes which are given in observation as material for a descriptive theory of the noticing process. The first alternative would not, as far as I can see, meet the requirements of science, and so only the second remains. In this second case we would thus investigate in all detail the abundance of phenomena which occur here and which simply demand exploration (but under a different name, a new chapter, so to speak). We would run into the same difficulty with a descriptive theory as if we were to treat everything as processes of the sensations themselves. So it follows that the argument advanced in favor of unnoticed sensations cannot accomplish its purpose, for we still could not avoid the difficult task of a descriptive theory of these phenomena. In a discussion with my respected teacher, I have become convinced that he himself would never draw the other conclusion and demand less of a descriptive exploration of the process of noticing than of the sensations of tone. But that argument of Stumpf's in favor of the basic assumption, and especially in favor of unnoticed sensations, if taken strictly, does force us to such conclusions. Just because these conclusions are unformulated, I would like explicitly to point out the danger that threatens here without our being aware of it: If the assumption of unnoticed sensations could inadvertently lead to the consequence that a whole region of phenomena which threaten the simplicity of our acoustics would be excluded from more exact descriptive investigation, then I must see in this fact a further very clear indication that the theory of unnoticed sensations tends to retard the progress of science.

This argument for unnoticed sensations is rather similar to the following argument for errors of judgment, which I would like to discuss briefly, although it may not in itself retard the progress of psychology. The tendency to regard perceptions and sensations as much as possible as unambiguously determined by peripheral stimulation, and to plead for errors of judgment in cases where observation shows departures from stimulus boundedness, has sometimes been based on the following argument: if sensations could really be changed so very much, we would be entirely unable to understand this fact teleologically; and specifically the existence of a highly developed science of physics would be incomprehensible. How could creatures survive who would be informed about reality by sensations corresponding so little to it? How could these creatures construct a useful physics, since sensations necessarily constitute the primary material of this science? We might say, first of all, that the enormous teleological and biological value of many "illusions" is obvious. I think it is sufficient to refer to "apparent size," "apparent form," and "memory color" in this connection. In the second place, somewhat closer inspection shows that for all cases where an argument exists over errors of judgment and of sensation, it simply does not matter biologically or teleologically whether we interpret them one way or the other. The illusions are there, and only special training which some psychologists undergo reduces a number of them. The vast majority of people are subject to them every time the appropriate conditions are given. If these illusions are teleologically incomprehensible and biologically harmful, then they are just as bad if they are errors of judgment as if they are changes of sensation. Teleological considerations, therefore, provide no argument at all for or against either side. But none of us experience possibilities of harm in the Müller-Lyer illusion, the "apparent" unity of a clang, the octave illusions, but blithely survive the struggle for existence (in relation to biological "reality") despite such terrible illusions (in relation to the stimuli). Thus the thought suggests itself that illusions, whether of judgment or sensation, are biologically completely indifferent,[37] insofar as they are not of tremendous value, as mentioned above.

With regard to physics, anyone who has worked much in physical laboratories will admit that the sense perceptions involved in physical research, for example in measurement, are limited to a very small number of types. These have proved to

[37] This fact might easily be explained if we regard as the "immediately given," and in any case as the biologically primary "reality," not "sensations," but (for the most part) *things.*

be the most useful, especially for quantitative purposes, through a kind of process of elimination. Of these, the perception of complete or approximate coincidence of some contour (a pointer, a mercury meniscus, etc.) with another (scale mark), as well as the perception of an adjacent number, constitute the most frequent and most important cases. The rest are mostly methods of equality and null methods, in which the sensations in question have, in general, just as little reason to deviate at all from the usual stimulus-sensation laws.[38] From the existence of physics, therefore, no more can be concluded than these cases of perception important for physics permit, namely that these cases correspond to the "basic assumption." Whether the whole field of sensations and perceptions conforms to the basic assumption cannot at all be decided by the existence of physics.[39]

Enough of this. The two auxiliary assumptions, that of unnoticed sensations and that of unnoticed errors of judgment, are shown to be, in fact, general and incapable of being disproved in most concrete individual cases. This is the first reason why these assumptions do not recommend themselves from a scientific and technical point of view. I do not hesitate to say that it is a kind of scientific instinct that seems to me to forbid our making hypotheses that cannot be tested. It has been shown, in the second

[38] On the use of sensations in physics, cf. also H. Bergson, *Essai sur les données immédiates de la conscience.* (8. éd.) Paris: Alcan, 1911. Also G. v. Allesch, Über das Verhältnis der Ästhetik zur Psychologie, *Zeitschrift für Psychologie*, 1909, 54, 440f. and 445. In chemistry, sensory qualities (colors and smells) as such are of even greater concern, but also without any great "danger of illusion."

[39] Three further points are so obvious that I almost hesitate to mention them specifically. In the first place, the same reasoning applies, of course, to the argument from the possibility of physics as to the teleological argument, i.e., illusions considered as wrong judgments are exactly as dangerous or as harmless for physics as they are if they are regarded as sensory changes. In the second place, physicists have long known about certain illusions, such as those that occur in transit observations. How many physical measurements are necessarily beset by the errors that we investigate in "complication experiments"! Does physics therefore become impossible? Not at all Finally, as far as sensory changes are concerned which, in my view, can be brought about by attention, we naturally accept no more of these phenomena than are present as facts and than the opposition has to explain by degrees of noticing. Since the facts are there and physics apparently does not suffer from them, no difficulty remains.

place, that no independent criteria exist in specific cases to decide when we must have recourse to these assumptions and when we must, rather, accept an observation that represents an exception to the basic assumption (of strict determination of our sensations by stimuli). Thus the door is opened to arbitrariness (moreover, a door that seems passable in only one direction). In the third place, it has been shown that there is an obvious danger that, on the basis of these assumptions, whole groups of phenomena might be excluded from research, and thus opportunities for advance would be lost. Finally, it has been shown that the auxiliary assumptions, by their very nature, undermine confidence in observation, thus in the facts of psychology, and that they therefore destroy the joy of observing, the zest for progress.

It might therefore be recommended tentatively that, of these *assumptions,* that of unnoticed sensations and that of unnoticed errors of judgment be given up entirely, and that the *facts* of inadequate judgments not grounded in perception be used only where they can really be established. After every other possibility of decision has been eliminated, let the decision be based on success alone, and let us see whether progress may also lie in this direction. It is obvious that, at the same time, the basic assumption will thus tentatively be given up, the direction of thinking in sensory psychology according to which the stimulus and its peripheral reception almost completely determine sense data. This assumption is not tenable without the auxiliary assumptions. A simplicity of sensory psychology which I believe is premature and artificial will thereby be sacrificed. For, in accordance with observation, we now assume that, in general, apart from the stimuli and the well-known peripheral conditions, a number of other factors, primarily central ones, also play an essential role in the determination of sense data. We assume that those simplest relations between stimulus and sensation, which the basic assumption considers as absolute as possible, represent limiting cases. Such cases can be achieved through isolation, so that the influence of the stimuli and of the peripheral conditions can be completely decisive because the other factors influencing the sensory processes are either eliminated or invariable, and thus relatively indifferent with respect to these laws. In accordance with the observations, we hold further that (especially in cases where "complexes" are present) a description of the sensory data must remain incomplete and divorced from reality as long as we try to get along with the current variables of our sensory psychology (according to the basic assumption). Rather, we believe that in the usual description, a large and significant part of the properties of perception is neglected. These properties actually recede into the background in those limiting cases achieved by means of isolation, but are often much more important for a psychology of perception than the usual sensory attributes—as soon as the remaining factors, apart from peripheral conditions, also exert their influence. This applies particularly to the psychological correlates of stimulus complexity, and specifically to the everyday perception of *things*. Anyone can see that the theory of perception will at first become less simple in this way. But research so oriented will also find laws and constants in the greater richness of its material and perhaps will finally be able to attain a deeper understanding of the whole field than can be achieved by means of the assumptions which we have opposed.

2: *An aspect of gestalt psychology*

WHAT we call Gestalt psychology means a new point of view and a new procedure in various respects, and in several parts of psychology; it is far beyond my power to give a complete and adequate idea of it in one lecture. If I try to speak about it in general terms, my statements will necessarily sound vague, and you will not be able to see how they are to be applied in concrete cases. And if I try to show, in a more special field of our science, how the problems and the procedure of Gestalt psychology develop, many aspects and consequences of the new concepts cannot pos-

From *Pedagogical Seminary and Journal of Genetic Psychology*, 1925, 32, 691–723, and Carl Murchison (ed.), *Psychologies of 1925*. Worcester, Mass.: Clark University Press, 1926, 163–195. Reprinted by permission of The Journal Press and Clark University Press. Originally a Powell Lecture in Psychological Theory at Clark University, May 1, 1925.

[Since this is one of the very first papers Professor Köhler wrote in English, minor editorial corrections have been made. It seems appropriate to add that, not very many years after publication of this article, Professor Köhler was correcting the written English of this editor and others of his younger American-born colleagues. Certain sections of this paper have been omitted; in these cases, references are given to treatment of the same problems elsewhere.—Ed.]

sibly become visible, and you will probably take as a central position of Gestalt psychology what really is only one of its applications. Since, in my judgment, the second danger is less serious than the possibility that very general statements will not give you any concrete idea at all, I prefer the risk which is the natural consequence of exemplification in a special kind of problem; and I shall try to show you how Gestalt psychology treats some aspects of our sensory experience—more especially, how the new ideas deal with the visual field in a state of rest.

One of the fundamental methods of natural science is *analysis*. The psychologist, therefore, confronted for example with a complex field of vision, feels naturally inclined to analyze this field into smaller and simpler entities whose properties he may study more easily and with greater hope of clear results than an immediate consideration of the whole field would yield. Generally he does not ask himself what this procedure means and if, perhaps, the term analysis has more than one connotation. He simply analyzes down to very small parts of the sensory field— let us call them the sensations—which do not contain differences, which show a minimum of area, and so seem to constitute the simplest parts of the field. Only gradually have we become aware of the fact that at this very starting point of investigation at least two ambiguities must be carefully avoided.

Let us take an instance from the physical world. If we want to study the air which surrounds us in this room, we also shall feel inclined to analyze it. We may do that in different ways. Either our attention picks out a "differential" of this volume of air, i.e., an extremely small volume which may be regarded as homogeneous in density, temperature, etc.; or we concentrate our attention on one molecule, say O_2. In the first case, everybody knows that we are not dealing with a *real* element of the air. We know that the differential is not defined by objective physical properties, as if its interior were kept together somehow, while there is no such holding together beyond the limits of the differential, between *different* differentials. We know, therefore, that the limits of the differential exist in thought only. On the other hand, if we take the molecule as the final product of our analysis, we mean an element of the other kind. It is well defined physically as a real unit; mutual inner forces which keep the interior of it together do not, in comparable degree, unite parts of one molecule with those of another. In order to get differentials, we imagine arbitrary separations in the medium; where a molecule is, begins, and ends is a matter which nature has decided. The molecule is an *objective* unit.

Does a sensation belong to the first or to the second type? If we do not want to answer this question for the sensation as a supposed part of consciousness, I will ask the same question with respect to the physiological processes underlying the sensory field. It would hardly be indifferent for the sensation or the sensory field whether the process corresponding to the sensation must be treated as a differential or as a molecule of the total field. We should probably construct different theories of sensory experience corresponding to our choice of one or the other of these fundamental possibilities. In the psychological literature, however, the existence of these alternatives is hardly ever mentioned. Sensation has been a vague concept, and the consequences of our use of it correspond to this state of affairs.

The second ambiguity of our concept, certainly related to the first, may again be made clear by an example from physics. I can connect two rooms by a number of tubes or pipes; and I can, in one room, press water into each of them separately, so that, in the other room, jets of water come out of each pipe separately and fall in separate receptacles. In this case we have real elements before us, isolated streams of water, which are so totally independent of each other that, from the standpoint of physics, no problem remains that refers to the whole of streaming water. On the other hand, I can connect two points of a network of wires with the two poles of a battery of galvanic elements. The electric current through this network is immediately established, forming the so-called stationary distribution in the net, in the wires connecting it with the battery, and in the battery itself. Nobody can prevent me from concentrating my attention on one small part of this conducting system and on one small part of the physical process constantly going on in it. I may do that in my attempt to make a theory of the process. But the next step I have to take, if the theory is to agree with the facts at all, must consist in my admitting that the small part of the process I have in view is *as* it is, not for its own sake and independently, but only insofar as the corresponding processes are going on in the other parts of the system. The stationary distribution of electric current in a given system is a dynamic equilibrium of the *whole* system, not to be reduced to independent branches of current.[1] What occurs in one wire of this system, therefore, cannot be compared functionally with the stream of water in one of the pipes of our other example. In this pipe I shall find the streaming absolutely unchanged, whatever may happen and whatever is changed in the other pipes; the streaming in one of them is a function of the local conducting properties in this pipe only. In the case of electric currents in a conducting network, any change in any place will immediately alter what happens in "the small part" of it which we were considering. If, therefore, I like to analyze, in the case of the pipes I may do so. No harm will be done, provided my analysis finds the real elements (independent streams in each pipe). But if my analysis picks out a part of that stationary current distribution, I must confess at the next moment that here analysis cannot mean the same thing, since I find a local state of affairs which cannot be understood as long as I do not consider the whole process. It cannot be understood because it does not exist without the dynamic influences throughout the whole system (and vice versa).

Is a sensation, or is a physiological process corresponding to it, like one of those streams of water in separate pipes, i.e., functionally independent? Or is it like that "small local process" in the network conducting the electric current, i.e., does it exist in its actual state only as dependent upon the dynamic equilibrium distribution in a larger area? Evidently, this decision is at least as important for our theory of sensory experience as the choice between the meanings of analysis discussed above. But, although dynamic equilibrium is a word mentioned in some of our more modern textbooks, we do not see that the fundamental

[1] It is instructive to know that, in the early days of the investigation of currents, this situation was exactly as embarrassing for physicists as the problems of Gestalt are now for us.

difference between the two assumptions has as yet been recognized and the concrete consequences worked out. For a long time we have all, in practice, applied the standpoint of the pipes when treating the sensory field. When, now, we are told that the other point of view seems to be more probable for several reasons, and that we should not go on with the pipes, we easily become angry and say that we never did formulate such a radical principle as that of the pipes. In this we are probably right, because we never had a clear idea of the functional alternatives, no idea that there was something important to decide one way or the other, and rather unconsciously *worked* in that one line only. But I think somebody *should* have stated that radical principle, because it is of so much higher scientific value to make a clean, clear mistake, which is the best antecedent of progress, than to remain in that phase of vagueness where not even mistakes can be made—and afterwards be displaced by something better.

One remark may be needed here to show that the two kinds of theoretical choice are not simply identical. The molecule as representative of an objective unit and the independent stream in one pipe seem to be similar; yet we must not exaggerate the parallel between them because, although a molecule in the air is a physical unit held together by forces which do not connect in a comparable degree parts of one molecule with those of another, still what happens with the molecule may be determined by its being part of a larger whole. If it has a charge for example (i.e., if it is an ion), it will move in the electric field and influence other charges by its own field, so that perhaps its movements will finally become one dependent little part of just such a whole process as we described above. Therefore a molecule or any other physically defined unit may either be an altogether independent unit like the stream in one separated pipe or it may, while still retaining its property of more specific unitedness, have a life which can only be rightly understood if we consider a larger system in which we find it.

Is sensation of the same type as the molecule? Let us try to answer with complete naïveté, as if there were no psychology.

I look up at the homogeneous blue sky and find it continuous. I find not the slightest indication that it is composed of real units, nothing of limits or of any discontinuities. One may answer that my simple observation is not the method by which to decide this point; but I cannot agree with this argument since we need, first of all, concepts for the description and the understanding of our immediate experience. The sensation loses considerably in its importance as a fundamental concept if, taking it as something of the molecule type, we find nothing to substantiate this idea in direct observation. The continuity of that region of the sky or of any homogeneous field is one of its positive properties. And we see that, in this form, our fundamental theoretical concept does nothing to make this property understood. On the contrary, a special hypothesis would be needed in order to explain how, in spite of the existence of sensation molecules, the homogeneous field becomes a continuum. Therefore the only thing accomplished by this useless assumption is a complication of theory. And I lay the more stress on this fact as we shall see very soon that parts do exist in sensory fields which are real, objective units, though they certainly are not sensations. The concept of sensation tends to hide from us the importance of these other realities and has done so for a considerable time, very much to the detriment of psychological progress.

Since the concept of a *differential* does not mean anything like a real unit, but only signifies the small uniform part of a medium, field, or process which our thinking has selected out at a certain moment of our theoretical consideration, sensation as a differential can evidently not be verified in experience. It has nothing directly to do with experience. Perhaps it does not help us very much in our thinking, but at least—so long as we remain aware of its completely arbitrary nature—it will not lead us into error.

Having found that we may keep sensations in our system as differentials, if we want to, we have to ask whether these differentials we are considering in a quiet field of vision are to be regarded as independent or as dependent differentials in an equilibrium distribution of larger area. Feeling that this is the very kernel of our problem, we should give our answer slowly, gradually approaching the decision by a series of observations. . . .[2]

We began our observations with a view to deciding whether or not the sensation is an *independent* differential. Our first result, however, has led us back to another concept, namely that of an objective unit. In order to show what I meant by this term, I mentioned the molecule in the atmosphere as a unit which is not arbitrarily conceived in thought, but objectively given by the strong interaction of interior forces which hold the molecule together, in contrast to the comparatively low dynamic interrelation between the molecule and its surroundings. I chose the very small molecule as a model because the question was whether we have to regard sensations, supposedly small things, as similarly small objective units; and we found no indication of their existence as such. But the concept of an objective unit in the defined meaning is not necessarily restricted to small things. A crystal, for instance, in the saturated solution in which it forms, is an objective unit, in a meaning so similar to that of the molecule that some physicists have actually called it an enormous molecule. Are there objective units in a field of vision? Yes, there are. It is not arbitrary and abstract thinking that makes groups or spots or rectangles or things in my visual field. I find them there as optical realities not less real than their color, black or white or red. As long as my visual field remains the same, as long as it is not changed by internal or external influences, there is little doubt about what belongs in one of those units and what does not. And if we have found that in the visual field there are units of different rank, a group, for instance, containing several spots, the larger unit containing smaller ones of still stronger unity, exactly the same occurs in physics; there the molecule, as one larger objective unit (defined by a comparative break of inter-

[2] [There follows a discussion of the formation of visual groups and of continuous two- and three-dimensional units. The question is raised, Why do visual units generally correspond to entities in the physical world? Again, the role of past experience in perception, and its limitations, are considered. For discussion of these problems, cf. W. Köhler, *Gestalt Psychology.* (Rev. ed.) New York: Liveright, 1947, Chapters V and VI; cf. also Chapter 7 of this volume, "Human Perception"; also M. Wertheimer, Untersuchungen zur Lehre von der Gestalt. *Psychologische Forschung,* 1923, 4, 301–350.—Ed.]

connection at its limits), contains smaller objective units, the atoms, whose interior is again enormously more strongly united than the molecule. There is no contradiction and no vagueness in saying that objective units contain smaller units. And as it remains an objective fact, in the case of the physical material, where the boundaries of its units and perhaps its subunits are, so in the visual field, no arbitrary analyzing thought should interfere with observation. Experience is spoiled if we begin to introduce artificial subdivisions where real units and boundaries of one or the other rank are open and clear before us. This is the principal reason why I think that a concept like sensation is almost a danger. It tends to absorb our attention, obscuring the fact that there are observable units and subunits in the field. For the moment we give up our naïveté in description and theory, and think of the field in terms of unreal elements, these unreal little things appear to our thought side by side, indifferently filling space, some of one, some of another color or brightness; and the observable units with their observable boundaries do not occur in this pseudodescription. I do not exaggerate. Look at the development of the psychology of vision. All the more important observations relating to real units, etc., began to be made only in the last thirty years, though the facts were before us for thousands of years, wherever psychologists or other people looked into the world. Artificial theory made us a little blind to them.[3]

It will be worthwhile to mention here one more ambiguity of the term analysis in psychology. Either I may consider in theory one little part of the visual field, i.e., when thinking about such a field—about this we have been speaking up to now; or, looking at an actually given field, I may proceed by *actual analysis in vision*. In the second case, for example, if I find the letter *K* in Figure 2.1, I have really changed the visual field, the units and the boundaries in it.[4]

[3] G. Humphrey, The psychology of the Gestalt. *Journal of Educational Psychology*, 1924, 15, 401–412.

[4] [This example of camouflage was discussed in a section of the paper omitted from this selection. The drawing, when viewed naïvely, is seen as consisting of three parts, two irregular hexagons, with a longer irregular figure between them. The *K* is not usually seen spontaneously since its parts are absorbed in the contours of the closed forms. Cf. discussion of Figure 7.14 in "Human perception," Chapter 7.—Ed.]

Figure 2.1

There is a letter now which did not previously exist in the field, and the units which were given before are seriously changed. Really to see the letter and the closed areas of that figure at the same time and undisturbed is more than I can achieve. Probably it is as impossible as to have the two really separate atoms of O and the molecule O_2 at the same time. Of course it is highly interesting to produce such a change in the field; what happens or what does not happen in such an operation may even give very valuable hints as to the nature of the units in question. But in no case must one expect to find the whole truth about a given unit by transforming the field and creating new units in it. I would not find out all about a molecule O_2 by describing two atoms O which I have separated; also, the separate atoms O which I describe did not really exist as the same things in the molecule. This is a point we shall treat more thoroughly later on.[5] For the moment it is more important to mention that, from the standpoint of Gestalt psychology, there is, after all, *one* analysis which is perfectly genuine, permissible, and productive in all cases: the simple description of the field in terms of real units, of subunits as their real parts, in terms of their boundaries, subboundaries, etc.

The question we wished to answer was whether or not the local state of affairs in a sensory field is an independent process, so that the whole field may be regarded as a mosaic of such processes. On our way we learned something about extended units in the field, and the same facts we were considering there give an

[5] The fact that the change of subjective attitude toward the field can, to a certain degree, alter its properties, units, etc., must be regarded as a very interesting problem. It has not yet been studied thoroughly enough. Cf. W. Köhler, Komplextheorie und Gestalttheorie. *Psychologische Forschung*, 1925, 6, 396ff.

answer to our present question too. How can local processes which are independent of, and indifferent to, each other be at the same time organized into larger units of well observable extent? How, again, can relative break of continuity at the well observable limits of those areas be understood, since these limits are not limits between all the little pieces of a mosaic, but only appear where one group or unit ends? The hypothesis of independent little parts is unable to give an explanation. All the concepts we found necessary above for the description of the field have no relation whatever to the conception of independent local elements. And more concretely, where our groups or units are formed can certainly not be deduced from a consideration of the conditions at one point, then independently those at the next, etc. Only a consideration which takes into account how the local conditions of the whole field *relate to each other* begins to approach an understanding of these facts. It is not the local white along a white line drawn on a black field which makes this line a real optical unit in the field; there is no specific unit, and no line, before the surroundings have a *different* color or brightness. This difference of stimulation around, as against equality of stimulation within, the line must be the fact which produces a specific unit in the given arrangement. And it is the same for units of higher order: It is not the independent or absolute conditions in one of our parallels, then the conditions in the next one, which make them form one group, but that these lines are *equal, different from the ground,* and *near* to each other—three prerequisites which again show the decisive role of *relations* of local conditions (see Figure 2.2). And let us be careful not to forget the ground. For, if a certain group is formed, say two parallels half a centi-

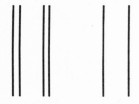

Figure 2.2

meter apart, I have only to draw two more parallels on the outside
of this group, much nearer to the first lines than these are to each
other, and the first group is destroyed; two other groups are
formed by the parallels which are now nearest to each other (Figure 2.2). Only so long as we had uniform white in the neighborhood of our first group did this group exist. I change conditions in
this neighborhood, and what was the interior of a unit now becomes a gap between two others. One additional consequence follows immediately: The characters of "figure" and "ground" are
so absolutely dependent upon the formation of units in the field
that, since these units cannot be deduced from an aggregate of
independent local states, the appearance of an area as figure or
ground cannot either. And still another fact is relevant to our argument. We draw two parallels and produce a group; we draw
another congruent pair considerably more distant from the first
than the distance between the lines of the first pair; and we go on
increasing the length of our series. The result is that *all* the
groups in the series become more solid than each of them would
be if given alone. Even over such great distances, the conditions
in one place influence what happens in another place, and vice
versa.

Thus not the local properties of given stimuli, but the relations of these properties to each other (the total constellation of
stimuli, to use a better expression), are decisive for the formation
of units. This fact at once suggests the idea that dynamic interaction in the field decides what becomes a unit, what is excluded
from it, what is figure, and what falls back as mere ground. Indeed, at the present time not many psychologists will deny that,
given these real units, etc., in the visual field, we have at once
to draw certain consequences for that part of the brain whose
processes correspond to our field of vision. The units, subunits,
boundaries, the difference between figure and ground must exist
there as physiological realities.[6] There must be a unitary process

[6] M. Wertheimer, Experimentelle Studien über das Sehen von Bewegung.
Zeitschrift für Psychologie, 1912, 61, 161–265. W. Köhler, *Die physischen
Gestalten in Ruhe und im stationären Zustand.* Braunschweig: Friedr.
Vieweg & Sohn, 1920, 173ff.

containing three comparatively separate subunits when we look at Figure 2.1; and this unitary physiological process must be at least partially disturbed and give place to a new one, not existing the moment before, when we begin to see the K. Remarking now that relative distance and relations of qualitative properties are the main factors that determine the formation of units, we remember that exactly such factors ought to be decisive if unit formation is the effect of dynamic interaction throughout the field in the physiological process. Most physical and chemical interaction we know of depends upon the relation of properties and on mutual distance between the material in space. Now, differences of stimulation produce points, lines, areas of different chemical reaction and in certain spatial relations to each other on the retina. If there is transverse connection between the longitudinal conductors of the optic nerve somewhere in the optic sector of the nervous system, dynamic interaction ought to depend upon the relations of qualitative properties and distance which, at a given time, exist in the total optic process, streaming up to or into the brain. It is not astonishing, then, that we find phenomena of distribution, etc., showing direct dependence upon these relations.

But physiological conclusions of this kind will appear better founded if first we consider another side of our descriptive problem. Intimately related to the existence of real units and boundaries in the field of vision is the fact that there are *forms* in this field. It was practically impossible to exclude them from the foregoing discussion, because wherever we see these units, they have forms; this is why, in German, these units are called *Gestalten*.[7] Again, the reality of forms in visual space is a fact which cannot be understood from the theory that the visual field consists of independent local elements. If there were elements of this kind forming a dense and perhaps continuous mosaic as the "stuff" of the visual field, then we would have no real forms in this field.

[7] I do not think that the term "configuration" is quite adequate as a translation of the German word "Gestalt." The word configuration seems to refer to elements put together in a certain manner, and this is a functional idea which we must carefully avoid.

Mathematically, of course, some aggregates of them might be considered together, but that would not correspond to the reality in which, at a given time, some concrete forms *are simply there* in vision, no less than colors and brightnesses. And first of all, mathematically, *all* imaginable patterns might be considered in such a field of independent elements, whereas in vision quite *individual* forms are always before us under given conditions.[8] If, now, we examine these conditions upon which real form depends, we naturally find again the qualitative and spatial relations of stimulation. Naturally, because the now well-known *units* appear in the individual forms we see, and we earlier came to realize that these units are somehow a function of those relations. I remember from my own slow development in this respect how difficult it is to make a sharp distinction between any aggregate of stimuli, i.e., geometrically existent patterns of them, and optic forms as realities. On this page there are certainly some black points which, considered together, would constitute a large group of the form shown in Figure 2.3. Do we therefore *see* such a form as a visual reality? Certainly not. But let these stimuli be red and perhaps nearer together, and all people who are not color blind or half blind for forms because of brain lesions will immediately see this group as a form. Also, to use our previous example, we first did not see the form of the letter *K*, but another form containing three separate units; only when these units gave way, at least partially, the definite form of *K* appeared at once. And do not think that these are exceptional cases, painfully sought for the purpose of my argument. There is no field of vision in everyday life in which you might not find thousands of geometrical patterns of all varieties; but you do not see such forms because other *existing* units with other forms have, as it were, spent and distributed the field among themselves.

All this is not only true for forms in a plane or on paper; it is equally true for the things or objects in our surroundings. And so I wish to warn you against the misunderstanding that these problems of real units and their forms might perhaps have

[8] W. Köhler, Komplextheorie, *op. cit.*, 386ff.

Figure 2.3

some importance for aesthetics or for other considerations of a supposedly higher level only, whereas they are foreign to the practical affairs of everyday life. There is no object, no man you have to deal with, whose optical reality is not a concrete demonstration of the same scientific situation. If, in thousands of years, people have never become fully aware of it, it is not astonishing that we still have difficulties in realizing how full of problems one glance into the world is.

"Perhaps you are right," somebody might say, "insofar as your units and their forms have psychological reality and importance. It also seems probable that, for units and their forms, the constellation of stimuli is at least as important as the absolute stimuli themselves. But why not assume that some psychic factor, which we might look for, collects the local elements into units and gives them form at the same time? Your tendency is to deny the existence of independent sensory differentials and to consider units and their forms as the outcome of dynamic interaction in the total stream of the optic process itself. But surely you would not go so far as to assert that the real nature of a local process is determined by the relations of stimulation in a large area. Is not, after all, the color or brightness which is somewhere in the field the fundamental reality in it? And this color, at least, does depend upon its local stimulus. White is white, black is black on the surface of this paper, whatever may be the units and forms in which they occur. They *are* independent local processes."

There are two points in my answer. That color is a more important or more fundamental aspect of our visual field than the objects in which it appears, or the form of these objects, would not be easy to prove. Our vital reactions are determined by objects, one single property of which is color. And if a color, however extended, is at the same time the mere ground on which an object appears, what determines our naïve reactions—from thinking down to eye movements—will, in 99 cases out of 100, be the *object*, though its color might be a poor gray. And the second point: Colors *are* dependent on the constellation of stimuli throughout, the field. The black on this page is at once transformed into a white, the white around it into a black, a gray spot may become a red one, a red one white, without the slightest change in local stimulation, if only you change sufficiently the total constellation or quality of stimulation around the spot. Everybody knows that we have only to reduce drastically the light reflected by the white on this page, and to keep the black letters reflecting exactly the amount of light they are now reflecting, in order to get white letters on a black ground. No need to dwell upon the other cases. For simple physical reasons, really strong changes of this kind in the surroundings of one smaller area, which itself remains unaltered, are rather rare, and so we do not easily become aware of these phenomena. Neither are we much struck by the more frequent fact that a change of stimulation, produced for instance by change of illumination in a part of the field, leaves the white of an object there much more constant than the radically different local stimulations can account for. Since the relation of stimuli is not changed when only the illumination becomes stronger or weaker both for our object and its surroundings, the nuance, the white of this area, does not change very much either.

"I know," you will say, "but that is contrast!" Whatever the name of it, we have to do with the facts behind the name and the type of functional interrelation involved. The facts are that local color also shows its dependence on a *set* of stimuli, whenever we change the average properties of stimulation in the surroundings a little more than is usually the case. If we make the experiment with this printed page, for example, the result shows clearly enough that the black of the letters is really black only when a much higher brightness surrounds it.

And there is one fact about contrast which makes it altogether impossible to eliminate it from our discussion as something old, well-known, and not connected with this problem. Quite a number of observations have recently shown that the tendency to treat the visual field as a mosaic of elements is particularly dangerous in the work on contrast. All of these new observations agree in one essential point, namely that the existence and the amount of contrast is in the highest degree dependent upon the units or forms which appear in the field. We find contrast of various degrees, but we also find the opposite of contrast under different conditions of unit formation. Even without any change in the constellation of stimuli if, by change of subjective attitude, we produce a real change in the units of the field, the effects which are ascribed to contrast may suddenly appear in striking degree or disappear altogether, depending on the units present. Apart from contrast, and more generally, several investigators were able to show that it is easy to alter local colors thoroughly by making their area enter one group or another in the formation of real units.[9]

Instead of small units of the type of molecules, we have found larger units and forms in the visual field which come into existence and disappear, depending mainly on the actual conditions of stimulation. The manner in which stimulation determines these units shows that the physiological foundation of their existence must be dynamic interaction in the optic stream, the units being *dependent* real parts in this stream, and every local process, if we want to consider it more particularly, being a *dependent* differential. It follows that such a differential and its properties, as we consider them in the abstract, cannot rightly be understood without going back to the total sensory constellation in which, only, they are what they are.

We may draw a physiological consequence: If the local pro-

[9] K. Koffka, Zur Grundlegung der Wahrnehmungspsychologie. *Zeitschrift für Psychologie*, 1915, 73, 11–90. K. Koffka, Über Feldbegrenzung und Felderfüllung. *Psychologische Forschung*, 1923, 4, 176–203. W. Fuchs, Experimentelle Untersuchungen über das simultane Hintereinander auf derselben Sehrichtung. *Zeitschrift für Psychologie*, 1923, 91, 145–235. W. Fuchs, Experimentelle Untersuchungen über die Änderung von Farben unter dem Einfluss von Gestalten. *Zeitschrift für Psychologie*, 1923, 92, 249–325. W. Benary, Beobachtungen zu einem Experiment über Helligkeitskontrast. *Psychologische Forschung*, 1924, 5, 131–142. W. Köhler, Komplextheorie, *op. cit.*, 411ff.

cess in an extended system is a dependent differential, it will change, and so will the process in the whole system, until equilibrium is reached in a stationary distribution without further change. We have been treating visual fields in a state of rest. They must be the psychological correlates of a stationary equilibrium distribution in the corresponding processes of the brain. There are enough cases in physics where a process originating in a system under a certain set of conditions develops its stationary distribution in an extremely short time. The time in which the equilibrium of an optic process is developed must also be rather short. Because, if we present a set of stimuli suddenly, say by projection, the phase of "something happening" which we observe is extremely rapid, and in a moment we see the field, its units and their forms, at rest.

To avoid misunderstanding, I may add that, in a state of stationary equilibrium, the field is by no means "dead." The mutual stresses in the phase of field formation (which of course are themselves interdependent) do not disappear when the stationary distribution is accomplished. Rather, they now have (together with the processes) those intensities and directions in which they balance each other. The total process in stationary distribution is still a *store of energy* distributed in the field. . . .[10]

Furthermore, we have reason to believe that the coordination of certain simple motor reactions to a visual field depends directly on our principles. If, in the stereoscope, one vertical line is exposed to one eye and a second to the other so that, with a given degree of convergence of the two eyes, the lines appear nearly parallel and at a rather short distance from each other, we find that they unite into one line almost at once. It is well known that in this case our eyes turn without our intention to that degree of convergence which brings the two lines upon two

[10] [Omitted here is a discussion of assumptions about the physiological processes in the nervous system which would account for the perceptual properties described. The conceptions of machine theory and free dynamics are contrasted, and illustrations of dynamic theory are given. For a more extended and a more recent treatment of these issues cf. W. Köhler, *Gestalt Psychology*, Chapter IV. Also omitted is a section on perceptual units as prerequisites for recognition, recall, and the acquisition of meaning. Cf. *Gestalt Psychology*, Chapters VIII and IX.—Ed.]

corresponding verticals of the two retinae, the two physiological *processes* probably becoming more intimately united under these circumstances than with any other degree of convergence. But we have already seen that parallel lines near to each other in a monocular or binocular visual field form a group or belong together as if under mutual attraction. Doesn't it look as if, under the conditions given in stereoscopic observation, these forces accomplish the same thing more thoroughly by really uniting the parallels? An examination of the situation from the standpoint of physics seems to show that such a thing might really occur. We saw that in the equilibrium distribution of process, the field is still full of stresses which are for the moment in balance, but which represent a store of energy. So in vision there seems to be stress tending to bring the two parallels together. In physics, if such a field is functionally connected to movable parts, of which some definite form of motion would release the still existing stresses of the field, this movement will immediately occur, produced by the energy of those stresses. These only "waited," as it were, for an opportunity to let their energy work, for instance influencing movable parts in the direction of a better equilibrium. The better equilibrium in physics always lies in the direction of those stresses which tend to produce some change, but which in our physiological case *cannot do it directly in the field.* If possible, then, they will do it by a detour influencing the muscles of the eyes, as movable parts, in the direction of release of their energy. There is nothing supernatural in such an orderly physical process; no process with or without detour can ever produce changes which are not directed toward a more stable equilibrium of the whole system. We have only to adopt this view for the case of the optical part of the brain and its nervous connection with the muscles of the eyeballs in order to have a new explanation of fixation movements which is founded on principles of Gestalt theory and physics.[11] Of course the hypothesis needs to be worked out carefully for the concrete conditions given in the nervous sys-

[11] W. Köhler, Gestaltprobleme und Anfänge einer Gestalttheorie. *Jahresbericht über die gesamte Physiologie und experimentelle Pharmakologie,* 1924, Band III (Bericht über das Jahr 1922), 536f.

tem and in the muscles of the eyes. But the more we work in this direction, the more facts seem to show that we are on the right path.

About one other, and far more important, extension of Gestalt psychology only some brief remarks are possible here. We have dealt with forms or groups of very different degrees of solidity. There are cases in which all attempts by analysis to destroy a given form in favor of a certain other form are in vain. But distribute furniture in an irregular manner in a room; you will have rather solid and stable units, the single objects, but no equally stable and firm *groups* will be formed spontaneously with these objects as members. Equality or similarity and dissimilarity of color and other properties, relative distances, etc., still tend to form groups; but you will observe that one group formation is easily displaced by another, depending on slight changes of conditions, probably in yourself. It is evident that, under such circumstances, the influence of changes in the subjective attitude toward the field will be much greater than in the case of solid units or stable groups. Even forces of no particular intensity will now be strong enough to produce new groups in a field which, with the exception of the objects in it, does not resist very much because its own tendencies to group formation are too weak. (If we wish our theory to remain consistent, subjective attitude and change of it must also be represented in the physiological field as physical states or stresses and changes in them, which influence the formation of physiological groups.)

The members of these groups, the objects, are however more than purely optical entities under most conditions of life. They commonly appear as imbued by experience with meanings, functional properties, and so on. And these secondary properties, when actually present, must be almost inherent now in the optic physiological process units of objects, because in extreme examples we have the strong impression of actually *seeing* the acquired properties in the objects, even if there is no possibility of their having a purely optical origin. I cannot tell you briefly how Gestalt psychology would treat this fact. For the moment we may state only that in practical life, of course, seen objects have more properties than we have treated here. Do not forget, however, that if seen objects are to become imbued with their functional properties, a prerequisite is their real optical existence as forms in the field. If you camouflage them, or if the optical units do not actually exist for some other reason, the functional properties do not appear either.

Suppose now that a field is given in which objects have no strong optical tendency toward formation of stable groups; our subjective attitude will often tend to group them with regard to acquired functional properties—not necessarily so that objects of equal functional value are grouped together; rather, more frequently so that objects which *belong* together in one practical task or performance stand out together in the field. Here, however, we must be careful to avoid a mistake. The subjective attitude may easily be taken as something foreign, acting from without, like an independent power, on the content of the field, for instance forming groups in it. In real life quite a different thing usually happens. A chimpanzee sees a banana beyond the bars of his cage, too far away for his arm to reach. If he is healthy and not overfed, a well defined subjective attitude immediately appears: the banana arouses his appetite. That is, the relation between his inner condition and the sight of the fruit makes the banana outstanding in the field, makes its functional value very alive, and produces the corresponding stress toward the fruit— both things being sides of one and the same fact. *There is no arbitrary subjective attitude;* the appearance of this object and the animal's attitude toward it are changed correspondingly and at the same time, depending on the relation between the animal's inner condition and one real part of the field. If we consider not the visual field separately but the larger whole in which it actually occurs, namely the total situation including the inner condition of the animal, we find the subjective attitude and the functional value of the object produced *in mutual dependence.* The subjective attitude, then, does not come out of the blue any more than do the changes which it produces in the visual field; and we become aware of this fact if we do not restrict our consideration arbitrarily, that is, again, if we do not make an artificial analysis.

Let us continue with our example. After a short while we see the chimpanzee looking around for a stick. Evidently this attitude is no less determined by the total situation than was the direct tendency toward the food. But again this new attitude has remarkable consequences for the objects in the field. A man can easily observe in himself in a similar situation, and one can see in the behavior of the ape, that many objects which are not real sticks but similar to them, very soon appear as "sticks" in the functional meaning of the word, if no real stick is found.[12] The tree with its branches, however, may remain "one thing" for a long time; it is too much a unit optically to permit the functional value of a stick to enter its branches, since these are not seen as optically real parts—at least by the chimpanzee. If, finally, this unit is destroyed under the pressure of the subjective attitude of "seeking a stick," we certainly have a case of a unit changed by the subjective attitude. But once more, this attitude itself is changed at the same time and in a corresponding manner: as soon as the attitude of seeking makes the branch a real part of the field, that attitude itself undergoes the change from "seeking" to "breaking off." After all, we seldom have the subjective stress alone; it is a stress *between man* (or animal) *and the field* or some part of it, determined by the relative conditions of both sides in this *total situation*. Therefore, in principle, no change will occur on one side without a corresponding change on the other.

I draw some conclusions: Reorganization of the field by subjective stress, if the field is not too stable, seems to be an important part of intelligent behavior. We suspected this before when describing the behavior of apes. But the subjective stress is as much a function of the field as the field is of the stress, both being dependent sides in the total situation. And, of course, only if the subjective attitude is so concretely related to the ac-

[12] W. Köhler, *The Mentality of Apes.* Ella Winter (Trans.). New York: Harcourt, Brace & World, 1925, 37.

tual field, can the corresponding stress have effects on the field which lead to the solution of the problem given in this field. In the total situation, the inner and outer conditions seem to be in a functional interdependence similar to that which prevails, for example, between the dependent areas of the visual field. If this is true, the dynamic interaction between field and subjective stress must follow the same rule, that is, develop in the direction of equilibrium, which I have so far applied only to the field, to eye movements, etc.

With these remarks I return to my starting point. Though here I have mainly tried to explain the procedure of Gestalt psychology in its treatment of the visual field, this is by no means the only application which its functional concepts admit. They can be applied as well to the full reality of mental life, and we are beginning to do it. But since we need firm ground under our feet, we prefer to *introduce* our standpoint by showing how it works in vision, because there we have the best methods for concrete, experimental decisions.

3: The mind-body problem

AMONG the problems with which philosophy and the various sciences have to deal, the mind-body problem is still the most intriguing. No completely convincing solution has so far been offered. I do not claim that I have found such a solution. Recent advances in philosophical thinking and in experimental research have made the problem even more challenging than it was, say, thirty years ago. For now we have begun to realize that almost any imaginable solution is likely to affect our interpretation of what we call the physical world. I will try to explain this statement in the following paragraphs.

In present discussions we do not assume, as the philosophers of the past did, that the mind and the body are two substances. In the first place, we have the very best reasons for regarding the bodies of animals and men as processes or, more specifically, as approximately steady states, which maintain their shapes and other characteristics by self-regulating activities. Biologists know that the material of all organs of the body is con-

From Sidney Hook (ed.), *Dimensions of Mind.* New York University Press, 1960, 3–23. Reprinted by permission of the publisher.

tinuously being eliminated, and at the same time replaced, in the course of metabolic events. Similarly, there is no evidence that mental functions represent the activities of a mental substance. What we call, in a purely empirical sense, the *self* is not a permanent entity with constant characteristics—although, among the various states through which this important part of the mental scene passes, there is a great deal of coherence. The relative constancy of a person's self is likely to be basically of the same kind as the relative constancy of his heart, his muscles, his brain, and so forth—that is, a constancy of a state of affairs.

All this does not alter the fact that the events which occur in our organisms appear to us to be of one kind, and those that we call "mental" events to be of another kind. It is this prima facie dualism which makes us speak of a mind-body problem.

We are less and less inclined to believe that the dualistic view can be accepted as final. For one thing, we prefer unitary knowledge to the view that certain groups of facts will never become parts of one cognitive system. Secondly, numerous observations, particularly in medicine, tend to show that, however different from processes in nature the mental phenomena may seem to be, they only occur when certain conditions are fulfilled in a particular part of nature, the brain. Causal relations between processes in the brain and mental facts are, of course, readily recognized by the dualists. But mental facts depend upon biological conditions in a much more radical fashion. I need not mention details. One example will suffice. When the oxygen supply to the human brain is lowered beyond a certain crucial level, the mental world of the person in question disappears entirely—until the oxygen level rises again, and sufficiently. We do not usually speak of interaction when the presence or absence of one of the allegedly interacting entities or events depends upon variations in the state of the other. This and similar arguments against the dualists' thesis may not be fully convincing, but they have made most of us feel that the solution of the mind-body problem must lie in another direction. Meanwhile, the dualists have not yet surrendered. Some philosophers and also some biologists remain convinced that certain achievements of the mental world will never be explained in terms of natural science. On the contrary, such authors sometimes add, even the most important activities of the *organism* cannot be understood in such terms, for these activities exhibit the same characteristics as do the irreducible mental processes. Although the more extreme form of this thesis, namely vitalism, has so far proved to be singularly unproductive, the dualists' factual arguments may at least serve as warnings. To be sure, those who claim that certain mental processes have no counterparts among the facts of the physical world often offer examples for which people more familiar with natural science will find physical partners without the slightest difficulty. In other instances, however, no such simple answers to the dualists' arguments are available. This ought to prevent their opponents from proceeding too rashly. The tremendous store of knowledge which natural science has accumulated in the past may sometimes make them overconfident. There is a risk that, when now approaching the mental world, they will inadvertently crush rather than recognize some outstanding facts of this world or (what would be just as bad) that they will simply ignore such parts of the less familiar field as do not immediately yield to the impatient demands of the conquerors. Some geneticists and evolutionists have actually proceeded in this fashion. But can we be interested in a unity of knowledge that only destruction or partial omission of the evidence makes possible?

We wish to compare psychological facts with the facts of natural science. We must, therefore, make sure that we know the characteristics of these facts as such. For our present purposes, an inspection of some psychological evidence and a consideration of a major biological issue will suffice. We may regard ourselves as fairly well acquainted with the behavior of inanimate nature, but we do not always have sufficiently clear concepts in psychology and biology.

I begin with psychology. Here, early behaviorism made an error, the consequences of which still disturb the psychologist's work. It is quite true that, in natural science, all observation of systems is observation "from the outside." But does it follow that, when the psychologist deals with human subjects, he must always use the same procedure? Must he also restrict his observations to behavior as watched from the outside? Why should he not be interested in mental life as *experienced* by himself or others? If a certain scientific enterprise which we admire has unfortunately only one kind of access to its material, why should psychology, which has two, refuse to make use of both? In the meantime, the behaviorists themselves have discovered that, when a physicist observes his systems from the outside, the content of his observations as such consists of certain perceptual facts, mostly in his visual field, and that the same holds for the behaviorists' own observations of animals and of men. But perceptual facts belong to the mental world, the world of experienced phenomena, and it therefore follows that such phenomena play a decisive role in any scientific enterprise. Hence, modern behaviorists no longer maintain that the phenomenal world has been invented by the metaphysicians. What is left, however, is their preference for observation from the outside, which under the right conditions yields clear quantitative results, in contrast to phenomenological procedures, which in this respect are generally inferior. In this methodological sense, most American psychologists now seem to be behaviorists. Under the circumstances, not only details but also most impressive aspects of the phenomenal scene are often ignored in the psychologists' work. Their admiration of method, of precision, prevents them from paying attention to phenomenological evidence even when this evidence could hardly escape the very simplest observation. Naturally, the psychologists' sin of omission makes them incapable of contributing to the solution of the mind-body problem in its most serious form, in which it refers to the relation between the *phenomenal* scene and the characteristics of events in nature. Once more, one cannot study the relation between two groups of facts without knowing the facts in each group per se.

I have just implied that, when trying to solve the mind-body problem, we actually have to answer more than one question. The reason is that the expression "mental processes" is sometimes given one and sometimes another meaning. But so abstract are many discussions of the problem that, at a given moment, it may be almost impossible to decide whether the term is being used in one sense or the other.

In its first meaning, the term refers to all facts which are directly accessible to a person, the facts which are phenomenally given. I have repeatedly been asked to indicate more clearly what I mean when I refer to "phenomenally given facts." It seems quite possible that in this case no actual definition can be given and that, if the attempt is made, one undefinable word is merely substituted for another. But I also doubt whether such a definition is really needed. Everybody will recognize the meaning of the expression if I tell him that objects as felt, sounds as heard, colors and shapes as seen, and movement perceived in any fashion are all phenomenal facts. To avoid misunderstandings, I should have to include a person's hilarious or dejected moods, the direction of his attention, his awareness of relations, and the values, both positive and negative, with which objects or ideas seem to him to be imbued, and which thus establish his motivations. It is the task of phenomenological psychology to study these facts; and, in its first form, the mind-body problem refers to the relations between the characteristics of such facts and those of facts in nature.

The psychologist's work is not restricted to the study of the phenomenal scene; he investigates other facts besides, which often are also called "mental." The phenomenal facts as such do not constitute a functionally complete material. There is a coherence among the phenomenal experiences of a person which transcends these experiences themselves. A person may suddenly have a new idea which he has just begun to elaborate when circumstances arise which force him to do other things first, and only after they have been done is that idea, with the reasoning which it had barely started, likely to emerge again as an experienced fact—whereupon the reasoning may be continued. This is memory in the strictest sense of the term. In the present case, it makes temporally separated stages of the phenomenal flux coherent in spite of an interruption. Most probably, if a person's mental life were crowded with phenomenal experiences, but deprived of the coherence established by memory, this life would be of very little value. Memory is generally regarded as a fact which the psychologist has to study, and so are its gradually developing *defects* which we call forgetting. But neither retention in memory per se nor forgetting per se are generally experienced in the sense in which we experience the emergence of a new idea and, afterwards, its recall. Retention, often for considerable periods, and gradual forgetting are facts which do not belong to the phenomenal scene. This holds also for memory in its more general sense, in which the word refers to our habits and to our cognitive, motivational, or emotional dispositions. Habits and dispositions as such are not parts of the phenomenal, the experienced, world. Only their temporary *effects* will generally be experienced—although not necessarily *as* effects of the underlying more permanent entities, the habits and dispositions themselves. But again, if all our habits and dispositions were suddenly to disappear forever, our mental life would probably no longer deserve its name.

Even though the effects of memory in all its meanings are so closely related, and so necessary to most mental processes in the phenomenal sense, it is perhaps not wise to refer to retention in memory, to our habits, and to our dispositions as "mental facts." After all, the existence of retention in memory, of habits, and of dispositions can only be inferred from certain achievements within the phenomenal field, which they make possible. And, from the point of view of epistemology, this means a fundamental difference between these products of the past and the experienced facts, however much these may owe to such hidden entities. Consequently, when dealing with the mind-body problem, we must try to keep two comparisons separate: that of the phenomenal world with the facts of natural science, and that of memory, and so forth, with the same facts.

All merely inferred "mental" states seem to have much in common with certain facts in nature. For instance, memory as a mere retention, as an aftereffect of events which have taken place in the past, is by no means a rare fact in physical nature. It has therefore been suggested that memory in psychology simply *consists* of more or less permanent physical states which earlier events have established in the brain. Thus, the comparison of merely inferred "psychological" facts with certain facts in the physical world may perhaps be expected to yield positive results. But, when we compare phenomenal situations with the various facts which occur in nature, we have reasons for being far less optimistic.

Some difficulties arise only when particular classes of phenomena are being considered. It would, for instance, not be easy to find in nature anything like Dilthey's *"verständliche Zusammenhänge."* What, in the physical world as such, would be comparable to such *understandable,* as distinct from merely *factual,* relations? And also, what physical fact would be capable of what we call "understanding"? But, far more generally, present epistemology refuses to attribute *any* phenomenal characteristics to *any* fact in nature—whatever these characteristics may be. It seems to follow that, in this respect, not a single part of the phenomenal world fits the premises on which the system of natural science rests, and that therefore the dualists are right.

If we do not wish to accept this radical conclusion, we must obviously examine the thesis from which it is derived. How did it happen that the epistemologists excluded all phenomenal characteristics from our picture of nature? There is, I believe, no question that, as children, we have all been "naïve realists." The rocks, trees, houses, and so forth, which we perceived were at this stage regarded as permanent entities which happened to be thus accessible at the time, but were not at all dependent upon our presence. When we were absent, they continued to exist, and still had characteristics of the same kind as they had in our presence. These characteristics were, of course, phenomenal characteristics. Obviously, we had no difficulty in ascribing such characteristics to objects outside the field of actual awareness. In less sophisticated populations, adults share this view with their children. This we can safely say because even the most sophisticated physicists and epistemologists among *us* still think in the same fashion whenever they do not happen to remember the arguments against this simple view of the world. We are all naïve realists most of the time. It will not be necessary to mention the observations which gradually destroyed naïve realism in the thinking of scientists *as* scientists, and eventually made it necessary to distinguish, as a matter of principle, between all facts of phenomenal experience and an independent physical world. So gradual was this development—its final stages occurred during the nineteenth century—that even now a physicist may think of the behavior of molecules in a gas in concrete phenomenal terms, as though he were considering a *visual* scene and *visual* events. It is this behavior which obscures to us the consequences of a more consistent discrimination between all phenomenal facts and all facts in nature. I repeat, according to the epistemologists of our time, not a single phenomenal datum is, as such, a characteristic also of situations in the physical world. The content of all statements about this world is only a matter of inferences, of a construction in thought—although some simple perceptual facts used in actual observation are supposed to have somehow comparable partners in nature, and thus to control the direction in which the construction can proceed. From this point of view, what ingredients, what building materials, are being used in the construction? So far as I can see, only one material is available. Although we have been told that we must sharply distinguish between the characteristics of nature and those of the phenomenal world, the contents of this world remain the only stuff at our disposal when we do the constructing. What else could we use? To be sure, as scientists we are free to select such particular characteristics of the phenomenal scene as seem to us most adequate for our purposes; and, being parsimonious people, we do the constructing with a *minimum* of concepts taken from the phenomenal world. Thus, the various sensory qualities are never used, nor are our feelings, our experiences of value, and our motivations. As a consequence, the resulting picture of nature is, of course, a most colorless affair when compared with the world of which we are directly aware. Even so, any concept actually used in the process must contain one or several components which are known to us from phenomenal experience. If something in nature were totally different from *all* phenomenal facts, then this part of nature would forever remain inaccessible to us.

How well the process of construction has so far worked we

all know. However, I have not yet been able to overcome a certain difficulty. I said that, in constructing the physical world, we have to equip it throughout with attributes directly known to us only as properties of the phenomenal scene. But we are also told that no state or event in nature has any phenomenal characteristics. It seems to follow that when, for example, the term "intensity" (the meaning of which is derived from certain experiences) is used as it is nowadays in physics, it is deprived of all phenomenal content and yet remains a term with a meaning. What exactly is left under these circumstances? Suppose we were told that "intensity" in nature must be understood in a far more abstract sense than it is when the term is applied to a phenomenal fact; that, in nature, the meaning of "intensity" is reduced to a system of mere *relations*. If this were said, I should be inclined to ask from what sources anybody derives his knowledge of such *relations;* and the answer would be that *their* meanings, too, must stem from relations experienced in the phenomenal world—whereupon the same difficulty would once more arise. Obviously, there would be no such difficulty if, contrary to present convictions, states and events in nature actually had phenomenal characteristics. It is a curious fact that a physicist as advanced as Galileo still regarded the behavior of the planets as partly determined by values. This is a strange situation. Epistemologists may, of course, be able to clarify the present issue entirely. I can only repeat that, as I see it, all parts of recognizable nature must more or less resemble *some* aspects of the phenomenal world. If this is a true statement, it may sooner or later have to be remembered in discussions of the mind-body problem.

I NOW turn to a fundamental issue in biology, namely, to certain consequences of the theory of evolution. Unavoidably, the following discussion will be concerned with problems in natural science with which few philosophers are accustomed to deal.

Until recently, one part of the theory had remained disappointingly obscure. We were unable to explain the *beginning* of life on this planet. We knew that, in the absence of large organic molecules, there could be no living cells. But we also knew that, in present organisms, these molecules are built up in the cells. Where, then, did such molecules come from when cells did not yet exist? Thanks to Oparin in Russia, and to Urey and Miller in Chicago, a great step forward has now been made at this point. The early atmosphere of our planet contained no oxygen. Could not organic molecules, which cannot survive in the present atmosphere, originate and survive under such conditions? Miller found that, in the absence of oxygen, a mixture of exceedingly simple molecules did produce several amino acids, if energy such as that of electric sparks was supplied to the original material. Amino acids are, of course, organic compounds—in fact, some such acids are essential components of protein molecules. To be sure, their molecular weight is still comparatively small, but the very procedure used by Miller may have prevented the formation of much larger molecules. At any rate, we can safely say that what used to be the weakest part of evolutionary thinking has now become a matter of precise experimentation.

If the theory of evolution wishes to unite inanimate nature with the various manifestations of life, then the theory cannot permit itself to introduce principles of action at *higher* levels that never operate on *lower* levels. From this point of view, the theory of *emergent* evolution can hardly be called a theory of evolution. For emergent evolution is said to mean that, when systems become more and more complicated, entirely new forms of action are added at certain crucial levels to those which are valid on lower levels. An evolution in which such things happened would involve discontinuities which the scientist could not understand. Emergent evolutionists may not always realize that their theory is incompatible with physics as applied to inanimate systems. When the physicist formulates the general principles according to which his systems operate, he does not refer to degrees of complication beyond which these principles would no longer permit him to predict what the systems will do. But the theory of emergent evolution clearly implies that, in this respect, the physicist is mistaken, because he fails to realize that the validity of his laws depends upon the simplicity of the systems to which they are being applied. Only as a result of this error would he have given his laws their present *general* form. Emergent evolution, therefore, cannot be defended without attacking physics at the same time. On the other hand, if the physicist is right, no place is left for new principles which suddenly take over when systems become particularly complicated. The concept of emergent evolution in the present sense does not appeal to the scientific mind. We shall later see, however, that most attempts to deal with the mind-body problem tacitly accept *other* forms of emergence. For the moment, we will return to evolution as the term is now most generally understood.

It is obvious that the theory of evolution tries to give us an explanation of amazing *changes*. But, if nothing is added to this statement, it is practically bound to cause grave errors. What has to be added to prevent such errors is a statement of this kind: While evolution took place, the basic forces, the elementary processes, and the general principles of action remained the same as they had always been, and still are, in inanimate nature. As soon as any new force, any new elementary process, or any new principle of action were discovered in some organism, the concept of evolution in its strict sense would become inapplicable. *This is the postulate of invariance in evolution.* Similar statements are generally made on the first pages of books on evolution, but they are seldom mentioned thereafter, and the remaining pages are filled with discussions of evolution only as a matter of changes. Many discussions of this kind are plausible contributions to science. Occasionally, however, an author makes assumptions which are, obviously without his being aware of it, incompatible with the postulate of invariance. The fundamental concepts of physics have seldom played an important role in evolutionary thinking. The factors which make for change —namely, accidental variations of germ cells or, in more recent thought, mutations of genes, the selective action of this or that environment, and so forth—tend to occupy evolutionary thinking to such an extent that the postulate of invariance and its consequences are not always given sufficient attention. This is a dangerous situation. According to the postulate, a tremendous number of physical and chemical processes occurs in all organisms, although often in combinations hardly ever found outside these living systems. The postulate claims that these processes follow the laws of physics and chemistry, including such principles as govern the combination of more elementary events. At every step, evolution must have come to terms with this store of invariant physical facts which has, therefore, been just as relevant to the tremendous development as have been gene mutations and environmental influences. For instance, not every characteristic of a given organism need be the result of an "adaptation." Some such characteristics may simply be physical or chemical consequences of the conditions which, at a certain time, prevailed in that living system. And yet, in well-known evolutionary explanations, the postulate of invariance has been completely ignored. I will mention only a few examples.

We remember that natural science proceeds in a most parsimonious fashion and that, when developing its picture of nature, it strictly excludes some forms of action which play a most important part in our lives. As examples, consider value and motivation. If value and motivation were suddenly removed from human life, not much of this life would be left—nobody would take trains any longer, nobody would read a book, no man would be interested in any woman (or vice versa), in fact, nobody would move from one room to the next, and so forth. For we generally do such things because, in doing them, we approach valued objects or goals we have in mind, some only mildly, but others intensely, important to us. Nothing of the kind, the physicist tells us, ever happens in inanimate nature. There are no values in this realm. Events in nature are supposed to occur as mere matters of fact. But what have we often read in books on evolution? Not a few authors have claimed that human values originated when, in the genes of our ancestors, certain mutations followed one another. In the history of evolutionary thinking, there have been times when no part of this thinking was so popular, and so widely accepted, as precisely this curious invention. And yet, it should have been obvious that the invention is

incompatible with the basic premise of the theory of evolution—
that is, the postulate of invariance. If, as a matter of principle,
no event in inanimate nature has anything to do with value, then
no mutations, however great their number, can have brought
values into the life of man. For, according to the postulate, action
in organisms still follows the basic rules which are valid in inanimate systems.

But the fact that evolutionary thinking sometimes ignores
the supposedly invariant aspects of nature has caused a further
most disturbing mistake. Biologists, psychologists, and laymen
alike now seem to take it for granted that individual human
achievements in perception, in thinking, and so forth, are either
inherited or are products of learning. This alternative is unacceptable. It is only a minor point that given human activities
may depend on inherited gifts and *also* be influenced by learning. The worst part of the alternative is that it leaves a most
important third factor unmentioned. I said that countless processes which occur in organisms are merely repetitions of well-
known events in inanimate nature, or combinations of such
events. For instance, diffusion, electric currents, and a host of
fairly simple chemical reactions are the same processes in living
systems as they are elsewhere. When, in organisms, they assume
more complicated forms, such complications are still supposed
to be in line with the principles of natural science as applied to
one histological condition or another. Under such circumstances,
do they follow such principles because our genes are of a particular kind? In other words, are the rules of their behavior
prescribed by inheritance? If the postulate of invariance is accepted, these rules must be independent of what has happened
in evolution. On the other hand, are those processes or their
laws products of learning? Clearly no learning is involved, if
electric currents and chemical reactions follow the same laws in
organisms as they do in outside nature. All these facts are obviously being ignored when we say that events in living systems
are brought about *either* by inherited conditions *or* by learning.
Actually, when trying to explain the achievements of animals or
human beings, we must, of course, always consider *three* classes

of facts. In part, such achievements are made possible by inherited conditions; they are often, in part, products of learning;
but, in each case, they must also exhibit the characteristics of
processes which, as such, neither evolution nor learning has
affected. According to the postulate of invariance, there cannot
be a single action in living systems to which this third statement
does not apply.

SINCE the present discussion is relevant to our thinking about
the mind-body problem, I had better add the following remarks.
If evolution could not introduce new basic forces or events, and
also could not alter the principles of physical and chemical dynamics, what *could* it change? For our present purposes, a very
short answer will suffice. The course taken by a physical process
depends not only on its own nature but also on properties of the
medium in which it takes place. An electric current, for instance,
may spread in a medium of high or of low conductivity. Moreover,
the conductivity of the medium may be the same throughout, or
it may vary from one place to another. In both cases, the intensity of the flow as a whole depends on such conditions and, in the
second case, its particular spatial distribution is determined by
the inhomogeneity of the medium. More specifically, a current
may be forced to follow a linear conductor because this conductor
is surrounded by an insulating medium. In this situation, the in-
sulator plays the part of a "constraint," a term originally applied
to analogous conditions in mechanics. It goes without saying that
the current obeys the general laws of electric currents which
spread in conductors, whatever the particular characteristics of
these conductors may be. Such laws contain terms that refer to
such properties of the medium. Similar considerations apply to
the distribution of *fluids* moving in conducting arrangements of
one kind or another, and to many other processes in nature.
    While evolution could not affect the basic forces, processes,
and laws of physical nature, it was free to establish or to modify
the conditions under which those invariant factors of nature operate in organisms. In actual fact, a great deal of what we call

an organism simply *consists* of special configurations of cells, by which events are given particular directions, distributions, localizations, and so forth. I need hardly give examples. Everybody knows about the role of the bones in constraining the movements of animals, of the blood vessels in prescribing the flow of the blood, and of the fibers of nerve cells in determining the direction in which nerve impulses are propagated. No fact of this kind is at odds with the postulate of invariance, if the processes which gave the tissues their forms and their other characteristics followed the laws of physics and chemistry. It might be argued that, in the organism, we cannot sharply distinguish between *action* and the *conditions* to which it is subjected, because the conditioning tissues themselves are not objects in the usual sense but, rather, steady states, and hence also processes. Such a statement would be slightly misleading for two reasons. First, the steady states in question are generally so stable that they do serve as conditions which prescribe the course of what we usually call functions. Secondly, far from weakening the thesis that invariant dynamics plays a decisive role in living systems, the statement actually emphasizes that this is true. For it rightly insists that even the most stable-looking anatomical entities are maintained by processes which are not creations of evolution.

In passing, I should like to remark that events in organisms cannot be properly understood unless we realize that organisms are *open* systems, that is, systems which absorb energy from the outside. Under these conditions, the direction of events in living systems need not be the same as it is in closed systems. But, since many systems in inanimate nature are also open systems, no difficulties arise at this point.

WE CAN now turn to the mind-body problem itself. Since what I have just tried to explain applies to all processes in animals and man, it also applies to the processes which occur in brains—whether or not these processes are directly related to psychological facts. No actual *event* in a brain can be a product of evolution. All action in brains must, as a particular kind of process, be known to natural science; and, if a brain process is a new combination of such known events, then the behavior of the combination must be derivable from the general principles which *other* combinations follow in *in*animate nature. For, if this were not the case, we should be forced to discard the postulate of invariance and, with it, the theory of evolution in its strict form. Naturally, the characteristics of the brain as a medium, and special histological conditions within this medium, are bound to influence the course of brain action, just as certain histological facts influence action in other parts of the organism. But this fact cannot affect the following general conclusion. It is not quite correct to speak of "those unknown processes in brains which are related to psychological facts." Whatever we may mean by "related to," these processes (or their components) must belong to that well-known class: the basic events studied by the physicists and the chemists. In this class we must find the processes directly related to perceptual facts, to our feelings, our motivations, our thinking, and, of course, all forms of memory and recall. What remains to be done is the selection of such *special* members of the class as actually occur when those psychological events take place. Professor Feigl has rightly pointed out that the mind-body problem is to a large extent a problem of empirical science. Philosophical analysis alone cannot discover the right solution. At least the selection of those processes will have to be based on physiological evidence, which we shall then have to compare with the corresponding psychological facts. Only after such comparisons shall we be able to tell what exactly the expression "directly related to" means, that is, whether the dualist's or the monist's or the parallelist's views are to be accepted. For instance, if the comparison were to show that, say, in perception, brain processes with a certain functional structure give rise to psychological facts with a *different* structure, such a discrepancy would prove that the mental world reacts to those brain processes as a realm with properties of its own— and this would mean dualism.

At this point, it becomes necessary to consider concrete situations rather than psychological facts and their possible physiological partners in general. Unfortunately, so long as available physiological evidence is not yet conclusive, speculation must play a certain part in such considerations. As a simple example, I will discuss a problem in visual perception. I hope to show, first, that an apparently clear answer to a question in this field cannot be regarded as satisfactory and, secondly, in what direction a better answer may be found.

From the eyes to the visual cortex of the human brain, nerve impulses travel along separate fibers. So far as we know, the points of origin of these fibers in the eyes determine the particular places in the visual cortex at which the equally separate neural messages arrive—although it is actually a *sequence* of neurons with their fibers in which the propagation occurs. In one hemisphere, topological relations among the arriving messages are apparently the same as those of corresponding stimulated points on the retinae. The separation of the messages and the preservation of their topological order are undoubtedly important facts. But can we go farther, and assume that these facts explain the spatial order in which points or objects appear in the visual field? If it is always *processes* which are related to phenomenal data, then the merely geometrical distribution of functionally unrelated events in the brain cannot, as such, be responsible for any visual characteristics. And, at the present time, few will be inclined to believe that the human mind fabricates visual distances, directions, and shapes after having inspected a purely geometrical arrangement of separate events in the cortex. But, if it is a process which underlies our experience, say, of a certain visual distance between two points, then this process must arise after the local messages corresponding to the two points have arrived, and must now translate their merely *geometrical* relation into an aspect of its own spatial distribution as a *function*. A physicist will be inclined to assume that the process in question is a "field" which relates those points across their distance, and in doing so expresses this distance in functional terms.

There is a further fact which points in this direction. If it were true that local brain processes are functionally separate events, we could not expect visual objects to show symptoms of *interaction*. But, as a matter of fact, such interactions occur all the time. The color seen in one part of the field is affected by the colors of other parts. Under certain conditions, the place of a visual object is strikingly changed by the appearance or disappearance of another object. Both attractions and repulsions may be demonstrated under such circumstances. Again, it is perfectly easy to change the size, the shape, or the orientation of an object by showing properly chosen other objects in its neighborhood. There is no evidence that interactions of this kind take place within the phenomenal field as such. Only their *results* are phenomenally represented. Hence we are again forced to assume that, far from consisting of functionally separate local actions, the physiological processes related to the visual scene spread as fields, and so cause interactions. There seems to be little doubt as to the more specific nature of these processes. Some interactions in the brain occur across considerable distances, and yet very fast. In the brain, only one kind of process can operate so fast, namely, the electric field and the current which it establishes. It has therefore been suggested that parts of the brain which are affected by afferent neural messages are sources of electric currents, and that the spatial characteristics of visual facts depend upon the distribution of these currents in the tissue as a continuous volume conductor. Physiological evidence that active brains *are* pervaded by such currents has been offered by several investigators.

It would take too much time if I were to tell you how currents would cause interactions between parts of the brain. From the point of view of neurophysiology, the explanation is fairly simple, and sooner or later such matters will have to be studied by the philosophers. For, to repeat, in the near future discussions of the mind-body problem in a general and abstract sense will no longer satisfy us. Presently we shall be forced to consider questions which refer to particular psychological and physiological situations.

IN THE meantime, philosophers may wish to hear of any conclusions, however tentative, which follow from our present discussions. I will, therefore, add the following brief remarks.

1. We have distinguished between phenomenal facts and psychological facts in a wider sense, such as retention in memory, our various dispositions, and our habits. Since more or less persistent states of this kind have no phenomenal attributes, their interpretation in terms of natural science may not be too difficult.

2. When dealing with the relation between any *phenomenal* facts and events in brains, we always seem to be confronted with a problem of *emergence*.

a) Take the dualist's interpretation of that relation. Nobody who has studied physics would predict that, when physical processes occur in brains, they will affect events in an entirely different realm, the mental world, and that, in turn, they will be affected by such mental events. The laws of inanimate nature are formulated in a way which seems to exclude this possibility. Surely, no such causal traffic across the boundaries of nature is envisaged when the physicist refers to the conservation of energy. If, nevertheless, brain processes and phenomenal events *were* causally related, this fact would argue against the scientists' laws as now interpreted. From the point of view of science, causal relations of this kind would have to be regarded as instances of an incomprehensible emergence.

b) Parallelists do not assume that phenomenal facts and brain events are causally related. Nonetheless, their view also implies that what happens in brains when we perceive, feel, think, and so forth, is a *novum* from the standpoint of natural science. No processes in inanimate nature are said to be "accompanied" by phenomenal facts. And yet, according to the parallelists, certain physical and chemical processes in brains *have* such companions. Even if it is not assumed that new laws of *physical* action are involved, this once more means emergence. And, like other forms of emergence, this form would again suggest that the scientists do not give us an adequate picture of nature. If their picture were entirely adequate, they would have foreseen what *now* appears as the unexpected emergence of phenomenal facts as partners of brain processes.

c) The thesis of isomorphism as introduced by the Gestalt

psychologists modifies the parallelists' view by saying that the structural characteristics of brain processes and of related phenomenal events are likely to be the same. If this should prove to be true, it would be an important fact under all circumstances. But, so long as phenomenal events are still said to "accompany" structurally similar partners in the brain, the Gestalt psychologists would find themselves in the same situation as the parallelists: structurally similar or not, those phenomenal events would appear as partners of physical facts only in brains. And this would mean emergence.

d) Professor Feigl defends the view that phenomenal facts are *identical* with certain events which occur in brains. He derives this view from the consideration of a cognitive network in which both phenomenal facts and corresponding brain events must find a logical location. It turns out that the location of both is the same. Feigl realizes that we do not generally identify facts unless they have the same characteristics, but I doubt whether he convinces his readers that such an identity as to content has been made plausible in the present case. Quite apart from such questions, his view again implies a form of emergence. For he does not claim that *all* physical and chemical events are identical with some phenomenal facts. On the contrary, he assures us that this holds only for certain particularly complicated processes in brains. If this were true, and if the postulate of invariance were accepted at the same time, we should be led to the following conclusion: At a certain level of complication, physical and chemical events which have shown no such tendency when investigated on simpler levels unexpectedly become identical with phenomenal facts, and therefore assume the characteristics of such facts. This would seem to me to be a clear case of emergence. If it were not emergence, that is, if the possibility of such a change were foreshadowed on simpler levels of physics and chemistry, then we should once more have to criticize the men in natural science who did not suspect that their materials contained such capacities for a radical change.

3. The difficulties inherent in the concept of emergence would, of course, disappear if we were to take a particularly bold

step. Suppose that *all* events in nature have phenomenal characteristics of a more or less primitive kind. On this premise, it
would simply follow that this holds also for the processes which
occur in brains. But, if this were true, it would again show that
the scientists have not given us an adequate description of nature. In fact, their error would be greater than it was in the
various instances of apparent emergence. Bertrand Russell would
be prepared to make the radical assumption which I just mentioned. This assumption would also answer a certain question
in epistemology to which I referred in the beginning. Professor
Feigl could not seriously object for this reason: let us assume
that, in the not too distant future, physiologists will be able to
study some brain processes which, according to Feigl, are identical with certain phenomenal facts. But, being accustomed to
studying physiological events "from the outside," and not having
heard of Feigl's thesis, their description of such events would be
given in terms of potentials, chemical reactions, and so on. It
would never occur to them to mention any *phenomenal* facts
when describing their observations. Why, then, should we expect
natural science to discover phenomenal facts when it studies the
behavior of systems in *in*animate nature? Obviously, natural science would not be aware of them even if they were present.

In this situation, I prefer to reserve judgment. Even a casual
inspection of phenomenal facts, on the one hand, and facts in
nature, on the other hand, leads to questions which defenders of
the present assumption could not easily answer. I am not a
skeptic. But much may have to happen in natural science and
in psychology before we can seriously approach such questions.

4: A task for philosophers

AT the sixty-sixth annual convention of the American Psychological Association, in 1958, Herbert Feigl delivered an address which he called "Philosophical Embarrassments of Psychology" [4]. Early in this lecture he declared that at the present time an important function of the philosopher in his contacts with the sciences resembles that of a psychotherapist; for work in a particular discipline is often impeded by disturbing influences, the nature of which a calm philosopher who looks at this discipline from the outside will easily recognize, while those who are deeply immersed in that work may remain utterly unaware of the disturbance itself and of its causes. When applying this principle to psychology Feigl was careful not to offend the psychologists, and therefore restricted his therapeutic suggestions to fairly mild remarks. I have the feeling that present-day psychology may need a more drastic treatment. Could Feigl perhaps visit his pa-

From Paul K. Feyerabend and Grover Maxwell (eds.), *Mind, Matter, and Method: Essays in Philosophy and Science in Honor of Herbert Feigl.* Minneapolis: University of Minnesota Press, 1966, 70–91. © Copyright 1966, University of Minnesota. Reprinted by permission of the publisher.

tient, psychology, again but now be more outspoken, and discuss her mental troubles more specifically? I will go a bit farther, and ask Feigl whether he would allow me to accompany him on such a visit. I know the patient and her symptoms quite well. Actually, the following paragraphs are written for the purpose of telling him what I discovered when recently watching her once more.

After a short while, I found myself particularly interested in behaviorism. Since Professor Price of Oxford has recently discussed this school in an interesting article [7], my remarks ought to be compared with his statements. It seems to me that Feigl will not object if occasionally my remarks refer to questions which the philosophers of science are thoroughly accustomed to deal with. The transgression is unavoidable because the behaviorist's lapses originated in this region when he decided to ignore the only part of the world which is directly accessible to a human being.

In order to avoid misunderstandings, I must now briefly explain what I mean when I call one part of the world directly accessible. At first, this explanation may seem to be superfluous because the same topic has often been discussed by others. Apparently, however, such older statements have not been sufficiently explicit, for even in modern philosophical writings I sometimes find arguments which are at odds with basic facts in this field.

Among the directly accessible parts of the world, *perceptual* scenes are, on the whole, accessible in a particularly satisfactory fashion. I will begin with these. Perceptual scenes are roughly divided into two regions. One contains the perceptual facts around the self, such as a street, trees, automobiles, and other people; the other contains this self. When understood in one sense, what we call the self is just one more directly accessible *percept*. Its owner can see, feel, hear, touch it, and so forth. I will call it the "body," a name which, in the following, will always refer to this perceptual entity. When dealing with perception more in detail, we shall find it necessary to distinguish sharply between the self as a percept and the physical organism in question. Apart from the body-percept as a whole, human beings also have a self in a second, less tangible sense. This somewhat elusive entity is perhaps not a part of the directly accessible world in the same sense as is the body-percept, for it appears mainly as a center from which such directed states as attention and related vectors, all as such accessible facts, are felt to issue. The center itself seems generally to be experienced only *as a place*, the place of origin of such vectors, but not as a place with particular characteristics of its own. Curiously enough, this place is nevertheless fairly well located within the body-percept, namely, in frontal parts of the head-percept, a short distance behind the perceived nose. Obviously, not everything is quite simple in the directly accessible world. I should perhaps add that this location of the self in the narrower sense within a particular region of the body-percept must, of course, be clearly distinguished from the localization which the physiological representation of this self may have in the brain as a physical system.

Before we continue our primitive survey of the directly accessible world, it seems advisable to emphasize the difference between its accessibility in general and another property of this world, which its parts exhibit in varying degrees. This other property is "clearness." Not all perceptual situations, for instance, are equally clear. Thus, when we compare central regions of the visual field with more peripheral regions, we realize at once that the latter are less clear, if not actually "vague." I hope it will be obvious that, when using such terms in the present connection, I am referring to characteristics of the compared perceptual facts themselves rather than to the clearness or vagueness of any cognitive operations that refer to these facts.

Now, the same distinction applies everywhere within the directly accessible world. Everywhere what is accessible as a matter of principle may at the same time be experienced as more or less clear or as relatively vague. On the average, perceptual facts tend to be clearer than are other parts of the accessible scene, for example, than merely remembered scenes that, in the past, may have been clearly perceived. Again, when considering our own planning, thinking, deciding, and making efforts, or our moods and our emotions, we often have every reason for calling such states and activities (or parts of them) directly accessible; but this does not mean that such experiences are always as clear as, say, a simple house perceived on a clear day. Even when extraordinarily intense (as emotions, of course, sometimes are), such facts need not, for this reason, be particularly clear in the present sense. Moods, especially, often make the impression of being fairly vague clouds in our interior.

At this point a word of caution must be added. Most of us, especially the philosophers and scientists, like to deal with clear situations just as we try to keep our own thinking clear. We tend to have a low opinion of facts that look or feel vague. But it is not the philosopher's or the scientist's task to prescribe to any part of the world how it ought to look. Can we be sure that facts that in my present sense look a bit vague are invariably less important than optimally clear-looking facts? This applies also to the parts of the directly accessible world that have no clear outlines or structures. If, because of their intrinsic vagueness, we keep away from such states or events, we project upon them a valuation which is justified so far as human cognitive processes are concerned but cannot be applied to the materials to which such processes refer. The projection is not permissible—even if the scientist's work is sometimes made difficult by lack of clearness of what he wants to investigate. When the psychological world first originated, it was probably not meant to be, first of all, a world which the psychologist could easily study.

Some among the directly accessible facts which I have just mentioned are somewhat vague not only per se. Their *localization* within the directly accessible scene is also seldom as clear as that of many percepts. Where, for instance, are our moods and our emotions experienced? Mostly, it seems, in certain regions of the body-percept; but where precisely within this percept they are located we often find it difficult to tell. Nevertheless, some such states are felt to be fairly clearly related to other parts of the accessible scene. For example, expectations, intentions, fears, and the like are generally experienced as being related to this or that particular object within the scene—just as in physics field-vectors relate one physical object to others. Within the directly accessible world, the "other objects" in question may be percepts; but often they are things or situations of which we are *thinking* at the time. No fact could be more important for the purposes of what we now call physiological psychology than the observation that certain functional relations among psychological facts are not matters of mere inference but rather are directly represented within the directly accessible scene. Why our physiological psychologists do not seem to be impressed by this simple but nevertheless fundamental evidence, I do not know.

I have called one part of the world "directly accessible." Another name of this part is the "phenomenal" world. I have not used this name because it almost sounds as though it referred to mere appearances of other, more substantial, and therefore more important, facts. As I see it, we ought not to introduce value judgments of this kind when we have hardly begun to inspect our material. Moreover, if we *have* to use terms that imply values, I am, with others, inclined to attribute a certain value to the directly accessible facts for the simple reason that they *are* so accessible and, in this special sense, clearly superior to anything that is only *in*directly accessible.

Actually, our main difficulties tend to arise when we now ask ourselves how the content of the directly accessible scene is related to the parts of the world which are not directly accessible. These parts constitute, of course, what the physicists, chemists, astronomers, biologists, and so forth, call *nature*. So long as naïve realism was not yet overcome by powerful criticism, and sturdy percepts were simply regarded as parts of an environment that existed independently—that is, whether or not there were perceivers around who "had" these percepts—so long, of course, the physical world did seem to be directly accessible. I need not enumerate the steps that gradually made this original (and most natural) attitude untenable. Suspicions that certain nonperceptual contents of human experience do not also occur in nature probably arose fairly early. Then the secondary qualities of percepts became suspect of being merely "subjective" ingredients of the otherwise objective perceived world, and only their primary qualities survived the attacks of skeptics—until, during the late parts of the nineteenth century and the first decades of the twentieth, some began to doubt whether what is called the extension of perceptual facts in space or time is quite the same thing as the spatial or temporal extension ascribed to facts in the physical world. It was mainly investigations of nature itself, particularly early work in neurophysiology, that led to this radical separation of the perceptual world from an altogether objective nature.

Eventually, of course, the conclusion became inevitable that no property of physical systems is directly accessible to the scientist, and that, therefore, all statements about physical nature must be based on inferences, that is, must be results of constructions in the scientist's thought. Observation of physical facts remained possible only in the sense that certain simple perceptual facts used in the scientist's observations have structural characteristics in common with states or events in nature, and thus give the scientist the foundations on which he can erect his constructions. The assumption that some perceptual, that is, directly accessible, facts share certain structural properties with facts that are not so accessible has never been subjected to serious doubts. The constructional part of the scientist's procedure is, as a matter of principle, also generally accepted; for, its results and consequences are thoroughly examined all the time in further perceptual observations of the kind just mentioned, which either prove or disprove that given constructions are acceptable.

This again is a well-known story. I have to repeat it because occasionally we still find statements in the philosophical literature which do not seem to agree with it. Thus, a philosopher's argument may begin with the words "When I perceive a physical object. . . ." Even if such expressions may merely be used as convenient abbreviations, that is, not as implying a form of naïve realism, they ought, it seems to me, to be avoided. Otherwise, misunderstandings and errors are almost bound to occur. I do not yet know whether at this point Feigl and I entirely agree; for in a recent article [3] he mentions certain questions which, he says, can quickly be shown "to rest on elementary conceptual confusions." Does Feigl not want us to discuss such questions? Some among those he mentions really deserve no answer. But one example is: "Do we really see physical objects?" I like to answer questions of this kind because only when they are answered will the conceptual confusions to which Feigl rightly refers finally disappear. When we consider the long chain of events that connects physical facts in our physical environment with directly accessible percepts, our answer to this particular question can only be a clear No. It is dangerous to use expressions which imply that in such situations the beginning of a long causal chain may be identified with its end. My doubt as to whether Feigl completely agrees with what I have just said arises from his interpretation of certain everyday expressions. These expressions, he says, combine phenomenal and physical terms, as for instance when one person, referring to another, makes the statement, "Eagerness was written all over his face." I hesitate to admit that, when used in common language, this statement refers to any physical facts in our present sense of the term. Rather, the "face" which is here mentioned is a *percept* that, in the spirit of everyday naïve realism, is supposed to exist independently of the perceiver; and "eagerness" is a tertiary quality of this percept "face" which, at other times, might be replaced by such qualities of the same class as "fatigue" or "depression" or "haggardness."

My sharp distinction between percepts and corresponding physical objects may be in need of more explicit support. The next paragraphs are meant to give it this support. Unavoidably, I have now to consider what may seem to be mere details in the fields of physical optics and elementary neurophysiology. What is an object or thing in perception? It is a particular area or, because of its possible extension in three dimensions, a kind of block in visual space, in both cases an entity that is, as a whole, segregated from its background and from other things. If somebody were to tell us that this segregation simply follows from the existence of a corresponding image on the retina, he would not be aware of a simple fact. Generally speaking, a physical object affects the retina by the light which its surface reflects. Now, small parts of this surface reflect light independently of one another, and so do the small parts of the physical background and of the surfaces of other physical objects in the neighborhood of the first. Some such locally reflected beams reach the refractive parts of the physical eye, and in this transmission and in their final projection upon the retina the spatial order of the local beams is fairly well preserved according to the laws of optics. As a result, the mosaic of the reflecting physical surface-elements is rather adequately repeated as a corresponding mosaic of the retinal stimuli in the eye. (It does not essentially affect this description that actually retinal stimulations do, to a degree, overlap.) Now, if local retinal stimulations are mutually independent facts, just as the elements of all physical surfaces before the organism reflect light independently, then these stimulations must be regarded as a mere mosaic. Consequently, we use a seriously misleading expression if we refer to what happens on a particular area of the retina as "the image" of this or that physical object. In doing so, we inadvertently ascribe to the retinal projection a segregation of circumscribed molar entities from the rest of the mosaic, for which, up to this point, there are no grounds in the physics of the retinal situation—however clearly such a segregation of particular molar entities may be present in the perceptual field of the owner of the retina.

How does this segregation of visual things arise? It is the outcome of neural interactions which begin within the neural tissue of the retina, continue to occur at higher levels of the neural medium, and seem to be completed in occipital (and perhaps also parietal) parts of the brain. Such interactions mainly depend upon the properties of given local events in the anatomical visual system, or rather upon their distances from each other and upon their similarities and dissimilarities. Now, since these properties are everywhere determined by the nature of the local beams which at each retinal point contribute their local share to the total mosaic of the stimuli, the interactions ultimately depend upon the physical and chemical characteristics of the surface-elements in the physical environment where the beams started. In visual perception the final result is the organized character of the perceived scene, the segregation of circumscribed molar entities from their visual surroundings, the formation of visual groups of such entities, and so forth.

It is this dependence of the interactions involved upon the physical characteristics of surface-elements in the physical environment which often makes the final outcome, the structure of what we see, a more or less adequate representation of the physical objects before our physical eyes. Do the perceptual structures always have this "veridical" character? Of course they do not. Anybody familiar with visual perception can fabricate physical patterns, the visual counterparts of which are mild or crude distortions of the physical originals. He can also arrange these physical conditions in such a way that in the resulting visual scene the presence of a particular physical object in physical space is not at all announced by a corresponding segregated percept.

I do not believe that, after this description of certain physical and physiological facts, I need defend the strict distinction between percepts and physical objects any further. But why is it so difficult to convince people that this distinction is necessary? Some philosophers may hesitate to make perfectly clear statements in this respect because they do not wish the content of physical science to be too loosely connected with observational, that is perceptual, evidence. Others may not yet have been able to discard the last remnants of naïve realism from their philosophy of science. I admit that this is a hard task for all of us. Part of the trouble, I suspect, arises from the fact that even distinguished authors sometimes confuse one particularly important perceptual entity with the corresponding physical object. Since this mistake always causes further errors in the philosophy of science, I must now describe both this error and the way in which it can be corrected by more consistent thinking.

Recently an outstanding philosopher explained his interpretation of the relation between perceptual facts, such as colors, and cortical events. I need not discuss this interpretation. In the present connection, only the way in which he deals with that particularly important percept is relevant. The physical event, he says, which is directly related to a seen color takes place in the organism, namely in the brain. Nevertheless, he continues, this color is, through conditioning, referred to the surface of an object in the environment of the organism. In other words, what is actually "inside" now appears "outside." More generally, he adds, all distance perception, whether visual or auditory, is in this fashion established by conditioning. In evaluating this thesis, I have to refer first to some experimental findings and second to the fact that, when the meanings of the terms "inside," "outside," and "organism" are kept clear, the philosopher's problem disappears immediately. The experimental evidence is that, when the distance-perception of rats reared up to that time in darkness is quantitatively tested in a lighted room, it proves to be highly adequate at once, although these animals have had no opportunity to learn by conditioning that visual contents have to be transferred to the surfaces of distant objects in the physical environment—and what the right distances from the organism are in each case. But, secondly, the philosopher's explanation is quite unnecessary for the following reasons. We have to distinguish between percepts and their physical counterparts not only when the physical objects in question. are tables, chairs, and so forth, but also when we consider our physical organism (as investigated by anatomists and physiologists, and not directly accessible) and the directly accessible body-percept that each of us has, that entity combining visual, auditory, tactual, and kinesthetic components, to which I referred when first describing the content of the directly accessible world. Once this distinction between the organism and the body-percept has become clear, and naïve realism has thereby lost its last stronghold, we realize immediately that the relational terms "inside" and "outside" do not refer to the same facts when we consider the organism and its spatial relations to other physical objects, on the one hand, and the body-percept and its spatial relations to other visual percepts, on the other hand. Suppose the author is not astonished when a chair-percept and a table-percept appear in separate parts of visual space. Why, then, should it surprise him that the surface of a certain visual percept (with its color) and the visual body-percept are separated by a visual distance? He will not, I assume, claim that all visual distances between all visual percepts are products of learning by conditioning. Since the author is interested in cortical events which are directly related to perceptual facts, I should perhaps add that, when visual percepts are clearly separated in visual space, the cortical events directly related to those percepts also generally have separate places in the *brain*— with all the functional consequences that follow from this separation. Therefore, the cortical representation of the body-percept is located in *certain* cortical regions, and the cortical representation of such visual percepts as chairs, etc., in *other* parts of the cortex. Consequently, there is no reason whatsoever why our seeing other percepts outside our body-percept should be regarded as a problem that can only be solved by a reference to learning. The *physical* distance between a *physical* object and our *physical* organism is, of course, a fact that does not, as such, appear in our perceptual field at all—because it is not a directly accessible fact. And also, the further fact that all our percepts and their distances from each other are functionally related to certain events within our physical brain does not appear in what we perceive; for the physical brain and the physical processes in its interior are just as little parts of the directly accessible scene as is the physical distance between the physical organism and, say, a physical table.

The decisive point is, of course, that the body-percept must be clearly distinguished from the physical organism. Does our philosopher doubt that the body-percept really *is* a percept, that is, by no means the physical organism? If he does, there is a simple demonstration experiment that will probably remove his doubt. Suppose that a small object is shown on the surface of a larger object, and that the latter object can be physically moved without moving the former. Actual movement of the larger surface while, physically, the small object remains stationary now causes the small object *as a percept* to move in the opposite direction. Karl Duncker [1] has thoroughly investigated this phenomenon, which is called "induced movement." Similarly, when wind moves scattered clouds across the moon, the perceived moon performs a visual movement in the opposite direction. Now, precisely the same thing, an induced movement, occurs when a physical person is quietly seated on a physical chair while a pattern of alternately black and white vertical stripes (on a curtain) slowly moves around him. In the perceptual field of this person, his own body-percept now begins to turn in the opposite direction. I can assure the philosopher that this is a most striking and convincing experience—and that it occurs when the physical organism involved does not turn at all. It follows that we *must* distinguish between the physical organism and what I have called the body-percept; in the situation just mentioned, the perceived self behaves exactly as other percepts do under comparable circumstances.

It is only fair to add that our philosopher finds himself in excellent company. For instance, Helmholtz regarded it as a curious fact that "red," "green," and various other sensory qualities seem to cover objects in space "in spite of the fact that such qualities belong to our nervous system, and do not extend into outside space." It is actually simpler to find authors who commit this error than people who have recognized it as an error. The mistake was first corrected a hundred years ago, in 1862, by Ewald Hering—an extraordinary achievement, since in 1862 little was known about the way in which perceptual facts and their spatial relations are represented in the cortex. Characteristically enough, in his publication Hering made a pessimistic remark about the chances that his explanation would be understood by his contemporaries. As a matter of fact, few ever became acquainted with it during the past hundred years, and not very many seem to know about it now. How, under the circumstances, can philosophy give us a clear account of how, in physics, an observer is related to what he is observing?

I have, however, offered my assistance to Feigl not for an application of therapeutic measures to philosophers but, rather, when the patients are psychologists. I will, therefore, now turn to a symptom I have observed in this part of the population. One of my major findings is that psychologists are astonishingly liberal in their use of certain words. At one moment a given term is meant to refer to a certain fact, but the very next moment it may be applied to a different fact. One is seldom told which meaning it is supposed to have in a particular situation. Many

examples of such conceptual confusions are available. I will restrict my remarks to a few examples, and begin with the various
meanings of the terms "subjective" and "objective." A lack of
precision in the use of these words is as dangerous as failure to
distinguish between the physical organism and the body-percept
has just proved to be.

A psychologist (who has not yet become a behaviorist, and
therefore permits himself at times to inspect the directly accessible world) might be inclined to use the terms "subjective" and
"objective" in a purely descriptive or geographical sense. He
would call all percepts that look solid, and independent of his
own self, "objective," while anything that seems to be part or
action of this self he would call "subjective." It would not always
be easy to tell whether a certain directly accessible fact belongs to
one or the other category, particularly since the self and the "objective" parts of the experienced scene are so often related by
experienced vectors (see above, page 85). But then, where does
the eastern part of this country stop and the Middle West begin?
And yet this distinction is quite useful, since when we have arrived from somewhere else in the "real" Middle West we cannot
miss the difference. In the same sense the distinction between
"subjective" and "objective" parts of the directly accessible world
may also often be convenient. But if our psychologist were actually to use these terms in such a descriptive sense, he would almost surely be misunderstood by other members of the profes-
sion. For the words "subjective" and "objective" have long since
become imbued with other meanings, meanings which they acquired in the history of natural science.

In physics the term "objective" refers, of course, to the independently existing facts of nature per se, but occasionally also
to such *procedures* as give us adequate knowledge of such facts.
From this point of view, the physicist once looked with some
suspicion at the psychological equipment of man because, research in physics being done by humans, intrusion of such
"merely subjective" human factors might have endangered the
objectivity of physical science. They "did not belong." Nowadays
physicists no longer believe that there is such a danger and there-

fore look at psychological facts with complete equanimity. But the name "merely subjective" still adheres to whatever is a psychological state or event, and it does so even when we are not concerned with the physicist's business at all. Obviously this use of the term is entirely unrelated to a possible descriptive use of the same word in a description of the directly accessible world. For, however the physicists may *now* feel about psychological facts, their former reserve in this respect implied a distinction of *values*, "objective" facts and operations being *good* facts, and "subjective" influences that might have come from the psychological world being *bad* facts. It is these value-characteristics of the two adjectives which still strongly affect us when we hear one or the other. One has to do with truth, and the other with untruth, or with truth-in-danger. While we cannot object to the former connotations of these terms in physics, it is most unfortunate that they are still being applied in the same sense when now used in a purely psychological context. To a degree, it is true, such selected perceptual facts as the physicist himself uses in his observations seem to be excepted; they are regarded as "less subjective" by those who are sufficiently acquainted with the physicist's actual procedures. But to others the word "subjective" continues to sound bad, particularly when applied to any part of the directly accessible world. Or am I mistaken? According to some philosophers the directly accessible world is perhaps not really dangerous; rather, while it remains bad, it is now bad only because it is in a way *inferior*. Its contents, we hear, are barely discernible phenomena in a remote region, mere shadows, if not simply illusions. Most probably this curious attitude would not have developed if young psychology had advanced more rapidly, and if similar views had not been held within this discipline itself by the behaviorists.

I have to say a few words about the directly accessible world as a world of thin, subjective shadows. We remember that in everyday life we all are naïve realists, who regard the more robust percepts before us as independently existing entities—*because that is how they look*. They still look the same even when we have learned that, when considered in a wider scientific context, percepts cannot be identified with the real objects of natural science. And this is, of course, the reason why we remain naïve realists in everyday life. The periods of sophistication during which we do consider that larger context are rare and short indeed, and so we practically continue to live and to think within the directly accessible scene. Does it consist of mere shadows? To be sure, some parts of the scene actually have the fleeting character of mere shadows as, for instance, weak and moving shadows in the usual sense of the word. But what about the extraordinarily firm ground (-percept) on which I (my body-percept) am now standing? What about the very hard and resistant wall (-percept) against which my hand and arm (-percepts) are now exerting a considerable (felt) pressure? Again, the heavy weight (-percept) which I yesterday tried to lift—does it deserve to be compared with a mere shadow? Such percepts simply look and feel utterly substantial. I do not like to be in (perceived) places where big rock-percepts are just beginning to tumble down a steep slope-percept right above my body-percept. And do not tell me that I have just used expressions which are borrowed from physics, and are now merely projected upon the perceptual world. For the concepts of physics are defined in extraordinarily abstract terms. If, occasionally, such expressions as I just used are applied to facts in physical nature, then just the opposite happens: properties of the *perceived* world are then projected upon entities and events in *physics*.

Perhaps the philosophers who tell us that the directly accessible world may practically be ignored will here raise the objection that, when referring to faint and remote phenomena, they mean the moods and feelings of man rather than his percepts. But have they never heard of the terror of extreme fear, or of how people feel who are suffering from a deep depression? Surely the rapture of overwhelming joy cannot have remained entirely unknown to them. And what about the scientist's unshakable insistence on proper procedures in the pursuit of knowledge? Faint phenomena? Clearly, the mere fact that an event occurs within the directly accessible world need not prevent this event from being extremely powerful—even if it is located within the self.

I now turn to behaviorism, the school that shares the views of such philosophers, and therefore claims that the directly accessible world is not worth a true scientist's attention. Behaviorism originated when students of psychology had just heard about the tremendous achievements of a strictly objective natural science, in which nothing subjective was ever permitted to play a part. Some such students now developed what, I believe, teenagers would call a crush. The crush referred to that majestic enterprise "science." I have to add, however, that (just as it is with other crushes) this science-crush grew up with particular ease among people who did not know too much about the actual makeup of the admired being, and also showed little inclination to learn more. Now, one of the outstanding characteristics of a crush is that objects which might otherwise be of interest lose their valences. A neat scale of values is soon established. The more positively something seems related to the idol, the better it is; anything that appears to be at odds with the idol's actions and intentions is obviously bad. The crush that grew up in our particular instance exhibited the same symptoms. Those who were caught lost the ability not only to look carefully at the specific content of natural science but also to consider other enterprises in an impartial fashion. Such enterprises were now good or bad, important or without interest, depending upon their relation to the ideas and procedures of the scientists. Hence, since the scientists of the time wanted to deal only with objective facts, and seemed to have a low opinion of the "merely subjective" psychological facts, those young psychologists decided to become behaviorists, that is, to study only the objectively observable actions of their subjects, and to do so with methods comparable to those of natural science.

I suggest that the crush which led to this decision be now replaced by a more mature feeling of great respect, by serious efforts to become more familiar with the specific achievements of natural science, and also by a more natural distribution of interests. Do we really know that, in psychology, one may safely ignore certain facts merely because natural science was once afraid of them? Did not the very fears of the scientists imply that some such facts might have fairly important even if (in natural science) undesirable effects?

At first, behaviorism could be regarded as a special form of materialism, for some leaders of the new movement virtually denied that there was a directly accessible world in my sense of the term. Most probably, all members of the school would now say that they are simply not interested in this question, and that they prefer to define behaviorism in purely methodological terms. This means, they would add, that all psychological phenomena as seen from the inside had better be left alone, because no proper way of dealing with such phenomena is available, and that therefore so-called introspection ought to be replaced by observation from the outside, i.e., by observation of truly objective behavior, which occurs in a just as objectively given environment. Since, in experiments, the observed behavior mostly consists of responses to particular objects (called "stimuli"), the behaviorists often call their work a study of stimulus-response connections.

The main advantage of the transition from "introspection" to the observation of behavior is sometimes said to be as follows. Whatever other weaknesses introspection may have, the psychological facts observable from the inside are, in each case, accessible only to the one person who does the observing, while facts observable from the outside may always be observed by any number of people, and can thus be established in a strictly reliable fashion.

Sophisticated members of the school may also have been impressed by a further argument against the study of private human experiences, an argument that was first formulated by certain positivists. Suppose that observations of such experiences are possible. Then we still must ask whether they are really valuable from the point of view of science. To be sure, a person may find in his private world such qualities as "red" and "blue" or "loud" and "soft." But this means no more than that this person becomes *acquainted* with such phenomena; and mere acquaintance with certain data is something quite different from what a physicist or philosopher of science would call "knowledge."

In discussing the behaviorist's arguments, I will concentrate on the following issue: Do these arguments force us to conclude that psychologists ought to ignore the directly accessible world? My answer will be closely related to this further question: Is the behaviorist right in claiming that his observations "from the outside" permit him to answer all questions that psychology must be expected to answer?

Once more, the argument that, because of their "subjective" character, psychological events as seen "from the inside" do not deserve our scientific attention suffers from the vague meaning of its main term "subjective." The fact that the objective study of nature once seemed endangered by the operation of factors located in man's interior made caution with regard to such influences a fully justified attitude. But, as an independent discipline, psychology should not primarily be concerned with bad (or good) effects which certain psychological processes might have in other enterprises; its foremost task is that of studying psychological facts as such and of discovering the principles involved in their occurrence. Consequently, those fears of the scientist can no longer be allowed to affect the psychologist's choice of what he will investigate.

Is there any further cause for calling the directly accessible world a collection of merely subjective phenomena? The behaviorists are quite prepared to answer this question. According to them, we remember, psychological facts as observed "from the inside" are accessible only to the person who observes them. Such psychological phenomena are, therefore, subjective facts in a further sense of the word "subjective," and it is this sense of the term which must be regarded as decisive from the point of view of science. I will not deny that other people are unable to look into the world that is directly accessible to me. But whether it follows that this world should not interest the psychologist is an entirely different question. In order to answer it, we have next to examine the behaviorist's claim that his own observations can be repeated, and checked, by any number of other persons because all these persons observe precisely the same objective facts. Take my experiments, the behaviorist would say. There is, for instance, that jumping stand which I am now using, that is, opposite a screen with two doors in it, one platform, and, behind the doors, a second platform. All these are physical objects, accessible to any observer. A rat which I place on the former platform is, of course, also a physical object; and when the rat now jumps against one of the doors, opens it by the impact, and thus lands on the second platform where it begins to eat—these events are again physical facts which everybody can observe.

My answer to this report follows from our earlier considerations. The behaviorist's account of what he observes in such experiments is a striking example of naïve realism. For how does he know about platforms, a screen with doors, and a rat? And how about the rat's jump, the opening of a door, and the rat's eating? As he observes these facts, they are without exception accessible to him only as *perceptual* objects and events in his private visual field. Physical objects and physical events as such are just as inaccessible to him as they are to a physicist. I need not repeat the arguments that make the identification of perceptual facts with their physical counterparts impossible. I must therefore conclude that, in all his observations, the behaviorist relies on facts that appear in his private experience, the only experience in which he can do any observing. Moreover, when other observers are present, and describe what they have seen during his experiment, their descriptions again refer to occurrences within *their* private perceptual worlds. Hence, when the behaviorist says that the private, "subjective" content of the phenomenal world cannot interest a true scientist, this statement is plainly contradicted by his own procedure. He actually proves that certain contents of the directly accessible world must, and can, be used as reliable tools in his science. Why, then, should they not also be accepted as materials which may be studied by psychologists? If the behaviorists are convinced that, in a given situation, observations of one behaviorist tend to agree with those of another, then this holds also for observations within the perceptual scenes of psychologists who believe that such scenes are worth their full attention. Such scenes are accessible to only one person in each case? This may be true; but then, they are accessible *at least to one*, while the independently existing objects in the

sense of physics, including the physical behavior of physical men
and animals, are directly accessible to *nobody*.

Behaviorists do not show much interest in perception. Few
naïve realists do. Members of the school might therefore be inclined to raise this objection: "Even if you are right in your interpretation of our observations from the outside, you overlook an
important point. All our observations refer to very simple facts
such as platforms, screens, doors, rats, and jumping. Under such
conditions perceptual facts may practically be regarded as copies
of corresponding physical facts so that the former tell us what
is also true of the latter." I will answer as follows. In the first
place, the behaviorist does not realize that even the simplest perception of individual molar objects is the outcome of organizational processes in the nervous system. In the mere mosaic of
local physical stimuli on the behaviorist's retina there are no individual molar objects such as platforms, doors, and rats (see
above, page 90). If the behaviorist is not interested in this part
of neurophysiology, other psychologists find it a fascinating part.
They therefore study not only perceptual facts which have proved
to be veridical from the point of view of physics, but also others
of which this cannot be said. For only when, in this respect, the
study of perceptual facts is strictly impartial will the psychologists' investigation of perception give them an adequate view
of how the neural processes involved organize themselves, and
thus produce our organized perceptual fields. Actually, this study
now begins to yield results in which, as admirers of objective
science, behaviorists ought to be intensely interested. Nowhere,
it is now generally admitted, are important events in the physical
world more closely related to psychological facts than they are in
brains. It therefore seems natural to use the characteristics of
such psychological facts as evidence concerning the nature of
their physiological foundations in the brain. Among the psychological data that might be used for this purpose, the percepts of
human beings can be studied with particular ease and accuracy.
Indeed, investigations of this kind now seem to give us more adequate information about related brain-processes than even otherwise excellent physiological procedures have so far brought to

light. I once more conclude that the behaviorist's low opinion of the directly accessible world is mistaken. At least from the perceptual part of this world extremely short and reliable paths appear to lead into the most interesting province of physical nature. Nor is this access restricted to those brain-events which are directly related to perception; for, the organizational aspects of brain function which were first revealed by studies in this particular field have now been found to be also relevant to the solution of certain problems in memory, learning, and thinking.

After these remarks, I need not spend much time on a discussion of the thesis that inspection of the directly accessible world makes us merely acquainted with its contents, but cannot yield what is called scientific knowledge. This thesis may have seemed plausible when the examples mentioned in this connection were sensory qualities. But in the meantime Gestalt psychology has taught us that many facts of *organization* are just as directly observable as those simple qualities, and that on this basis knowledge in a very good sense is possible not only within the directly accessible world but also beyond it, namely, in brain physiology.

How could early behaviorists develop their radical views, if simple considerations such as those contained in the preceding paragraphs actually show that those views were based on simple misunderstandings? Most probably their mistake was facilitated by a further conceptual confusion. The term "stimulus" (which behaviorists so often use) now has no fewer than three different meanings; but authors do not always make it clear which of these meanings it is supposed to have in a given case. Psychology first used the term "stimulus" in the sense in which it was then used by physiologists who studied the reactions of sense organs to physical agents such as light waves, sound waves, pressures, electric currents, and certain chemicals. It is these agents as actual stimulants of sensory cells (or of nerve fibers and muscles) which were originally called "stimuli." But in the case of perception such stimulating agents could be regarded as outposts or effects of objects in the physical world. Thus, in order to abbreviate their verbal references to such objects, psychologists began to speak of "stimuli" also when they meant those objects rather than, for instance, the light which they reflected and which actually stimulated retinal cells. For a while it was customary to specify in which sense the term "stimulus" was being used in a given situation by calling the actually operating stimulants *proximal,* and the related physical objects *distal,* stimuli. We no longer hear or read these specifying adjectives very often and as a consequence the term "stimulus" is now being used in an ambiguous fashion. Unfortunately, there is even a third entity to which psychologists give the same name. When studying the formation of associations or conditioned reactions, they call the effects of such connections "responses" and, in referring to the facts with which these responses are being connected, they again use the term "stimuli." The "stimuli" in question may now be the distant physical objects involved, or the proximal stimulating agents such as light waves, or also the *percepts* which finally appear in the subject's psychological scene. Particularly when psychologists speak of "the stimulus-object," the ambiguity begins to be quite disturbing. What, for instance, is being associated with a "second item" in certain experiments on learning, the physical object in question or its perceptual counterpart? What is the "stimulus-object" with which a response is being connected in an experiment on conditioning? We are seldom told. For example, in a recent article that explains what is now called the probabilistic theory of learning, the term "stimulus-object" plays an important role; but the author does not say whether it is the physical or the perceptual object in question to which this expression refers. Combined with the usual lapses into naïve realism, this ambiguity tends to deprive not only this particular theory of learning but also other theoretical discussions of a sufficiently precise meaning. To what does the behaviorist refer when he uses the "stimulus-response" formula? Since all his terms are supposed to have strictly "objective" meanings, we must assume that in this formula "stimulus" means to him, say, a physical door with a physical pattern on it as a part of a physical jumping stand. Now, of course, the confusion is complete, and the behaviorist virtually *must* make the mistakes which I have criticized. Placed at a certain distance from the behaviorist's physical rat, the door and its pattern do not, as these physical objects, affect the physical rat on its platform. These objects are not, as such, "stimuli." The optical (proximal) stimuli which impinge on the rat's retinal cells *do* deserve this name; but they cannot, as such, explain the rat's behavior. We remember that they produce a mere mosaic of local alterations in those cells, while the behaviorist tells us that the rat's jumping refers to such circumscribed molar entities as a "door" or a "pattern." Since these entities are actually products of perceptual organization, they should never be called "stimuli." At any rate, the behaviorist has now equipped the rat with more or less the same perceptual scene as he himself sees. But since he is a good naïve realist, he will nevertheless continue to call such percepts "stimulus-objects," as though they were the *physical* objects "door" or "pattern." Once this mistake is made, we need not be surprised by other results of the behaviorist's thinking, particularly not by his thesis that the interior worlds of individual men (or rats) play no role in his work.

While I cannot agree with the behaviorist's interpretation of his own procedure, I do not, of course, suggest that investigations done in his style should not be undertaken. In certain instances, as for example in animal psychology, no other procedure is available; and some results obtained with this method are obviously important contributions to general psychology. This holds, first of all, for several discoveries made by Skinner; but it is also true of recent investigations in which the interests and techniques of the behaviorist have been combined with physiological questions and procedures. Still, only if in the future the school decides to use its terms in a less ambiguous way can the full and precise import of such findings become apparent. At the same time the school will naturally have to discard its objections to work which deals with the directly accessible world. Thus at least *one* unnecessary limitation of its studies may at last disappear.

But in the meantime I must mention a further restriction which many behaviorists impose on their own activities. Not only do they want to deal only with what they regard as "objective" *facts;* the term "objective" is also being used in a second sense in which it refers to certain special *methods.* In the behaviorist's system, "objective" methods are those which permit him to subject the reliability of his findings to severe statistical tests. These tests are excellent. But at the present time not all forms of behavior permit us to apply these procedures. The behaviorist, therefore, now restricts his investigations by a further rule. Within his own realm, the study of behavior, he investigates only such aspects of the subject's conduct as can be described in numerical terms, and thus permit the application of those statistical tests. A great many forms of behavior cannot be handled in this fashion and are therefore never investigated by the behaviorist. Perhaps he does not realize that, when new problems arise and new forms of observation become necessary, it is not always possible to use at once the most satisfying quantitative techniques. At any rate, the behaviorist is now in danger of imprisoning himself. One understands that life in a small apartment, where familiar furniture can easily be kept in the right places, has its attractions. But neighbors are sometimes surprised to see that the inhabitants pay so little attention to the larger world outside. Why should, at times, details in the field of conditioning be almost the only items of which these retiring people wish to hear? The very meaning of the name "behaviorism" is now tending to change. Since the school cares only for those few aspects of behavior which happen to fit the requirements of particular procedures, its name is beginning to sound as though it referred to an almost *subjective* trend in psychology. A strictly objective science would hesitate to derive general convictions from a few selected data, particularly when the selection is based on standards of technical approach rather than on the objective importance of the data themselves.

In concluding, I should like to ask Feigl whether he approves of my first, tentative suggestions in the therapeutic field. At the beginning of my remarks I stated that some patients of ours are in need of a firmer treatment than he has applied to them. Does he believe that in what I have just said I have been *too* firm? I hope I have not. For in a few patients I now seem to discover the first indications of a slight spontaneous improvement. It would be unfortunate if my frank discussion of their predicament were to aggravate their symptoms again.

REFERENCES

1. DUNCKER, KARL. "Ueber induzierte Bewegung (ein Beitrag zur Theorie optisch wahrgenommener Bewegung)," *Psychologische Forschung*, 1929, 12, 180–259.
2. FEIGL, HERBERT. "The 'Mental' and the 'Physical,' " in Herbert Feigl, Michael Scriven, and Grover Maxwell (eds.), *Minnesota Studies in the Philosophy of Science*, Vol. II, Minneapolis: University of Minnesota Press, 1958, 370–497.
3. FEIGL, HERBERT. "Mind-Body, *Not* a Pseudoproblem," in Sidney Hook (ed.), *Dimensions of Mind*, New York: New York University Press, 1960, 24–34.
4. FEIGL, HERBERT. "Philosophical Embarrassments of Psychology," *American Psychologist*, 1959, 14, 115–128.
5. KÖHLER, WOLFGANG. *Gestalt Psychology* (Rev. Ed.), New York: Liveright, 1947.
6. KÖHLER, WOLFGANG. "Gestalt Psychology Today," *American Psychologist*, 1959, 14, 727–734.
7. PRICE, H. H. "Some Objections to Behaviorism," in Sidney Hook (ed.), *Dimensions of Mind*, New York: New York University Press, 1960, 78–84.
8. ZENER, KARL. "The Significance of Experience of the Individual for the Science of Psychology," in Herbert Feigl, Michael Scriven, and Grover Maxwell (eds.), *Minnesota Studies in the Philosophy of Science*, Vol. II, Minneapolis: University of Minnesota Press, 1958, 354–369.

5: Gestalt psychology

WHAT we now call Gestalt psychology began to develop in 1910. At the time, there was not much psychology anywhere in Germany. People were doing experiments on memory, with the technique introduced by Ebbinghaus, and on the problems of psychophysics. Fechner, a physicist-philosopher, somewhat optimistically regarded difference limens, as investigated by Weber, and the quantitative relation between stimulus and sensation from his own studies, as the beginning of a real science of the mind. Max Wertheimer, in 1910, was disturbed by the narrowness of such enterprises. He tried to study more interesting psychological facts and, as a first example, he chose apparent movement, the

From the *Psychologische Forschung*, 1967, 31, xviii–xxx. This paper was written shortly before Wolfgang Köhler's death, in response to an invitation to address the American Psychological Association at its 1967 meetings. It is the last scientific paper that he wrote. The manuscript is published here in the form in which he left it, except for minor editorial revisions by Solomon E. Asch, Mary Henle, and Edwin B. Newman. The original manuscript has been deposited with the Library of the American Philosophical Society as part of the Wolfgang Köhler collection. Reprinted by permission of the publisher, Springer-Verlag.

movement seen when two objects appear in fairly rapid succession, one in one place and another in a different location.

Apparent movement as such was known; but many psychologists regarded it as a mere cognitive illusion. Since no real objective movement occurs under these conditions, it was believed that apparent movement could not be a real perceptual fact. Rather, it was felt, it must be a product of erroneous judging. The explanation went like this. First, I see one object; immediately afterwards I see an object of the same kind in a somewhat different place. Naturally, I regard this second object as identical with the first, and conclude that the first has simply moved from the one place to the other.

This is a tranquilizing explanation. No longer need we worry about apparent movement. But this is also what we would now call a case of "explaining away." A striking perceptual fact is observed which we cannot immediately explain. Then we invent an explanation for which there is no factual evidence, an explanation according to which there simply is no perceptual fact that has to be explained, but only a curious cognitive blunder.

"Explaining away" has not entirely disappeared from psychology even now, although such extraordinary constructions as the one just mentioned are no longer used for the purpose. The procedure may kill important problems. When tempted to do this kind of thing, we therefore ought immediately to test our proposed explanation in experiments.

This is what Wertheimer did. He studied the conditions under which apparent movement is seen. He varied the spatial locations of the objects involved, and the rate at which they followed each other; he observed the variations of the movement itself which occurred under such conditions, and so on. He also showed his subjects optimal apparent movement and similar movement of a real object, side by side and simultaneously. He found that the two could not be distinguished by the observer. Eventually he added a most important test which, it was afterwards discovered, had once before been done by a physiologist. First, a great many repetitions of apparent movement are shown in a given place. Later, when a stationary pattern is shown in the same place, subjects clearly see a negative afterimage of the apparent movement, just as negative afterimages are seen after repeated presentations of a physically real movement.

Wertheimer's was a masterpiece of experimental investigation in the field of perception. It was also the beginning of extremely fruitful studies in general Gestalt psychology. Much thinking and many discussions followed. The number of basic questions which Wertheimer now began to consider increased rapidly. At the time, he did not publish what he found; rather, he told Koffka about his questions and his tentative answers, and Koffka in turn began to tell his students what he had learned from Wertheimer and about further ideas that he himself had developed in the same productive spirit. These students investigated one interesting possibility after another in the new field. For a brief time I was able to take part in this development. It was Koffka who, realizing that Wertheimer hesitated to write down what he was thinking, formulated first principles of Gestalt psychology in an excellent article which was published in 1915.[1]

Similar questions had begun to be discussed in Austria. Years before Wertheimer began his work, von Ehrenfels had called attention to a serious omission in the customary treatment of perceptual facts. We are accustomed, he said, to regard perceptual fields as collections of local sensations whose qualities and intensities are determined by corresponding local physical stimuli. This simple assumption, he added, cannot explain a large number of particularly interesting perceptual phenomena. For, quite apart from such local sensations, we often find in perceptual fields phenomena of an entirely different class—Gestalt qualities such as the specific shapes of objects, the melodic properties of this or that sequence of tones, and so forth. These Gestalt qualities remain practically unaltered when the stimuli in question are transposed. They seem to depend upon relations among the stimuli rather than upon the individual stimuli as such.

[1] K. Koffka, Zur Grundlegung der Wahrnehmungspsychologie. Eine Auseinandersetzung mit V. Benussi. *Zeitschrift für Psychologie*, 1915, 73, 11–90; see particularly 56–59.

From these, and other obvious perceptual facts, the Austrian psychologists developed an interpretation of perception which differed radically from the views developed by Wertheimer. Since the Gestalt qualities could not be derived from the properties of individual sensations, the psychologists in Austria felt that they must be products of higher mental operations which the mind constantly imposes on mere sense data. This theoretical approach, the so-called production theory, did not seem particularly inviting to Wertheimer and Koffka. Nevertheless one has to admit that at least one member of the Austrian School, Benussi, sometimes seemed to forget the curious production theory, and then invented most original experiments.

At this point, I have to say a few words about my own experiences during this period. I was aware of what Wertheimer was trying to do and found it not only objectively interesting but also most refreshing as a human endeavor. He observed important phenomena regardless of the fashions of the day and tried to discover what they meant. I had a feeling that his work might transform psychology, which was hardly a fascinating affair at the time, into a most lively study of basic human issues. My own work, however, was not yet related to Wertheimer's investigations, although I did write a fairly energetic paper against the tendency of others to invent explanations which served to get rid of many most interesting facts. Just when Wertheimer's work came near its most decisive stage, I became separated from my friends in Germany when I was sent to Spanish Africa by the Prussian Academy of Science. They wanted me to study a group of chimpanzees, just captured for the purpose in western parts of the African continent.

The chimpanzees proved to be extremely interesting creatures. I studied their sometimes strangely intelligent behavior and also the curious restrictions to which such achievements were often subject. Somewhat later, I occasionally interrupted these studies and investigated the perception of chimpanzees and, for the sake of comparison, that of chickens. It soon became clear that in the visual field of both species constancies of size and of brightness are almost as obvious as they are in humans.

In further experiments these animals, particularly the chimpanzees, learned to choose between two objects of different size or brightness. I was able to show in tests of transposition that what they had learned was relationally determined. (I later discovered that experiments of the same kind had been done, a short time before, by American psychologists.)

I was kept in Africa for more than six years by the First World War. During that long period I did not always feel inclined to continue my work in animal psychology. Ideas with which I had become acquainted in Europe would come back to me, most often the changes in psychological thinking which Wertheimer had just introduced. But I was also very much aware of what I had learned as a student of Max Planck, the great physicist. He had just discovered the quantum of electromagnetic radiation, but at the time taught us mainly what physicists called field physics. Under Planck's influence I had dimly felt that between Wertheimer's new thinking in psychology and the physicist's thinking in field physics there was some hidden connection. What was it? I now began to study the important works on field physics. The first discovery I made was that, fifty years before Wertheimer, some of his basic questions had already been asked not by psychologists but by physicists, first of all by Clerk Maxwell, the greatest physicist of that period. The Gestalt psychologists, we remember, were always disturbed by a thesis which was widely accepted by others. One psychologist, strongly influenced by traditional convictions, had formulated it in the following words: "I do not know whether perceptual fields actually consist of independent local elements, the so-called sensations. But, as scientists, we have to proceed as though this were true." An extraordinary statement—an a priori general conviction about the right procedure in science is assumed to be more important than the nature of the facts which we are investigating.

From its very beginning, Gestalt psychology ignored this thesis and began its work with simple and unbiased observations of facts. Independent local sensations? Consider again what happens in apparent movement. After a first visual object has appeared in one place, a second visual object does not appear in its normal location but nearer the place where the first has just disappeared, and only then moves towards what I just called its normal location. Clearly, therefore, the process corresponding to the second object has been deflected, has been attracted by a remnant of what has just happened in another place, the place of the first object, and has only then approached its "normal" location. Consequently, under the conditions of such experiments, the second object does not behave as though it were an independent local fact at all. The statement, quoted earlier, that perceptual fields must be assumed to consist of independent local sensations, is therefore at odds with the behavior of percepts even under such fairly simple conditions. Or take any of the well-known perceptual illusions, say the Müller-Lyer illusion. Can there be any doubt that in this case two lines of objectively equal length become lines of different length under the influence of the angles added at the ends of the distances to be compared? And so on, in a long list of examples, all of them incompatible with the statement about the nature of perceptual fields.

Ours was an uphill fight. I felt greatly relieved, as mentioned above, to find so fundamentally similar an approach from the side of physics. In his great treatise, *Electricity and Magnetism*, Clerk Maxwell had remarked that we are often told that in science we must, first of all, investigate the properties of very small local places one after another, and only when this has been done can we permit ourselves to consider how more complicated situations result from what we have found in those elements. This procedure, he added, ignores the fact that many phenomena in nature can only be understood when we inspect not so-called elements but fairly large regions. Similarly, in 1910, Max Planck published lectures which he had just delivered in New York. In one of these, when discussing the second principle of thermodynamics, the entropy principle, the author states emphatically that those who try to build up physics on the assumption that a study of local elements has to precede any attempt to explain the behavior of larger systems will never understand the entropy principle, the principle which deals with the direction of physical processes. Or take Eddington, the astronomer, who once wrote the following sentences: "In physics we are often invited to inspect all tiny elements of space in succession in order to gain a complete inventory of the world." But, the author objects, if we were to do this, "all properties of the physical world would be overlooked which cannot be found or understood as matters of tiny elements in space."

I was greatly surprised by these statements of eminent scientists which so obviously agreed with statements made by Gestalt psychologists. Did these great physicists merely add further mysteries to the mysteries in which, according to many critics, the Gestalt psychologists were mainly interested? Actually, these physicists did not refer to mysteries at all. Rather, they studied a great many specific physical situations and did so in an extraordinarily clear fashion. They handled these situations as wholes rather than as collections of small, local, independent facts; they had to because of the nature of such situations, the parts of which are all functionally related (or interdependent) so that what happens at a given moment at a place happens only so long as conditions and events everywhere else in the system are not altered, so long, that is, as all interactions within the whole system remain the same.

Most of us are probably familiar with Kirchhoff's laws which describe the distribution of a steady electric flow in a network of wires. When looking at the fairly simple expression which indicates what occurs within a particular local branch of the network, we see at once that this expression refers to the conditions of conduction not only in this particular local branch but also to conditions in all other branches. This is, of course, necessary because, in the steady state, the local currents throughout the network must balance one another—which means that, while a current develops in the local branch, its flow is influenced by the flow in all other branches as much as by the condition in the interior of its branch. What could be more natural when function is balanced everywhere within the system as a whole? Obviously, there is no mystery in this behavior of physical systems. And there would be no mystery either if the same kind of thing happened in a brain rather than in a network of wires. To be sure, networks of wires are exceptionally simple examples; other systems in which functional interrelations determine local facts in a far more radical fashion are not so easy to handle.

I was much impressed by such facts in physics. They offered a striking lesson to psychology in general and seemed to give Gestalt psychology a most welcome justification. I wrote, in Africa, a book about this part of exact physics and its possible application to psychology and to the understanding of brain function. The book has remained practically unknown in this country, partly, I think, because it uses the language and the logic of field physics, a part of physics with which not all of us are familiar.

When the book was published in 1920, both Wertheimer and Koffka greatly enjoyed its content. It showed that the alleged mysteries of Gestalt psychology agreed with perfectly clear procedures and facts in natural science. In a sense, Gestalt psychology has since become a kind of application of field physics to essential parts of psychology and of brain physiology.

When I was able to return to Germany, I found a most lively group of students just appearing at the Psychological Institute of the University of Berlin. They were attracted by Wertheimer, by Kurt Lewin, and, to a degree, by what I had discovered when experimenting with chimpanzees and reading physics in Africa. Not all our work referred to Gestalt psychology. For instance, we managed to prove that the famous moon illusion is by no means restricted to situations in which the sky and the moon play the decisive role. But Gestalt psychology remained the central issue. A few simple examples. One student, Scholz, examined the distance between two successively shown parallel lines when the rate of their succession was varied. He found that the second line appeared clearly too near the first line long before the rate of the succession approached that needed for apparent movement. Hence, the second line was attracted by some remnant of the first, just as Wertheimer had said. Or again: in an attempt to investigate time errors in the comparison of shapes, and the connection of such errors with the fate of young memory traces, Lauenstein did some beautiful experiments. Also, just about the same time, von Restorff and I applied Gestalt principles of perception to problems of memory, and in doing so discovered the so-called isolation effect. Kurt Lewin, too, did experiments in memory. But his main achievements were experiments in which he boldly transferred psychological situations from ordinary life to the laboratory and thus enlarged the range of psychological investigations in a highly productive fashion.

The most important person of our group, however, remained Wertheimer, who at the time was completing his most significant study in perception, his investigation of the way in which objects, figures, and patches are segregated from their environment as circumscribed entities. Perhaps it was not emphasized at the time, but for most of us it became the main result of his observations that, in this fashion, he gave a perfectly clear meaning to the term "perceived wholes" which, before, had sounded so mysterious to many colleagues. Obviously, the appearance of wholes of this kind is just as much a matter of division or separation within the visual field as it is of their coherence, their unitary character.

So long as Wertheimer's observations referred only to well-known unitary things, many authors were inclined to believe that it was merely learning ("previous experience") which makes them appear as firm units detached from their environment. But Wertheimer continued his investigation of perceptual wholes when the units in question were unitary groups of individual objects rather than simple things. In such situations one can often demonstrate that the formation of specific group units is not a matter of prior learning. Wertheimer did not deny that sometimes past experience does influence perceptual grouping. But, on the other hand, one should not forget what Gottschaldt once demonstrated: that, in many cases, purely perceptual organization is too strong to be affected by past experience, even when this past experience is, as such, most powerful.

In the meantime, several European and American psychologists who were not members of the Gestalt group became intensely interested in its work. They had begun independently to work on similar problems. One such person was Edgar Rubin who concentrated on what he called the relation of "figure" and "ground" in perception. For instance, even when an object is part of a large frontal-parallel plane, this object appears slightly separated from the ground and stands out in the third dimension. We now know that this separation is not only a qualitative curiosity but a real perceptual depth effect which can easily be varied in a quantitative fashion, and may then establish quite specific shapes in three dimensional space.

Other psychologists who turned in the same direction were David Katz and Albert Michotte in Europe, Lashley, Klüver and, to a degree, Gibson in America. I wish more people would study Michotte's marvelous publications, and also a lecture which Lashley delivered in 1929, when he was president of the American Psychological Association. The spirit of this lecture was throughout that of Gestalt psychology; later, it is true, Lashley became a bit more skeptical. Once, when we discussed the main tenets of Gestalt psychology, he suddenly smiled and said, "Excellent work—but don't you have religion up your sleeve?"

Time is too short for a discussion of the great achievements of Wertheimer and Duncker in the psychology of thinking. Their work in this field may be regarded as the last great development in Gestalt psychology that occurred in those years. Since then almost all members of the old school have died, and only a few younger psychologists are left whose investigations are clearly related to those of the earlier period: Asch, Arnheim, Wallach, Henle, Heider—all of whose work is well known to us.

When the Nazi regime became intolerable, I emigrated to the United States which I knew well from earlier visits. In America, I tried to continue the investigations which had been started in Berlin. For instance, when actual perceptions have disappeared, traces of them must be left in the nervous system. They are supposed to be the factual condition which makes recall of those perceptions possible. My first question was: traces of what in perception? Perceptual fields contain not only individual objects but also other products of organization such as segregated groups, sometimes groups which contain only two members. Grouping of this kind may be just as obvious in perception as are the individual members of the groups. Now, this means a perceptual unification or connection within the group, and there is no reason why, in the realm of memory traces, this connection or unification should not be just as clearly represented as are the members of the group. Consequently, when the group has only two members, we must expect these members to be connected not only in perception but also as traces. How would this fact manifest itself in memory?

Among the concepts used in the psychology of memory, the concept "association" may mean, for instance, that two items in a perceptual field are functionally so well connected that, when one of them is reactivated, the same happens also to the other item. This is precisely what one has to expect if, in perception, the two items form a pair-group, and if the unitary character of the perceived pair is represented as a correspondingly unitary entity in the realm of traces. If this were true, the concept of association would be directly related to the concept of organization as applied to pairs in perception.

This assumption can be tested in simple experiments in the following manner. The formation of pairs in perception depends upon the characteristics of the objects involved; it is, for instance, most likely to occur when these objects resemble each other—or when both belong to the same class of objects. Consequently, if association is an aftereffect of pair formation in perception, association must be most effective precisely when the objects are similar or at least obviously members of the same general class. Tests of this conclusion could be quite easily arranged and showed, for instance, that association of members of a given class is far more effective than association of objects dissimilar in this sense. I fully realize—and some, Postman in particular, have emphasized—that this result may still be explained in another fashion; therefore, I have just begun to do further experiments which ought to tell us whether or not the organizational interpretation of our results is correct. Work in a young science is an exciting affair. It becomes particularly exciting when new functional possibilities have just been introduced. I am grateful to those who make the present issue even more exciting by their objections. They force me to do further

experiments which will decide whether the concept of organization is applicable to basic facts in memory.

Objections have also been raised against the Gestalt psychologist's organizational explanation of the isolation effect, or
the Restorff effect. Here again, some investigators, including
Postman, believe that the intrusion of dangerous concepts developed in the study of perception may be avoided and replaced
by older, well-known, and therefore (according to them)
healthier ideas. I recently constructed sets of experiments which
had to have one result if the Restorff effect can be understood
in the conservative way, but just the opposite result if this effect
must be interpreted as a consequence of organization in perception and in memory. The results prove that, in this case, the
unhealthy organizational explanation is undoubtedly correct.

Another more recent investigation referred to a problem in
perception. Wallach and I tried to discover whether, after prolonged presentation of visual objects in a given location, these
objects (or others) show any aftereffects such as changes of size
or of shape. When numerous objects and combinations of objects
had been used for the purpose, it became perfectly clear that
prolonged presence of a visual object in a given place not only
causes distortion of this object but also displacements of other
test objects, displacements away from the previously seen inspection objects. Practically any visual objects may serve as inspection objects in such experiments. Eventually it became obvious
that the well-known distortions observed by Gibson in the case
of some particular figures such as curves and angles were special
examples of a veritable flood of what we now call figural aftereffects.

When we had studied the figural aftereffects which occur
in a frontal-parallel plane before the observer, Wallach and I
asked ourselves whether there are not similar distortions and
displacements in the third dimension of visual space. These
experiments clearly showed that there are displacements of test
objects in the third dimension, and that these are often even
more conspicuous than the displacements which occur in the
first two dimensions. Next, I tried another perceptual modality,

namely kinesthesis, where Gibson had already observed a figural aftereffect. We could not only corroborate Gibson's findings, but could also observe such effects in further kinesthetic situations. Again, not only in the kinesthetic modality, but also in simple touch were examples of figural aftereffects immediately observable. Once, when I tried auditory localization, displacements of the same kind seemed to occur. Obviously, then, figural aftereffects can be demonstrated in most parts of the perceptual world. This made us look with some suspicion at facts in perception which had generally been regarded as facts of learning. The Müller-Lyer illusion, for instance, can be abolished or greatly reduced when the pattern is shown repeatedly. This fact had previously always been regarded as a matter of learning how to observe the pattern better and better. But one look at this pattern suggests that it is most likely to develop considerable aftereffects, effects which would surely reduce the size of the illusion under conditions of continued or often repeated observation. Fishback and I found that such aftereffects, not learning in the usual sense, were probably the right explanation of the reduction of the illusion so often found by other psychologists.

Now, what kind of change in the nervous system is responsible for all these aftereffects? Or, what kind of process occurs in so many parts of the nervous system and always has about the same result? This question I regarded as particularly important because it seemed probable that the very process which is responsible for normally organized perception also causes the figural aftereffects when perception continues to occur in a given place for some time.

The nature of figural aftereffects in the visual field made it fairly easy to discover a good candidate for this fundamental role. The candidate must be able to explain the following facts:

1. The figural aftereffects are the result of an obstruction in the nervous system. Why else should test objects recede from the places where inspection objects have been seen for some time?
2. The process in question and the obstruction which it causes cannot be restricted to the circumscribed area in which the

inspection object is seen. Otherwise, why does even a fairly remote test object recede from that area?

3. The intensity of the process which causes the obstruction has to be particularly great near the boundary between the inspection object and its background. For simple observations show that the displacements of test objects are particularly conspicuous just inside and outside this contour, in both cases, of course, away from the contour.

These simple statements almost tell the physiologist what kind of process occurs in the brain when we see visual objects, and which then produces the figural aftereffects. Among the processes possible in the brain, only steady electrical currents spreading in the tissue as a volume conductor have the functional characteristics just mentioned. Such currents would originate when a circumscribed area with certain characteristics is surrounded by a larger area with different properties. The current would pass through the circumscribed area in one direction, and would then turn and pass through its environment in the opposite direction, so that a closed circuit and current result. Consequently all together just as much current would pass through the environment as flows through this circumscribed area, a behavior which fits our condition 2. The current would be most intense near the boundary of the two regions, because here the lines of flow will be shortest and thus the resistance lowest—a behavior which fits our condition 3. Condition 1, the fact that the processes in question must cause an obstruction in the tissue, is satisfied by any currents which pass through layers of cells. In fact, the flow has several kinds of effects on the tissue, all of them well known to the electrophysiologists. When the flow continues for some time, these effects are obstructions. Physiologists in Europe call these obstructions electrotonus, a name which (for unknown reasons) has not become popular in the United States. The term means that where currents enter cells, a kind of resistance or, better, obstruction develops in the surface layers of the cells, and this reduces the local flow— whereupon the current is forced to change its own direction and distribution. Thus the current has precisely the effects which appear in perception as distortions and displacements, in other words, as figural aftereffects.

We have now returned to field physics, but field physics applied to the neural medium. I need not repeat what I explained in the beginning of my report. What happens locally to a current that flows in a volume conductor is not an independent local event. What happens locally is determined and maintained within the total distribution of the flow.

Although this explanation seemed plausible enough, could we be sure that the brain is really pervaded by quasi-steady currents when we perceive? We could not, and therefore I tried to record such brain currents when visual objects appeared before human subjects or animals. This was not an easy task. To be sure, several physiologists (in England) had recorded steady currents from other active parts of the nervous system, but not from the striate area, the visual center of the brain. After initial attempts made in order to discover optimal conditions for what we planned to do, we did succeed, and could record many such currents not only from the visual, but also from the auditory cortex. I am surprised to see that, so far, no physiologists have repeated or continued our work. Too bad: the microelectrode inserted in an individual cell seems to have abolished all interest in more molar functions of the nervous system.

Our observations lead to one question after another. For instance, how do currents of the visual cortex behave when the third dimension of visual space is conspicuously represented in what we see? Or also, are currents of the brain capable of establishing memory traces in the brain? And so forth. The situation is exciting. What we now need more than anything else are people who get excited. Sooner or later there will be some people who enjoy the atmosphere of adventure in science, the atmosphere in which we lived when Gestalt psychology just began its work. If that could develop in Germany, why should it not also happen in America, the country which once produced so many pioneers?

two

===

COGNITIVE PROCESSES

6: An old pseudoproblem

WHY are the objects of the phenomenal world perceived as before us, outside of ourselves, even though today everybody knows that they depend upon processes inside of us, in the central nervous system? A psychologist will, as a rule, immediately be able to give a simple solution to this curious problem. But that it is generally known may not be assumed. It is not only a philosopher like Schopenhauer who uncritically accepts the erroneous premises implicit in that question and must then make the wildest assumptions to answer it. Many of the greatest physiologists, among them even Helmholtz, have failed to achieve full clarity on this question.[1] Mach and Avenarius attempted to lead the scientific world away from the errors already implicit in the formulation of

Ein altes Scheinproblem. *Die Naturwissenschaften,* 1929, 17, 395–401. Reprinted by permission of Springer-Verlag and translated by Erich Goldmeier.

[1] From the principles of his theory of space, Helmholtz proposes to derive "an astonishing consequence": "the objects present in space appear to us clothed in the qualities of our sensations. They appear to us red or green, cold or warm, they have smell or taste, etc., while these sensory qualities belong, after all, only to our nervous system and do not at all extend into outer space." (H. v. Helmholtz, *Die Thatsachen in der Wahrnehmung.* Berlin: August Hirschwald, 1879.)

the paradox. But either their explanations remained little known, or they did not sufficiently elucidate the problem.[2] For only a few years ago a well-known physician raised the question anew: "How is it that consciousness, which is bound to an organism, relates the changes in its sense organs to something located outside of itself?" All attempts to explain this "compulsion to project" appeared useless to him, for he felt that here is one of the eternal enigmas, related to the mind-body problem. It seems clear that this contemporary physician is not alone; rather he represents the majority of natural scientists. Students, at any rate, even those of the natural sciences, always have to go through a sort of revolution in their picture of the world as they try to transform what appears so strange into a simple, transparent matter. Under these circumstances, it may indeed be worthwhile once more to correct in somewhat more detail the error inherent in this question.

We have here a typical case of a difficulty which we create ourselves, in which we proceed on a correct line of reasoning for a while, but not consistently to the end. If new knowledge is gained in one area, while in a neighboring area an earlier stage of knowledge is inadvertently retained, contradictions *must* result. The path in the present case is directly determined by the development of physics from Galileo and Newton on. Consequently, the way to discover and to eliminate the core of the difficulty that developed leads over this same road of natural science. Little would be gained if we tried to demonstrate by philosophical speculation that there must be an error, while science would find itself, just as before, led on *its* way to the same old paradox.

The physics of the late baroque period destroyed naïve realism. The objects which exist independently of the observer and are to be the subject of scientific study could not possibly possess

---

[2] A much clearer attempt, correct in its essential points, to give a concrete, positive solution of the paradox was made by Ewald Hering as early as 1862, at least for visual perception. (E. Hering, *Beiträge zur Physiologie.* Leipzig: W. Engelmann, 1861–1864. Heft 2, 1862, 164–166.) By the way, Hering himself expressed great pessimism about the understanding of his arguments that could be expected among his contemporaries.

all the variegated characteristics which the phenomenal environment certainly shows. Thus the physicist subtracts many so-called sensory qualities if he wants to extract what he considers the objective realities from the phenomenal manifold. I do not venture to judge whether the greatest minds of that time were immediately aware that much more is needed, namely a radical departure from the identity of phenomenal object and physical object. Sometimes it seems that for them the phenomenal object was simply the physical object itself, somewhat changed by all kinds of subjective trimmings, thus both basically still one and the same existence. Whatever the historical truth, after the elimination of the "secondary qualities," physics developed so rapidly that soon its way of thinking had to be applied to the relation between physical events and the organism. For example, whether a sound wave impinges on a violin string or on the human eardrum can, after all, make no difference in principle. From this moment on, there seems to be no escape from the paradox. Anatomy, physiology, and pathology teach us that about *one* point there can no longer be any possible doubt. The physical processes between object and sense organ are followed by further events which are propagated through nerves and nerve cells as far as certain regions of the brain. Somewhere in these regions processes take place which are tied to the occurrence of perception in general and, therefore, also to the existence of phenomenal objects. Thus a physical object which reflects light differently from its surroundings will be the source of a long series of successive processes of propagation and transformation through rather different media, until finally a complex of processes takes place which can be considered the physiological carrier of the corresponding phenomenal object. Now it would obviously be meaningless to identify with each other the starting point and such a late or distant phase of this sequence of events. Therefore this reasoning might well allow for similarities of some degree between the phenomenal object and its partner in the physical world; but in any case the two represent existences at least as different as the physical object and—in an entirely different spatial position —the brain process on which the existence of the phenomenal object directly depends. If I shoot at a target, nobody will claim that the hole in the target is the same thing as the revolver from which the bullet came. By the same reasoning, we may not identify the phenomenal object with the physical object from which the stimuli in question came. Under no circumstances has the phenomenal object anything to do with the place in physical space where the "corresponding" physical object is located. If it has to be localized at all at some point in physical space, then obviously it belongs most properly to that place in the brain where the directly corresponding physiological process takes place. It is immediately apparent that Schopenhauer, Helmholtz, the above-mentioned physician, and everybody for whom this paradox exists would regard just such a localization of phenomenal objects and phenomenal qualities as the natural one. But instead, without any doubt, we have the phenomenal objects before us and outside of ourselves.

We might be tempted to say that parts of the phenomenal world should not be thought of as localized in *any* place in the physical world as a matter of principle, since phenomenal and physical localizations are incommensurable. Therefore localization of a phenomenal object within the brain is also ruled out. But we should not make the answer to our question *too* easy. Such a purely negative statement certainly does not solve the problem before us. For the problem lies in the fact that phenomenal objects are localized in a definite position *relative to our body*, only not *in* it, but *outside* of it. Thus the simplest experience seems to contradict the epistemological argument just considered. One finds, therefore, among biologists and even philosophers, the assumption that the phenomenal object is somehow again withdrawn from the body into physical space and, wherever possible, precisely to the place of its physical counterpart ("compulsion to project"). Fantastic as such an idea may be, it is unfortunately not uncommon to find all kinds of hypotheses in psychology so confused that nobody would tolerate them in the natural sciences proper. There are surely also those who see in such an extraordinary achievement an expression of the superiority of mind over mere nature.

As to the epistemological argument of the incommensurability of physical and phenomenal localization there is, however, this to say. Let us assume that it is absolutely correct and that, therefore, the total phenomenal world of a person is simply not definitely localizable anywhere in the physical world, because it is not possible even to conceive of the relative localization of phenomenal and physical facts. Then it follows that we may arbitrarily think of the *totality* of a person's phenomenal world wherever in the physical world it would help our thinking. Such a procedure, if followed systematically, can never lead to an inconsistency precisely because, in fact, we are always dealing with the relative localization either of physical data or of phenomenal data among themselves, but never with localization of the one relative to the other.[3] Now, according to our basic assumption, the totality of a person's perceptual world is strictly correlated with certain processes in his central nervous system. It will then simplify our discussion and our terminology if, in what follows, we do not consider spatial relations of the phenomenal world as entirely separate from those in physical space, but think of the totality of the phenomenal world and its subdivisions as being mapped on those brain processes which certainly at least correspond to them. After what has been said, this procedure will prejudice nothing. Whoever believes that he can cautiously avoid this assumption and prefers to conceive of the totality of the phenomenal world as permanently set apart in an incommensurable space, must reach exactly the same result, the same solution to the paradox which we will reach. And besides, I want to show that this solution succeeds entirely even if one maintains, with Helmholtz and so many biologists, that phenomenal data "belong only to our nervous system."

Phenomenal space everywhere offers examples of the relationship "outside one another." *Next to* my book, *outside of* it, is the pencil; still farther from both is the phenomenal object, the

---

[3] Similarly, I am completely free to think of the "pyramid of concepts" of classical logic or of the color pyramid in any arbitrary regions of space, precisely because their quasi-spatial nature neither excludes nor requires coincidence with a definite region of "real" space.

inkwell. This seems entirely natural to us. The only consideration required for the solution of our curious problem now consists in the fact that "my body," *before* which and *outside of* which the phenomenal objects are perceived, is itself such a phenomenal object along with others, in the same phenomenal space, and that under no circumstances may it be identified with the organism as the *physical* object which is investigated by the natural sciences, anatomy and physiology. Since at first, as long as this distinction is not yet obvious so that the pseudoproblem disappears, the situation is necessarily somewhat confusing, I shall explain it step by step. If I put my own hand next to the pencil and the inkwell, the hand reflects light and this stimulates my eye, exactly as the other two objects do. In that brain field which contains the physiological correlate of our perception—and, according to our assumption, also this perception itself—there thus occur not only two total processes corresponding to the external objects pencil and inkwell, but also a third process of generally exactly the same nature, connected with the appearance of the phenomenal object "hand." Nobody is surprised that the phenomenal object "pencil" is outside the phenomenal thing "inkwell." But it is no more astonishing that the hand as a third phenomenal object appears *next to* the other two and that they, in turn, appear *outside of* the hand. The processes in that brain field undoubtedly possess some properties on the basis of which perception in general is spatial; but also, more particularly, specific behavior of several brain processes corresponds to the phenomenal relations *next to* and *outside of* the respective phenomenal objects. If this particular behavior exists for the processes corresponding to pencil and inkwell, then in the case just discussed, it certainly does so in exactly the same way for both of these in their relation to the "hand process."

Now, as I sit at my desk, besides my hand there is also visible in the more peripheral field a good portion of both arms and the upper part of my body. Obviously arms and body are phenomenal objects just as the hand or the pencil and inkwell. They arise, physically and physiologically, in exactly the same way as the others, through retinal images and the ensuing processes in the nervous system; consequently they are subject to the same rules of relative localization as those objects. If there are understandable reasons why, under the conditions of our example, those other objects appear external to each other, then exactly the same reasons apply to their being external to my body as a phenomenal object.

To enable us to see the situation still more concretely, we shall introduce an assumption which is certainly not entirely correct in this form and will need later correction. We shall assume that if two objects, such as pencil and inkwell, exist phenomenally side by side at a particular phenomenal distance, the corresponding brain processes simply exist next to each other at a particular distance, in short that phenomenal space and the spatial distribution of the directly corresponding processes in the brain field are, to some extent, geometrically similar or even congruent. Then consideration of the example just discussed shows that the complex of processes for my body as a phenomenal object is localized at a particular place in the physical brain field, that the processes for other phenomenal objects take place all around it, and that, because of the relative geometrical relationships of these processes, phenomenal objects must be next to each other everywhere in phenomenal space, and at the same time they must all lie outside of one (for me) especially important phenomenal object which I call my body.

This is the first essential step to the solution of the paradox. If Schopenhauer and many natural scientists after him were astonished by the "external localization" of phenomenal objects, the reason was only that they failed to apply to their own body an assumption which had become natural to them in considering other objects. For the body they retained the naïve identification or confusion of physical and phenomenal object. But if we say some object is in front of "us," then what we mean by "us" is *not* the organism in the physical, physiological sense, but a phenomenal object among others which must show the same kind of localization relative to them as they have among themselves. And *both*, the other phenomenal objects as well as the "self" (in the everyday phenomenal sense) depend functionally on certain processes in one's own *physical* body; and likewise all relative phenomenal localizations depend on the distribution of these processes. Nobody has ever seen a phenomenal object localized relative to (outside of) his *physical* body.[4]

At this point the reader might still be slightly uneasy because now, to be sure, phenomenal objects are understandably outside of the phenomenal self but still, according to our assumption, both of them exist *inside* our physical body. Later all doubts in this respect should disappear. But first an extension and a correction of what has been said so far are needed.

An extension is necessary because our phenomenal world contains very much more than just visual facts. So far the discussion has been confined to the visual content of phenomenal space because we know, and are accustomed to this knowledge, that visual processes occur in orderly fashion in *one* connected physiological field. Therefore the arrangement of the visual phenomenal body next to other visual phenomenal objects is immediately convincing once we know that the phenomenal body may not be identified with the physical organism.

Sound is also localized in phenomenal space but, in general, less precisely so. Likewise I *feel* the hardness of the table under my hands (as phenomenal objects), thus again in phenomenal space. An old controversy is concerned with the relations to vision of such phenomenal spatial data in other modalities. But in any case one fact is phenomenologically certain: Whether sharply or diffusely localized, sound appears to us in places of the same phenomenal space in which we *see* phenomenal objects (in the same or in different places). It is only because of this that I can say, for instance, "Just now I heard a rustling sound in the bushes over there," and thus relate the place of a sound to the position of a visually given phenomenal object. In just the same way I feel the hardness of the table, for instance, somewhat to the left of the place where the phenomenal object pencil lies,

---

[4] When we speak of the phenomenal self, the personality in a deeper sense remains entirely outside of our discussion. We speak here of the self which is intended when we say, "I lie down on the couch," "I sit down," "I go downstairs," etc.

and thus I localize a felt place in relation to a seen one. Anyone who is in the habit of letting his judgment about the facts of perception be determined by his knowledge of the peripheral sense organs may not at once agree at this point, since the organs of sight, hearing, and touch represent separate receptor surfaces, and certainly the primary regions of entrance of the respective nerves into the cortex are also separate from each other. But as to the first point, the two eyes are also two separate peripheral sense organs, the stimulation of which nevertheless unquestionably results in *one* connected visual phenomenal space. Furthermore, there is no good evidence at all for the assumption that the primary regions of entrance of the several sensory nerves are also the last stations of the sensory processes. The alternative hypothesis would correspond much better with direct experience—that all sensory processes finally enter a field common to them all, and that here they interact according to their respective relations; this would be the basis for their localization in a single phenomenal space. This is the physiological version of a view which at one time was considered almost obvious, and which more recently has been advanced again by William Stern. It would be a bad argument if someone wished to object that not infrequently discrepancies are observed between the localization of a sound and the position of the visual source of the sound, and that there are similar inconsistencies between the felt object and its seen form. The above assumption by no means implies that this could not happen; the observation of such a discrepancy indeed presupposes that acoustic location and visual location of the source of sound, that the tactual and the visual image, have in principle comparable characteristics since, in fact, I *do compare* the two. Normally, of course, not only does the localization of the phenomena of different sensory modalities take place in one and the same phenomenal space but also, at least by and large, whatever belongs together is perceived together; thus the locus of the sound and the locus of the source of the sound as a visual object coincide, etc. It is not essential for our question whether this approximate "fit" of the relative phenomenal localization of visual, auditory, and tactual objects is partly based on anatomy (as the unitary spatial order of seeing with the two eyes), or if an almost inconceivable amount of learning brings the locations of sounds, tactile objects, etc., into an approximately fitting relation to the unitary spatial order of the visual world, or if, finally, still other possible explanations might be considered. At any rate, this coordination of localization already exists very early in the life of the human being. And thus the other phenomenal data fit into the one phenomenal context which was described at first in its visual extension before the visually given body-self. Therefore we may also conceive of the sensory processes of nonvisual origin as taking place in the same regions of the cerebral field where the corresponding visual process complexes take place (but see below, pages 136ff).

But a corresponding extension must also be made in regard to the phenomenal make-up of our bodily self. For it and its changing states, sensory data of nonvisual origin are undoubtedly even more important than its visual appearance which, for ourselves, always remains rather incomplete. Just as our phenomenal world is enriched by the sense of touch, but at the same time preserves to a high degree the correct correlation of visual phenomenal objects and tactile data in *one* phenomenal space, so what we perceive of ourselves through the sense of touch incorporates itself in and attaches itself, on the whole correctly, to the visual object, "our body." Into the same region of phenomenal space, again in proper context, a great deal of data are included which exist essentially only for one's own phenomenal body and its members, and about whose physiological foundation in sense organs of the skin, muscles, joints, etc., we are actually very poorly informed. These are what we experience even without looking: the phenomenal positions of our limbs, the felt tension or relaxation of extremities and parts of the body. In the consideration of the immediate phenomenal data, we need continually to guard against slipping what is meant by these words into the physical-physiological states and changes in the corresponding regions of the physical organism. Obviously one of the most important groups of phenomenal data may not be forgotten, the one that concerns the change and motion of the phenomenal body and its limbs. It is well known that stimulation of the vestibular nerves gives rise, in a sense, to the purest perception of spatial dynamics. And all these states and events occur in and on the same phenomenal structure for which we have—phenomenologically quite properly—a single name, the self (in the everyday sense), without concerning ourselves with the enormous variety of different sensory inputs which, physiologically, contribute constantly to its make-up. This is again possible only because all these data, whatever their peripheral physiological source, may be ordered, in general, so entirely adequately in *one* structure of phenomenal space. The tension which I just now feel in my right arm as I make a fist is localized in the structure which I experience visually as my right arm, etc. Again there is a conclusion to be drawn for brain physiology: the data from all these different sense organs contribute to the determination of one single segregated process complex, whose phenomenal correlate is called "self." Neither from considerations of brain physiology nor of phenomenology, therefore, does the "sensory heterogeneity" of the phenomenal self and of the phenomenal environment change anything of the fact that the one is *surrounded by* the parts of the other. There is then no reason whatever why the phenomenal environment should appear *within* the phenomenal self. This actually occurs only in special cases where it is a consequence precisely of the principle of normal appropriate organization of all sensory data in one phenomenal context: In taking food, I certainly perceive phenomenal objects, just now objects of the phenomenal *environment,* in the interior of the phenomenal body self—that is to say, *in* the mouth—for a few minutes. But, of course, this has nothing to do with the paradox from which we started. It only means that in a unitary perceptual field (and, correspondingly, in a brain field of unitary structure) it is quite possible to have continuous shifts of a phenomenal image (and likewise of the underlying brain processes) from a surrounding area to a surrounded one (the complex of self processes).

In addition to the above generalization of our considerations, from the visual facts only to perception in general, the solution of the paradox still requires the correction of a simplifying assumption which is not seriously tenable, but which has been made up to now. It is impossible that the spatial relationships in phenomenal space simply correspond to the geometrical relationships of their respective processes in the brain field. G. E. Müller pointed out a long time ago that this is not conceivable because, for example, visual space acts like a fairly uniform continuum, while the corresponding processes of the brain field are anatomically-geometrically distributed over the two hemispheres; and therefore, from purely geometrical considerations, something like a gap or at least a gross disturbance of continuity would have to be brought about by this inhomogeneity of the geometrical distribution of the processes. The same thing follows from the irregular arrangement of blood vessels in the nervous tissue (also emphasized by Müller). Quite aside from such considerations, phenomenal space has a large number of characteristics which would be altogether incomprehensible on the assumption that its structure and its articulation in each concrete case were determined by nothing but purely geometrical relations of individual local processes. The new psychology of perception has demonstrated beyond any doubt that only the *functional* distribution of processes, as well as gradations and articulations in such a context, can be regarded as the physiological basis of the phenomenal spatial order. Accordingly, the physiological theory of phenomenal space must be *dynamic,* not geometrical. The symmetry of a perceived circle, for example, would not depend on the mere geometrical relationships between the loci of independent individual processes, but on the fact that, in an extended whole process which underlies the visual circle, a corresponding symmetry of the functional context exists. A more detailed discussion would lead us too far from our topic.[5] It will suffice if we show, by means of an analogy from elementary physics, how this changed assumption permits us also to solve those difficulties arising from the anatomical peculiarities.

[5] But cf. M. Wertheimer, Experimentelle Studien über das Sehen von Bewegung, *Zeitschrift für Psychologie,* 1912, 61, 161–265; and W. Köhler, *Die physischen Gestalten in Ruhe und im stationären Zustand,* Braunschweig: F. Vieweg & Sohn, 1920.

Let a three-dimensional network or lattice be formed from filiform conductors, such that the conductors may be considered the edges of many equal small cubes. Consequently, at the corners of each such cube six filaments are in electrical contact, while they are otherwise encased in insulating sheaths. If such a network is connected to the poles of a battery in a certain manner, then the distribution of the stationary current may, of course, be represented purely geometrically. But this is a rather superficial procedure, since purely spatial data mean very little for what takes place here, and since the distribution of the current must essentially be related to portions of the *conductor*. As far as geometry is concerned, the stationary distribution of current would be very different—it would be distorted—if the network were "bent," if some filaments were curved, etc. At the same time, however, in terms of length of conductor or amount of resistance, the distribution would be the same as before. Indeed, in these terms the distribution could still be considered the same even if some of the filaments (between two junctions) differed in length from the others but had the same resistance. Under these conditions there would certainly be considerable discrepancies between a description of the current in purely geometrical coordinates and one (the only adequate one) in functional coordinates. For instance, in the latter terms a certain distribution of current would have to be characterized as "homogeneous" while its density per square centimeter would vary considerably from place to place.

Since the distinction between functional and geometrical coordinates may be applied to other events, and thus must not be restricted to the case of stationary electrical currents, it may well be applied to the central nervous system and especially to that part of it whose processes underlie the spatial order of our perception. It is clear, then, that only functional coordinates may be used and that, therefore, the geometrical-anatomical position of the individual conducting structures and cells relative to each other becomes meaningless (a position partly determined by all kinds of secondary factors). With this step, the difficulties discussed by Müller disappear. As a very rough approximation we can, of course, still assume a correspondence of geometrical-anatomical and functional coordinates of the system. For functionally neighboring parts of the tissue are usually also geometrical-anatomical neighbors, and functionally very distant parts are also separated anatomically from each other by a certain distance in space. But this correspondence will not hold in detail and will not apply strictly. It will be irrelevant for the understanding of the ordering of events in such a field since the functional distances are the only ones that really matter.

Without this principle it is impossible to understand even the relation between *visual* ordering of space and the corresponding brain events. It is all the more necessary if we want to make comprehensible in physiological terms the fitting coordination of the phenomena of the various sensory modalities in one common space. (This needs to be considered in relation to the simplifying formulation on page 131.) But perhaps this point of view is most important for the understanding of the construction of the phenomenal self from such different sensory material. Again, it cannot seriously be maintained that in the brain region in question the corresponding process complex represents a kind of geometrical copy of the phenomenal body. For what matters are precisely the functional coordinates, and these may be "distorted" in a great many ways. This correction of the relevant coordinate system will not in the least change the relative localization of phenomenal self and phenomenal environment. "Being outside" and the changing distance of phenomenal objects relative to the phenomenal body are again to be thought of as *functionally* determined only, as a gradation in the extended context of processes which the purely geometrical distributions reflect only very roughly.

After this, nothing at all remains of the paradox of the localization of our phenomenal environment around us. Whatever relative phenomenal localization may take place is determined by functional proximities and distances in the underlying nervous process distributions. The fact that in their totality these are contained within the meninges and the skull in no way enters into these functional connections. Therefore they could not possibly appear in our perception, whose spatial character, indeed, depends only on those functional connections. Only if, during the analysis, we shift from one kind of coordinate system to an entirely different kind, can we possibly still find difficulties here. If the phenomenal self depends on *one* process complex, the phenomenal environment on *other* such complexes, and if the relative phenomenal localization of the two corresponds to functional externality (just as two different phenomenal objects in the environment are outside of each other), then there is no problem left.

I do not wish to give the impression that this discussion leads to nothing more than to the disappearance of the old paradox. So far the emphasis has been on the fact that, in general, separate localization of phenomenal environment and self is natural and necessary for consistent thinking. From a slightly different point of view, however, these same considerations lead, rather, to a functional equivalence and kinship of the phenomenal self and phenomenal objects, which again cannot be understood as long as this self is not recognized as a separate part of the phenomenal world. Physiologically, the self and the objects of the environment represent complexes of processes in one and the same brain field. It is by no means necessary, and not even likely, that these process complexes are functionally entirely indifferent to each other. The psychology of perception is full of instances of mutual influences between the objects and occurrences of the phenomenal environment. For example, forms, sizes, and directions of seen objects may be strongly influenced by a suitably chosen surrounding visual environment. Because objectively and physically these are nothing but independent and mutually practically indifferent objects, forms, or contours, because there is thus no corresponding influence outside the organism, these distortions are usually called "illusions." But psychology is coming more and more to realize that, physiologically in any case, this is a matter of true influences on visual process complexes by their neighbors in the field. After what has been said, it is not astonishing that among the processes which underlie the phenomenal organization of space, more intimate functional connections exist than between the individual objects in physical space, whose forms, sizes, etc., are independent of each other under ordinary circumstances. Particularly striking influences are often observed in phenomenal space when there are movements in the field. Everybody has noticed, for example, that the moon clearly moves in the opposite direction when clouds pass in front of it. This is called "induced" movement of a phenomenal object, and recently Duncker has been able to offer a satisfactory explanation of its remarkable properties.[6] If, now, the phenomenal self belongs to the same interconnected field in which objects of the phenomenal environment can exert such an influence on one another, we may then expect that the same influence which is exerted, for instance, on the moon by the passing clouds may, under suitable conditions, also be exerted on the phenomenal self by vigorous movements of the phenomenal surroundings. Now, it is well known, and has even become a favorite amusement at country fairs, that obvious rotation of the visual environment leads regularly to rotation of the phenomenal self in the opposite direction, while the physical organism remains at rest. This phenomenon becomes, in principle, fully comprehensible if we consider the organization of the process complex which underlies the phenomenal self as part of the whole field of connected processes corresponding to everything phenomenal.

This simple example shows particularly impressively that phenomenal space and the underlying physiological field structure have qualities which do not exist in the same way in physical space. In particular, there are dynamic relations between the process complex of the self and the environment processes in the brain field which have no correlate in any analogous causal connections between the physical organism and its physical environment. But if we have gone this far, to be consistent, we must go very much farther. For, considerations of continuity demand that every kind of behavior in which we are directed toward a part of the environment will have to be understood as the expression of a vectorial state or event between the momentary process of the self and the environmental process in question. Depending on

[6] K. Duncker, Über induzierte Bewegung, *Psychologische Forschung*, 1929, 12, 180–259.

the actual characteristics of the two which, of course, always determine such a vectorial state, very different directions may occur. Such psychological facts as "attending to," "feeling attracted or repelled by," "hesitating before something," etc., occur in experienced space as directed from a phenomenal object to the self or vice versa. If one wants to be consistent, these will have to be incorporated in the schema outlined here of a correspondence between phenomenal order and functional connections in the brain field. But a more concrete development of this idea is hardly possible without also treating the phenomena of memory; it would therefore lead us too far from our problem.

7: *Human perception*

TODAY I should like to discuss human perception. But it seems appropriate to start by recalling an experiment performed with animals. This experiment will introduce us to an essential problem. You remember the simple method widely used in animal psychology: The animal is placed in a situation in which it can go to one or the other of two objects which differ in one property only. For example, these objects may be two doors of the same size and the same shape, but one is a light gray, the other a dark gray. If the animal receives food when it chooses the dark object, and if it is punished when it goes to the light one, it will learn to prefer the dark object, and after a sufficient number of trials, it will choose only this one. Let us merely note that, during the experiments, the psychologist must change the relative positions of the two objects in an irregular order, so that the dark object is now on the left, now on the right. Under these conditions, the

La perception humaine. *Journal de Psychologie normale et pathologique*, 1930, 27, 5–30. Reprinted by permission of Presses Universitaires de France and translated by Mary Henle.
Lecture given at the Collège de France, November 19, 1929.

animal's choices cannot depend upon the position of the objects, but only on their color.

How can we explain this fact? It is generally believed that the task of science is primarily analytic. Do not the great successes of physics consist of analyses, complex phenomena being reduced to simpler events and simpler facts? When we adopt this point of view, we are tempted to offer the following theory. Being rewarded when it goes to the dark door, the animal will associate a positive tendency to this nuance, i.e., approach; being punished when it chooses the light object, it will develop an inhibition, a negative tendency, in relation to that side. In short, training which leads to consistent choice of one particular side really consists of two independent trainings relative to the two objects or properties presented.

Such a theory doubtless explains the animal's choices. Besides, it is in perfect agreement with the results of the experiments of the famous Russian physiologist Pavlov and, as pointed out above, with our general scientific convictions. But these considerations are not enough to demonstrate its correctness. It remains a hypothesis, so that we must test it by varying our experiments.

This is easy to do. After training has been completed, we set up a new situation. All shades of gray may be represented graphically by a straight line drawn between the extremes of black and white (see Figure 7.1). Two points on this line represent the two grays used in the experiments described above. Now, eliminating the light gray of the original pair, we combine the dark gray with a new one toward the black end of the series. According to our hypothesis, the animal will have to choose between the positive color of the training trials and a new, indifferent nuance. Consequently we will predict that, in most of its choices,

Figure 7.1

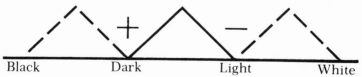

Black   Dark   Light White

it will go to the positive color, as it did before. Or again, eliminating the dark gray of the original pair, we may combine the light gray with a new one nearer the white end of the series. Now, according to our hypothesis, the animal will have to choose between the negative nuance of the training and an indifferent color. Since it has acquired an inhibition with regard to the negative gray, we will expect to see it choose the indifferent nuance. Why should the effects of training to one color change with the addition of an indifferent color? Such a result would be altogether contrary to our hypothesis, according to which training depends on the nuances considered in isolation.

But the animal does just the opposite of what we predicted. Confronted with the positive gray and a still darker gray, it prefers the latter, and only rarely chooses the positive color of the training series. Likewise, when we present the negative nuance and a still lighter one, it persists in choosing the former, as if it had not learned to avoid it in the course of many trials. Our hypothesis is thus refuted by critical experiments. It is impossible to explain the animal's choices as products of two independent trainings, each to a particular color as such. In this sense, the true explanation cannot be analytical.

You will no doubt already have found a better explanation: The animal has not learned to choose a more or less definite nuance, a point in the series of grays, independent of the other color presented. It has learned to choose *the dark side of the given pair*. The dark gray of the original pair is not only an isolated color, it is also the relatively dark side of the pair, and it is *this* property that determines the choices. Now, in the first pair of nuances of our critical experiments, i.e., in the pair transposed toward black, it is the new gray that plays the role of the dark side, while the dark gray of the original pair has now become the light side and, as such, the negative side. Likewise, in the other case, the pair transposed toward white, the negative gray of the original pair becomes the dark side, i.e., the positive gray of the new pair, while the new very light gray plays the role of the negative side.

Let us summarize this result. The animal treats the pair as

a whole, whose parts play a specific role, not independently, but according to their place in the given whole. It is not this nuance or that nuance in isolation that determines the results; it is always the role that a gray plays in the given pair. Consequently, when the pair is transposed, the roles of the nuances likewise change, and a gray that has just been the positive side of a pair of colors will easily become the negative side if it is given a suitable companion.

In psychology, then, we have wholes which, instead of being the sum of parts existing independently, give their parts specific functions or properties that can only be defined in relation to the whole in question. *Physically,* the two objects of our experiments can be separated without any alteration in their properties. With regard to *perception,* on the contrary, they always lose something if we isolate them.

I have done these experiments with chickens. American and German psychologists have done them with these and other birds. They have been performed with rats, with apes, with fish, and also with children. Differences of size have been used instead of differences of shades of gray. Always the results have been the same. Obvious conclusion: We are dealing here with a very general finding.

Now, neither chickens nor fish possess pure reason, a faculty which, according to the rationalists, would permit the adult human being to conceive the abstract relation between two grays or two sizes. We would, therefore, be forced to admit a physiological organizing function which, in the sensory processes of these animals, would make the two grays into a whole and which would add a specific character to each of them inasmuch as these grays are members of this whole.

But enough of animal psychology for the moment. We will come to quite analogous conclusions if we examine some general questions concerning human perception.

How do we perceive—visually, for example—the objects that surround us?

Suppose that, on the dark table before me, a piece of white paper has been placed. The table is *one* physical unit and the paper is *another*. This means that the material that constitutes the table is maintained as a unit by forces of cohesion, and that the same holds for the material of the paper—while between the material of the table and that of the paper, there is no analogous cohesion. We can say, then, that in physical space we do not merely have a simple geometrical distribution of materials. Beyond the statement that there is *one* material in this cubic millemeter, and *another* at that other point, we recognize the fact that the material of a certain volume forms a mechanical unity, and that between this material and the neighboring materials there exists no connection of this kind. In general, then, the physical world which surrounds us consists of well defined units having very definite limits.

Now let us examine our visual field. What we see there is certainly not physical reality, it is a psychological reality, the function of sensory processes of our nervous system. But this visual field nevertheless exhibits corresponding units. It contains *two* kinds of order, precisely as the world of physical objects. And we may say at the outset that the order of distribution of the parts in the visual field corresponds very well to the order of the superficial parts of physical objects. There is thus no confusion; relations of neighborhood are quite well preserved. But, in addition, the visual field is not a mosaic, an aggregate of indifferent local elements. Just as the physical world, the visual field contains clearly defined units with definite limits. Just as there is cohesion in the interior of one physical object, while such a connection is absent between two different objects, the visual field appears to contain *visual* objects, and it is easy to believe that forces of cohesion also operate in the interior of these visual objects or, rather, in the corresponding physiological processes. The perceived table seems to be a visual unit just as the physical table is one, the paper seems to us to be a segregated whole, just as the physical paper is, and in this sense the existence of more or less extended units seems to be a very common phenomenon in the visual world. This observation raises *two* problems. The first lies in the very fact of this organization of the visual field. Are there really forces of cohesion in the sensory processes that underlie this field? A second problem is that of the correspondence between visual units and physical units or objects. Why should sensory processes organize visual units that correspond so well to the physical units that exist outside the organism?

Few people realize the full importance of these questions. But for those who have recognized it, the world suddenly takes on a new and enigmatic aspect, even in its commonest phenomena. A very simple consideration will suffice to show how much there is of the unexpected in this visual organization. Let us take the case of the table and the paper. Reflected light waves are the only messengers which, leaving the physical surfaces, arrive at our retinas. Now, in the transmission of these waves, all the units and the specific cohesions existing in the physical objects disappear completely. A small part of the surface of the white paper reflects light in a manner that is absolutely independent of what happens in a neighboring particle. Thus the rays reflected by different parts of the paper are mutually independent to the same degree that all the rays reflected by the paper are independent of those reflected by the table. Likewise in the course of visual transmission, there is no specific cohesion between the waves leaving one particular physical object. Thus the projection of the table and the paper on our retinas consists of entirely indifferent points of stimulation, in a word, of a mosaic which, at first, contains nothing of that kind of cohesion and functional connection which characterize the physical world around us. Nevertheless, as has been remarked above, such an order is one of the most marked properties of our perception, the visual field containing visual objects as well defined units. Besides the table and the paper, there are before me a door, a chair, a pencil, a lamp, a window, and so on; all these objects constitute visual units and thus reveal clear signs of an organization which cannot be explained on the basis of what happens on the retinas.

May I be permitted a more general remark. In many respects our position in psychology is quite different from the situation in which we find ourselves in physics. In the latter science, it is often difficult to discover the most important facts because they are hidden or because they cannot be established without the development of very complicated methods. It seems to me that in psychology the greatest obstacle is quite the opposite. Often we do not observe the most important psychological facts precisely because they are too commonplace, because their presence every moment of our lives blinds us to them.

Thus it is in the case that now concerns us. But nature seems to have done everything to hide from us the importance of this problem. For, hardly have we seen it, when we are already tempted, and often seduced, by the possibility of a simplistic explanation. As a matter of fact, we are *familiar* with almost all the objects that surround us; that is, we have a great deal of information about their practical behavior, about their movements as units, about their resistance as units—resistance which opposes their destruction—about their use, which generally presupposes their unitary construction. It occurs to us at once that memory, or the reproduction of these earlier experiences, combines with our actual visual sensations and gives them a secondary, indirect organization which they did not possess before undergoing this influence of the past. Here is an application of empiristic theories which abound in all branches of psychology. There is hardly an interesting but difficult psychological problem that is not treated in this way. The explanation is too convenient not to be used constantly. And it seems so natural that, in general, it hardly occurs to us to regard it as a hypothesis and to examine it as we have to examine all our hypotheses. However, in our case, the fact that we know many of these perceived units, that is, the fact that they are "associated" with many other experiences, does not at all prove that they owe their existence to the influence of these previous experiences. I am acquainted with the color green, for example; I know its name, and many ideas are "associated" with it. And yet I cannot explain its existence as a color by these secondary experiences. The new movement in psychology which has been called Gestalt psychology has led to a deeper study of this problem, and the result of these researches has been decidedly neg-

Figure 7.2

ative. At present it seems to us altogether impossible to explain visual organization as a phenomenon that is in principle secondary and indirect. We believe that it has become inevitable to recognize real, direct sensory organization.

First, it is easy to construct cases where the units favored to the highest degree by past experience do not appear spontaneously in the visual field, because natural or autochthonous forces of organization distribute the material in a different manner, certainly a less familiar one. How would one describe Figure 7.2? Everyone will say that it consists of two rather unfamiliar shapes and a horizontal line. However, geometrically this pattern contains a well-known unit, the number *4*. The visual field seems rather to have a tendency to form *closed* units. Thus the number *4* is, so to speak, *dissolved*, its lines being absorbed in the organization of the other units. I could present a whole series of such facts. Many examples of what is called camouflage are nothing but an application of the same principle because, in these cases too, we make a well-known visual unit disappear by creating conditions which favor the formation of different, unfamiliar units. It has been objected that, in the case of the number *4*, we have never before seen this number in such an unusual environment, and that this is the reason why past experience remains ineffective. This is not, however, where we must seek the explanation of the observed fact. In the following case (see Figure 7.3), I will again give you a number in an environment that is no less unusual. It is nevertheless seen as a unit. It is evidently the *total configuration of stimulations* rather than their more or less *unusual* environment which makes

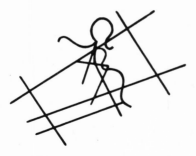

Figure 7.3

us see a unit in the second case, while suppressing it in the first.

There are many arguments which show the same thing. From an empiristic point of view, we expect to find units where we *recognize* a part of our visual field. Past experiences cannot be reproduced by parts of the field which are definitely unknown. Now it has happened many times that, while strolling at night, I have found myself before something unknown which, without any doubt, appeared to me as a unit, although I had not the slightest idea what this thing could be. In this case, the visual field has not yet reproduced definite past experiences concerning the use and the practical significance of an object. However, I have a unit before me and, consequently, it can be said that this unit does not owe its existence to such reproductions of the past.

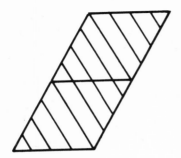

Figure 7.4

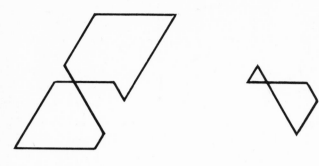

Figure 7.5

Furthermore, we have tried experimentally to produce the effects of previous experience on which, according to the hypothesis in question, what appears to be visual organization depends. If the hypothesis is correct, it should be possible to produce specific organizations by appropriate practice. Logically, a complicated drawing permits numerous organizations. I could see it as a whole or as a collection of several figures, and it is easy to see that in a given case perhaps a hundred or more possibilities exist. Let us take the example of Figure 7.4.

It is possible to see there a single whole, a parallelogram with lines running through it, but a priori a division or separation producing smaller figures would be equally possible. The drawing could be seen as one of the two forms of Figure 7.5, and quite differently besides; the possibilities are numerous even in this rather simple case. For whatever reason, we perceive the drawing as *one* unit, as long as we look at it naïvely and passively. Now, if the empiristic theory is correct, it should be easy to transform this perception so that a specific whole detaches itself from the rest. Here (Figure 7.6) is a simple part of the drawing. Such a shape has the advantage of being somewhat

Figure 7.6

familiar at the outset. Geometrically, it is contained in our drawing. It will be seen as such if we present it in isolation. If now, under some pretext, we show it two hundred times to our subject and if, soon afterwards, we suddenly present the more complicated drawing—from the empiristic point of view we should expect an effect of so many previous experiences, the hexagonal form tending to appear as a whole detached from the rest of the drawing. Gottschaldt has done this kind of experiment, using many drawings with many subjects. The result was entirely negative. As long as the subjects do not know what the experiment is about, and as long as they do not *intentionally search* for the hexagon, for example, this preliminary training has not the slightest effect. The subjects do not have the least idea that the given drawing contains the lines corresponding to the form seen so many times before. We infer that, if past experience influences organization, it does not do so automatically, easily, and generally. The empiricists must, therefore, produce new data if they want us to be able to admit their theory as a solution to the problem of sensory organization. It is no longer enough to indicate in an abstract and general way the enormous importance of past experience; it is necessary to show it *rebus et factis*.

Besides, if visual organization, for example, is interpreted as a product of previous experiences, this means that reproductions of these experiences introduce into the visual field some properties which were not there without this influence. Now we shall soon see that, in every case of organization, there are specific qualities characteristic of this organization. If the reproduction of past experiences introduces *organization* into the visual field, it must also introduce these specific qualities. From where do they come? They must be contained in the same previous experiences that are now reproduced. Thus we are faced with the question of how these specific qualities of organizations arose originally. We see, therefore, that the problem has only been shifted. Instead of solving it, we have hidden it by saying that it is a matter of an effect of past experience.

Finally, although visual organization generally supplies us with visual units corresponding to the physical units or things

Figure 7.7

around us, it cannot be said that there are *always* physical objects where we find visual units in perception. The latter are
much more numerous. To show this we need only consider the
innumerable cases of discontinuous units or *groups*. Well known
in everyday life, these groupings did not arouse the scientific
interest they deserved until my friend Wertheimer studied them
in depth. Why do the lines of Figure 7.7 form three groups?
Once more, they could be seen as nine indifferent lines, or perhaps as forming two groups with four and five members, or again
as two groups enclosing the greater interior distances, each with
two additional outside lines. I do not know any past experience
that could teach us to recognize known objects in these lines!
There is no experience according to which nine equal objects,
distributed as these lines are, behave as units in groups of three.
The heavenly constellations offer remarkable examples in this
connection. What practical experience has made the Big Dipper
a segregated whole? The only thing that experience could teach
us in this case is that *all* fixed stars move together. But does not
the popular name "Big Dipper" prove the influence of very definite previous experiences? Perhaps; but certainly the constellation could not remind us of these specific experiences before
there existed a definite group whose *specific properties* favored
such a reproduction. Instead of proving the indirect origin of
the constellations, this argument thus *presupposes* a spontaneous
and direct organization in our visual field. I know that it is
difficult to avoid such errors. No one enters this area of psychology without making them at first. Naturally, many sensory organizations *evoke* previous experiences. But if we examine these
cases a little more carefully, we will almost always find that they
evoke these experiences *as a consequence of their natural or-*

Figure 7.8

ganization, which reminds us of the more or less similar organization of well-known objects. Obviously this does not explain how sensory organization could result from the reproduction of past experiences!

Since discontinuous groups are generally less stable than compact visual objects, one might wonder whether they are as elementary as continuous units. Animal psychology has recently made advances which enable us to answer this question. Hertz used the delayed reaction method to study the behavior of certain birds (*Corvidae*). Sitting on a branch, the bird notices that food is placed under a reversed flower pot. It soon approaches and, lifting the pot, seizes the objective. But Hertz was not interested in the reaction to the invisible objective. She wanted to study the perceptual conditions of a correct response. If several like pots were irregularly distributed, the bird was obviously puzzled and was unable to orient itself to the correct pot, although it had seen that the food was hidden there. In this case there is no clear organization or grouping in the whole, even for human perception. In the next case, diagrammed in Figure 7.8, a very marked grouping is introduced, at least for man. Once more a number of indifferent pots are given in addition to the correct one. But these indifferent pots form a group in our vision, and the correct object remains apart. Now the bird reacts correctly without hesitation. It still does so if the distance between the group and the

Figure 7.9

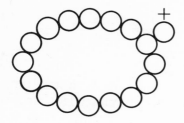

Figure 7.10

right object is less than were the distances in the irregular distribution—so much does the grouping make the correct object a separate thing. Even in the following case, where all the pots are arranged in a straight line (Figure 7.9), there is no difficulty; the grouping is sufficiently clear for the bird, as it is for man. One of these experiments is particularly important inasmuch as it shows the effects of grouping independently of all differences of distance. The right object touches its neighbor, but all the indifferent pots form a closed whole, so that the correct object remains outside, a thing apart (Figure 7.10). The bird chooses it at once. But is our interpretation justified by the facts? Until now we have described only a single case of confused and incorrect reaction. To confirm our explanation in terms of more or less clear perceptual grouping of objects, we will have to study cases in which the grouping gradually becomes less clear for human perception. On this problem Hertz has done the following experiments. Three pots are placed in the arrangement shown in Figure 7.11, the distances separating them being 6 and 2 centimeters respectively. For us, the grouping is still quite clear. And, as a matter of fact, the bird chooses correctly. But now

Figure 7.11

Figure 7.12

more nearly equal distances are used, 3 and 2 centimeters, for example (Figure 7.12). Then the grouping is much less clear and, although man can, with a slight effort of attention, easily determine the correct object in the configuration, the bird loses its orientation and reacts in a confused manner. As I have observed many times with my apes, these animals likewise seem incapable of assisting the given sensory organization by voluntary effort. They are much more tied to their sensory field than are adult human beings.

After what has been said, the hypothesis that, in principle, would explain what appears to be sensory organization by the influence of past experience can no longer be maintained. Sometimes, it is true, we observe a modification of organization which results from previous experience. But it seems to me that, in all the cases in question, we are talking about the influence of an *earlier sensory organization* on the present organization; that is, it is not past experience *as such,* but rather its specifically organized character, which contributes to determining the present organization. Once more, we must assume the existence of an *organization* in the earlier experiences in order to explain the changes produced in subsequent organizations.

The fact that the majority of sensory organizations do not correspond to units in the external world protects us against the objection that our ideas would lead to the admission of a miraculous pre-established harmony between the products of nervous processes and the units or objects of the physical world. This objection would be well taken if there were a general correspondence between the two. A certain number of sensory units, all of the continuous type, represent, it is true, the corresponding physical units. But, as I have shown in a recent article,[1] it is perfectly possible to derive this partial correspondence from the nature of the forces operating in the nervous system, forces which are probably of the same physico-chemical nature as the forces of cohesion which form or maintain the units of the external world.

It is thus to the sensory part of the nervous system that we attribute the processes of organization. In physical systems, such an organization can be more or less stable. In colloidal chemistry, for example, we know systems with two phases, one external, the other internal, such that in the external and continuous phase we find drops from the other phase. For purposes of comparison, take milk, which contains drops of fat suspended in water. Such a system is not necessarily stable, because a minimal change of conditions can often transform the external phase so that it becomes the internal phase, and vice versa. Thus there is nothing astonishing in the fact that there are also more or less stable sensory organizations. It goes without saying that such phenomena are particularly appropriate as examples of what we have called sensory organization. Although stimulation is constant, there is something that disappears and something else that takes its place in a striking manner.

At first sight, Figure 7.13 appears to consist of three narrow sectors. Thus we are confronted by a whole consisting of three parts. The lines *a* and *b*, *c* and *d*, *e* and *f* respectively form distinct groups. But if you fixate the center of the figure for some time, a change will probably occur, and all of a sudden another figure consisting of three wider sectors will appear. Now *b* and *c*, *d* and *e*, *f* and *a* form the respective groups. What has changed here is what we call organization. Since the colors have not changed at all, it is clear that we do not sufficiently describe a visual field when we indicate all the local stimulations or local colors. So long as we limit ourselves to speaking of colors, of

[1] [W. Köhler, Bemerkungen zur Gestalttheorie. Im Anschluss an Rignanos Kritik. *Psychologische Forschung*, 1928, 11, 188–234; cf. Pt. II, Sec. V. Cf. also W. Köhler, *Gestalt Psychology*. (Rev. ed.) New York: Liveright, 1947, Chapter V.—Ed.]

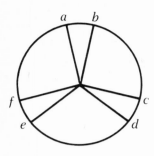

Figure 7.13

different shades of gray, of black and white, we fail completely to recognize a remarkable reality, one which, in this case, is particularly vivid, precisely because it does not remain constant. Now, in our opinion, visual objects—this chair, this table, etc. —are only more stable cases of the same phenomenon. May I give you evidence of the sensory reality of this reorganization. Some years ago I made observations on the rhythm of spontaneous changes of a figure just like this one which, however, consisted of illuminated lines in an otherwise totally dark room. My subject was a young physicist, already well known for the bold but very precise experiments he had performed in his field. He indicated to me by accurate signals the moment the organization changed from one form to another, while I measured the times; I stayed far enough away from him not to disturb him. When the experiment was completed, the young man turned to me and said, "Excuse me, Professor, but I am so much interested in the technical procedures of the various sciences that I must ask you how you are able to substitute one figure for another so suddenly, when you stay far away from the instrument." You see that, under these conditions, where the darkness of the room excluded any indirect cues, our physicist, however accustomed to critical observation, took all these changes—there were perhaps twenty of them—for objective modifications produced by some physical apparatus. So far was he from suspecting that the modification took place in his nervous system! It is probable that cases of periodic reorganization can lead us to rather important discoveries about the processes of organization in general. McDougall has, indeed, devoted himself to interesting research on this problem and, in recent years, I myself have often been surprised by the number of physiological factors that influence these phenomena to the highest degree.

It follows that organization is not at all a rare or exceptional thing which can be demonstrated in the laboratory, but which has no practical and biological importance. The truth is only that our *scientific* attention is rarely directed to organization. But it is involved, in fact, in all the experiences of our daily life. If I have cited an example of the rarer cases of unstable organization, it is because here everyone must recognize the reality of organization and the resulting problems. Practically, the innumerable cases of very stable organization that we call objects are much more important.

It must be added that there is also organization beyond the visual field and that, in the course of experiences extended in time, this is no less so than in the simultaneous extension of a stationary visual field. In hearing, for example, continuous units are more or less clearly segregated in music and in spoken language. Wertheimer has even found that almost the same rules govern both successive organizations and the formation of simultaneous units. (Compare rhythms or successive discontinuous groups in which the relations of qualitative similarity or difference and of relative temporal distance play approximately the same role as similarities, differences, and spatial distances in simultaneous visual units.)

A historical remark is relevant here. Our concept of extended unit and of organization is opposed to the atomism of classical experimental psychology, for which sensory fields are mosaics of independent local sensations, able to form extended units only through the influence of learning. Now everyone knows that two eminent philosophers have protested against this distorting and artificial atomism with such cogency that, in support of my critique, I would only need to repeat what Bergson and William James have said on this subject. However, in order to understand exactly what Gestalt psychology is, we must distinguish between their criticism of sensory atomism and the positive doctrines that they developed. If I understand it correctly, the philosophy of James does not recognize any original sensory organization. James believes that visual fields do not contain limits or specific units, that on the contrary they exhibit an uninterrupted continuity. According to him, it is our practical experience that gradually segregates definite regions and makes them appear as units. Likewise in the philosophy of Bergson, it is intelligence, with its aims of practical mastery, that introduces well defined boundaries, surfaces, and volumes into a milieu which otherwise would remain a continuous whole, incapable of any adequate analysis. On *this* point, then, our views are altogether opposed to those of these two eminent writers because, for Gestalt psychologists, as I have tried to show, there is an original sensory organization on which are based all developments of secondary organization produced by learning or by practical intelligence.

Because of this conception of an original organization, we have often been accused of a Kantian apriorism. Words are truly the most dangerous things in the world. "Original organization!" Does this mean preestablished units or organizations in man's nature, for example in his brain? Not at all! Perhaps there are some in the brains of certain animals who surprise us by their very special and very accurate reactions to particular objects which have a certain importance for their instinctive life. But our theory of sensory organization in man would be entirely compatible with the idea that the cortical field of visual excitations, for example, is an absolutely homogeneous medium without the least special preparation for particular forms. What we call original sensory organization depends on the distribution of retinal stimulation. It is "original" in so far as its primary development does not require learning or the operations of intelligence. In any homogeneous or indifferent medium, dynamic distributions of different processes will take place according to the different conditions at the surface of the system. In my opinion, the study of theoretical physics will give a clear appreciation of Gestalt psychology much better than the history of philosophy.

However, it is important to know a little of the history of *psychology*. Our interest in extended sensory units is considerably increased by the fact that they possess specific qualities which cannot be derived from the properties of their parts. Two thousand years ago Aristotle said that a whole is more than the sum of its parts. This is approximately correct. Only, a specific sensory whole is *qualitatively* different from the complex that one might predict by considering only its parts in isolation. We owe this discovery to the Austrian psychologist von Ehrenfels, and his favorite example can serve again to show us the problem. In classical European music there are two principal modes, the major and the minor. (Earlier there were more, and certain exotic music still has more modes.) We have enough in Europe for our present scientific purposes. A melody or a chord is played on the piano. A person who is at all musical can immediately recognize it as belonging to the major or the minor mode. We would try in vain to explain such a whole quality in terms of the notes taken in isolation and their separate properties. Neither the major nor the minor character can be found in isolated notes. In music, then, extended wholes possess specific, irreducible qualities. The same is true in the visual field. Let us take the case of the unstable organization (Figure 7.13). When we perceive the three narrow sectors, we would not describe this form precisely enough by saying that the lines *a* and *b*, *c* and *d*, *e* and *f* form groups. Even though the background is of the same white throughout, there is a difference between the white of the figure and the white of the intervals. Organization does not concern only the lines; it modifies the space in the interior of the three sectors, giving it a quality of solidity and substantiality which is lacking in the case of the empty intervals separating the three sectors. As soon as the organization changes, these characteristics of the surfaces also change. What was solid or full becomes empty and, on the other hand, substantiality and solidity suddenly appear in the surfaces that were previously empty. Here is another specific quality of extended units as such. This quality seems to be of particular importance inasmuch as it is found in all those continuous units that we call objects. Rubin of Copenhagen was the first to call attention to this visual property. Truly, we do not exhaust the properties of a visual field if we limit ourselves to enumerating the colors of all the points of this field.

But why should we insist on little known qualities, when generally accepted properties give us much stronger arguments? What is a *visual shape*? Some authors tell us that a visual shape is nothing but a plurality of local sensations, provided that we do not forget the spatial relations which exist among these local sensations. This is an axiom that seems altogether innocent and even plausible at first, but which is easily recognized as wrong under more rigorous examination. Indeed, we can see at once that, according to this doctrine, every visual field would contain an infinite number of visual forms, because there is always an infinite number of mosaics of local points which I can consider with their spatial relations and which, according to the axiom in question, would necessarily be visual forms. Consequently, each visual field would contain *all possible forms,* because I could always choose suitable mosaics which, with the relations existing among their points, would correspond absolutely to this definition of shape and to the concrete shapes in question. Every visual field would contain the word "French" and also the word "German." But this is really too wrong for serious discussion. In a given field, either we find no form or we find definite and specific shapes to the exclusion of all others. Let us distinguish between these imaginary forms, present only geometrically, and real visual forms which are *seen* at a given moment. Clearly the axiom of local sensations and their relations tries to escape the problem of shape by reducing the idea of shape to very simple conceptions already acknowledged. But this procedure can only appear to be successful because of an implicit assumption which contains the whole problem. Which are the specific mosaics of sensations that, with their spatial relations, become visual shapes? If this doctrine does not give us an answer, every visual field will contain all imaginable shapes. If, to escape this con-

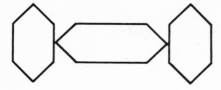

Figure 7.14

clusion, an answer seems necessary, a factor has been forgotten in the doctrine, a factor of vital importance for real shapes, and the axiom as such collapses.

Let us see if our description of the field, in which specific extended units play an important role, cannot give us the key to this theoretical situation. You remember Figure 7.2 which, for the unbiased observer, consists of two extended units crossed by a horizontal line. Our observer sees two unfamiliar shapes and the horizontal, but he does not see the shape of the number 4. Thus the units which he sees *have* shapes—whereas there is no shape where the corresponding unit does not actually exist. Now, it *is* possible to see the shape of the number 4. And, indeed, as soon as we see it, the corresponding unit also appears. I could give you any number of examples. Perhaps a single one will suffice.

In unbiased observation you see in Figure 7.14 a group of three shapes corresponding to three visual units. Have you seen the letter *K*? Not at first! And at the very moment that you discover it, a new extended unit also presents itself. At first the lines of the *K* are differently distributed, the vertical being absorbed in the unit on the left, and the other two lines in the middle unit. Consequently *K* does not exist as a visual shape, because the unit which could have this shape is lacking. Make an effort to see the shape of *K* and, if you succeed, you will produce the unit with the shape.

It follows that the existence of visual shapes is intimately tied to the existence of those sensory units that we have interpreted as products of a sensory and physiological organization. And, since real shapes are found only in sensory units, we conclude that it is the same organization that produces both the units and their shapes. Visual shape is, then, one of those qualities which became a problem for von Ehrenfels, inasmuch as they are properties of specific units as such, and cannot be reduced to local stimulations. Once more, on a given surface we may have all the local colors and all their relations; this mosaic will not, however, have real shape before it is segregated as a visual whole.

Of all the specific qualities that characterize extended units, *shapes* are probably the most important, at least from the point of view of man and his biological needs. It is probably for this reason that von Ehrenfels, in looking for an appropriate general term for all the properties he discovered, decided to call them all *Gestaltqualitäten,* that is, qualities analogous to visual shapes. It is difficult to translate this word: "form qualities" does not convey its full meaning; "structural qualities" would perhaps be more exact. But my French colleagues will know better than I what French terms convey the thought of von Ehrenfels. And that is still not the greatest terminological difficulty. In German, the word *Gestalt* means, in general, a shape or form, and may be translated by this term. But the same word *Gestalt* has long had another, more concrete meaning; for the *whole having* a form is also called *Gestalt.* It is in this sense, for example, that Goethe says, "Naht ihr euch wieder, schwankende Gestalten?" and, in his scientific works, he speaks of *Gestalt* in the same concrete meaning. Now, in psychology, we use this word in the same way, so that the term "Gestalt psychology" hardly means what its translation "Psychologie de la forme" would make one believe. Gestalt psychology is, in fact, a psychology that takes as its basic subject matter this tendency to organization, to the development of specific units, of which we have spoken. And "shapes" in the narrower sense constitute only a rather limited area of its research. Our principal efforts concern the dynamics of organization, so that our researches go well beyond the problems of perception. Indeed, in embryology and also in neurology there are some problems so like those that concern us this evening that we do not hesitate at all to treat them too from the Gestalt point of view. Fortunately we are not the only ones to do this. Some biologists and, more recently, some physicists have recognized the legitimacy of this procedure.

It remains for us to make the connection with the experiment from which we started this evening. Earlier we were surprised by the fact that the animal treated a region of the given situation as a whole, the parts of this whole having properties determined by their relative positions in the whole. It is thanks to this fact that, after a transposition of the whole (i.e., of the pair of grays), it is not the same part—taken absolutely or in isolation—that was treated as positive part, but the same part defined by its role in the transposed whole, or the same part in the structure of the new whole. Let us, therefore, examine human perception to see if the same phenomenon is found there. First, we know already that the specific properties of extended units discovered by von Ehrenfels cannot be derived from the qualities that we attribute to the isolated effects of the local stimulations taken separately. Now, to demonstrate this fact in a convincing manner, Mach and von Ehrenfels made use of the procedure of transposition. Thus a melody remains itself, the major and minor modes are maintained when we modify the absolute pitch of the notes without altering the relations of their frequencies. It is precisely this method of transposition that will bring us back to the experiment performed with animals.

If a melody has a whole character, that is, a property that belongs to it as a musical whole, the notes of this melody are subject to the influence of the melodic structure of which they become parts. For example, one of the notes, which we call the tonic, is characterized by the altogether decisive role that it plays in the melody, in this sense, that the musical movement cannot come very near to it without there being a very lively tendency to complete the transition. It is thus the note of equilibrium of this movement and, indeed, when the transition has been completed, we feel ourselves at the end of the road, at the point of natural rest. But this highly characteristic quality of the tonic and its dominant functional or dynamic role do not at all depend on a definite stimulation taken in isolation and absolutely.

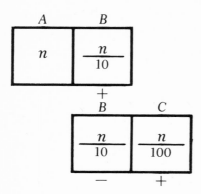

Figure 7.15

In F major it is the F that acquires it, while in A major it is the A that possesses it. After the transposition, the note A has the same relative position in the musical structure that the note F had at first. Consequently, our musical reaction to the A in the transposed melody is the same as if it were the F of the original melody. We have thus returned to our point of departure. In human perception as in that of animals, the functional role and quality of a part are determined by the whole in which this part is integrated.

One more task remains for us. In our opinion, sensory organization, with its somewhat surprising properties and consequences, must be understood from the point of view of physiology. And, if the physiological processes of the nervous system may be understood as special cases of physical dynamics, we will even be obliged to give a physical theory of such phenomena. However, such a goal seems to me to exceed our present powers. Therefore, instead of giving a concrete theory of sensory organization, I will raise the more modest question of whether, at least, there are physical systems which show the same functional properties that we found in the perception of man and animals. It is very simple. In our first experiment, where a whole contained two parts, two grays—let us call them A and B—the role of A was determined, not by the properties of A in isolation, but by the position of *A* in the whole. Very well. Let us form a physi-cochemical system by combining two solutions of hydrochloric acid, such that between them there is a functional contact by diffusion (see Figure 7.15). Concretely, let us give the first a normal concentration and the second a dilution ten times as great. An electromotive force will then develop immediately be-tween them, *A* being the electronegative solution and *B* the positive part. Let us transpose the system just as we transposed the melodies or the perceptual whole presented to the animal. Solution *B* will then be combined with a new solution *C* with a concentration ten times more dilute than *B*. Solution *C* now plays the same role that *B* played before, that is, *B* will lose its electropositive quality and *C* will assume this quality, while *B* will be transformed into the negative part.

We see, then, that the properties characteristic of percep-tual units exhibit traits that are well known in physics. The functional units that are observed in that science determine the roles of their parts, just as perceptual units do in psychology. Nothing could be easier than to demonstrate this by any number of physical examples. Why should we be astonished if, in mod-ern physics, ideas very like ours are beginning to appear? As Eddington says, ". . . the centre of interest is shifted from the entities reached by the customary analysis . . . to qualities pos-sessed by the system as a whole. . . . Physics is the study of . . . organization."[2] On this path, let us add, it will meet biology and psychology.

[2] A. S. Eddington, *The Nature of the Physical World*. New York: Mac-millan and Cambridge, England: The University Press, 1929, 103–104.

8: The nature of intelligence

YOU will find most psychologists today little inclined to talk about the nature of intelligence. It is the same in this case as with "memory" or "attention" or "the will." As long as we ask about them as faculties or parts of the ego, we can answer at best with feeble allusions or shallow definitions. We will become more eloquent only when, instead, we speak of specific kinds of psychic *processes* in which, as we say, memory, attention, will, and intelligence manifest themselves.

Even if we speak of "intelligent behavior," we can by no means report existing knowledge as yet; we can almost only refer to problems which are gradually becoming clearer. Even such references must, for the time being, remain somewhat indefinite. This is unavoidable. Last year the American psychologist Lashley characterized our situation in psychology in this way: We have the choice between a clear presentation which is undoubtedly misleading and a certain vagueness which may conceal within

Das Wesen der Intelligenz. In Arthur Keller (Hrsg.), *Kind und Umwelt, Anlage und Erziehung*. Leipzig und Wien: Franz Deuticke, 1930, 132–146. Reprinted by permission of the publisher and translated by Erich Goldmeier.

itself a yet unknown clarity of the future. Nowhere is this more true than in our field. And since I do not want to mislead you, I shall speak somewhat vaguely.

In the expression "intelligent behavior," the word "behavior" must not be understood in the sense of American behaviorism, which refuses in principle to admit any data in psychology other than those which can be obtained with scientific methods on *other* organisms, men or animals. Here one must make up one's mind at the outset. Methodological purists cling to a procedure which seems to them to be particularly precise. They thereby limit their field of vision to what little experience can so far be grasped by this method. Anyone who does not want to have his view narrowed, thus missing some essentials, will, in a young science, take the most fundamental data from almost anywhere, since what is essential may often be discerned independently of the degree to which details can be established with certainty. The problem of intelligent behavior so far certainly belongs to those questions whose solution a methodological purism could seriously hamper. We would be glad if a felicitous observation on ourselves helps us along, even if it means incurring the displeasure of the behaviorists.

In any case, typical events in this area definitely tend to express themselves significantly in overt behavior, and equally significant is the absence of such an event where the situation demands its presence. *Understanding* or *grasping* is the first important kind of intelligent behavior. What a radiant smile spreads over the face of a small child who has just grasped the meaning of a game that an adult has started to play with him. The sudden grasping of a connection in an entirely different direction than was first expected is the functional core in the understanding of many good stories.

Understanding, grasping, comprehending could easily be overlooked in simple cases when it is merely a matter of passive taking in of the given material without any performance on our part. Do we do anything more than take in the meanings of the words passively when we follow the ordinary lecture of a professor or read a book? But there must be more to it, even if we can do it easily and surely; for we can always find individuals who are by no means capable even of such tasks, however simple they may be. At any rate, there is a demonstrably close connection between understanding and other performances which anybody would call intelligent behavior. In such cases a situation, a problem presents itself: for a while, surely, a door without a key, a stream without a bridge. Suddenly one of us clicks his tongue or strikes his forehead with his hand and tells us how we might yet open the door or cross the stream. Such "inventions" or "discoveries" appropriate to the situation appear in every case to contain a specific accomplishment. Psychologists usually contrast them with "understanding" and "comprehension" as the second kind of intelligent behavior.

That the two are intrinsically closely related becomes evident in the fact that we generally try to explain both types of event together. What kinds of explanation have been proposed?

Faced with such problems, popular psychology tends to revert to a particular kind of psychological materialism. When it encounters a specific function or form of process, it likes to refer to a particular kind of psychological material which is involved, as if the mere appearance of this special psychological material constitutes that function, that process. But in chemistry, it is no explanation of combustion, for example, to say that oxygen is required. This would disregard the formation of specific oxygen-containing microstructures or molecules, i.e., a kind of dynamics about which we deceive ourselves if we believe we can properly characterize combustion as "something with oxygen." I am afraid it is not much better to conceive of intelligent behavior, understanding, or invention in the following manner.

The given material as such does not produce the achievement. Therefore it depends on additional material which one person possesses, while another does not. Such material obviously consists of ideas which different individuals have at their disposal to different extents or—particularly in science—concepts, the addition of which to the material constitutes understanding or invention.

Obviously the main thing is missing here, just as in the chemical example above. It is incomprehensible how an accumulation of material beyond what is given could essentially change the situation in the sense in which it is undoubtedly changed in cases of true understanding or invention. Such an increase of material can certainly remain just as useless as the starting material was at the beginning before it was understood. Does the profusion of ideas in "flights of ideas" illuminate processes of understanding or invention? It hardly seems so. And who does not know one or another of those awful people who bury problems and situations under an avalanche of inappropriate concepts, rather than bring them to a solution?

Quite obviously, a principle of selection is missing which either takes care of the appearance of very definite and "appropriate" ideas right from the start, or at least selects those which are appropriate from among the blindly appearing ideas, if they are already present, and rejects the others. So far, a theory of the first kind has hardly been attempted. Many would consider it a mystical idea that, as a rule and from the start, "fitting" ideas, i.e., precisely those which are conducive to a solution or to understanding, should arise in a given situation. They are all the more convinced that these ideas occur at first in accidental variety, but that there is a simple principle according to which the objectively unfit are eliminated from this variegated display and the appropriate ones selected.

In this connection they have gone back to Darwin's basic idea, according to which accidental variations in the nature of the germ cells of one generation give rise to a corresponding multiplicity of somewhat different young individuals of the particular species. But now the environment, which does not have space, food, and sex partners for all, permits those to live and propagate who by chance turned out to be better adapted, while the less fit soon perish.

This idea has long ago been applied to the adaptation processes which are observed again and again in the individual life even of animals relatively low in the evolutionary scale. In a new situation, it is said, for which there is no ready-made behavior, such a creature produces all kinds of chance responses. Some sequences of such responses, which occasionally occur accidentally among entirely unsuitable ones, would by chance be such as to constitute objectively suitable behavior precisely for this particular situation. A very practical arrangement in the nervous system provides that those sequences of responses which lead to success become physiologically fixed and acquire a tendency to be repeated in similar external situations, and adaptation thus comes about. This is the famous theory of trial and error which plays such an important role in animal psychology, and which is rather widely considered to be the explanation of early adaptive behavior in the life of the individual, even in the human child.

To be sure, this procedure would not be very intelligent: the blind production of just any responses in relation to which the external situation acts like a sieve, allowing only objectively adaptive sequences through. But with only a slight change, it seems for a moment to come out much better. A more intelligent creature, one psychologist has said, will not actually produce all possible responses in overt behavior. Endowed with a wealth of ideas, it will rather produce them internally according to the laws of chance. Once more, most of these randomly produced sequences will, of course, not be adaptive; but a few of them will be, will be translated into reality, and then will be stamped in for similar reasons. Soon, in related situations, they will be called forth more easily, like the adaptive chains of responses in the theory of trial and error. It is emphasized how much more economical, and therefore more valuable, it is if the play of chance is shifted in this manner from the sphere of overt behavior to that of mere ideas.

This does not sound bad at all; but I fear that the problem remains unsolved in the proposed theory. For if ideas really occur as much by chance as do responses in trial and error, then "the sieve" is still needed, to take care of the selection of what is suitable, as does the environment at large for Darwin and the actual situation for the theory of trial and error. And furthermore this sifting must occur purely mechanically, on the basis of the purely objective usefulness of the ideas in question. For otherwise this theory could not be recommended as a simple transfer of the doctrine of trial and error to the world of ideas. Rather, it would have to bring forward a new principle of selection, which would be altogether foreign to the idea of trial and error. But at any rate one thing is excluded, namely that the external situation as such would still serve as "the sieve." For then, to every sequence of ideas, the corresponding overt actions would have to be added, since the situation could exercise its sifting function only in relation to these—and we would have returned basically to the old form of trial and error. Thus nothing is left but that the individual compares, so to speak, the chains of ideas arising randomly in him with his perception of the situation, and that in this process he is able to grasp which sequences of ideas, if converted to action, would fit the situation objectively, and which would not, which, in other words, might be considered for actual execution. But this would, in fact, introduce a principle of selection of an entirely new kind, so new that it can scarcely be compared any more with the purely practical "survival" of certain accidental products in Darwinian theory and in trial and error. Such creatures would still be led to appropriate behavior by chance; but they would see what was appropriate from the objective relation of this behavior to the given situation, without any trial and error. But then the main issue is obviously no longer the actual production of ideas as material, but whatever it is that is called insight, the grasping of the essential features of a situation in the given or incoming data.

This would be a step forward. The kind of psychological materialism which I mentioned above would basically be given up, and it would be conceded that the problem of intelligence concerns a type of function, a grasping of relatedness within the material, but not a particular kind of material or its "being added" to the original situation.

But there is still need for caution lest this advance be spoiled by too easy a short cut. Nothing is accomplished if we say: Naturally the higher animals and man have not only what is called the "contents" of consciousness in the narrower sense, but in addition all relations among all such contents. If this is supposed to be a clarification of our problem, we must be on guard against it. First of all, such a thesis is entirely contrary to experience. Fortunately, by no means do we experience all possible relations among all the "contents" of our actual situation.

Just imagine everything actually present in a perceptual field at any one time. Could it possibly be maintained that I am conscious of all relations among all distinguishable parts of this field at all times—for instance, all relations of brightness, size, position in time and space, hue, etc.? Since I know very well what it means to be conscious of a really existing relation when it occurs, I must emphatically deny that I would have some hundreds of such relations simultaneously, or even that I could do so. We may not invent facts in psychology any more than in physics or elsewhere. The claim that relations are ubiquitous in consciousness is, however, not only false, but also entirely unsuitable as an explanation of intelligent behavior. For most of the relations in the indifferent network of relations which, according to this view, are contained in every experienced situation, would be completely irrelevant for understanding or invention in this situation, if not downright disturbing—just as are most of the ideas which might at times occur to me at random in this situation. Understanding and invention undoubtedly have something to do with relations, but only with particular ones in a given situation, specifically those which are essential in the context. And so this theory, which would offer us too many relations, only leads back once more to the need for a principle of selection.

I will not describe the attempt in so-called constellation theories, in spite of everything, to derive the orderly and appropriate conscious processes, which seem to us to be characteristic of intelligent behavior, from the blind play of individual associations, or rather from recall of them. Here, too, facts have been assumed to be obvious and, therefore, to occur quite generally which, one fine day when somebody undertook to put them to actual test, immediately turned out to occur only exceptionally or not at all.[1] Moreover, Selz was able to show convincingly that even if these facts could be assumed, their explanatory value for the present problem would be exceedingly small, and that com-

---

[1] I refer to experiments by J. F. Shepard and H. M. Fogelsonger (Studies in association and inhibition, *Psychological Review*, 1913, 20, 290–311) and to the conclusions correctly drawn from them by G. E. Müller (*Komplextheorie und Gestalttheorie*. Göttingen, 1923). For the explanation of these experiments, see also W. Köhler, Komplextheorie und Gestalttheorie, *Psychologische Forschung*, 1925, 6, 358–416.

pletely inadequate sequences of ideas would still remain possible and frequent. In his positive suggestions, to be sure, even this author holds that a given experienced situation possesses no tendency arising out of its objective nature to bring about that articulation and restructuring which are at the heart of understanding and invention. According to him, what I have called insight does not really play the decisive, i.e., productive, role. Therefore, everything essential still has to be left to some happy accident; and what this cannot do must be accomplished by prescribed, reliably operating mechanisms of the nervous system, acting like machines made for the purpose.

Is this skepticism necessary? Our problem, which more and more is seen to be going in the direction of remarkable processes of organization, will perhaps become somewhat less puzzling if we consider for a moment other organizations, which were likewise for a long time not taken for what they are, but which we are forced to accept today.

We find these organizations in our perceptual field. For too long the perceptual field has been treated analytically, in an artificial and unrealistic manner, as though, e.g., in visual space, individual local sensory qualities were essentially determined by individual local stimuli, so that an incoherent mosaic of such qualities would have to result. Of course the phenomenal world does not look like this to anybody. We have before us patches, bounded surfaces, and things or groups of these; also we see, hear, or feel events of definite form. Thus there is a concrete structuring of the whole field in its spatial and temporal extension, and frequently also further substructuring of such segregated wholes into their true, i.e., their phenomenally real, parts (Wertheimer). What could our analytical procedure achieve in this variegated world? But if it is possible and necessary to analyze, then this process must be directed to the divisions and structurings which our subject, the perceptual world, exhibits of itself. If, instead, we introduce an analysis in terms of arbitrary local elements, then there disappears before our eyes not only the unity of particular phenomenal wholes, but also the true contours and articulations of the field.

Sensory organization has not been taken seriously enough,

but has been interpreted so that no problem of "structuring of the field" seemed to remain. According to this interpretation, we would have *learned* to treat certain sets of local sensory data as units, because they always occurred together or because they were of practical significance for us in this grouping. Gestalt psychologists have gone to a great deal of trouble to make clear the implausibility of this basically empiristic interpretation of field organization. But now most psychologists, at least in Germany, have understood that every attempt at a purely empiristic theory of structuring must somewhere be circular; that is, in applying its principles, it must tacitly assume the autochthonous organization which was to be derived from these principles in the first place, and therefore not meant to be autochthonous. Since we have therefore, in principle, to abandon the empiristic interpretation, what then produces the organization of the perceptual field? It has become clear that we must have the courage to abandon the basic view from which it became necessary to treat field organization as a secondary, derived phenomenon: If there is a multitude of local stimuli, the organism by no means reacts with separate local sensory processes for each of them. A now tremendous body of experience forces us rather to think of the sensory processes as a functionally connected continuum in which local conditions may at once acquire more than local significance. Therefore distributions, specific connections, and separations are formed and re-formed in reciprocal dynamic interaction across the whole system until the whole comes to rest. The path to such equilibria shows itself as a process within the field; if it comes to a balanced state, usually in a fraction of a second, we have before us a world of stable objects and enduring qualities.

In this sense we speak of sensory dynamics in which the perceptual field as a whole assumes, wherever possible, an organization which is stable in itself and relative to the total stimulus array of the moment. If we investigate what determines the actually occurring organization, we find that under given internal conditions it is certain features of the stimulus conditions in relation to each other—we might say of the total constellation of stimuli. This is just as in physics, where a system under the influence of an actual constellation of conditions at its boundaries always forms an organization of its states which, as a whole, is compatible with this constellation. There, too, it depends on the relatedness of certain features of the constellation of conditions. We are not surprised that the physical processes "know," so to speak, how to direct themselves so that this organization results. Therefore we should expect as much from sensory dynamics. Of what happens in detail we may have satisfactory knowledge in several decades. For we already have the *results* of such sensory organization continually before us in the form of perceptual structures, and we also frequently get a hint of the processes by which they are produced; such evidence does not remain silent with respect to the concrete physical (physiological) forces at work. Most of the forces at play in this case lie outside of consciousness, below or before it, in nervous processes. The very fact that the sensory processes are hidden makes it especially clear that a sensory situation finds the path to its own organization by itself, in an autochthonous manner. Sensory organizations can be formed, in their basic features at least, without need for the participation of other psychological regions. But then it also follows that, right from the start, the organism is not a copying machine for stimuli, but that it is already creatively at work on these external influences.

Not all sensory organizations, however, remain so lastingly stable as, for example, phenomenal objects—which are practically most important to us—essentially do. For instance the following figure (Figure 8.1), after its center has been fixated for some time, usually changes suddenly from one organization—

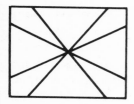

Figure 8.1

a phenomenal form in the region of the four narrow angles—to an entirely different organization—a phenomenal form in the region of the four wide angles; then it usually changes again to the first form, etc. Such a case teaches us two things. First, by the very alternation, it demonstrates particularly clearly the reality of what has been called organization or structuring, and secondly, it certainly shows that structures need not necessarily be unchangeable, but under certain circumstances can be restructured. The influences at work in the present example are of no particular concern for our problem. We must be all the more intrigued by those cases in which our self is intently directed to a given situation. Where objects or figures do not form compelling organizations, but stand in relatively loose juxtaposition, it is not particularly difficult to produce certain groupings intentionally and to transform these again, at will, into certain others. Still, one certainly cannot claim complete arbitrariness in these transformations; and the forces of the field themselves impose very noticeable limits to such activities. Besides, tendencies to arbitrary organizations or reorganizations of this kind do not even occur to people. Rather, in a specific relation of self and situation, very specific organizations usually arise from this relation itself. Let us consider, for example, the case in which two complex drawings are presented in the two sides of a stereoscope, and do not at once fuse in depth into a solid object, but for a while produce a confusing tangle of lines. Anybody who has seen something like this knows that this field situation is experienced as painful. This seems rather generally to be the effect of unclear fields, in which there is a blocking of the organization. Again, as a rule, a still stronger direction toward the field at once develops out of this painful state, in the same way that it is difficult not to pay attention to a shoe that is too tight. In the case of the stereoscopic picture, however, it is remarkable that there often occurs a sudden restructuring of the field (in which suitable eye movements will have taken part), and suddenly the clear three-dimensionality of a single organized picture stands before us. To my knowledge, there have as yet been no investigations of whether different degrees of subjective directedness to the field correspond to different speeds or delays of this kind of "crystallization." But we may assume it with considerable probability. Still, it is not the subjective directedness as such which achieves the specific organization that suddenly appears. For in such a case we would not at all know which lines would have to fuse with which others for the desired outcome, nor how we would have to turn our eyes. Thus our directedness to the at first painfully confused field must be a really necessary, but still only a very generally favorable, condition for the decisive process. The specific forces within the field, which in the concrete case permit just these and no other changes, must arise from the nature of the thing, i.e., from the specific nature of the confused, unclear situation itself, after that generally favorable condition has been met. Just as characteristic as the painful effect of the beginning condition for these processes are the release of tension and satisfaction with which we perceive the transition to the clear organization. Gradually we approach processes which also exhibit the characteristics of intelligent behavior, of understanding and discovery.

In some situations understanding means precisely this, that a perceived event changes to a definite, stable organization. Understanding or not understanding then usually shows itself in the ability or inability to coordinate one's own actions to the event as its meaning, i.e., its principle of organization, demands.

The chimpanzees that I studied in Tenerife loved to perform a kind of primitive dance in which they trotted one behind the other around any kind of center, a pole, a box, or some such object, in easy, rhythmic motions. As usual with such games, there were frequent variations on the basic principle, and one of the most attractive consisted in dancing around *two* focal points instead of *one* center, so that the animals described a kind of ellipse. But there were too few chimpanzees to fill out this elongated pattern very densely. Thus to a spectator or a participant, there were *objectively* only individual apes in motion, separated in space; the principle of the dance could be clear, participation in the intended manner would thus be possible, only if the moving "markers" were correctly organized as the periphery of a rotating ellipse. That understanding is really required here easily escapes the normally intelligent adult, because for him this process of understanding occurs at first glance, too obviously and too quickly. But let an adult only be asked to participate in a somewhat more complex and more structured dance pattern, and he will find himself confronted by just this difficulty of organized seeing and understanding into which the elongated dance around two centers plunged one particularly unintelligent chimpanzee. This eagerly participating animal might have been particularly hampered in grasping the new pattern of movement by the after-effect of the previously practiced simple circling around a single center—as often happens with us human beings in the transition to new situations. At any rate, this animal, after turning around one center, again and again blundered out of the movement pattern he had not understood, into the interior of the ellipse and then, to his great astonishment, collided on the other side with those fellow dancers who had correctly gone around the second center. The example shows clearly how much understanding enters, or can enter, into what we are usually inclined simply to call "seeing." The expression is misleading insofar as we often speak of seeing without consideration of the problem of organization, or else where a very simple sensory organization is present, ready-made, for everyone. On the other hand, the word is entirely appropriate where the understanding of an event which takes place before our eyes really brings about organization in the visual field, so that from then on we see in it something which previously did not exist there. Of course, stupid creatures are particularly able to make clear to us the reality and decisive importance of such organizations, since they are unable to bring them off even in situations where—for purposes of psychological observation—we achieve them too quickly and too easily. In the example of the chimpanzees, the oldest animal finally grabbed the poor fool by the hair and dragged him several times over the required path. But even this did not help.

In a further example from animal psychology that, by the way, was provided by the same chimpanzee, the required organization is no longer so simply geometrical-kinematic. But that there, too, understanding depends on the formation of a specific connection in a perceptual event becomes clear enough from the behavior of the animal who did *not* understand. Several apes at the station on Tenerife had discovered or learned to reach objectives attached at a great height by dragging a box nearby and grabbing or jumping at the desired object from this stool. The stupid animal mentioned above had been present a number of times, watching this performance; now he had to show whether he was able to employ this simple method himself. A banana was attached to the ceiling of a room, and a box stood a few meters to the side. It was immediately clear that this ape had "seen" the action of the model only in pieces which, as pieces, could not contribute to the solution of the problem. Either he tried it with the very primitive method of jumping from the level ground under the fruit, a method that had nothing to do with the demonstration and was necessarily unsuccessful; or he climbed on the box just where it stood and, looking at the objective, made repeated preparations to jump. The solution was demonstrated several times more, but the only effect was that the animal showed still more clearly how little he had grasped the connections of the several actions. For he climbed again on the box just where it was, mustered all his strength, ran as fast as he could toward the fruit, and jumped from the floor. As though the advantage of standing on the box would be transferred to this place by sheer speed! It was pitiful how the chimpanzee tried to connect this position and the objective, after he had failed to grasp the necessity of the action that would make the connection, and therefore did not carry it out. That the movement of the box was not "seen" in its necessary role within the demonstrated sequence was shown most clearly when the other animals once again demonstrated this little performance. Now the ape being tested actually seized the box and began to push it around on the floor—but not to the place where it should have been used as a stool. This shows directly that the error consists in a failure of processes of organization. Moving an object in space may belong to a larger context in a variety of ways: one may "remove an object from the place" where it originally stood; one may "remove it from another object" which was at first its neighbor; one may "drag it along" in its own movement, i.e., without relation to external space, as chimpanzees frequently do when they get excited; one may "bring it between two other objects"; and, finally, one may "transport it to another object" in a particular position. Depending on the existing circumstances, one or another very definite organization of the movement will be required for the understanding of the whole activity, while at the same time *any* or almost any of the types of organization mentioned would usually be possible if the situation were considered purely out of context. This observation once again makes it clear how extraordinarily simple sequences of events may not be understood if the one appropriate organization does not occur. The unintelligent ape has at first seen "movement" of the box so much outside of any connection with its use as a stool that this aspect of the demonstration remains irrelevant and is omitted in his own efforts. Later, when this aspect became more impressive, the required organization still failed to occur, and only some "pushing on the floor" was seen. It was a long time before this animal understood the movement of the box in relation to the too great vertical distance between floor and objective.

This example also enables us to judge, at least for the present case, the relation between understanding and processes of recall. Does not the ape simply "forget" a part of the demonstration in the short interval between it and his own efforts? The answer to this is the question why he forgets just this particular part and not also the role of the box as a stool. To this, the answer must again be that this last part, by virtue of its immediate transition to the reaching of the goal, can much more readily be seen as organizationally united with it, while the movement of the box is, so to speak, too remote from the goal for it necessarily to be included in the same context with it. But if, for the observer, the movement did not at all have a particular function in the demonstration, why should he reproduce it in his own action—any more than any head or arm movements which occurred in the demonstration and which were likewise not included in the goal-directed structure? Thus we come to the conclusion that recall certainly has a significant function in intelligent behavior, but that in a situation like the one described here, it depends on the organizational process itself whether or not recall occurs.

In speaking of the relation between understanding and the recall of ideas, we usually do not mean recall as repetition of what has been understood or not understood, but rather we consider recall of any ideas to be decisive for understanding itself. This question may be examined by means of the following example, which has the further advantage of bringing us from the animal experiment to observation on human beings. Again it deals with the understanding of a demonstration. But this time the task is made somewhat difficult by the fact that a part of the action, and indeed just the decisive part, is not visible, and also by the fact that a wrong organization of the demonstration is suggested. Someone stands before a group of people and promises to furnish evidence of the physical effectiveness of very intense concentration of the will. A stick, merely touched on the side by the palm of the hand, will remain freely suspended in space if the necessary will power, conducted through the two arms, overcomes gravity. Then the demonstrator, stick in the left hand, and right hand clasped around the left wrist, turns to the right (to the left of the spectators), lifts his arms together with the stick, and pretends that he is making the most intense effort by strenuous tensing of all the muscles of the arms until they tremble and by appropriate facial expressions; now he slowly opens the hand in which the stick lies until the hand forms a flat surface in front of the stick. It is astonishing how slowly some, even very intelligent, people realize that one finger of the second (right) hand behind the first (left) does not take part in clasping the wrist, but presses the stick against the invisible palm so that it does not fall. If the performance is skillful, the perceived tension of the right arm and right hand is concentrated on the left wrist to such an extent that this impressive connection does not readily allow contradictory tendencies to arise. Thus, in the face of this very stable organization, the practical and very obvious idea does not occur at all to some people that one finger, against all appearances, might have an entirely different direction and the really decisive and banal function which it actually has. This means, in turn, that the appearance of ideas in such a situation depends on the organization in which the situation is viewed. Here an inadequate organization is intentionally created. Anyone who wants to understand what is happening, on the contrary, must achieve an objectively required organization which cannot be formed entirely in terms of the visible aspects of the situation. He misses a visible support for the stick and will therefore be directed toward something invisible in the region of the stick that could hold it up. The idea of a very definite position of the fingers is the most obvious recall that can complete a suitable organization in the unseen part of space; and this succeeds in those who are not permanently dominated by the phenomenal role of the right hand in a misleading organization. Accordingly, the success of the trick must depend on how well and how convincingly the wrong organization is achieved. This agrees with my own experience. If the right hand is simply placed on the left wrist from behind, this "magic" will make little impression.

This explanation assumes that (in the positive case here and also generally) those ideas will be recalled, in a situation viewed as incomplete, which are objectively somehow suited to making a stable organization out of the incomplete situation. The specific kind of incompleteness in an otherwise perceptually given situation seems sufficient to determine this completion. In fact it cannot be denied that understanding in such cases involves the appearance of particular ideas. But their appearance would presuppose the formation of a tentative organization which has a situationally determined gap. The pressure to close this particular gap would evoke objectively suitable ideas and tend to incorporate them into the tentative organization. Understanding would be the achievement of the complete *organization,* not the recall process as such. Is it too bold a thought that an organization which is unclosed in a particular way tends to closure, in a way suited to its particular structure, by means of selective recall? Such a process in itself seems to me no stranger than the fact that, in the visual field, those unit formations and segregations occur *selectively* which result in a clear overall organization. We have only to assume that the total field in which this pressure toward organization exists consists not only of the actual sensory processes but, beyond these, also of the realm of past experiences, which must, of course, somehow be represented in the nervous system. Perhaps, then, it makes no difference in principle whether a particular region of sensory events enters into an organization because of its objective appropriateness or whether, just as specifically, a particular product of past experience is incorporated in it and thus permits the organization to become complete and stable.

A generalization of the above ideas is almost inescapable. At first it may appear a sort of leap if we proceed from the consideration of largely perceptual situations, and of understanding in such cases, to the understanding of situations which are only imagined or thought. But essentially this seems to be exactly the same problem. It will perhaps be difficult to describe to somebody the situation of the sleight of hand with the stick, so that he can imagine it in the same way the actual spectator does in the above case. But if this succeeds reasonably well, then in this "thought" situation the same closure of an incomplete structure with a particular kind of gap would have to be effected; and it would again be hampered by the same misleading organization as in the perceived situation. Once more, understanding would amount to an organization fitting the situation and including a suitable idea which brings about closure. And it seems, in general, to be similar where the situation to be understood remains in the sphere of thought. The fact that, in this sphere, organizations may be more diffuse is obviously only a secondary difference. Nor do I believe that the transition to specifically conceptual material, as in science, could make any difference for understanding as a process of objectively determined and objectively demanded organization.

Finally, invention and discovery are, in general, closely related to understanding in cases where considerable parts of the event to be understood cannot be observed. There is a situation with a task, and initially everything will depend on seeing the core of this situation as a very particular kind of incomplete organization; thus the problem will be properly understood. From this there results, as before, a pressure toward incorporating further fitting parts of the situation, as well as appropriate knowledge, so that, insofar as possible, a complete organization may occur as the solution. We shall not deal further with these processes because, in human life, understanding goes on continually, invention and discovery unfortunately much less frequently.

What does it mean that the organizations in question come easily to some individuals, to others only with difficulty? If we put the question in this manner, intelligence is not a fact of consciousness, nor is it the occurrence of intelligent behavior, but it is the general condition for the fact that objectively required organizations are achieved easily or only with difficulty. There must be nervous systems which are favorable media for such organizations and others where this is not the case. This is not to say that some individuals have special nervous arrangements, lacking in others, which automatically produce intelligent performances. Rather, it is comparable to the fact that, for example, one fluid medium facilitates crystal formation and another medium makes crystallization difficult, without special arrangements for the process in one case and their absence in the other. Nor need we think in terms of an entirely constant condition of the medium. Rather, it is clear that there are variations in the ease with which a given nervous system permits processes of organization. Thus there is no doubt that above a certain intake of alcohol, the possibility of understanding and of creative intelligence is reduced. Strangely enough, a heavy cold has, according to common experience, an enormous effect on the suitability of the nervous medium for such organizations. And again, when our emotions are strongly aroused, the medium seems to get into a condition which allows only the simplest forms of organization.

What should we do to get on the track of these properties of the medium? It will be best if we first try to clarify the characteristic *processes* which take place in this medium as organizations. When we know more of their nature, it will be easier to infer what kinds of properties of the nervous system facilitate or hinder such processes. On the other hand, I am somewhat suspicious of the tendency to neglect these highly interesting questions because it is getting to be the fashion instead to employ so-called intelligence tests. A gifted teacher talks with a child for a few minutes and then has quite a vivid picture of his abilities, his interests, and his difficulties. This is now to be replaced by an intelligence test. A glance at the test items which often appear in such intelligence tests shows immediately that it is not always quite clear what really should be tested. A kind of potpourri of demands is put together and presented to the child. His intelligence is measured by how many of these tasks he solves. In some circles, this procedure is particularly valued because of the quantitative results it yields.

How does anyone know that such tasks are specifically intelligence tasks and therefore able to replace the more qualitative personal judgment of the born teacher? The scores obtained are compared, for example, with later achievements in school or at work. I must say that this seems to me to be a rather misleading kind of procedure. For anybody who is not a very naïve prisoner of the values of his particular civilization and cultural era, of his country and social milieu, will surely have to realize this: By standardizing against scholastic or occupational performance, we call *intelligence* in our children something which merely corresponds to those particular requirements which the present-day school, the present-day city in Europe or America, the present-day middle class consider important. But how do we know that something so arbitrarily taken out of history, geography, and all cultural possibilities can serve as a suitable measure of a basic psychological attribute? And yet we can scarcely proceed otherwise if the test is not based on an analysis of the decisive processes involved.

Still, this may suffice for some practical purposes, as long as what is wanted is a prognosis of achievement in school, in our time, in the city, in a particular milieu, and if one is not really interested in finding a basic psychological attribute.

How is it, then, that so many very vital teachers, and others who enjoy life, dislike the tests? And why, on the other hand, are the tests so highly recommended? I think I know why. To appreciate the intelligence and the *type* of intelligence of a child is itself one of the most difficult and noblest processes of understanding, and this is required of the teacher unless we give him the test instead. Will they all succeed? It is the same as in a bureaucracy. Not all officials can be very wise and judicious. Therefore a substitute must be sought in exact regulations, in the bureaucratic machinery within which there is not too much room left for individual understanding and initiative. Anxiety begets bureaucracy. In our field, too, it is anxiety and the desire for an automatically guaranteed result which would substitute the quite automatic, if also quite limited, intelligence test for the living understanding which cannot be guaranteed in all. Those who hold this point of view might say that "understanding" is something about as intangible as artistic creation; they would rather not get into that. Not all teachers, they would add, are such unfailing artists of understanding that we can trust to their judgment. Let us give them the machine! This is the intelligence test.

9: On logic and psychology

so far we have not dealt with the cognitive part of the mental world, and I propose to do so in this last lecture of the present course. The connection between problems of value and the problems of the cognitive realm is not immediately clear. In fact, it is one of the more serious omissions of modern thought that, on the whole, little attention has been given to the relations between the more strictly intellectual occupations of our minds and our valuations. The reason for the omission seems to have been that, at their best, our cognitive activities satisfy certain strict rules, the rules of logic; but pure logic can be handled in a way in which it appears to be utterly remote from *all* human concerns, including the actual cognitive or thought processes which satisfy, or fail to satisfy, the laws of this remote realm. Few have tried to separate in a similar fashion abstract principles of value from concrete value experiences, probably because no such principles have ever been clearly established. The contrast

This is an excerpt from the Gifford Lectures which Professor Köhler delivered in Edinburgh in 1958. The American Philosophical Society is in possession of the original and has granted the privilege of publication.

between abstract logic and the utterly concrete and human processes to which we mostly refer when talking of values is very
striking indeed. As a result, my friends in philosophy are almost
shocked when I insist that not only our cognitive operations, but
also the content of systematic logic, appear to me significantly
related to our value experiences and corresponding motivations.
Why do I insist that even logic is still a member of this large
family? My reason is that logic has one essential characteristic
in common with thinking and with value experiences: Logic does
not describe the mere occurrence of certain facts; actual thinking is not merely a matter of such facts, for it aims at *valid*
results; and, of course, the "good" or "bad" which is inseparable
from values and corresponding motivations can also not be reduced to mere or neutral facts. Why should we not recognize that
all these concerns of the mental world resemble one another, and
differ from all neutral psychological facts, in containing an
element of "ought to" or "should be," as distinguished from mere
"being" and mere "occurring"?

For the most part, philosophers do not like to see logic
grouped with actual thinking and with valuation, because they
fear that, when brought together with *any* psychological events,
logic might lose much of its extraordinary cleanliness and objectivity. As a psychologist, I do not like to see logic escaping
into a realm of its own, because such a radical separation of
logic from the study of mental events appears to me as a threat
to this study, to *psychology*. If so sharp a line is drawn between
the discipline which deals with the principles of truth and the
investigation of all actual mental events, then within the latter
realm the altogether necessary distinction between mere psychological facts and experienced *demands* will easily be obscured;
for now everything that happens in the mental world will, by
contrast with the noble timeless world of logic, be pressed together into one mass of mere occurrences. Nothing could be
worse. Even without being pushed in this fashion, present psychology is too eager to imitate the natural sciences somewhat
blindly, particularly in handling all mental facts as though they
were neutral events and in ignoring experienced values. Natu-

rally, this unfortunate tendency is greatly strengthened by the philosophers' insistence that all connections between logic and psychology be severed. So long as these connections are recognized, the mere existence of logic can serve as a warning—a warning against the powerful factualistic trend in psychology.

The logician's aversion to any contact with psychology has historical reasons. During the past century, attempts have been made to replace philosophy by fairly naïve extensions of scientific thinking. One such attempt referred to logic. It was suggested that what we call the principles of logic are simply factual laws which indicate what actually happens when we think. No refutation of this curious doctrine will be needed. If the doctrine were correct, all thinking would have to follow those allegedly factual laws; and, if these laws really coincided with the principles of logic, wrong thinking would be impossible—which, unfortunately, it is *not*. Now, those so-called natural laws of thinking were, of course, supposed to be *psychological* laws. Hence, the trend which expressed itself in this doctrine was called psychologism, and ever since that time, "psychologism" has remained the name of the worst sin which can be committed in, and in the neighborhood of, logic. Again, hence, the tendency of the logician to deal with his subject as though it were entirely unrelated to *anything* in psychology.

When I said that logic ought not to be separated entirely from the psychology of thinking (and not from the study of other mental events which contain values and demands), did I mean that we ought to return to psychologism? Surely, I did *not*. It is not my wish to identify logic with the psychology of just any events which occur in thought processes. But I do believe that logic has its roots *in certain phases* of these processes, namely, in demands which arise while these processes take place. When they arise, they generally do so with a claim of being strictly valid, of following from the very nature of the material with which the thinking person is occupied, quite regardless of any tendencies located in this person's self. But those demands do not always arise when they ought to, and then, actual thinking is likely to make bad mistakes. It is a factual question whether or not they do arise at the right time. On the other hand, their content if and when they arise is far from being a merely factual matter; for this content leaves no doubt at all as to what conditions thinking ought to fulfill at the crucial point. With those who insist that logic must be distinguished from mere descriptions or laws of thought processes as they really occur, I agree. But I no longer agree if they conclude that logic is not related to anything that happens in thinking. For, whenever those demands emerge in thinking, this thinking exhibits a particular aspect of itself which is plain logic in action—not, of course, logic as an abstract system, not logic as a special discipline, not a logic which dictates merely from the outside what is correct and what is not, but rather logic immanent in the thought process. Surely, this process is not determined by those demands of acting logic alone. Much too often, it is also influenced by tendencies which do not belong to the class of valid demands. In the course of time, however, the various threads have been disentangled; the truly valid demands have been recognized as a special group of mental states; any effects of other mental influences have been thrown aside; and eventually the genuine material has been assembled in a clear system. The result, I believe, is what we now call logic. But, originally it has come from particular experiences in thinking. Without such experiences in actual thought, how could we know about any principles of logic? How could Aristotle have known? This, of course, is not psychologism. For, what I just said does not imply that logic is concerned with everything that occurs in thinking. My statements refer *only* to those particular experienced demands; and whether these demands really arise, whether they then win in the competition with other factors, and therefore whether our thinking follows these way signs—this is an entirely different question, a factual question with which pure logic as such need not be concerned. I can therefore not be accused of trying to pull logic down to a lower level. I emphasize the connection between logic and the psychology of actual thinking only in order to prevent psychology from lowering its own level. Psychology ought not to deal with mere facts alone, or to proceed as though human experience consisted only of such facts. If this science is to do justice to its own subject matter, it must realize that human experience is to a large degree experience of demands. Why just the strangely cool demands of acting logic have the character of being binding under all circumstances—this is a question which we had better not discuss today. Values in the usual sense of the term are seldom felt to be so utterly or absolutely right.

One more distinction. The demands which arise in cognitive processes, and are now handled by the logicians, are not the only demands experienced in this field. The same domain exhibits other demands also, and these do resemble the demands of values in general. Thus, a particular intellectual task may appear interesting or even fascinating; while another may rather impress us as tedious or boring. Such positive and negative value characteristics are, of course, of the same kind as those which we discussed in preceding lectures. They show this at once by being positive or negative in relation to a given self—while the demands of acting logic are felt to be entirely independent of this subjective center of experience.

three

ANIMAL PSYCHOLOGY

10: Methods of psychological research with apes

THE research methods used specifically for the psychological study of apes need to be presented as such only insofar as phenomena appear and are to be investigated in these primates which lower animals do not exhibit in the same way. The "anthropoid" in the literal meaning of the word is the reason for this special position. On the other hand, to the extent that the methods of animal psychology apply to apes just as to other mammals, and to vertebrates in general, they will not here be discussed further.

Since even the highest apes lack essential human characteristics and remain far behind man in the degree to which they possess other characteristics which, in principle, they share with man, methods of psychological research with apes must be dif-

Die Methoden der psychologischen Forschung an Affen. In Emil Abderhalden (Hrsg.), *Handbuch der biologischen Arbeitsmethoden,* 1921 (Abt. 6, Teil D), 69–120. Reprinted by permission of Urban & Schwarzenberg and translated by Mary Henle.

ferent from those of human psychology. But since we have only recently begun to turn seriously to this new branch of research, the methodological problem represents almost the main issue in a treatment of methods in this area.

Under these circumstances we can as yet say little about special techniques of investigation, and in the present descrip- tion or discussion of methods there will even be a certain inten- tional disregard of purely technical points of view. For the further development of this branch of science depends much more on the clarity and sharpness of our questions (the way of thinking) than on the details of experimental procedures. Why take pains to achieve technical refinement when we do not quite know how to proceed validly in essentials?

Just one variety of overestimation of technical points of view—a danger to objective psychology—is to try to achieve the quantitative, the numerical, the experimental record as quickly as possible, or to regard as really valuable only those experiments which yield numbers and curves. Every research must employ those methods which are appropriate to its subject and to its state of development; what matters is not simply the imitation of the trappings of the exact sciences. In the most important areas of objective psychology, there is very much to observe which so far cannot be studied quantitatively either directly or indirectly. Thus the investigator will necessarily find himself on a bypath if he observes only the quantitative and leaves unob- served—and therefore without influence on his questions and his thinking—the other behavior of the creatures studied. Then he will not at all see the major part of his task; his theories will necessarily be one-sided and narrow. Where behavior assumes such high and diverse forms as with apes, this error will lead to the neglect of the most important phenomena. The essential determining forces in these animals are undoubtedly *affective,* and we still have no methods for discovering in quantitative experiments how these forces act.

Findings and problems of the rapidly advancing human phenomenological psychology can, it is true, lead immediately to quantitatively formulated experimental questions for objective psychology as well. But the scope of quantitative proof in this region has remained just about the same as its scope in human psychology. And even in the latter field, were not the points of view which are now being applied to objective psychology first achieved entirely in *qualitative* experience? Thus if every good question and also every meaningful quantitative experiment go back ultimately to such qualitative observation, then a simple methodological conclusion follows: The investigator must wander—again and again and over its whole extent—through this foundation of all inquiry and all experimentation. Of the total range of psychological investigation, even contemporary human psychology knows only parts. In this science we know how to make observations in special areas like perception and memory, but according to what laws a man, for example, reacts as a whole, "as a system," to life situations in which he is highly involved emotionally—about this we know astonishingly little as psychologists, and from such slight knowledge we cannot properly derive sharp questions for objective psychology. Thus for such cases, which concern the behavior of the organism as a whole, we remain dependent on observation *within* objective psychology. This will have to be *qualitative* at first precisely because we want to learn later somehow to bring such higher questions to an experimental and quantitative decision.

I. OBSERVATION OF ANIMALS LEFT TO THEMSELVES

Basically, only such apes may be said to be "left to themselves" as are observed in their own habitat and in their native climate, under natural conditions, particularly in freedom. The amount of knowledge so obtained is extremely slight; it derives from chance encounters or quick and exciting hunting episodes during which nearly all conditions for objective observation are lacking. If, with captive apes, it takes weeks and months of continuous association with them to learn to understand them, at most the crudest outlines can be seen in such short encounters where there has been no previous experience in observing. In general, only a few aspects of anthropoid nature will show themselves under such conditions. Systematic observation at a safe distance,

which the apes do not suspect, suggests itself; with the only
moderate sense of smell of the animals, this is feasible, especially
with noisy, gregarious animals like chimpanzees, for example,
more difficult with the most important anthropoid, the gorilla.
For all apes, observation in captivity will be more productive in
detail—if only account is constantly taken of what is without
any doubt (and also of what is only probably) different in captive animals as compared with free ones, and if, at the same
time, the conditions of living in captivity retain at least some
similarity to those of the free life of the animals.

I have the impression that we underestimate the influence
of a number of external conditions on such higher animals. To
be sure, we assume that an ape behaves differently in Germany
than in India or in the forests of the Congo, just because the
climate is so entirely different; but even in the same place his
mood fluctuates depending upon the weather, very like man's,
and an ape who is unhappy anyhow because he has been separated from his fellows easily falls into despair if, in addition,
cold, damp weather sets in. It means a drastic change if the
apes are confined in small spaces. Insofar as we are dealing with
gregarious animals, of course, very characteristic occurrences
are never seen, or seen only in rudimentary form, which are
typical of the group of animals when it moves about—just as
no migration takes place in an aviary. But, in addition, the continuous existence in the same few square meters, always in the
same surroundings, exerts a stultifying, dulling influence which
produces a false impression in every respect. Anyone who has
come to know the nature and ways of higher apes under somewhat favorable conditions must greatly pity the animals in zoos,
who sometimes have not much more space than very dull lower
mammals; after a short time we can no longer expect a sem-
blance of natural behavior. It is the same with the inside equipment of the apes' quarters. Since the animals destroy everything
they are strong enough to destroy, it is difficult to provide them
with permanent and changing material with which they could
occupy themselves in the lively and diverse ways that are natural
to them. But if we are interested in observing their behavior,

how should it be brought to any richness of expression, if not through things in the living space which give rise to this or that behavior? Anyone who does not know apes in other settings will never get a sufficient picture of them if a trapeze or the like is their entire equipment. Observed under such conditions, most men would not be very interesting either.

That "equipment" which must first of all be present, however, if the ape is to be observed with any view to a genuine result, is the company of other animals of the same (or at least a closely related) species. In the ape, the most important "stimulus" for the appearance of scientifically interesting behavior or actions is another ape; and very many observations can only be made or correctly interpreted if their object is the *group* of animals or the individual *in it*. By way of comparison, a single animal simply acts unlifelike, since in isolation the biologically most important expressions of life, through which the species in question shows its character most clearly, do not appear. A single orangutan, for example, whom I observed for years, makes on the whole a very friendly and human impression; but because he is alone, the best opportunity for the lively expression of his nature is lacking; and within that very general impression, the animal remains very poor in nuances. And this is not the only reason why the observation of only one animal must give an entirely insufficient picture. For often the best means of understanding the ape's behavior correctly is the effect of this behavior on others of his species. Their reaction in and for itself can have a more easily understandable form, so that now the behavior of the first ape also becomes more understandable; and also, apart from this, sometimes the total process in the group (between apes in a natural social setting) is more meaningful than if, for example, an ape plays his part without the natural answer from a man who does not know how to behave in relation to an ape. A person seeing solitary apes, as they are generally kept in zoos, will not get the slightest idea of what remarkable phenomena this species shows in the group and how meaningful the observed modes of behavior are. But even the particular composition of different groups will color the resulting observational picture very differently. Among the chimpanzees of the Anthropoid Station, for example, things would have happened differently, certainly not only for directly sexual reasons, if an adult male had been present. Of course, we do not come to know "the" orangutan, "the" chimpanzee, etc., from observation of a single animal also because such an individual shows in his behavior very individual characteristics combined with those of the species as such; again, only experience with several apes of the same species would teach us which characteristics of a given individual are not at all typical of the species. I may take it for granted that we can, without joking, designate as "personalities" individual animals of a higher species of apes, and that the greatest differences can be found among individual personalities. Therefore any conclusion from the observation of only one animal is especially suspect.

Since the quiet of captivity is unnatural—for example, no enemy appears, the question of food may perhaps be left to the animal to deal with occasionally in an experiment but not permanently, since marches or extensive climbs in search of food or water do not occur—apes in captivity come to be more passive and quieter than they would be in freedom. Cameroon hunters confirm this impression when they miss in the chimpanzees on Tenerife the constant, excited noise which is apparently heard from afar from the groups of animals in the bush. To be sure, the "drumming" on tree trunks and the like is observed here too, but in descriptions of African safaris, apes are so frequently detected from afar by this characteristic sound—sometimes because of it they are even mistaken for signal drummers in distant native villages—that this activity must take place almost constantly in freedom. And like every other acoustic expression of the animals, this too only occurs in an active to a strongly excited mood; thus they have occasion for much more lively behavior under natural conditions than in captivity.

Finally, however difficult it is to control the ape or, for reasons of hygiene, to break him of some habit (perhaps through punishment), there is no doubt that the continued supervision, control, and other influences of man gradually produce certain changes. With valuable species one must, for example, prevent older females from having frequent sexual intercourse with a much too young male. After repeated prohibitions, something unfree, something shy comes into the sexual relations, which could lead to far-reaching interpretations, but which might be treated simply as a regrettable by-product of human control.[1]

If so much has to be taken into consideration in the observation of apes kept under the most natural conditions possible, it is obvious that animals which are trained for circus performances, while still, perhaps, in many respects suitable objects of research outside the trained performance, can teach science little during these acts. In order to produce an astonishing effect, such performances are usually chosen much above the level of relations and activities that the ape can grasp, so that the animal is forced mechanically, by any means, into essentially ununderstood sequences of actions, necessarily meaningless to him. Almost the only meaning of the whole is that no punishment—or a reward—follows the smooth performance of the required activity. If, under such circumstances, gross errors can take place with slight changes of conditions, this follows from the nature of the situation and permits no general unfavorable judgment about the abilities of the animal. I must, however, go still farther. Even activities which, for example, an ape carries out occasionally on his own, just because they give him pleasure, are easily undertaken in a different manner —indeed in a meaningless way—if man forces him to do them, and particularly if he does so repeatedly. Chimpanzees often gather objects for nest building, often also food to be eaten later, and in general this happens intelligently, very much as in man. But if one wants to make the same animals collect exactly the same material in one place (perhaps to "tidy up"), the process now seems entirely different and gives the impression of a faltering sequence of movements performed without insight, mechanically. The animals work unwillingly. It is thus essential for a natural process that the ape's own interest be the driving force: if one resorts to compulsion, the animal

[1] Coprophagy seems to belong to the very unnatural phenomena of captivity; we were not at all able to break chimpanzees of it. I once saw young orangutans drink urine, but never eat their excrement.

carries out blindly and mechanically even actions he can perform intelligently if they come about spontaneously. In the face of the complete ignorance of these facts that appears here and there in the literature of animal psychology, one can scarcely warn emphatically enough against conclusions from the behavior of circus apes.

Free observation without any influencing of the animals permits various reliable statements. Some examples may show what kind of knowledge of apes may be gained in this manner.

A new chimpanzee enters the living space of a group of chimpanzees very much accustomed to one another. There follows a moment of fixed but excited staring by the old animals. Immediately afterwards a furious cry by one ape is taken up by all the others. In the next instant the newcomer is covered by assailants who sink their teeth into his hide. Human intervention separates the wild animals, even if it does not restore peace. The new animal struggles to his feet, staggers forward and, with all haste, throws himself around the neck of a woman who has taken care of him for the last fortnight. This place he absolutely refuses to leave; he clings more firmly as soon as the woman wants to remove him and, with an excited motion, strokes her shoulder and back with one hand.

In playing around with a very young chimpanzee male, a little female orangutan comes into the earliest diffuse sexual excitement. As this increases perceptibly, the female lies on her back and presses her sexual organs toward the male crouching before her. The chimpanzee remains indifferent. Already in the first sexual scenes, and also after maturity, the female ape always presses her hind part toward the male.

Thus, without experiments, numbers, and curves, we can very well make observations on animals whose objectivity there is no reason whatever to doubt. Such observations are certainly of just as great interest as most of the experiments and results of animal psychology that are now feasible. In the same way, with repeated and long continued observation, generalizations are also possible.

During his crying and howling or other acoustical expressions of feeling, the chimpanzee produces, on the whole, so many

phonetic elements which resemble those of our speech that it
is certainly not for peripheral-phonetic reasons that he is without speech.

Volatile, unstable behavior, which we regard as characteristic of apes, is not nearly so marked in the African apes as in
lower primates of the African continent.

Apart from this, in a number of characteristics of what
we might call everyday behavior, kind of movement (especially
in affect), sound production, etc., many baboons act extremely
like the chimpanzee. In just such matters of ongoing behavior
there is a tremendous difference, almost an incomparability between species, between the chimpanzee and the orangutan
(thus also between baboon and orangutan).

I have said that observation of the apes, without any apparatus, can be entirely trustworthy. But we know that, by its
very nature, this practically simplest method of collecting data
is by no means clear enough. Therefore I raise some questions
which we must answer sooner or later if we wish to make use
of this method with full insight into its meaning.

1. What do we report when we describe the behavior of
apes? An animal "struggles to his feet," he "staggers," he
"strokes" a person; lower apes often show "volatile, unstable behavior," etc. All the words here used for description reflect *total
impressions* which correspond to movement *complexes* in the
observed animals. Is it therefore a matter of *unanalyzed* perceptions, and does this not also mean unclarity? Must we not undertake the analysis of complexes if we are to discover their true
parts—what is really there? But if we change to this method
and direct our observation and description to *parts* of these
movement complexes, the result turns out to be entirely un-
satisfactory: It provides detailed examples of the mechanics of
movement and of the pure physiology of muscles and glands.
The farther we push the analysis in striving for this kind of
objectivity, the less are we inclined to call the description one
of the "behavior" of apes, and the more it dissolves into purely
physiological statements. But this is scarcely the intention of
objective psychology. We suspect that a train of thought that
leads to such conclusions must contain an error, even if it is

not at first clear where to look for it. Is it, then, incorrect that the more highly analytical observation is always of greater objective value?

The rejection of this kind of conclusion, to be sure, leads to conceptions of description in the psychology of higher animals which contain something very unfamiliar. If the subject matter of objective psychological observations disappears as soon as one tries to describe it analytically beyond a certain point, then *there are realities in the animals investigated which are perceptible to us only in those total impressions.* How is this possible? Do any objective total processes in the animal correspond to the whole properties that we see, processes which would be designated as their "behavior" of the moment? And again, what would their nature be? At first we do not see at all what their relation could be to the objective elementary processes in the sense of pure physiology; and only this one thing would be clear, that they do not simply consist of the latter. For it will be assumed that something objective in the animal—the very subject matter of objective psychology—eludes observation if this is directed to those part processes. But here another problem arises and remains, in the end, to be solved: In what manner do the total *processes* in and on the body of the ape produce total *impressions* in our perception? what is the nature and the degree of the correspondence between them?

It is easily shown, indeed, that just as in the observation of apes, natural perception of other persons in daily social life also occurs in this way, in terms of whole properties; that this manner of perceiving is therefore a thoroughly everyday affair; and that, moreover, it is cultivated by teachers, physicians, judges, customs officials, etc. Nevertheless, even a first attempt to give a more exact account of this occurrence leads to remarkable questions; and if we may regard as somewhat reliable what commonly proves of value to us in the practice of everyday life —still, more will be required of observation as *method.* It will not do that the psychology of higher vertebrates, which depends entirely upon this method of observation, continues to remain in the dark about its possibility and its nature.

2. We have seen that we cannot do without such total impressions if our observation of the animal is directed by psychological interest. This leads immediately to further questions: What connection exists between these unanalyzed characteristics and the *psychology* of apes? Or, since some total *processes* in the animal seem to correspond to our total impressions, while "behavior" iş otherwise supposed to be something objective, what have these total processes to do with the psychology of the animal? Yet they must also produce bodily changes in him— otherwise how could they give rise to perceptions in the observer? In general, how does it happen that *any* perception, analytical or not, reflects "behavior" as psychologically meaningful?

It seems to me that the usual answer to such questions misses the mark. According to it, expressions like "in all haste," "stroke," "in excited movement," etc., have unthinkingly been brought into the description of the perception of others (men and higher animals); but the meaning of the words is then no longer purely descriptive, but lies in the additions, really psychological in nature, which man himself automatically makes to the perception of those movement complexes and which, indeed, he must make on the basis of earlier experience. Logically, this procedure is of the order of inferences by analogy,[2] psychologically, a recall or assimilation process. In order to acquire psychological interest in general, the purely phenomenal body perception must necessarily assimilate to itself such unnoticed components. The older psychology is accustomed to treat a large number of the mysteries confronting it in this manner; but in this case there exists every reason to exert ourselves more strenuously on behalf of the problem.

First, the most important and intensive group phenomena certainly depend upon that perception of whole properties between ape and ape—for example, the spreading of rebellion and aggressive mood, but also enthusiasm in a group. Anyone who has once seen and heard how the furious excitement of one chim-

---

[2] [The reference is to the doctrine that we understand the emotions of others by analogy with, or inference from, our own experience which, in the past, accompanied similar expressions.—Ed.]

panzee is instantly taken up by his fellows, and how all mutually intensify it to an ever wilder outbreak, will have to regard the connection between the animals as much more directly dynamic than would follow from that other view. Does an animal, too, understand the other only by way of associative detours, by means of unceasing reproduction of his own psychological experiences? Without this completion, does he see in the other ape before him only a meaninglessly moving puppet?

Second, as observers, we believe that we *see* the characteristics indicated by these expressions in full reality in the ape; they are thus localized in the visual field before us; and we do not at all succeed in analyzing them (in our own consciousness) into "purely visual facts" without trimmings and recalled admixtures from mere experience. And if someone says that, very generally, the residual effects of past experience appear inseparably worked into perception, then we must refer the advocates of the inference doctrine to their own basic ideas. According to these, the truly psychic and the visible body or its movements constitute two entirely incomparable worlds; just for this reason mechanical habit alone is supposed to be able to supply the whole properties of certain percepts with psychological meaning. Thus, in our case, what belongs to two incomparable worlds would have to combine into such a unitary whole that we could no longer separate the one from the other! Is this not rather remarkable? And how can the *recalled* psychic content suddenly appear localized within the visual field if the corresponding *primary* experience of the phenomenal bodily world and its spatial characteristics is alien to it in nature?

But if the inference doctrine is in this manner self-contradictory, any other conception which we now have at our disposal seems likewise to be incapable of a real explanation. We assume generally that the perception of other individuals, their movements, etc., can have no direct, objective relation to their conscious processes. Will we not then be forced to go the way of the inference doctrine? And must we not add at the same time that there can really be no such thing as "objective psychology"?

Nevertheless this retreat remains closed to us, and we find

our thoughts going in a very different direction: For not only do we fail in the attempt to separate experiential trimmings of psychic content from a purely visual (or acoustic) part in those total impressions, but also a large number of expressions used to describe *behavior* may just as well be applied to purely *conscious processes* and at the same time also to certain purely perceptually given processes even in the *inorganic world*, where there is certainly no question of a "psychological" interpretation or addition.

The "restlessness" of behavior may "increase or decrease"; I can say the same of inner excitement as a conscious event, but also of the movements of an eddying stream. Behavior such as fright may be represented graphically as "abrupt rise" and "slow decline"; an entirely similar curve would reflect the dynamics of the corresponding phenomenal process, but also those of purely electromotive processes in a suddenly and briefly exposed photoelectric element. In its posture (limbs and eyes), an animal is "directed to the left"; these words may also be used for attention as a conscious process and are always applied to vectors in the physical sense.

These examples may suffice. If the meaning of such expressions as "directed to the left" remains somehow the same no matter whether we use them to mean, subjectively, the behavior of attention or, perceptually, the posture of a chimpanzee or, equally perceptually, the direction of a hydrodynamic stream, then the inference doctrine loses its foundation. For then it is in principle quite possible that an objective relationship exists between the psychic processes in an individual and the phenomenal whole impressions which his body movements produce in our perception. To be sure, the change to such a different point of view leads at first only to new questions. If some perceived processes can be similar in certain characteristics to some psychic processes, this is still not to say that whole impressions of overt bodily changes of an individual will turn out to be related precisely to the simultaneously occurring psychic processes; and we have to investigate under what conditions that particular correspondence could be expected which alone would be of value for us. It is certainly not universal. Only when we learn how the coordination takes place where it seems to exist at all, will we be able to judge all this; and it would also have to be explained why it is just the *whole* impressions of an observer that tend to have psychological meaning.

Here I can only indicate that these problems belong to methodology. We should be more deeply aware of them in order gradually to develop approaches to a solution. These seem to lie very much in the direction of the new Gestalt theory, thus to be directly related to the central questions of contemporary psychology.

Meanwhile, we are dependent on such observation even without sufficient theoretical insight into its nature; such things are often enough necessary in science. Perhaps this procedure seems bold and, in fact, it is not very popular among contemporary animal psychologists. But we have no choice if we want to investigate more than details of the behavior of higher animals, for which strictly experimental methods already exist, and especially if we wish to be led to new experimental questions. Besides, even the opponents of free observation constantly make use of this very procedure if they believe that they must supplement the purely numerical results of quantitative experiments on the animal with description of his behavior in these experiments. That description often succeeds more easily and more surely under such conditions than with free observation is related to the fact that it concerns only limited aspects of behavior.

There is certainly no doubt that this kind of observation is subject to error, that it requires practice to use it successfully, and that perhaps even with the same amount of practice, different talent for this procedure will produce results of very different value. But is this not true also of other sciences and their methods? We must admit the same thing for phenomenological observation in human psychology; and even in such an objectively minded science as the histology of the central nervous system, not everyone achieves, as we say, the same sure art in grasping structures and structural differences of fields or layers. The introduction of this analogy also indicates that the case for the free observation of animals should not at all encourage the activity of undisciplined dilettantes. The latter are generally farthest from taking a detached view of what they see in the manner required here; and, on the other hand, as recent experience makes amply clear, even experimentation as such is no longer a sure way of distinguishing between animal psychologists and dilettantes in a pejorative sense.

> Training is needed to *observe* as much as possible without subjective additions; it is needed just as much afterwards to *describe* properly only what was observed. For if we want to describe the observed behavior of the animal to some degree, quite sharp self-criticism is necessary so that certain very primitive aesthetic needs do not make the description more rounded or more detailed than the behavior itself was. The task to be solved is distantly related to that of the artist, but the danger likewise arises of proceeding too freely under the more stringent conditions. A great help lies in the circumstance that language has provided a great abundance of words precisely for the description of perceptible whole properties of the behavior of others.

Since the rise of evolutionary ideas, highly emotional questions, wishes, and assertions have been directed to the nonhuman primates. Even the simplest observations, which can be made almost daily, easily meet with suspicion under these conditions, because lively prejudice is much more common than experience in this area. And, indeed, this danger threatens just about as much from those who wish to find the highest possible characteristics in apes as from those who would at all costs deny them anything human. In the face of such uncertainties, recording with photographic, moving picture, and phonographic apparatus is helpful. . . .[3]

II. QUALITATIVE RESEARCH

Anyone who approaches animals with definite questions from human psychology, or who has arrived at problems from free

[3] [A passage on the uses of these methods has been omitted in view of the enormous technological progress in this area since 1921.—Ed.]

observation of apes left to themselves, soon experiences the need not simply to wait until chance gives rise to interesting kinds of behavior. He will seek to create conditions which could bring about processes in which he is interested.

Such interventions become necessary if the behavior to be observed might never ordinarily occur under the usual conditions of captivity. How does the ape behave in relation to toy animals? Are such things so foreign to biological reality that they leave him indifferent? We bring a suitable toy of this kind to the apes and we can immediately make observations of the greatest interest, to which the everyday life of the animals would never have led.

Since an isolated animal lacks most opportunities for the rich expression of his nature, he must be specially assisted by stimulation, if we are even only approximately to make up for the behavior in the group without any human interference with the isolated animal. Young animals need prodding to lively behavior less than older ones. In my experience, chimpanzees after puberty (also as a result of the longer captivity?) gradually lose their lively activity, play, quarreling, etc., with which the younger animals spend their time; the older ones finally lie around most of the day in a half sleep, and one is frequently forced to interfere in order to produce behavior worth observing.

Since the observation of uninfluenced animals is directed to processes that cannot always be grasped sufficiently clearly in one perception, we also artificially introduce opportunities for the repetition of processes not yet fully understood. If, on the other hand, the *meaning* of an observation remains unclear, though the observation itself is not in doubt, we try to produce the phenomenon in question under conditions changed in such a manner that a decision can be made about possible objections or interpretations. It happens, for example, that an animal who must be punished in the company of his fellows turns to the attack—not alone, but with the support of the whole group. Against the interpretation that the others defended the one ape being punished, it has been objected that the foolish creatures would immediately relate the man's attack to themselves if they felt falsely that each one of them was threatened. If, now, we punish an ape in a remote place, in a special room where the others cannot see what is going on, but can only hear cries, etc., a room to which they know the way—then they themselves cannot feel directly attacked. Nevertheless, one of the other animals, hearing the wailing of his fellow, advances in the greatest excitement to stop the attacker; and if the man does not give in, this ape attacks for his part. Thus the reinterpretation of the event already becomes much more difficult.

A single observation so arranged can often characterize the ape better than many quantitative experiments in which he easily loses patience and, therefore, performs less well than under the freer conditions of the qualitative research. May I give an example. A chimpanzee is confined behind a grating of iron rods five meters long; perhaps a meter and a half in front of it, a nice piece of fruit is buried in the sand and then, over this place and within a radius of several meters, the ground is covered uniformly with sand, so that the spot is no longer distinguished in any way for human eyes; there are otherwise no conspicuous marks at the critical point. The ape, who has watched with the greatest attention, finds no stick in his room, with which he could at once reach out (as he frequently does on other occasions), and so he soon begins to occupy himself with play. During this time, not the least effect of the perceived events can be discovered, and besides, he constantly changes his position, as well as the orientation of his body in relation to the place outside. When, three-quarters of an hour later, a stick is thrown to him through the back bars of his cage, he takes it immediately, without any hesitation goes to the bars opposite the critical point, places the stick outside, begins to dig in the sand with an error of not even ten centimeters, and soon finds the right spot. It is obvious how the qualitative analysis of the behavior can be carried on with variation of the interval, of the animal's occupation during it, through change of the environment, etc. I found, for example, that the experiment (with other animals of the same species) succeeded immediately even after an interval of seventeen hours, thus with the interruption of a night's sleep.[4]

So long as neither human psychology nor animal psychology poses productive research questions for a field, we must depend on giving opportunities for the phenomena in question to appear over and over again until, one day, perhaps from purely qualitative observation, a first more far-reaching idea arises. This holds in particular for the area of feelings and their expression. The primitivity of the emotional dynamics of apes and the stormy intensity of the expression of affect in many nonhuman primates make it appear possible that in this way, rather than through human introspection, we will discover the simplest basic forces and directions of affectively determined behavior. And while it is always a ticklish as well as an uncertain undertaking, for experimental purposes, to create affect of any intensity in man, in many apes the same problem may be solved easily, often repeatedly, and with great precision. Chimpanzees, whom I know better than other species, in the course of time become downright disagreeable because of the wild intensity of their emotional outbursts, even at the slightest provocation, and the unreliability of their behavior, which corresponds to a very labile disposition. If we do no more than produce the various emotional processes frequently and, perhaps, finally succeed, after repeated descriptions, in deriving types and relations of types, much would be gained. Perhaps the primary dynamics of affect, as seen in apes and in nonintellectual people, follow much simpler laws than we usually assume. . . .[5]

Contemporary academic psychology has some tendency to regard emotions and affects as colorings or characteristics which become attached to the psychological event in accordance with its momentary content, as something external to it, while the laws

[4] Simple observation makes Hunter's method of testing "delayed reaction" unnecessary with the chimpanzee. (W. S. Hunter, The delayed reaction in animals and children. *Behavior Monographs,* 1913, Vol. 2.)

[5] [A paragraph on the recording of physiological changes in emotion has been omitted, since such procedures are now well known.—Ed.]

and thus the course of this event are always peculiar to it alone. I must warn that, from such a point of view, one can go astray in the observation of affective behavior of apes. If one proceeds directly from the description of emotional behavior, then affects and their directions appear, rather, as the driving forces, as the very center of the dynamics, which guide everything that happens in the animal. If, now, a particular kind of behavior (known from man) is "complex" in the sense that we are not able to see simple components in it, then the direction of thinking just mentioned makes us much readier to deny such behavior in the ape a priori. For we believe that we have to explain it in a very complicated way, and therefore we do not believe an animal capable of it, whereas the event might derive entirely from primary drive dynamics. Passing on punishment to others, taking out anger on innocent bystanders and on things, urgent attempts at reconciliation after a quarrel, giving food to an animal who begs, and especially primitive coquettishness in some female apes—are such processes to which we do not easily do justice because of theoretical prejudice. If the motivational dynamics occasionally look "deliberately purposive," no "intellectual" agency is needed to account for them; indeed, something like this is characteristic of a large number of organic processes, including even digestion.

INTELLIGENCE TESTS

. . . Lack of ambiguity in the experimental setup in the sense of an either-or has, to be sure, unfavorable as well as favorable consequences. The decisive explanations for the understanding of apes frequently arise from quite unforeseen kinds of behavior, for example, use of tools by the animals in ways very different from human beings. If we arrange all conditions in such a way that, so far as possible, the ape can only show the kinds of behavior in which we are interested in advance, or else nothing essential at all, then it will become less likely that the animal does the unexpected and thus teaches the observer something. Thus we must hope for nothing more than to be disturbed in our theoretical biases in this manner and to arrive at entirely new possibilities of theory. . . .[6]

In most of these experiments, effects of past experience are an essential precondition, since certain functionally important characteristics of objects in the situation are not first discovered in the experiment, but may be taken as given; but insofar as they cannot be found in immediate perception, they must necessarily be known to the animal from experience. Even the objective, say a banana, owes its drawing power only to experience, not to its primary visual properties. But by no means does it follow from this that a course of action appropriate to the structure of the experimental field now takes place merely according to the laws of memory. With continued observation of apes one may, rather, get the impression that simple reproductive tendencies in behavior, however helpful and practical they may often be, represent at the same time an ever present threat to higher forms of behavior, which would be governed more precisely by the actually given and varying conditions.

It is in principle impossible to perform the same test twice with the same ape with positive results since, with the repetition, there is a basis for reproduction of the form of the behavior which was lacking the first time. Now there exists a very general change of direction in the animals, so that modes of behavior discovered through high level, situation-determined actions are no longer produced in the same manner, but are more and more under the ever stronger influence of purely reproductive tendencies. The two are not mutually exclusive, and in the first repetitions the behavior of the ape still suggests consideration of all objectively essential conditions, although at the same time the faster appearance of the solution shows that reproductive forces are already effective. But at the end we see him "reacting with his solution" to the sight of the situation much too fast, on the whole, to be able to achieve the detailed survey necessary for action strictly governed by the situation. Since, now, according to the laws of

[6] [Much of this section has been omitted. The reader is referred to W. Köhler, *The Mentality of Apes*. Translated from the 2nd rev. German edition by Ella Winter. New York: Harcourt, Brace & World, 1925.—Ed.]

mechanical recall, even reproduction motifs which are only related to the original can have the same effects, the experimental
animal will always be in danger of mechanically producing the
accustomed behavior in a variation of the situation, thus of making foolish errors from habit in new experiments. In such simple
tests, each later experimental situation is in some way related
to earlier ones. Since our question concerns the degree of insight
possible at all, we will try to prevent this "secondary self-training"
from spoiling or preventing situationally determined behavior.
But it is not easy to avoid such deterioration of once new
performances, which appears most strongly precisely in the live-
liest individuals because of their impetuosity. For there is no possibility of influence such as that in the bringing up of children
where, at the appearance of such hasty reproduction, the words
"Think before you begin" may lead to a sensible survey of the
situation and to the inhibition of gross repetitive tendencies. If
the experimenter prevents the ape from making straight for the
goal by an external inhibition (intimidation, for example), the
animal will generally feel this only as a barrier to his drive ful-
fillment, and if it results in a delay, he will therefore scarcely
fill the time with closer surveying of the situation. Still, two
things can be done: The same animal is not used in too many
experiments or in too rapid succession; and, in particular, too
frequent repetitions in the same situation are avoided because
such a procedure directly favors the inferior secondary influence.
If we wish to use the solution of one problem as a reliable precondition for a further experiment, it will of course be necessary
to make that procedure familiar by several repetitions, but this
should not be carried farther than is absolutely necessary for the
particular purpose. The second remedy consists in a frequent
change of experimental place and of all those circumstances in
the test situations which do not need to remain the same for
objective reasons. The reproduction of familiar procedures is
induced not only if the test conditions proper are similar to conditions frequently used before; any other features of the surroundings in later experiments that look like those of earlier ones
have reproductive force in the direction of earlier behavior and

can hinder sensible new learning; for no boundary exists for pure association between objectively essential conditions and just any other circumstances. . . .

I HAVE already discussed qualitative observation and description. I shall now make a few remarks which apply to the special case of intelligence tests.

1. Observation and description should be sufficiently exact. If we hear only that "the ape has climbed on a box and from it has reached the objective," we know next to nothing of possible theoretical value about what happened. In such experiments, the meaning of a gross, external event always lies in the perceptually given whole properties of the behavior by which the ape moves from the entrance into the test situation to the objective reaching of the goal. For there can be no doubt that, in different cases, something very different can happen between that beginning and this end even if, for example, "the same tool," "the same detour" always play the decisive role in success. It depends precisely on the differences which remain despite this superficial sameness, and they exist not for theory alone, but also to a high degree for qualitative observation. The dispassionate and accurate seeing and describing of such properties, which characterize a process more exactly, require a much greater art than does the choice of favorable external and internal conditions for the experimental animal.

2. Perhaps the most important point of view for the description of the ape in the intelligence test is the *structuring of the event*. The course of each experiment from the beginning to the end exhibits neither a uniform, self-contained sequence, nor does the observed process divide naturally into an arbitrary number of elementary events of arbitrary length. Like a human action, that of the animal has its own most clearly recognizable *"phrasing."* And it is not so very astonishing that we are able to perceive it; for the changes at the periphery of the body and the total movements of the body are determined by the temporal structuring of the essential processes in the nervous system (of animal or

man), so that these external changes act, *in terms of the relations of their temporal sequence,* as a sort of translation or projection of the neural dynamics. If, now, an observer's visual perceptions are structured in accordance with that visible sequence, then such perceptual processes will, in turn, assume a temporal structuring similar to the one that existed in the neural dynamics of the individual observed.[7] An analogy from the acoustic realm: If a piano player, in accordance with his own feelings, structures the sequences of innervation of his musculature through phrasing of higher and lower intensity, then particular relations of temporal sequence, etc., arise for the resulting sequence of sound waves, which represent a sort of physical projection of that innervation phrasing and cause acoustic structuring in the (suitable) hearer in close correspondence with the neural structurings in the player. The ape in the experiment behaves as the player, the observer as the hearer; and if musical understanding presupposes that correspondence, the same is true, *mutatis mutandis,* for the understanding by the observer of what the ape does.

Thus we are saved from the danger of having to undertake the structuring of the behavior in the experiment from a purely subjective point of view. We can establish in observation where a unitary process exists, where a process of higher order includes another of lower order, where a gradual or an abrupt beginning or end of the "dynamic melody" takes place, whether or not several such motifs which follow one another have anything at all to do with each other. And these aspects of "coherence, incoherence, and degree of coherence" contribute directly to the appropriate evaluation of the events in the experiment. For if, for example, we see that the sequence of the animal's behavior consists of mutually independent single motifs one after another, of which the last leads to the reaching of the objective, then the ape has *not* achieved insight into the total process, but chance has allowed the independent dynamic motifs to combine in a suitable

---

[7] Besides, in this manner we could understand the significance of whole properties for observation in objective psychology, without immediately resorting to the inference doctrine. (Cf. above, pages 207ff.)

manner. On the other hand, a unitary process which is at the same time appropriate to the task will, in general, be recognizable as a "genuine" performance.

> If an animal performs several single actions one after another, which have no connection with each other, thus if the succession of motifs does not objectively constitute a *whole*, still the *single* activities need not simply be meaningless behavior. They can, for example, be "meaningfully intended" if they represent unrealizable attempts at solution (see below, par. 3).
>
> If the forces which motivate the ape in the experiment are weak and if, besides, the animal is constitutionally able to achieve longer dynamic processes of strong coherence only with difficulty, then the testing becomes much more difficult, because the animal abandons even good beginnings of solutions. At the slightest disturbances, the orangutan I observed breaks off, for a moment of play, activities which have clearly almost led to success, and which can only be seen as the greater part of a really planned total solution; and then, like someone to whom a forgotten intention comes back, he suddenly jumps up and carries out the solution—unless a new derailment intervenes. Such animals are unsuitable for the beginning of a research, because we can only understand what they are about with more experience.

The phrasing of the course of the experiment as purely temporal structuring is by no means the only perceptual characteristic of the process. We also observe whether a dynamic process is of increasing, decreasing, or uniform intensity, whether it is directed to this or that point, whether the basic character of the whole is restlessness, haste, calm, exhaustion, etc. This is not the place to go into all these aspects of the observed processes. In a good description, they should be reflected to such an extent that the resulting picture gains in sharpness and accuracy.

3. The behavior of the animals may not be considered and judged simply with regard to its objective feasibility. If an ape tries to reach the objective by a path which a man immediately recognizes as impassable, then it follows, to be sure, that the animal does not know, or has not understood, some factor in the

total situation; but apart from this one point, the behavior may possess all the characteristics of an insightful attempt at solution and, indeed, show them particularly clearly, because such a procedure is not to be traced back either to imitation or to trial and error in earlier experience. As an example of such (quite frequent) "good errors," I may mention that chimpanzees, prevented by a rock from opening a heavy door, try to raise it over the stone instead of rolling the stone aside.

The same holds for a sort of effort toward the objective which must necessarily remain unsuccessful, but which is carried on by the animal himself only as a "communication with the objective" if efforts actually to reach it have already failed repeatedly.[8] Such processes are seen particularly with young animals (as with small children); we may not regard them as meaningless responses.

4. If an evaluation in terms of practical feasibility is plausible, judgment according to similarity to man seems irresistible in the beginning. We are tempted to take as insightful what in some way looks particularly human and to regard as inferior that which strongly differs from human behavior under like circumstances. But the question, Insightful or not? is to be answered entirely independently of this other point of view. For example, we easily rate a performance good if an ape goes around with a human tool, perhaps a ladder. On account of a certain humanness "induced" only by the tool, the circumstance will be overlooked that the animal does not use this object exactly in the function for which it was made, but as some grossly similar natural object. On the other hand, insightful use of natural objects occurs which we scarcely ever see in man, and which we therefore tend to underestimate. The evaluation should be guided purely by the actual objective relation of situation and behavior of the animal.

5. Of particular value are observations of the following two kinds: In the course of many solutions, constant changes of the situation arise, and thus new subproblems which, to some degree,

[8] Cf. Köhler, op. cit., 87ff. and 125f.

depend on chance and are therefore unpredictable in form and sequence. For example, if an ape drags objects up to the bars of his cage with a stick, it generally happens that the ground, by its irregularities, etc., sets a series of such small special tasks, and since these will change with every variation of the experimental place or, indeed, with every chance change of the path, an activity established in a blind, mechanical way is entirely incapable of doing justice to these conditions. In the second place, if the genuine solution depends only on the essentials of the behavior, which ought to correspond to the objective relations of the parts of the situation as a dynamic whole motif, then its details may be carried out in many different ways without changing the meaning of the process. Nothing better characterizes the insightful performance than the animal's indifference to irrelevancies in its execution; nothing is more characteristic of ununderstood training than rigidity of a once learned procedure. This criterion is useful because a clear limit is placed on variations of behavior by the demands of the objective situation.

IF THE results of the first kind of intelligence test[9] are negative, we can give aids; by means of these we try to direct the animal's attention to particular parts of the constellation. It is no more than a strong help if we finally show the ape the procedure or allow it to be demonstrated by one of his more clever fellows. If the attempt succeeds, it is a matter of an intelligent performance when previously the test had never once showed signs of discovery and now, on the contrary, the solution corresponds to the essentials of the model. Besides, in the well-observed animal, it is generally easy to see how he takes the demonstration and whether it is this which enables him afterwards to achieve his own solution.

For methodological reasons also, we must learn to appreciate the great difficulties which, according to all experimental evidence, stand in the way of imitating solutions. The ape will

[9] [Tests in which the animal is given the opportunity to achieve intelligent solutions by himself, i.e., without help.—Ed.]

copy an action with understanding only after he has, at least once, experienced the behavioral sequence that takes place before him *in the correct emphasis and phrasing as a coherent path to the goal.* So long as this is not the case, he has not witnessed a visual movement complex which is meaningful as a whole. It can by no means be assumed as a matter of course that the animals experience the model in the same meaning as a human observer does; this can frequently be seen in the completely uncomprehending behavior of apes to whom a fellow has repeatedly demonstrated a simple performance in vain. The moment understanding comes, the behavior tends to change markedly: the animal then shows surprise and pushes into the place of his teacher on the next repetition of the experiment.[10]

[10] [The paper continues with a discussion of the experiment in the stricter sense.—Ed.]

11: *A new method for the*
psychological study of apes

THE superior performance of chimpanzees in many tests of intelligence contrasts with the way in which the same animals must be brought laboriously to a stable manner of choosing in so-called discrimination training. There seems almost to be a contradiction between the course of events in the two kinds of experiment. For lower vertebrates, which could not pass a single one of these tests of insight, nevertheless learn in approximately the same time as apes to solve tasks of the second type. One would expect, on the other hand, that the surprising degree of insight that chimpanzees display in tests of intelligence should, with suitable experimental procedure, also be a help to them in those investigations which have employed the method of mechanical training. But, by its very nature, this method hardly gives scope to the better intelligence of the ape, since it actually makes difficult the grasp-

Über eine neue Methode zur psychologischen Untersuchung von Menschenaffen. *Psychologische Forschung*, 1922, 1, 390–397. Reprinted by permission of Springer-Verlag and translated by Helmut E. Adler..

By permission of the Prussian Academy of Sciences, this report appears here [*Psychologische Forschung*—Ed.] rather than in its *Proceedings*.

ing of objective relationships. Thus it leaves the development of directed reactions, for example, to "darker" or to "larger," to blind habit and to "experience" (in Hume's sense). The apparent contradiction between the highly intelligent performances of apes and the slowness of their learning in discrimination experiments can thus be explained by the objective difference between the two types of task.

> In the *utilization* of this mechanical experience, differences are still possible. At some happy moment the principle of the sequence may, so to speak, come to the animal in a flash and govern further behavior. Apes, like children, may show this higher use of experience, so that even under these circumstances their superior talents are revealed.[1] But it is all the more absurd for the psychologist to leave it to the ape to speed up, by his comprehension, a procedure that in itself does not in the least encourage anything of the sort.

Is there no method that could be used with apes for questions which are now customarily investigated in discrimination experiments—a method that would allow their talents to play an essential role right from the start? The animals themselves lose interest so quickly in the usual mechanical type of experiment that their resistance is added to the clumsiness of the method as a greatly retarding factor. The experimenter's patience is greatly tried when he sees his animals become more and more careless. On the other hand, the introduction of a new method, which would replace the usual mechanical discrimination learning by choice based on some objective property, would constitute a kind of crucial experiment. If apes show insight in tests of intelli-

---

[1] Cf. W. Köhler, Nachweis einfacher Strukturfunktionen beim Schimpansen und beim Haushuhn, *Abhandlungen der Königlich Preussischen Akademie der Wissenschaften*, physikalisch-mathematische Klasse, 1918, (2), 48ff. In such experiments the animals even operate according to a "working hypothesis" that is primitive, but probably typical of apes: at the outset, they assume constancy of the relative position of the "correct" choice in the pair. (Cf. W. Köhler, Optische Untersuchungen am Schimpansen und am Haushuhn. *Abhandlungen der Königlich Preussischen Akademie der Wissenschaften*, physikalisch-mathematische Klasse, 1915, (3), 26f. Here it is shown that this behavior is not merely a matter of a motor set.)

gence, and if it is true that they do so poorly in discrimination training only because here they are given no real basis for specifically insightful behavior, then as soon as the method used provides a basis for objective choice, it must follow that they solve quickly and easily problems of the type previously presented in discrimination training. This is the theoretically important aspect of our question; it is at least as interesting as the prospect of a better and more flexible methodology.

By means of discrimination training, we investigate questions of perception in animals; we also study, if somewhat indirectly (after learning has been completed), their memory or still other functions. This always presupposes unambiguous and systematic responses to several (usually two) perceived objects— and this must first be accomplished. The new procedure must thus lead the animals to choose between the objects in a particular direction on an objective basis, because the nature of the given perceptions as such requires it. If this were accomplished, such choices could then be used widely for all kinds of "critical experiments," memory tests, etc., no less than the results of discrimination training, while the tedious complexities of the latter would be eliminated.

After several vain attempts to find a procedure of this kind, I finally succeeded with the method described below. It is so simple that it should have been obvious from the start. I was unable to test it in detail or to apply it practically to the study of new questions, since its success first became apparent immediately before the station at Tenerife was given up; and I have not had time since to return to this task. It is nevertheless worthwhile to make the beginnings known for the sake of future research with apes.[2]

The ape sits behind bars. Two choice objects, in the form of any containers which are perceptually sufficiently different from each other, are placed outside, in front of him. One of them is

[2] The method described below might be preferable to the somewhat different design that I presented in Abderhalden's *Handbuch der biologischen Arbeitsmethoden*, 1921 (Abt. VI, Teil D), 112ff. (Die Methoden der psychologischen Forschung an Affen).

slowly filled with fruit as he looks on, while at the same time he can see that the other one remains empty. Then both are closed, so that their interior is no longer visible. The animal naturally reaches for the filled container, so we can be sure that he has watched—but he is not permitted to pull it in. Now an opaque curtain is lowered in front of the containers. These are quickly set up side by side, at some distance, in such a way that the ape can see nothing of the experimenter's movements. The screen is raised again, and the ape can make his choice with a stick, as usual. We can only be sure that the choice is governed by the crucial perceptual quality of the containers if every other basis for choice is excluded. Most sources of error are to be eliminated in the same manner as in discrimination training; I need not go into it here. With this procedure special attention should, however, be given to spatial position. If the containers were filled before the animal's eyes in the same spatial relationship that they have later on, when the curtain is again removed, the ape could simply go by this cue. They must, therefore, not be in this spatial position on the "first presentation." But the opposite (left–right alternation from the first to the second presentation) is also not permissible. For if, on the second presentation, the containers always appear in the reversed position, then a very unfortunate source of error would be present—why should the ape not be guided by the spatial position? In time, on the contrary, the animal could simply become accustomed, on the second presentation, always to choose the spatial position which is opposite to that of the first presentation. Thus he would again choose "correctly," but in terms of an extrinsic criterion. It follows that the spatial position during the first presentation must have nothing at all to do with that of the second presentation. This may be achieved by showing the containers on the first presentation above or behind one another, while subsequently, for the choice, they stand next to each other (in random alternation of right and left).

The procedure will become clear with the description of a specific example. A larger and a smaller box of the same shape and color are placed in front of the bars, with the large one

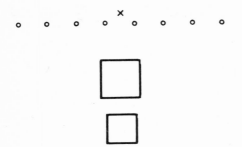

Figure 11.1   The animal sits at x.

nearer to the ape and the smaller one behind it (see Figure 11.1). The small one is filled with fruit before the eyes of the eagerly attentive animal, while the large one remains empty. The boxes are covered and, after lowering the curtain, the experimenter quickly places the small box to the right and the large one to the left, equidistant from the animal (see Figure 11.2), so that after only a few seconds the curtain can be removed again and the animal allowed to make a choice. If this choice turns out always or almost always to be correct on several trials, in which the spatial position is randomly changed on the first and second presentations (each in the appropriate spatial dimension), then the ape is deciding on the basis of the properties of the choice objects or their relational structure, since he is unable to recognize the "cor-

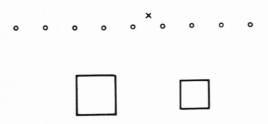

Figure 11.2   The animal sits at x.

rect" one by anything else. But the word "correct" now has a somewhat different meaning than in discrimination training. There, at least in the beginning, it only means "corresponding to an arrangement that cannot be meaningfully grasped, at most accessible through completely external experience and habit formation." Here it means "corresponding to a clearly grasped relationship of the events just observed."

The nature of this procedure allows us to check whether it really is this relationship that determines the choice between the two objects on the second presentation. For, in contrast to discrimination training, we are now in principle no longer dealing with a fixed effect of training, but with continuing insightful behavior of the ape, which could be equally effective with respect to a great variety of choice objects of the same kind. Thus, if the smaller box was filled in one trial, we can subsequently use the larger one in another trial with the same animal. If the experimental animal chooses in the same manner as in the first trial, he must now decide in favor of the larger container. Similarly, in further experiments, it must be possible to replace the boxes by quite different objects somehow distinguished from each other, as long as they can be given the shape of a container or can serve clearly to mark a container; and always, if the first presentation is effective, we would expect only choices in agreement with their attributes.

The first experiments using this procedure were made especially easy for the animals in this way: At first the two containers differed strongly in a number of respects. We used a basket and a wooden box of approximately the same size.

> "Box right" means that the box is the filled container and is located to the experimenter's right (the animal's left) on the second presentation (the choice trial). The rest of the descriptions are to be interpreted in the same way. The symbol + means "correct"; − means "incorrect choice."

SULTAN

5 / 6 / 1920		*Box right*	+
5 / 7	9 A.M.	*Basket right*	+
	5 P.M.	*Box left*	−

SULTAN (Continued)

5 / 8	9 A.M.	*Basket left*	+
	2 P.M.	*Box left*	—
	6 P.M.	*Box left*	+
5 / 9	9 A.M.	*Basket right*	—
	5 P.M.	*Basket left*	+
5 / 10		*Box right*	+
5 / 11	9 A.M.	*Basket left*	+
	5 P.M.	*Box right*	+
5 / 12	12 noon	*Basket right*	+
	6 P.M.	*Box left*	+

GRANDE

5 / 9 / 1920		*Basket left*	—
5 / 10		*Box left*	+
5 / 11	9 A.M.	*Basket left*	—
	5 P.M.	*Basket right*	+
5 / 12	12 noon	*Box right*	+
	6 P.M.	*Basket left*	+
5 / 13	10 A.M.	*Can right*	+
	5 P.M.	*Pot left*	+
5 / 14		*Can right*	+
5 / 15	9 A.M.	*Pot right*	+
	2 P.M.	*Small basket left*	+
		(Choice objects:	
		small vs. large	
		basket)	

The choices now seem completely reliable. The following day the box and basket were replaced by a tin can and an inverted flower pot.

SULTAN

5 / 13	10 A.M.	*Pot left*	+
	5 P.M.	*Can right*	+

Since Sultan makes these choices, too, with the greatest confidence, further trials used objects that differed much less. These were two covered baskets of exactly the same shape, but of different size.

SULTAN

5 / 14	10 A.M.	*Small basket left*	+
		Small basket right	+
		Small basket right	+
		Small basket left	+
5 / 15	9 A.M.	*Large basket left*	+
	2 P.M.	*Small basket right*	+

The theoretical question raised above (pp. 225–226) is thus decided in principle. The result is positive; therefore we can also proceed in practice in this manner and give up pure discrimination training with apes. Choice experiments with chimpanzees, even ones of only the present limited extent, never take such a course when they depend on chance rather than on objective properties; and I have never seen animals choose more quietly and more naturally than here, after a short time, when they had become accustomed to the general characteristics of the new procedure. The nature of the choice objects could be changed without difficulty. Specifically, the method does not break down even when, as in the final experiment with Sultan, the choice objects differed in only one respect (size).[3]

The fact that several errors are made among the first choices does not mean much, either from the practical or from the theoretical point of view. Perhaps this is an aftereffect of the many experiments with the pure training procedure to which the chimpanzees were previously subjected. They are used to relying on chance (because they do not have much else to go on), and therefore they do not at first get the idea simply of behaving in accordance with their perception on the first presentation. If this is the right explanation, we would expect objectively determined, correct choices from the beginning in chimpanzees who have not been spoiled by previous training, so long as they pay attention.

As the tables show, the individual choices are separated

---

[3] Sultan had earlier made choices according to size in training experiments (cf. W. Köhler, Optische Untersuchungen, *op. cit.*, 29). At that time, however, his choices were always of the larger object—not, as in the majority of cases here, the smaller one.

from each other by long intervals. Attempts to carry out the same procedure with a rapid sequence of individual choices, as in training experiments, failed and kept on failing if the animal was required to change the correct object in a constant pair of objects. It looks very much as if the aftereffects of the previous trial were too strong; the chimpanzee who had, for example, chosen the basket after having seen it filled, seemed unable to free himself from this observation on the next choice, and select the box, which is now the one he has seen filled. More precisely, it looks as if the rapid sequence of perceptions or their aftereffects merged for him, so to speak. Here, too, a chimpanzee who has not undergone prior training with a constant assignment of "correct" to the choice objects may possibly behave somewhat differently. In order to be certain to exclude the disturbing interference between the individual trials with the animals that were available to me, I made the intervals between any two choices very long, most likely longer than necessary. How near in time one can place the individual trials would still have to be determined in the interests of the method and of a more precise understanding of this process.

According to present experience, what can this procedure accomplish?

1. If we are interested in choices of only one particular kind (e.g., always according to size) and consistently in the same direction (e.g., always choice of the smaller object), then we can immediately substitute this method for the slow mechanical training technique; for under these conditions the interaction of the individual trials is not disturbing, but rather helpful. We may place the trials as close together as we wish; and often in a few minutes we will bring the ape to choice behavior as reliable as that achieved by the older method in a series of trials over a number of days. If this reliability is really achieved, one can later rely entirely on the aftereffect of earlier trials and simply eliminate the "first presentation." For example, Sultan, who one morning chose the small basket correctly four times in rapid succession (5 / 14), would have tended to make the same choice on a fifth trial immediately afterwards, even without the first

presentation; for it is, after all, just this kind of aftereffect which shows itself in errors when the prescribed direction of choice is changed in trials that follow each other immediately. Aside from the finding that the chimpanzee achieves what the method of objectively determined choices demands of him, the possibility of thus abbreviating the learning process to an extraordinary extent appeals to me particularly.

2. In the case just discussed, the objectively determined choice behavior presumably changes eventually to a more mechanical method. If, on the other hand, the experimenter can arrange to separate the individual trials sufficiently in time, they will remain independent of each other, and the animal continues to choose intelligently, in accordance with the first presentation. With an ape who achieves this, experiments can be carried on simultaneously with widely differing pairs of choice objects. In particular, we can let him choose, with pairs of the same kind, first in one direction, then in the other. It is not necessary to use different animals for each direction, as had to be done in the past, when (as often happens) the purpose of the experiment demands choices in both directions.

3. Two chimpanzees have demonstrated that they fulfill in principle the conditions for the procedure of objectively determined choice; they have thus passed a kind of intelligence test. The outcome of similar experiments in other species will also throw light on their degree of intelligence. We may expect, however, that most higher vertebrates are not up to such a task, since even for chimpanzees the procedure could only become useful after it had been reduced to this most simple form.

four

<hr/>

PSYCHOLOGY AND PHYSIOLOGY OF THE BRAIN

12: *The new psychology and physics*

ONLY a few psychologists are still convinced that the main subject matter of psychology is our direct experience. By direct experience I mean the content of our sensory perceptions, the properties of our mental images, the nuances of our feelings, and so on. Most of us realize that, regarded as events, the facts and sequences of our direct experience do not, taken by themselves, represent complete wholes; they are, on the contrary, merely parts of larger functional contexts. We recognize Mr. X on the street. Recognition involves a cooperation of the past with the present. Formerly this cooperation was interpreted as an interaction of a "memory image" of Mr. X with a fresh response of our senses. But where recognition occurs without difficulty, no "memory image" of Mr. X will take part in it. The past, therefore, cooperates with the present not by an experienced representation of past things but by something which remains outside our actual awareness. At the same time this "something" which makes it possible for us to recognize Mr. X must be a rather

From *The Yale Review*, 1930, 19, 560–576. Copyright 1930 Yale University Press. Reprinted by permission of the publisher.

accurate trace left in ourselves by past events, since, in general, it seems to operate fairly well in determining recognition. The same may be learned from perception. Our field of vision, for example, is not a mosaic of local colors indifferent to each other; it is not an indifferent continuum either. Usually it contains well-defined wholes or segregated units which we call things, and these things again appear frequently in definite groups. Whatever our theory of such facts may be, we must confess that very often things and groups are not made inside the field of our actual experience; in most cases, they enter this field ready-made. Something outside must be responsible for this organization. As an example, take the constellation of the Dipper as we see it. The constellation appears in our visual field as a definite whole. Yet this unitary effect is not produced by any experienced activity.

If, therefore, the psychologist is not satisfied with the mere description of experiences as the goal of his science, but wishes to investigate and understand the functional basis which under-lies them, their simultaneous structure and their sequence, his task cannot be confined to a study of direct experience as such. I cannot possibly learn to understand the principles of baseball if I look upon one-third of the field only and refuse to see the rest or even to speculate about influences exerted from the other two-thirds upon the corner I see. We may formulate it as a general rule that a system in which local events depend upon translocal dynamic interrelations can only be understood and handled scientifically as a whole.

What is the larger functional context, or whole, of which any actual human experience reveals only a restricted area? What kind of a trace in it makes possible, for example, one person's recognition of another or of a thing? What kinds of event produce the organization of this field of vision so that he sees, for instance, the Dipper as a segregated whole? I think I am in agreement with almost all American psychologists if I say that this and all our other direct experiences are based upon processes in our central nervous systems set up by outer stimulation of the sense organs, or by inner stimulation, and that these underlying processes represent only a fraction or province of a larger physiological context in our organism. In its explanations, therefore, psychology must be a branch of biology.

As yet, however, the physiologists have not told us very much about processes in the central nervous system and their dependence upon the functions of the whole human organism. Shall we wait for the help of physiology? Probably this is not advisable, since physiological investigation of brain action will hardly be possible in the near future, and in the meantime our mental experiences and special psychological experiments may give us valuable data. Still we must assume something definite about the nature of the "larger physiological context," if psychological research, together with our ideas about this context, is to lead to concrete conclusions. Only concrete conclusions can be examined, verified, or disproved by further psychological experiments.

By its very nature all theory in the sciences tends to become one unitary system of explanation. As soon as we admit an absolute gap among the explanations, with two principles, essentially different, dominant on either side, we get dissociation into two systems and a corresponding loss of scientific understanding. At the outset, therefore, any sound new theory will presuppose that principles valid in other realms of nature are applicable in its own field. And, by the way, this is also the only safe procedure by which we might hope to prove the existence of a plurality of fundamental principles and realms in nature with absolute gaps between them, if there be such gaps. If we do what we can in order to establish a unitary system of explanation, and if thereby we contradict the innermost structure of reality, nature in the end will not fail to give us the right answer.

For these reasons I regard it as a necessity of psychological method that we make the attempt to develop a theory of "the larger physiological context," upon which all our experiences depend, on the basis of the fundamental principles of physics. Vitalistic theories are mainly negative; they deny that certain goals of science can be reached and in so far do not invite us

240 Psychology and physiology of the brain

to examine definite consequences of vitalistic thinking. Only positive assumptions push us forward toward decisions.

For several reasons, perception seems to be the part of psychology in which a first attempt at a theory of underlying processes is most likely to succeed. Perception gives us experienced things and events distributed in a more or less orderly experienced space. From the standpoint of physics one feels at once inclined to conceive the processes underlying perception as a dynamic pattern that comes into existence in some field of the brain.

Neurology and pathology do not leave the slightest doubt that visual processes, for example, at least in man and the highest vertebrates, form such extended patterns not only on the retina but also in the occipital lobes, where they first reach the cortex of the brain. Furthermore, it has been shown that in this part of the cortex the most elementary spatial relations between local processes agree with corresponding spatial relations between objects seen in our visual field. Where visual things touch each other in our experience, as a rule the corresponding processes are immediate neighbors in the occipital lobes.

From this it does not follow, however, that the geometrical distribution of visual processes can be regarded as a real picture of our experienced visual field. If, from the center of a cube, I draw straight lines to all points of a plane surface upon which the cube rests, all relations of neighborhood existing between points of the plane will also exist between the corresponding points of the cube's surface where the straight lines cut it. Still this projection of the plane upon the cube will not be strictly similar to the things projected since, in general, equal distances on the plane will not be represented by equal distances on the cube's surface. But we have to realize anyhow that, in the case of brain functions, merely geometrical relations between local processes are of no importance for what we find in our visual field. I fixate the center of a circle which I find directly before me. Under these circumstances half of the processes corresponding to the experienced circle occur in one hemisphere of my brain, the second half in the other hemisphere; geometrically, the main fissure of the brain separates one half from the other. If merely geometrical relations between local processes were decisive for the distribution of visual experiences, there ought to be a gap or some other irregularity in the middle of the seen circle. Of course, we do not observe anything like that; the circle is one thing and symmetrical. It is easy to give more such arguments. But the most important is of a much more general nature. In all other respects, such as color and brightness, we conceive of our visual experiences as based upon properties of physiological processes. The spatial properties of the field are so intimately connected and interdependent with these other sides of our experience of it that, for consistency's sake, we cannot possibly attribute to experienced space a merely geometrical correlate in the brain. We must find a functional reality, some property of process underlying it.

During the last decades a new line of psychological work has developed which is called Gestalt psychology, or the psychology of functional wholes. One of the discoveries which we ascribe to it is nothing but the scientific acknowledgment of facts which, though they are open before us in common life, have never received a fair treatment in our systems of psychology. A melody has a "minor" or "major" character as a melody, that is, as an auditory whole. We may investigate the tones of the melody separately as much as we like; we find no "minor" or "major" character in them. But as soon as the same stimuli follow each other in appropriate sequence, our auditory experience contains the new character which evidently belongs to the melody as a unit extended in time. The same happens in space. "Regularity," "smoothness," "angularity," "slenderness," and so forth are characteristics exhibited by curves or figures in the visual field. These terms lose their meaning as soon as we try to apply them to any effects of local stimulation. In experienced space they belong to extended units. Consequently we must find translocal, extended functional realities, if a theory of brain processes is ever to explain the properties of our visual field.

About the year 1911 my friends Wertheimer and Koffka

and I became rather unpopular among the physicists of Germany because we asked them to give us an account of physical processes which might correspond to what we were looking for. Nobody could give us a satisfactory answer. A molecule, it is true, has some properties which are not found among its atoms. But evidently larger wholes, such as those given us in our visual perception, for example, could not be explained by any speculations about the tiny molecule.

We had therefore to trust to our own devices. After six or seven years of work, we have had some success in that we have found a simple and adequate parallel for visual figures in a state of rest in those extended self-distributions which are characteristic of dynamic equilibria. As a familiar example, take the stationary distribution of water current in a network of pipes. By mutual influence throughout the system, the extended process maintains itself *as a whole*. No local event in it exists *independently*. Anyone who grasps this essential fact in this example will realize that the same principle applies in all possible equilibria extended in space. Although we have not yet arrived at a concrete theory of brain processes underlying wholes and figures in our visual field, we have made the first decisive step toward such a theory. We know that everywhere in physics there occur extended functional units just as we conceive them. Our task is now to find the special dynamic equilibria which become possible and real under conditions prevailing in the brain of the higher mammals.

Undoubtedly this approach to our problems, which has become characteristic of Gestalt psychology, means a radical change in scientific point of view far beyond the boundaries of psychology. For generations physiologists and neurologists have tried to explain the order of processes in the nervous system by something like a machine theory. An orderly distribution of processes may be the consequence of either of two principles. I may suppose that elementary processes are conducted from the outer sense organs stimulated, through well-arranged and insulated fibers, to those places in the nervous system where they belong from the standpoint of order and adequate function of the organism. In such a view it is the preestablished anatomical pattern, exclusive of the interaction of events in it, which is considered responsible for the distribution; thus we may call this view a machine theory. I may, however, make another and certainly much bolder assumption which, by the way, is the only one left, if the first one should fail. This assumption, instead of *excluding mutual influence between local events* in the human organism, lays *the main stress upon such dynamic influence* because it is precisely this influence which, according to this second principle, is to lead to a definite distribution of the whole process. When this radical change in point of view was first proposed, biologists were inclined to look down upon it as a vague product of dilettantism. At present, on the other hand, there is a tendency on the part of biologists to deny that they ever took the machine theory seriously. The self-development of functional wholes in the operations of the nervous system is beginning to be a popular idea.

The essential difference between the two assumptions I have just mentioned may be summed up as follows: Whereas the machine theory of the working of the nervous system makes local processes in it indifferent to each other, from the dynamic point of view, with its admission of, and emphasis on, interaction, the outcome of a self-distribution will depend upon the actual properties of local events in the working of the nervous system. This is the case in all examples of physical self-distribution; the ways of interaction are always determined by the properties of interacting substances or processes in their relation to each other.

It is obvious that this second assumption, introducing into our conception of the action of the nervous system *the idea of dynamic interaction,* enlarges our view of possible forms of process in the brain in a manner altogether undreamed of by advocates of the machine theory. In this mechanical theory of sensory function, the possibilities of machine explanations are restricted to the number of those patterns which we would find by enumerating all possible patterns of peripheral local stimuli. On the assumption of interaction, however, a great many specific states and processes are to be admitted which are utterly foreign to the other alternative, since their manner of existence is essentially a matter of areas instead of points and, furthermore, since their properties depend upon constellations of stimuli instead of upon single stimuli taken separately. This brief description of the action of the nervous system, as Gestalt psychology conceives it, will give the reader an idea of what I mean by "sensory dynamics."

A first application of this new principle leads us back to our problem regarding the physiological facts underlying visual space as we experience it. The merely geometrical relations between local and independent processes in the brain could not be regarded as such a correlate of this experience. Is there more hope for a solution of this problem after it has become clear that there are no such *independent local events* in the brain? Indeed there is. Terms which generally are used in a merely geometrical meaning have another and more important connotation besides. Consider the term "between." If I say that, physically, there is a fence between your house and mine, my statement expresses a purely geometrical relation of three physical objects. In this statement the existence and the properties of the houses and the fence are mutually independent. Contrast with this a different case. In a network of pipes, water circulates under the influence of differential pressure existing at two open ends. The stationary distribution of current in this pipe system is an instance of a functional unit in which events at each point depend upon the actual events at all other points. But from the standpoint of physics, the influence exerted by one local event upon another, and vice versa, cannot jump through space. There is no direct influence of one point upon a distant point hydrodynamically. If I change conditions in this pipe system at one point, and thus the actual events at the same point, immediate alteration of the surroundings will be restricted to the *immediate neighborhood* of the changed point. Only after these surroundings have been altered, will their change exert an influence again upon their own immediate neighbors, and so on. It does not matter with what speed the change in the system is traveling from one point to other distant points; these distant points are only influenced after other points nearer the first have been influenced. Consequently, here the word "between," referring to different points of the pipe system, takes on a second meaning in addition to the geometrical, which was the sole meaning it had in the example given above of the fence. In cases of dynamic self-distribution, as with the water in the network of pipes, a local process of the functional context is "functionally between" two other processes whenever mutual influence of these two is mediated by an alteration of the third. In homogeneous systems the two meanings of the term will coincide for a superficial consideration, those events being functionally between two others which also are between them geometrically. This, however, is not necessarily so. I tell Mr. A a story which is meant for Mr. F, whom for some reason I cannot address directly. Mr. A is in the same situation and hands the story down to Mr. B, Mr. B talks with C, C with D, D with E and, at last, E with F. Thus A, B, C, D, and E are "functionally between" me and F in this case of an influence. At the same time F may be nearer to me geometrically than D; for example, he may even be "geometrically between" me and D. Still, functionally, the opposite is true.

The result of our consideration is, briefly, that merely *geometrical* relations between local events in the brain have no importance whatever for the structure of experienced space. This structure depends altogether upon *functional* relationships, as defined in the case of the term "between." Therefore, also, the main fissure between the two hemispheres of the brain does not disturb the homogeneity of the observer's field, if we suppose that the functional immediacy between the last cell of one hemisphere and the first of the other is the same as is the functional neighborhood between the first and a second cell in one hemisphere. We have not only found a functionally real basis of experienced space, we have, in the same way, eliminated the influence of geometrical inhomogeneity in the brain. Certainly, the processes in our brain do not represent a geometrical picture of spatial visual experience. But it is perfectly legitimate to assume that, measured in the only interesting "functional coordinates," their extended context is a true picture of the spatial structure of our visual field.

But in considering, as we have been doing, merely the processes of our visual experience, we have omitted all the rest of the lively play in our central nervous systems. We have sensory experiences besides those of vision. What is the relation of sounds and smells and objects perceived by touch and handling to the structure of the visual field? For naïve description, perhaps the most valuable tool of psychology, one thing is clear at once. All these other experiences, whatever their origin and peripheral genesis, appear in the same space in which the visual things and events occur. A sound is localized between two seen things in the same sense in which a third visual thing may appear between them. I touch a cool iron and its coolness and hardness is evidently to the right of the book I see before me; that is, it is localized in the same spatial system in which seen things have their places. From the standpoint of our theory there is no escape from one fundamental conclusion: The processes underlying these other experiences must belong to the same extended physiological context as the visual processes, which excel the others by their average clearness and accuracy of structure. It seems to me a possible assumption that all these sensory processes, wherever they start on the periphery of our organism, are finally conducted to one common final field inside the brain, the distribution in which determines the spatial properties of all sensory experience. Once more, however, I insist upon the principle that, here again, it is not a merely geometrical relation between local processes which determines their relative localization, but such functional relations as immediacy and neighborhood, which even in the case of mere vision we had to regard as essential. It is perhaps not altogether necessary that all sensory processes should finally reach one common field of the brain. For our present purposes we shall, however, suppose that there is such a common terminal.

To this common terminal we can now give its natural center. If I say that the desk is before me, the "me" of this statement is quite as different from my physical organism as the experienced desk is different from the physical desk. Much of what I call "myself" in common life is an organized complex of sensory experiences. I see my hands, my feet, my legs, and I experience myself by touch in a way quite similar in principle to the manner in which the experienced desk is built up on the basis of sensory processes. The organism as a physical object is not directly experienced at all. What, then, of the mutual localization of the "self" as an experience and of "things" as other experiences? Obviously, the "self" is experienced in one place, and "things" are experienced in others around it. It is one experienced space in which we find both. It follows that, in the brain field, there must exist the same relation between processes of "things" and the complex of processes corresponding to the "self" as exists between the processes of two things appearing outside each other. Again the term "relation" is to be taken in its functional meaning, as explained above.

By this extension of our field picture, which now contains the self and its surroundings as actors in one functional physiological state, we are immediately led to important consequences. Much is said in our textbooks about attention, striving, and fearing. We do not treat such states or attitudes wholly adequately if we discuss them outside the context in which they occur. There is no such experience as attention taken separately, apart from any objective; rather a person feels directed towards something, in the manner which is called attention. As soon as we realize this concrete nature of most attitudes, it becomes possible and even necessary to unite our functional ideas about them with the scheme of a field structure corresponding to the spatial structure of our experiences. Attitudes issuing from the self and directed toward definite parts of the environment will thus be regarded as based upon directed states of the field. These directed states must exist between the processes underlying the self and the processes corresponding to those definite things toward which the self is directed. Whether we experience such directed attitudes or not and whatever their direction and their qualitative nuances are, depend upon the actual properties of the self and the actual properties of our environment.

Physiologically, then, the corresponding states of the brain field depend upon the actual nature of the complex of self-processes and the actual properties of the environmental processes, or more correctly, upon the actual relation between the first and the second. Once more we find the content and the tendencies of experience determined not mainly by an anatomical machinery through which an indifferent "nervous activity" is conducted, but by the immediate dynamic consequences of some definite processes being in functional contact with other definite processes. Such is the case in physical dynamics. The same idea was introduced above as an explanation of sensory organization. Here this simple principle is made the basis for our understanding of the interaction between the self and its environment.

It hardly needs to be mentioned that, on this basis and in line with our general experience, the self-processes are not restricted to those sensory events which make us see parts of ourselves or feel how our experienced body moves or rests. Hunger and fatigue, restlessness and calmness, and other such states are localized inside the same self. Stimuli from inner sense organs or more direct influences exerted by changes in the actual properties of the blood may determine the variation of the self-processes which underlie these experiences, "subjective" par excellence. It is the inner situation of the physical organism which seems to be represented by such experiences, just as seen things correspond to physical objects outside the organism. But in the common brain field a much more intimate contact and far richer dynamics become possible between the self-processes and the environmental processes than we find between the physical organism and physical objects outside it. No outer physical force drives the physical organism toward food when food is needed. But in the brain field there is a directed stress when the self-process is altered in the way we experience as hunger and when, among the environmental processes, there is one complex which we experience as food. The stress, of course, exists in that region of the field which is functionally between the self-process and the food process. Its tendency is to decrease the functional distance between the two.

Any description of the brain field as a quiet or static pattern would be misleading. Distributions of processes which are dynamic contain energy in the physical meaning of the term. If possible they will transform themselves in definite ways depending upon their store of energy. In the field as we have conceived it, there are three main possibilities of development. Directed stress between the self and the environment can alter the processes corresponding to the latter. All psychologists know that, to some degree, an appropriate attitude will alter the organization of sensory processes. In other cases, the self will undergo a remarkable change as a result of a change in surrounding sensory processes, as when the mist dissolves on a gray morning and, with the new radiance of the environment, an active, cheerful feeling pervades the self.

The most important dynamic effects of stresses in the field are, however, produced by a physiological detour. Innervation of muscles during our movements undoubtedly depends upon the actual dynamic context in the brain field. Though the operation of the muscles involves energies far superior to the energies of nerve currents located in the muscles themselves, the muscles work under some influence which, from without, alters conditions for the processes constantly occurring in their interior. Small amounts of energy are needed to produce such a change of conditions or, as it is technically called, for "steering." Therefore, the most probable hypothesis is this: A stress in the brain field, between the self and, for example, food cannot directly bring the two together. But among all operations of the muscles possible at the time, certain constellations result in a locomotion of the physical organism toward the physical food outside. This will at once alter the situation in the brain field because, for obvious reasons, the outer approach brings about a corresponding inner approach of self-process and food process in the brain. So we assume that muscular activity is steered by innervations in such a way that the stresses existing in the brain between the self and its environment are released by the effect of outer action. The energy of lost stress is spent in steering.

While we are still occupied with extending our functional

scheme of brain physiology to the problems of learning and think-ing, the same ideas are gathering much strength from quite an-other side. Until recently physicists have not laid so much stress upon functional wholes, or Gestalten, as we have done in our attempt to bring psychological experiences into intimate relation with the physiology of the brain. But twenty years ago there was an intimation of a new point of view in physics. It came in a statement by Planck, the author of the quantum theory, who said in a lecture at Columbia University that, in all applications of the principle of entropy, we have before us functional wholes, the conduct of which cannot be deduced from the conduct of the molecules. And he added, casually, that the same theoretical situ-ation prevails almost everywhere in mental life. Ten years after-wards I tried to prove the same for those physical systems whose behavior, apart from entropy, is essentially determined by so-called dynamic laws. As physicists were then too much oc-cupied with the development of models of the atom, they did not take account of these investigations. During the last four years, however, we have been witnesses to a surprising revolu-tion among the physicists in their manner of thinking. In view of this sudden development, I would criticize my own attempt at Gestalt physics as having been too timid rather than too bold. A few months ago, in a powerful paper, Schrödinger stated quite definitely that problems of modern dynamics are problems of Gestalt dynamics, that is, dynamics of functional wholes. Again, in 1929 Planck declared that "in modern mechanics merely local relations are not sufficient for a formulation of the laws of motion; we do not obtain an adequate formulation of the laws until we regard the physical system as a whole." It has been shown that the quantum theory must be applied not to the single atoms of a crystal but to the crystal as a whole. In his recent book *The Nature of the Physical World* Eddington opposes a modern view to an older one. "There is," he writes, "one idea of survey which would look into each minute compartment of space in turn to see what it may contain and so make what it would regard as a complete inventory of the world. But this misses any world-features which are not located in minute compartments."

So we now have before us a "scientific reaction . . . in which the center of interest is shifted from the entities reached by the customary analysis . . . to qualities possessed by the system as a whole, which cannot be split up and located—a little bit here, and a little bit there." Strangely enough, Eddington asserts, physics has found it necessary to follow this second way. On the basis of these statements, then, we may say that the leading ideas of modern physics and of Gestalt psychology tend to coincide.

Physicists are gradually becoming aware of the psychological implications of their own work. Bohr, the great Danish physicist, has begun to handle psychological questions occasionally, and Eddington is astonishingly courageous in similar attempts to find the right connection between the physical properties of nervous processes and direct experience. It would be a pity if psychologists should lose the unusual opportunity offered to them to help in one of the most promising developments of modern science. We have now for the first time become able to handle certain essential problems concretely which, for centuries, have been discussed in a rather abstract way by metaphysicians. The physicists are working close to us. In the near future, I think, psychological investigation and theory will somewhere break through the thin wall which still separates the researches of physics from those of psychology. When this occurs, the whole scientific picture of the world will undoubtedly appear in a new light. Seldom has there been a more exciting moment in the history of science.

13: Psychology and natural science

MY subject concerns psychology and brain physiology. Now there are psychologists, especially in Europe, who easily become anxious when someone starts to talk about natural science, and particularly about the brain. I cannot quite understand this. By now psychologists ought to have more confidence in the findings of their own discipline. No finding and no theory of physiology could change any well observed psychological fact in the least. In many cases our methods are at least as good as those of neurophysiology, and we therefore have no reason whatsoever to be alarmed simply because there are brains and brain physiologists.

What I will now say goes a little farther. Not only is psychology now old enough to stand on her own feet; she is even, in my opinion, sufficiently grown up so that she can occasionally be of assistance to her older sisters, the natural sciences. In what

Psychologie und Naturwissenschaft. *Proceedings of the 15th International Congress of Psychology, Brussels, 1957*, 37–50. Reprinted by permission of the North-Holland Publishing Company and translated by Mary Henle.

follows there will be a good deal of discussion of physiology. But nowhere in my paper will rules be given which this natural science would impose on psychology. On the contrary, I will be concerned with tasks which psychological facts set for physiology. Fortunately, it will finally turn out that physiology is entirely in a position to meet these demands—even if she might not always like to do so.

First, however, I must mention certain basic ideas of natural science. In nature there are systems whose parts can freely follow the play of forces between them. Sometimes, however, this is not the case; then the dynamics of a system are subject to fixed conditions, so that only certain events are permitted and others become impossible. Such given conditions, which the dynamics are unable to change, are called "constraints" by English and American physicists, "Zwangsbedingungen" by Germans. How far this limitation of otherwise possible kinds of process goes varies from system to system. We human beings have a tendency to construct systems in which the influence of constraints is as great as possible in order to achieve practical ends, systems whose dynamics must thus follow entirely or almost entirely prescribed paths. In the terminology of the physicist, such systems have only one, or at most a few degrees of freedom. The systems themselves we call machines. Machines thus represent a very special kind of system and, of course, systems which are not machines in the above sense follow the same natural laws as machines do.

The powerful process which we call evolution has certainly been able to change no natural law; but it has equipped all higher organisms with anatomical constraints through which definite directions are prescribed for the operation of these dynamic laws —as in machines. Thus the blood flows in tubular structures, the blood vessels, to prescribed places; thus action currents follow paths or fibers which consistently make just the right connections. Nowhere does the machine principle seem to be more consistently carried through than in the nervous system. For if, for example, from each point of a sense organ an isolated fiber leads to the next neuron, if from here a next isolated fiber continues, etc., up to the brain, then an order will apparently be produced by means of a thoroughgoing splitting up of a total event into local single processes, an order in which everywhere only that can happen which the local histological conditions permit. I say "apparently." For all that I am going to say suggests that the above description cannot really be entirely correct. By no means does this sketch of nervous events agree with *psychological* findings. Almost sixty years ago it was attacked by the physiologist von Kries and, indeed, precisely because it does not do justice to psychological facts. Von Kries found what he called the "conduction doctrine" (*Leitungslehre*) in contradiction with characteristics of memory, especially with those of recall. But today we know so much more about perceptual processes that I prefer to take my arguments from this area. And the psychology of perception is practically a collection of evidence for the statement that the conduction doctrine or machine theory requires correction. For strong interactions take place continuously across perceptual fields. How would this be possible if local processes everywhere took their course in isolation from one another? A few brief examples. They are known to everyone with some knowledge of research in perception. Brightness and color contrast are interactions. The same is true, as Wallach has shown, of some of the well-known perceptual constancies. Likewise retinal disparity gives depth only because interactions between not quite corresponding images in the two eyes turn visual objects in space, displace them forward or backward. Even the simple segregation of visual objects from their surroundings depends upon interaction; for it happens only if certain relations exist between these regions of the visual field and their environment. We all know that suitable alteration of these relations can make a visual object simply disappear, even if objectively it is right there before us. Why do such facts play hardly any role in neurophysiological thinking? I am afraid because physiology does not quite regard them as "real." We find "real" facts, it seems, only if we concern ourselves with the nervous system as such, with the help of electrodes, amplifiers, etc. I cannot agree with this point of view. It is true that many fundamental questions of physiology can be answered only in this manner. But on other neurophysiological questions, good subjects who judge one way or the other in perceptual experiments give much more accurate information than even the best apparatus of the neurophysiologist. How is it that the interactions with which the perception psychologist deals are not quite real? I know one which is so real that veritable palaces are built to produce it. If two visual objects are shown at suitable temporal and spatial intervals, the second appears displaced from its normal position, much too near to the first, and then moves to its normal place. If still more favorable conditions are chosen, the first object too is immediately set in motion toward the second. Finally, under optimal conditions, the two movements fuse, so that in the perceptual field only *one* visual object carries the whole movement. What is it that is not "real" in stroboscopic movement? This is the condition for making films, and a very robust interaction in the nervous system has thus made possible an entirely new art form. For Michotte, however, even stroboscopic movement was not good enough. He has constructed sequences and has investigated in detail those that produce compellingly the impression of causality in perception. Thus he has opened up a completely new region of psychology.

I return to physiology. There are, in principle, two possibilities of interaction in the nervous system. In the first place, at particular places, connecting neurons can run from one neuron to others. If the activity of the first neuron gives rise to action currents in this transverse path, which are propagated to the second, this can have consequences which may be called a kind of interaction. Hartline has just shown that brightness contrast comes about in the limulus in this way, and there is no reason to doubt that still other transverse influences occur in this manner. But many interactions by no means permit this interpretation. For example, how can the segregation of visual objects as circumscribed units be brought about by action currents in connecting neurons? And figural aftereffects, which I will discuss presently? Thus we must also consider a second possibility of transverse interaction. It is that events which take place in histological elements do not actually remain confined to these, but spread freely in the tissue, far beyond them. For example, Lorente de Nó has been able to measure the "field" of action currents even at considerable distance from the active fiber. Again, the arrival in the brain of afferent impulses is announced by so-called evoked potentials, short-lived but strong electropositive waves. Monnier has now shown—and we can confirm his observation—that the same waves can also be recorded from the surface of the intact head. This process thus spreads even through the dense cerebral membrane, the dura, then through the skull, and finally through the scalp. The same is also true, of course, of the famous Berger rhythm, the alpha waves of cortical cells. Everywhere these waves are recorded for diagnostic purposes simply by placing the electrodes on the scalp. Each curve obtained in this way clearly demonstrates that the field of the alpha rhythm spreads completely without special conductors, even through considerable resistance. I cannot leave this subject without calling attention to Bremer's excellent experiments. Under the influence of strychnine, the motor neurons in the spinal cord of the curarized cat get into a state of rhythmic excitation. The frequency of the waves varies from about ten to thirty per second. What is remarkable, however, is that, from one end of the spinal cord to the other, the electrical waves are exactly in phase, i.e., synchronized. This can naturally be explained only by a mutual influence of the greatest speed, a speed never achieved by the propagation of excitation in fibers and through synapses. Bremer himself speaks, therefore, of an electrical interaction of the active cells. That this is really what happens he then demonstrated convincingly in a separate experiment. He completely severed the spinal cord in one place, so that between its two parts no histological connection existed, but only physical contact. When he then picked up the rhythm simultaneously from two places on either side of the cut, the synchronization of the waves on the two sides was not in the least disturbed. Since Gerard and Libet have also demonstrated similar phenomena in the frog's brain, there is no longer any doubt: active elements of the nervous system are surrounded by electrical fields or currents which spread in the tissue as a continuous conductor and in this manner make interactions possible over certain distances.

This conclusion will scarcely be misunderstood. For action currents in single fibers it is, of course, true—now as before—that their propagation is normally determined completely by these fibers. It is true that each such wave has its field which can be demonstrated outside of the fiber in question. But if this field also exerts a certain influence on neighboring fibers, yet in general it is not able to produce action currents in them. To this extent, then, the machine concept, according to which the distribution of processes in the nervous system is determined by prescribed paths, still remains applicable to the fibers and the waves propagated in them.

But fibers are not the only parts of the nervous system; they are only offshoots of cells. We must therefore ask ourselves what kinds of process take place in the cell body and its dendrites, i.e., at synapses. Once again, psychological observations first led us to raise this question. Our observations referred to so-called figural aftereffects, a name, I believe, that MacLeod first suggested. In 1933 Gibson discovered that prolonged presentation of certain visual forms leads to gradual transformation of these forms themselves and afterwards to striking distortion of other forms in the same region. Gibson at first believed that this phenomenon was limited to the transformation of forms of a particular kind. But then it turned out that this is really a much more general phenomenon. Gibson already demonstrated its appearance also in a case of kinesthetic perception. Later it was shown that not only most units in visual space, but also very different impressions in other sense modalities, give rise to such aftereffects. Only bounded shapes produce the phenomenon; prolonged presentation of a homogeneous visual field has no comparable consequences, even if this field is very bright. But a segregated visual object brings about the phenomenon not only when it is lighter than its surroundings, but also when black stands out against a lighter environment. Figural aftereffects are localized; they can only be demonstrated within or near the region where there was previously the prolonged perception. It is astonishing that, with a suitable procedure, they may often be demonstrated after hours, indeed after weeks and even months. We may assume that some relation exists between them and the very important phenomena that Ivo Kohler has recently investigated—even if this relation has not yet become quite clear.

How do figural aftereffects come about? According to the investigations which Wallach and I conducted, prolonged occurrence of excitation in a given part of the field produces an *obstruction* in this area. For afterwards, test objects which are presented move from the affected place; they appear displaced from it. This change probably takes place in the corresponding brain field, and indeed the process underlying a circumscribed percept may influence the cortical tissue simply by taking place. But what kind of process is it? Efforts have been made to derive figural aftereffects from influences which the afferent action currents exert in the brain. This hypothesis can hardly be correct because black objects on light ground have the same aftereffects as white objects on dark ground. Besides, several psychologists have shown that such an interpretation will not do justice to other characteristics of figural aftereffects. We soon found ourselves led to the hypothesis that in the region of a visual object, for example, a particular brain process takes place which has considerable intensity only here and in the immediate neighborhood, and that with prolonged existence, this process reduces the conductivity of the tissue. This conception immediately reminds us of facts which have been known to neurophysiology for more than a hundred years. Electric currents which are conducted through parts of the nervous system immediately change the condition of the cell surfaces which they cross. The kind of change depends on the direction of the current. After some time, however, the effect which appears where the current *enters* the cells predominates. This effect consists in a raising of the resistance (better expressed: the impedance) of the cell surfaces affected. Thus the current weakens itself and is at the same time forced to alter its spatial distribution. Essentially, this deviation consists in its receding from the self-generated obstruction.

If, now, the current is interrupted, this obstruction remains for a considerable time. Now, therefore, test currents which are conducted to the same or to a neighboring place must likewise take on a different distribution corresponding to the obstruction, as if they were repelled from the place of the earlier current. Physiologists call this effect of currents on the tissue they flow through anelectrotonus or sometimes, for the sake of brevity, simply electrotonus. Currents which do not issue from outside sources, but which originate in the tissue itself, have, of course, the same effect: they also raise the resistance of their substratum and leave this change behind as a sort of trace which persists when they themselves disappear.

It would be remarkable if there were no relation between these processes and figural aftereffects. Wallach and I therefore hypothesized that segregated visual structures are accompanied by currents, that these currents have electrotonic effects and aftereffects, and that consequently not only the currents of test objects, but also these objects themselves, are distorted or displaced. Further consideration showed that the effects derivable from this conception correspond well with the figural aftereffects actually observed. Our explanation has been considered very bold; but in reality it seems most natural to experts. Once when a well-known neurophysiologist visited us, I showed him particularly clear examples of figural aftereffects in the visual field. I did not mention the theory I have just outlined, and at that time no one but Wallach and I knew of it. After the physiologist had confirmed our findings, he turned to me and said with a smile: "Nice demonstrations of electrotonus, aren't they, Mr. Köhler?" As a physiologist he immediately recognized the striking correspondence of his observations with electrotonic effects.

At first we did not know in what way the postulated currents could take place. But we soon saw that they must originate in places in the brain where fibers of a lower level arrive at the cell bodies and dendrites of the next neurons, i.e., at synapses. It seemed to us that only in such a stratum could the afferent action currents produce the necessary electromotive forces. If they do this in a limited region of the stratum, however, then a current must immediately arise which flows all through this region and returns outside to the other side of its source.

Above all, it had now to be demonstrated that currents really arise when parts of perceptual fields are stimulated. This has finally been accomplished. But without the great perseverance and the exceptional skill of my collaborators, Held and O'Connell, I could certainly not have done it.

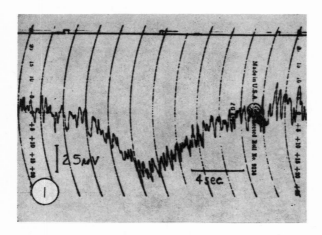

Figure 13.1   Current from human visual cortex in response to bright object moving across the visual field (Köhler and O'Connell, Journal of Cellular and Comparative Physiology, *1957, 49, Supplement 2, p. 5).*

It will not be necessary to describe technical details, such as the nature of our electrodes, our amplifier, and our recording apparatus. I will only mention that we usually placed the active electrode over the cortical representation of the fovea, thus slightly above the occipital protuberance of the head, the second (grounded) electrode on a presumably neutral point on top of the head. Almost all the records which are reproduced below date from recent years.

When this first curve (Figure 13.1) was obtained, a bright vertical strip of paper moved slowly and uniformly through the visual field before a dark ground. The subject fixated a small mark in the middle of the path of movement. The room was fairly brightly illuminated. As a rule we presented a moving object because we assume that the current of a stationary object would quickly be weakened by its electrotonic effect. The time line above the curve shows three marks, of which the first indicates when the object first became visible in the periphery; the second, when it passed the fixation point; and the third, when it disappeared again on the other side. The presentation lasted about sixteen seconds in all. Almost immediately after the appearance of the object, the curve drops, and this deflection grows until the object has reached the fixation point, whereupon it decreases again. This deflection indicates a current which is clearly produced by the slowly moving object. For the form of the curve corresponds exactly to the anatomical relations of the movement of the object and the position of the active electrode over the cortical fovea. As long as the object is seen far in the periphery, its cortical representation moves in parts of the visual cortex which are far from the electrode. Movement of the object toward the fixation point then brings its cortical representation nearer and nearer to the electrode; but beyond the fixation point, the distance from the electrode naturally increases again. Thus the recorded current must first become gradually stronger and then weaker—which is what the curve actually shows. The more rapid oscillations superimposed on these events are obviously alpha waves, which the optical stimulation has disturbed but not completely suppressed.

That the greater deflection has a downward direction means, under our conditions, that the appearance of the bright object raises the potential at the active electrode. All our records of visual currents from human heads shows this polarity. This could mean that the surface of the active regions of the visual cortex is really the positive pole of such a source of current. But we are by no means convinced that this is the case. For none of the currents we have recorded except the visual ones in man show this polarity, not even the visual ones which we have taken from exposed brains of monkeys. If the electrodes are placed

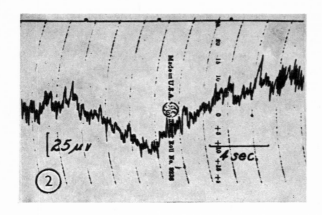

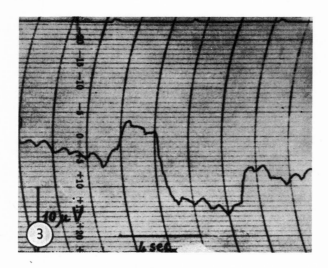

Additional records of human visual currents

Figure 13.2 *With a dark object (Köhler and O'Connell,* Journal of Cellular and Comparative Physiology, *1957, 49, Supplement 2, p. 5).*

Figure 13.3 *When one electrode is placed over the left, the other over the right half of the cortical fovea (Köhler, Held, and O'Connell,* Proceedings of the American Philosophical Society, *1952, 96, No. 3, p. 311).*

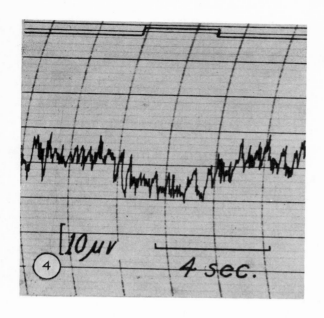

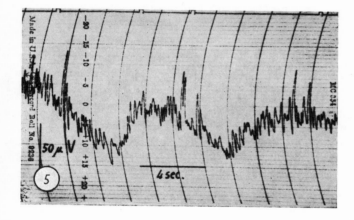

Figure 13.4   A stationary object (Köhler and O'Connell, Journal of Cellular and Comparative Physiology, 1957, 49, Supplement 2, p. 5).

Figure 13.5   When the movement of the object is interrupted (Köhler, Held, and O'Connell, Proceedings of the American Philosophical Society, 1952, 96, p. 316).

on the intact human head, their geometrical and physical relation to the visual cortex is so complicated that the direction of
the potential difference between them by no means permits sure
conclusions as to the polarity at the surface of the active region.
If this polarity were in reality opposite to the difference of potential between the electrodes, then we would simply have to
imagine the visual currents taken from human heads turned
through 180° in order to understand them correctly.

Figure 13.2 shows the result of a second record under
similar conditions; only this time a darker strip of cardboard
moves in front of a bright background. For purely physical
reasons, which have nothing to do with physiology but only with
our apparatus, this could not affect the direction of the recorded
current. This curve is thus almost a copy of the first. It merely
confirms what we already know.

If we place both electrodes over the cortical fovea, one on
the left side, the other on the right, then the cortical object must
move first under the one, then under the other. Consequently, the
object current must flow through the apparatus first in one direction and then in the opposite direction. Which direction appears
first depends, of course, upon the direction of the movement. We
have tried both possibilites, and in both cases we found what had
to be predicted from the known coordination of regions of the
visual cortex to parts of the visual field. The curve in Figure 13.3
corresponds to the case in which the prediction is: first deflection
upward and then deflection downward. The record clearly shows
the two currents of opposite direction following each other, and
the sequence of the deflections corresponds to the expectation.

I have already mentioned that, because of the electrotonic
effect of cortical currents, a stationary object must produce a
weaker current than a moving one. It is, however, entirely possible also to record the currents of objects at rest. The curve in
Figure 13.4 may serve as an example. In this case, an object suddenly appears near the center of the field and remains visible
there, without moving, for some seconds. Under these conditions
there is, of course, no slow increase in the intensity of the cur-

rent. The deflection downward is still clear, even if it is quite weak.

In the line of thinking to which our physiological experiments gave rise, electrotonic effects played a decisive role. Therefore we went on to demonstrate such effects still more clearly. The object first appeared, moving slowly, then came suddenly to rest, and resumed its motion only after some seconds. According to our thinking, the current had quickly to become weaker as soon as the movement was interrupted, and then increase again with renewed displacement of the object. Figure 13.5 reproduces the record of such a process. Of the four marks on the time line, the first corresponds to the appearance of the object, the last to its disappearance, and the two marks in between indicate the time during which the object did not move. The beginning of the curve shows the now familiar increase of the current with movement of the object toward the fixation point. Interruption of this movement leads, however, to rapid diminution of the intensity of the current, and the current remains weak until renewed displacement of the object permits it to increase again. We consider this record to be important for psychology, too. For moving objects are more impressive than stationary ones.

When physiologists were shown such records, they said, "These curves are interesting; but in brain physiology really conclusive experiments can only be performed if the active electrode is in contact with the brain itself." Thus Neff, Wegener, and I decided to undertake further experiments on the exposed brain of cats. In this connection, I must make a general remark. One can record perceptual currents of animals only when the anesthesia necessary for the operation has practically worn off. According to our experience, there are no such currents as long as the experimental animal remains in deep narcosis.

First we investigated the auditory currents of the cat. Figure 13.6 shows the effect of a tone of 500 cycles. The deflection upward, which is repeated in all the following records, is clearly recognizable. For purely external reasons it appears not to be as great as we might have expected. Actually, currents recorded

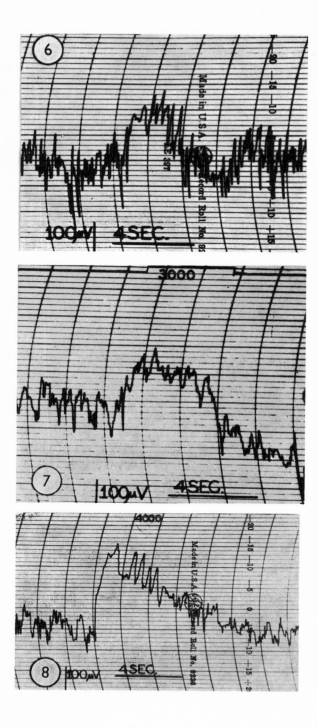

from the exposed brain are up to ten times stronger than the currents taken from the intact human head. Therefore, in the former case, we must work with considerably less amplification in order to limit the deflection to the width of the recording paper. This must be remembered when we consider this and the following curves. The next two records (Figures 13.7 and 13.8) show currents which were produced by tones of higher frequency, 3000 and 4000 cycles. In Figure 13.8 (as also in many other records of auditory currents) the intensity of the current falls off while the tone is still going on. This is not astonishing if it is true that each frequency corresponds to a particular place in the auditory cortex and, therefore, with frequency constant, the same phenomenon must appear as with a stationary object in the visual field, namely weakening of the current through its electrotonic effect.

Auditory currents can also be recorded from the human head, although this is no easy task. The human auditory cortex is located in the lower wall of the Sylvian fissure, thus for our purposes in a particularly unfavorable position. The best place for the active electrode is always opposite the source of the current, because here the current first reaches the surface of the head. In the case of the human auditory cortex, however, this place is 7–8 centimeters distant from the auditory cortex and is on top of the head. We nevertheless succeeded in recording many human auditory currents. Two examples will suffice. In the first record (Figure 13.9) the subject heard the noise of a buzzer. The second curve (Figure 13.10) shows a current in response to whistling. In both cases there is a deflection *upward*. Human auditory currents, like the auditory currents of the cat, thus have surface-*negative* polarity.

Recently O'Connell and I have also recorded visual currents from the brain of the cat. The active electrode was placed on the area in the brain which corresponds to the fovea of the cat. As

Figures 13.6–13.8 Auditory currents from the brains of cats (Köhler, Neff, and Wegener, Journal of Cellular and Comparative Physiology, *1955, 45, Supplement 1, p. 4, p. 13).*

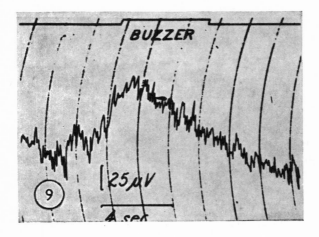

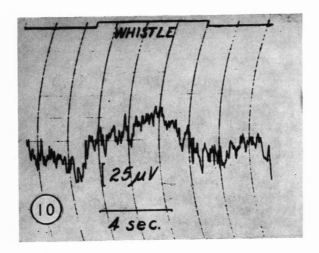

Figures 13.9–13.10   Human auditory currents (Köhler and Wegener, Journal of Cellular and Comparative Physiology, 1955, 45, Supplement 1, p. 35).

stimulus objects we projected bright areas or presented real objects. It was found that the visual cortex of the cat likewise produces surface-*negative* currents. The curves presented here (Figures 13.11 to 13.13) show this clearly. During the third record (Figure 13.13) a bright gray disk was shown twice in succession in front of a dark background. The corresponding deflections, which coincide temporally with the two presentations, are clearly recognizable. Could these currents have anything to do with eye movements? During the aftereffects of the anesthesia, cats seldom move their eyes. Nevertheless, in one cat, both eyes were immobilized by attaching them firmly to their anatomical environment, and records were also made under these circumstances. The curves which we obtained in this way did not differ from those recorded under other conditions.

Do our findings mean that we now know a brain event that is directly correlated with perceptual processes? Lashley and Sperry do not think so. They believe that such brain currents are mere by-products, to which no significance for psychological facts is to be attached. In order to show this, Lashley and his collaborators laid thin gold foil on the visual cortex of monkeys, on the assumption that this excellent conductor would disturb the flow of visual currents in the neighboring tissue. The animals had previously learned to choose one of two simultaneously presented forms. After the gold foil had been put in place, tests were undertaken with the same pairs, and it was found that the monkeys still always chose correctly. In my judgment, these experiments rest on a misunderstanding. If the direction of visual currents corresponded approximately with the direction of the thin gold strips, then these would presumably influence the distribution of current in the tissue. But in reality the source of the current in the brain is at right angles to the conductors that have been laid down, and therefore the distribution of the current which it produces can hardly be altered noticeably in this manner. Therefore I do not believe that Lashley's experiments prove what they were meant to prove.

The anatomist Sperry proceeded in a much more radical manner. First he inserted metal wires in the visual cortex of cats;

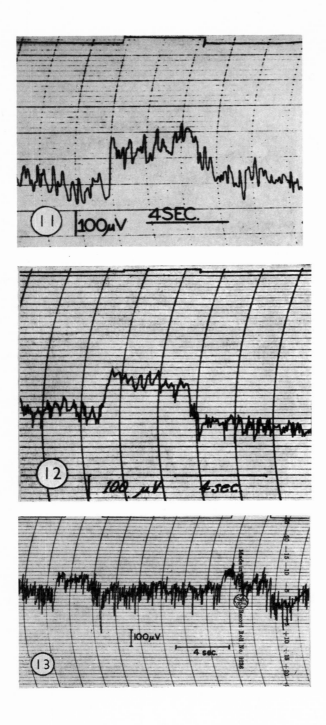

second, he split the cortex by vertical cuts in various directions; and finally, he even inserted thin sheets of insulating material in these cuts. The experimental animals had previously learned to make astonishingly fine discriminations between visual objects. Tests after the above procedures did not, as a rule, show very serious disturbances. These results would be decisive if they did not go somewhat *too* far. For a later paper contains the findings of autopsies performed on the experimental animals. According to these, serious damage resulted, not only in the visual cortex, but also in the subcortical visual fibers and in the thalamus, so that, in the last named region for example, sometimes more than half of the principal cells had disappeared. How cats, whose optical projection system has sustained such damage, can nevertheless still discriminate so well between two very similar objects, is incomprehensible not only from our standpoint, but is also difficult for the most conservative neurology to understand. So we can only hope that Sperry's experiments will soon be repeated with all possible sources of error strictly excluded.

I must add one more historical remark to my report on cortical currents. At first our investigation appeared to us to be an altogether new kind of undertaking. Then, when we made known our first results, others obviously had the same impression. Consequently, the most varied explanations were proposed, only not the one which, from the first, was the most natural. Almost twenty years ago our results could have been predicted with some confidence on the basis of facts discovered at that time. Thus I return to an earlier part of my report.

Neurophysiology does not deal only with action currents which are propagated along fibers. It is also familiar with electrical states in cell bodies and dendrites. These states are not propagated in the usual sense; rather they may remain in the same place for a considerable time. Again, they are not subject to the all-or-none law, like action currents, but appear in graded in-

Figures 13.11–13.13   Visual currents from the brains of cats (Köhler and O'Connell, Journal of Cellular and Comparative Physiology, *1957, 49, Supplement 2, p. 8, p. 18).*

tensity. The investigation of them began in about 1936. In contemporary neurophysiology they are called synaptic or postsynap-
tic potentials. Such potentials occur if the action currents of
afferent fibers arrive at synapses and now, probably with the
cooperation of chemical factors, depolarize the cell membranes
and dendrites of the next neurons. If this happens repeatedly in
rapid succession, these effects summate, and a local change of
potential can thus take place which sometimes remains constant
for minutes. Electrical states of this kind have been demonstrated at synapses in many different parts of the nervous system. Those which appear at synapses in the spinal cord are the
most important for us. They were first investigated by Barron
and Matthews, who used a somewhat indirect procedure. Since
then, however, Eccles succeeded in demonstrating them directly
in single cells of the anterior horn. Interest in this phenomenon
appears to be growing steadily.

In our connection, the decisive point is this. As soon as
synaptic potentials are formed in a circumscribed region, a current must arise which flows through this region and then, after
further spreading through the surrounding tissues, returns to the
other side of the source of the current. No one denies that this
happens; only, in general, the *source* of the synaptic current has
interested neurophysiologists more than the spreading current.
We may expect that synapses in the cerebral cortex behave in the
same way as those in the spinal cord. If this is the case, afferent
action currents produce synaptic potentials and corresponding
currents in the cortex too, and so we have again arrived at the
explanation of such currents given earlier. Only now the explanation can be made with greater confidence by reference to the
potentials and the currents in the spinal cord. These, in fact,
behave very much like the cortical currents in our records. Barron and Matthews have, however, gone farther than we have in
showing precisely how, with increasing frequency of afferent
waves of excitation, these gradually summate, and so finally produce a smooth current.

Thus a satisfactory connection has been established between our investigations and better known findings of neuro-

physiologists. It has therefore been worth while to trust psychological observation and from it to draw conclusions for the corresponding brain processes. The proof that cortical currents too have synaptic sources we would do well to leave to the physiologists. They will then also be able to ascertain which cortical synapses are involved. That active brain parts, in general, produce long lasting currents has meanwhile been confirmed by Goldring and O'Leary.

The present situation, however, gives impetus to new work in *psychology* too. For once we know about cortical currents, this knowledge also leads to questions which can best be answered by psychological research.

14: Unsolved problems in the
field of figural aftereffects

ABOUT thirty years ago, Gibson published his first observations of what we now call figural aftereffects, and thus gave psychology a chance to expand in a new direction. We have every reason to be grateful to Gibson.

When Wallach and I began our work on figural aftereffects, we happened to be concerned with effects of an apparently different kind. We had become interested in the behavior of extremely simple reversible figures. Their reversals suggested to us that continued presence of a visual figure in a given place operates against further presence of this figure, and thus causes a reversal. If this was true, *any* figure process was likely to affect its substratum, even when, in the given configuration, the effect could not be a reversal. We therefore now began to inspect a great many different patterns in order to discover what, if any, changes occurred when these figures were inspected for some time. We

From *The Psychological Record*, 1965, 15, 63–83. Reprinted by permission of the publisher.

Supported by Grants G-18635 and GB-2497 from the National Science Foundation.

found to our surprise that, under these conditions, the *size*, but sometimes also the *shape*, of the figures was affected. Moreover, after the inspection period, not only the inspected objects themselves but also other objects shown in the same region were often displaced or distorted. This meant a considerable expansion of the meaning of the term "figural aftereffects."

Gradually, Wallach and I developed a theory of such effects.[1] This theory applies well-known concepts of physics and electrophysiology to the visual cortex. It has often been misunderstood. Further discussion of it on the present level would be useless. I will therefore now attempt to correct the most disturbing errors made in the past, and to prevent further errors in the future. For this purpose, I must, first of all, briefly formulate the theory again. In order to simplify matters for readers not familiar with such issues, I will begin my explanation and the discussion of errors with conservative statements. Later, the meaning of several concepts will be made more explicit, because essential consequences of the theory cannot be understood without this clarification.

Our most frequent observation was that T-objects (test objects) *receded* from areas where other objects, I-objects (inspection-objects), had been seen for some time. Contours or boundaries of I-objects seemed to be their most important parts in this respect—as shown by the fact that, when T-objects were presented *inside* the area of I-objects, they were also displaced, namely, away from the boundaries of the I-objects. Such distortions and others happened so regularly that we had soon to draw a general conclusion: Figural aftereffects in our sense are surely not restricted to particular classes of patterns. Rather, prolonged inspection of any visual object establishes a condition which either affects this object itself or, afterwards, the location and other characteristics of properly chosen T-objects, or both. If this was true, Gibson's I-objects and his aftereffects had probably to be included in our general rule.

[1] W. Köhler and H. Wallach, Figural after-effects: an investigation of visual processes. *Proceedings of the American Philosophical Society*, 1944, 88, 269–357.

Soon, we became interested in this further question: What is the nature of all these effects? If any visual object, whether an I- or a T-figure, is cortically represented by a corresponding process, we had to assume that prolonged presence of such a process in a given cortical region affects this region, and therefore also both this process itself and new processes now introduced in or near the same region. Among all processes possible in the cortical medium, what particular process would affect its substratum in a way that would fit our observations? The process in question was obviously subjected to three conditions:

1. It had to be a process which affected its substratum in a particular fashion: the effect had to be an *obstruction*. If not, why did T-objects *recede* from the affected area?
2. It had to be a process that was stronger at and near the boundary of an object than in its interior. If not, why should the obstruction which it established be greater near the boundary than elsewhere, for instance far in the interior of the object?
3. It had to be a process which was not limited to the area of the visual object itself. For, in many cases aftereffects were observed when the T-object was shown at some distance from that area, *outside*. Obviously, therefore, the obstruction extended beyond the I-object. Hence, its cause, the hypothetical figure process itself, also spread beyond the object.

Psychologists familiar with physics will realize at once that these three conditions would be satisfied if the process corresponding to a visual object were an electric current which flows through the cortical tissue as a *volume conductor*. From the point of view of neurophysiology, it would by no means be surprising if such currents were established whenever we see a circumscribed object. Suppose that, in a limited area of the cortex, afferent impulses establish a high degree of brightness (or of its physiological counterpart), while in the environment of that area *less* frequent impulses cause a *lower* degree of brightness. Physiologists would probably admit that, under these conditions, a quasi-steady current is likely to flow through the former area, say, upward through the cortex, and to return to its other, the lower, side of the area in loops through its environment. Such a current would obviously satisfy our *third* condition. For, the current would not be restricted to the interior of the object area; rather, it would also spread around it.

Such a current would flow through the tissue in short loops near the boundary of the object, but the loops would grow progressively longer the farther inside the object, and the farther outside, they pass through the tissue. Longer loops mean higher, shorter loops mean lower resistance. Consequently, the intensity of the current would, on both sides, be greater near the boundary than farther inside and farther outside. Hence, such a current would satisfy our *second* condition.

Would a current that flows through cortical tissue establish obstructions in this tissue? Ever since the work of Du Bois-Reymond in the middle of the past century, neurophysiologists have known that, when a current passes through neural tissue, it immediately establishes an obstruction wherever it enters cells. The surfaces are rapidly polarized just as metallic electrodes placed in an electrolyte are polarized by a current that flows through the fluid and through the electrodes. This electrolytical polarization has the character of an obstruction which weakens the current by which it is established, and also tends to deflect it from its initial distribution. In the nervous system, electrolytical polarization is accompanied by a further, a more *biological*, change. Where the current enters cells, their surface layers rapidly become less permeable, that is, more and more polarizable. Physiologists call these two effects "physical" and "biological" electrotonus—or sometimes both, more briefly, just electrotonus. In our work on figural aftereffects both forms of electrotonus have been subsumed under the name "satiation." Obviously, the obstructions will be greater where the current is more intense than in places of weaker flow. The obstructions will, therefore, be maximal near the boundary of the object, because here the current is strongest. As a consequence, any currents, including the one responsible for the obstructions, will now be partially displaced—away from the boundary zone into less affected regions. Nothing of what has just been said is my invention. All steady currents, also those which flow in an orthodox inanimate conductor, say, in a network of wires, behave in this fashion as soon as local obstructions arise somewhere in their path. Thus, the *first* condition is also satisfied.

Other psychologists have called our theory extremely bold, and have added that a theory based on more familiar ideas would have to be preferred. I am surprised by such remarks. What is wrong with new ideas in a young science? In the earlier years of physics, new ideas were added to familiar concepts one after another. Are we timid, and therefore overconservative, in our young science? Moreover, there is only one, at least partially new, assumption in our theory, namely, the thesis that, when we see an object, an electric current flows through and around the corresponding part of the visual cortex. All our further statements simply follow from this one assumption and from well established physical and physiological facts. And is this basic assumption really quite unfamiliar? It may once have been a new statement that, under certain conditions, direct currents appear in the visual cortex. But in the 1930s Obonai had already developed a field, or induction, theory of visual phenomena, although at the time he probably did not identify his field effects with those of electric currents.[2] Soon afterwards, I suggested that electric currents flow through and around the cortical representations of visual objects.[3] This was meant to be an hypothesis. Actually, however, eminent neurophysiologists in England had just demonstrated that such currents really flow through some parts of the nervous system. When Adrian exposed the eyes of *Dytiscus* to light, a direct current could immediately be recorded from the optic ganglion of this creature.[4] Again, Barron and Matthews proved that, when afferent impulses arrive at synapses in the spinal cords of frogs or cats, direct currents are promptly established in these parts of the nervous system.[5] One cannot ask

[2] T. Obonai and Y. Sato, Contributions to the study of psycho-physiological induction. *Japanese Journal of Psychology*, 1937, 12, 451–464.

[3] W. Köhler, *The Place of Value in a World of Facts*. New York: Liveright, 1938, 214f.

[4] E. D. Adrian, Synchronized reactions in the optic ganglion of *Dytiscus*. *Journal of Physiology*, 1937, 91, 66–89.

[5] D. H. Barron and B. H. C. Matthews, The interpretation of potential changes in the spinal cord. *Journal of Physiology*, 1938, 92, 276–321.

for more convincing records than those published by the authors in the *Journal of Physiology*. Psychologists should also not forget that, in 1940 and 1941, most interesting investigations of steady brain potentials and corresponding currents were published by Gerard and Libet in this country.[6] As to the visual cortex, we did not wait for the neurophysiologists to test our main thesis. When observations in the field of figural aftereffects had shown that psychological evidence agreed with that thesis, my collaborators and I began to investigate the cortical responses of human subjects and of animals when their eyes or their ears were stimulated. In both situations, we obtained clear records not only of direct currents but often also of the fact that such currents promptly weaken themselves when stimulation is continued in a given retinal place.[7] I do not believe that any neurophysiologist would hesitate to regard this reduction of the current as the outcome of electrotonic obstructions. I do not think that Wallach and I should be accused of having started an unpleasant revolution. May I add that, when we had just published our first records of visual currents, Goldring and O'Leary discovered quite independently, that stimulation of the eyes gives rise to direct currents in the visual cortex of rabbits.[8, 9]

[6] R. W. Gerard and B. Libet, The control of normal and "convulsive" brain potentials. *American Journal of Psychiatry*, 1940, 96, 1125–1153.
[7] W. Köhler, Relational determination in perception. In L. A. Jeffress (Ed.), *Cerebral Mechanisms in Behavior*. New York: Wiley, 1951, 200–243. W. Köhler and R. Held, The cortical correlate of pattern vision. *Science*, 1949, 110, 414–419. W. Köhler, R. Held, and D. N. O'Connell, An investigation of cortical currents. *Proceedings of the American Philosophical Society*, 1952, 96, 290–330. W. Köhler, W. D. Neff, and J. Wegener, Currents of the auditory cortex in the cat. *Journal of Cellular and Comparative Physiology*, 1955, 45 (Suppl. 1), 1–24. W. Köhler and J. Wegener, Currents of the human auditory cortex. *Journal of Cellular and Comparative Physiology*, 1955, 45 (Suppl. 1), 25–54. W. Köhler and D. N. O'Connell, Currents of the visual cortex in the cat. *Journal of Cellular and Comparative Physiology*, 1957, 49 (Suppl. 2), 1–43.
[8] S. Goldring and J. L. O'Leary, Experimentally derived correlates between ECG and steady cortical potential. *Journal of Neurophysiology*, 1951, 14, 275–288.
[9] Lashley once objected to our thesis that the cortical correlates of visual objects are direct currents. (K. S. Lashley, K. L. Chow, and J. Semmes. An examination of the electric field theory of cerebral integration. *Psychological Review*, 1951, 58, 123–136.) If this were true, he said, one could

Nevertheless, many will be inclined to say: "Even if direct currents flow in the visual cortex when we see objects, have not Lashley and Sperry (and their collaborators) demonstrated that such currents cannot be related to what we see? For these authors took measures to disturb the flow of visual currents in monkeys and cats, and then gave these animals tests with visual patterns, between which they had learned to choose before those measures were taken. And did they not find that now their subjects performed practically as well as they had done before?" As a matter of fact, I admit, they did. But what were the disturbing conditions introduced by the two authors? Lashley laid strips of gold foil on the visual cortex of one monkey, and pushed pieces of the same material into the cortex of another.[10] These materials, he assumed, far superior conductors compared with cortical tissues, would deflect the flow of cortical currents from its normal course to such an extent that, if the currents had any visual significance, pattern vision would be severely disturbed. I object to Lashley's argument for the following reason. Why does one never use simple metallic electrodes when investigating a continued electric response of neural tissue? Because, when in contact with the active tissue, the surfaces of such metallic electrodes are at once intensely polarized so that little, if any, flow passes from the tissue through these surfaces, and thus into our recording devices. Similarly, when laid on the cortex (or inserted in the tissue) Lashley's gold foils must have been polarized at once, must therefore have become unable to conduct, to deflect cortical currents, and thus to disturb pattern vision.

Sperry and his collaborators took much more radical mea-

not understand how appearance of a visual object gives rise to efferent impulses and corresponding movements—as it so often does. Direct currents, he knew, do not establish series of impulses in nerve fibers. Obviously, he was not aware of the fact that this is by no means true of currents which flow through the *cell bodies* of efferent neurons—as, of course, they would do immediately when originating in the visual cortex. The discovery that, in this respect, the behavior of cell bodies differs entirely from that of fibers, was made by Barron and Matthews when they investigated the direct currents of the spinal cord.

[10] Lashley, Chow, and Semmes, *op. cit.*

sures.[11] Either metallic needles were pushed into the cortex of a cat, or the visual cortex was split by vertical cuts in various directions, or (also) sheets of insulating material were inserted at right angles to the surface. And yet, we hear, the cats now performed about as well as they had done before. When I read the authors' report, I felt that their results were just a bit too good to be accepted as reliable evidence. The animals were given a most difficult task; they had to distinguish between a standard figure and other patterns extremely similar to that standard figure. Under the circumstances, one would expect, Sperry's radical measures ought to have had rather striking physiological effects, quite apart from any reference to direct visual currents. My suspicions were confirmed when, in one of their papers, the authors reported on the post-mortem examinations of their animals' brains.[12] What had been found? The white matter, the fibers under the cortex, had often been cut below the cortex, occasionally near the lateral ventricle; in some cases, degenerations in the tissue had left cavities 2 by 3 millimeters large and, as a consequence, loss of principal cells in the geniculate bodies by degeneration amounted to 50 and 75 percent in some animals. The report gives a picture of utter devastation. From the geniculate region through the white connections with the visual cortex, little tissue was apparently left in a normal condition. The authors themselves say that "there may have been small scotomata and the like in the cats' visual fields." I do not believe that, when many deep cuts have severed the ascending fibers in large parts of the visual system, the necessary visual consequences should be described in such modest terms. Actually, the cats may have been partially blind when they were tested; and yet, their difficult choices are said to have been approximately normal. I can only conclude that, during their

[11] R. W. Sperry and N. Miner, Pattern perception following insertion of mica plates into the visual cortex. *Journal of Comparative and Physiological Psychology*, 1955, 48, 463–469. R. W. Sperry, N. Miner, and R. E. Myers, Visual pattern perception following subpial slicing and tantalum wire implantations in the visual cortex. *Journal of Comparative and Physiological Psychology*, 1955, 48, 50–58.
[12] Sperry, Miner, and Myers, *op. cit.*

early, most difficult, training, the cats had gradually learned to react not only to the visual patterns but also to other cues. The authors' statements do not tell us whether in this respect all the necessary precautions were taken. For instance, the *positive* object was always the same figure, while of highly similar *negative* objects there were forty. Consequently, unless new copies of the positive object were introduced quite often, this positive object could easily develop new distinguishing characteristics such as smells, and thus determine the animals' responses. I agree with colleagues who suggest that, for such reasons, Sperry's experiments ought now to be repeated by animal psychologists familiar with all the necessary controls. At any rate, so far neither Lashley's nor Sperry's findings can be accepted as conclusive evidence against our interpretation of figural aftereffects in terms of cortical currents.

I turn to critical statements which I find in the more strictly *psychological* literature. I can discuss only a few, but naturally I select those which seem to me particularly important.

1. A first criticism I find repeated by several authors. According to Köhler and Wallach, I read, no displacement can occur when a T-object coincides with the I-object. And yet, in numerous figural aftereffects, such displacements *do* occur. My answer is that, so far as I can remember, Wallach and I never said that coincidence of lines or contours of inspection- and test-objects must always prevent displacements. In fact, the statement that such displacements ought never to occur simply contradicts our theory. For this theory states that any T-object (or self-satiating I-object) will be displaced or distorted when satiation on one side of the object is greater than satiation on its other side. Why, then, should it never happen in cases of coincidence? The only instance in which it can probably not happen is that in which the I- and the T-object are straight lines in the same location; for, in this case, satiation is presumably the same on both sides of the I-line and, if this is true, neither the I-line nor afterwards the T-line can be displaced. The theory expressly excludes generalization from this special case to coincidence of just *any* I- and T-lines. I must ask the critics to read page 351

of our monograph where Wallach and I emphasize precisely this point.[13] Gibson's curved line, for instance, must distort itself in the observed fashion because, according to the laws of physics, the loops of its figure current *converge* on its *concave side*, and *di*verge on the *convex* side, which means that the current and its satiating action will be stronger on the *concave* side, particularly in its middle region. This will cause displacement of the more outlying parts of the line, away from the most strongly affected area, and therefore a gradual flattening of the curve, just as it was observed by Gibson.

Incidentally, even when a T-object coincides with a part of the I-object which is a straight line, the T-object may be displaced, namely, outward. For instance, Fox has done experiments in which the I-object was a rectangle and the T-object a dot—the dot being shown in various locations, in one of which it coincided with a contour of the I-object.[14] What does our theory predict in this case? It tells us that, in the rectangle, loops of current flow from all sides into the figure, while outside the current can freely spread, which means that outside the current is less dense, and therefore causes weaker satiation. Consequently, the T-dot placed on one of the straight contours lies between a strongly satiated area, the interior of the rectangle, and the less strongly satiated region outside. It must therefore be displaced toward the outside—which is exactly what Fox found.

2. In many excellent experiments, Japanese psychologists such as Obonai, Ikeda, Oyama, and Kogiso have measured the shrinking of T-circles shown inside previously seen I-circles, and also the expansion of T-circles surrounding smaller I-circles.[15] In both cases, the direction of the effects agreed with our predictions. But the authors also found that, under otherwise comparable conditions, the shrinking of a smaller T-circle within the area of a larger I-circle was far more conspicuous than the ex-

---

[13] Köhler and Wallach, *op. cit.*

[14] B. H. Fox, Figural after-effects: "satiation" and adaptation. *Journal of Experimental Psychology*, 1951, 42, 317–326.

[15] M. Sagara and T. Oyama, Experimental studies of figural after-effects in Japan. *Psychological Bulletin*, 1957, 54, 327–338.

pansion of a T-circle shown outside the I-circle. The difference, it has been said, cannot be derived from our theory. I do not agree. For, the loops of the current from a *larger* I-circle toward its center *con*verge, a fact which operates against the weakening of its current with increasing distance. But the loops of current of a *smaller* I-circle toward the outside *di*verge, a fact which enhances the weakening of the current with increasing distance. Conditions as to satiation are therefore quite different in the two cases. In the neighborhood of an I-circle, satiation *inside* must be stronger than satiation *outside*. Hence, under otherwise comparable conditions, a *smaller* T-circle inside an I-circle will be more strongly displaced than a T-circle *outside* the I-circle—a prediction which agrees with the authors' findings.

3. Our Japanese colleagues are also disturbed by another fact. When the T-circle and the I-circle *coincide,* then, they claim, the T-circle should, according to our theory, appear neither larger nor smaller, just because the I- and the T-object *coincide.* I have already said that coincidence of the I- and the T-object will prevent displacement only in the case of *straight* lines, and I have also given the reason why this is so. In spite of coincidence, a T-line will be displaced whenever the satiation caused by the I-object is greater on one side of the T-object than it is on the other side. But what is the *direction* of the displacement when an I- and a T-circle coincide? The psychologists in Japan have found that the I-circle is now *smaller,* an observation which agrees with the findings of others, including Wallach and myself. At first, I will admit, this observation does look surprising. For, if satiation *within* a circle is greater than satiation *outside* the circle (as one must expect it to be), then, it seems to follow, a T-circle coinciding with the I-circle ought to appear too *large*— since, all around, it would have to recede toward the outside, away from the more strongly satiated *interior.* Is this conclusive evidence against our theory?

It is not, because so far I have not mentioned one consequence of the theory. It is true that a circle must first rapidly grow; for, the high satiation inside turns part of the current of the circle toward the outside. This first stage I will explain in a moment. But what will happen when the outside current has thus been increased, and the circle has therefore become larger? The increased flow outside must now cause increased satiation outside—with the effect that, after having reached a maximum of expansion, the circle will, relative to this maximum, begin to *shrink*. Agáin, this is not an ad hoc hypothesis; it is a simple consequence of our theory. But now I have to answer the question: where is that first growth of the circle which ought to precede its shrinking? Wallach and I found that, in the case of closed figures, one often sees effects of self-satiation when the I-object has been seen only for a second. Psychologists in Japan have investigated the speed of satiation more systematically, and have demonstrated that clear, but short-lived, figural after-effects are generally observable even after a *fraction* of a second. With these findings, which have recently been confirmed by those of Fehrer and Ganchrow,[16] our Japanese colleagues have probably forced us to change our quantitative thinking in this field considerably. For instance, the immediate effect of self-satiation in a circle may also develop within such short periods, which means that such a circle should expand before our eyes when it is just appearing. But, if the satiation of its interior occurs so fast, the redistribution of its current toward the outside, and therefore also the corresponding increase of satiation outside, must also begin quite early—with the consequence that, after having reached maximal size in a few moments, the circle will now begin to look smaller. Subjects do not mention that first rapid growth of the circle to which I have just referred? That may be true. But at this point we have to remember a well-known perceptual phenomenon. When a closed object such as a circle is suddenly presented, for instance by projection, everybody sees a rapid expansion of this object—just at the time when strong satiation in its interior is first being established. The name of this first rapid growth is *gamma movement*. From what I have just said, I therefore conclude that *the gamma movement is the*

---

[16] E. Fehrer and D. Ganchrow, Effects of exposure variables on figural after-effects under tachistoscopic presentation. *Journal of Experimental Psychology*, 1963, 66, 506–513.

initial growth of an object by self-satiation. Unfortunately for our purposes, people are so accustomed to the gamma phenomenon (by having seen it when slides are projected and also when they look at changing traffic lights) that they no longer pay any attention to it. Even in experiments, I have sometimes found, the initial growth of suddenly appearing objects is often quietly ignored by the observers.

The spontaneous transition from the initial growth of an object to a reduction of its size later is only a special example of changes in the direction of satiation effects when a given pattern is seen for some time. Once more, strong local satiation always causes a redistribution of the satiating current, namely, a decrease of its intensity in places where it was, at first, most intense and an increase of the flow in places where, so far, the medium has been less satiated.[17, 18] In the Müller-Lyer figure, for instance, growing satiation in the interior of the angles (which reduces the illusion) must gradually increase the current and the satiation outside the angles, and thus operate against further reduction of the illusion. Satiation is not an effect which simply grows in a given location when its cause, the satiating current, continues to affect the tissue.

4. Occasionally, new observations are said to be at odds with the theory while, actually, such observations are confirmations of it. It has, for instance, been discovered that the shrinking of a smaller T-circle within the area of a larger I-circle is most conspicuous when, regardless of the absolute size of the two circles, the *ratio* of the radii of the circles has the right constant size.[19] We are told that the theory cannot explain this. As a matter of fact, however, this new finding is a corroboration of our theory. All self-distributing, functionally coherent processes, such as the cortical currents of the theory, follow one

---

[17] Köhler and Wallach, *op. cit.*, 329.

[18] Fehrer and Ganchrow, *op. cit.*, state that our theory requires an increase of figural aftereffects with an increase in the duration of the I-period. The present discussion shows that this cannot be generally true, because the direction of the changes caused by satiation is likely to vary during continued inspection. As we have just seen, the direction of the change may even be reversed.

[19] Cf. Sagara and Oyama, *op. cit.*, 329f.

main rule: When the system in which these processes distribute themselves is, as a whole, enlarged or reduced in size so that all parts of the system are enlarged or reduced at the same rate, then all functional characteristics of the flow are *transposed*. Everywhere, the intensity of the current will be reduced or increased at the same rate, but the distribution of the flow will remain the same—in the sense that, after the change of size, *relations* between corresponding parts of the flow are not at all affected. Within an I-circle of given size, for instance, the current distribution (and therefore the distribution of satiation) is optimal for the shrinking of a smaller T-circle when the length of the radius of this T-circle is a certain fraction of the radius of the I-circle. When now the size (the length of the radius) of the I-circle is changed one way or the other, the rule of transposition which holds for processes such as our currents must be applied as follows: In the new I-circle, the distribution of the current will be such that conditions for the shrinking of a smaller T-circle will be optimal when the radius of the T-circle is the same fraction of the radius of the I-circle as it was before the change of size. For, under these conditions, the quantitative relation between the current (and the satiation) on both sides of the T-circle will once more be the same as it was before the change.

What I have just said is not merely a defense of our theory from the point of view of physics; with their demonstration of transposition in the field of figural aftereffects, the psychologists in Japan have given us a convincing corroboration of this theory because their findings mean that the process responsible for figural aftereffects in vision must be a coherent self-distributing process. Only such a process can be expected to behave in this fashion, and the only specific process of this kind which seems possible in the visual cortex is the electric current.

5. A further criticism has come from Hebb.[20] His main objection is related to the concept of quasi-permanent statistical satiation which we must now consider in some detail.

In the course of a day, Wallach and I argued, images of

[20] D. O. Hebb, *The Organization of Behavior.* New York: Wiley, 1949.

objects of all kinds are constantly being projected on the retinae; the same happens the next day, and so forth. Under the circumstances, a considerable amount of satiation is likely to develop and to persist in the visual cortex. Even if, for the sake of simplicity, we assume that, statistically speaking, lines (and the contours of objects) are equally often formed everywhere on the retinae, the resulting cortical satiation will not be homogeneous; for, equal distances and areas on the retinae are, as a rule, not represented as equal distances and areas in the visual cortex. Statistical cortical satiation must be stronger where the cortical representation of given retinal distances is smaller than it is where the representation of the same distances is larger, because in the former cortical places contours and their satiating effects are more densely distributed. Since visual currents turn away from highly satiated parts of the tissue, distances in the small-scale cortical regions will, therefore, be visually enlarged, an effect which must tend to compensate for their geometrically smaller representation in the cortex. The compensation need not, of course, be complete. According to the observations of K. T. Brown, it is not complete. [21]

I do not agree with McEwen's statement that, according to Köhler and Wallach, "permanent satiation creates a cortical medium which is homogeneously satiated." [22] To repeat: Only if, statistically, the degree of cortical satiation *varies* directly with the anatomical irregularities of the tissue will statistical satiation tend to compensate for such irregularities.

Wallach and I applied the present reasoning to the curious fact that, while the representation of given retinal areas is much smaller in peripheral parts of the visual cortex than it is in and near the cortical fovea, there are only moderate distortions in the periphery of the visual field, surely no such reductions of the size of visual objects as the small-scale cortical representation

[21] K. T. Brown, Methodology for studying figural after-effects and practice effects in the Müller-Lyer illusion. *American Journal of Psychology,* 1953, 66, 629–634.
[22] P. McEwen, Figural after-effects. *British Journal of Psychology,* Monograph Supplement 31, 1958, 38.

of the retinal periphery would lead one to expect. We suggested that the crowding of contours in the periphery of the visual cortex and the correspondingly increased peripheral satiation explains this fact.

Hebb raises the objection that we seem to overrate the crowding of contours in the periphery of the visual cortex. The lower visual acuity in the periphery, he says, the fact that here contours must retinally be separated by considerable distances if they are to give rise to separate visual contours, reduces the peripheral crowding of contours and therefore their total satiating effect. It seems to me that Hebb's argument applies only to simultaneously given contours. When statistical reasoning is also applied to what happens successively, then the fact that, in the periphery, simultaneously given retinal contours are often not represented by visually separate contours no longer weakens our argument. When given successively, many contours may not have different spatial locations in the peripheral visual cortex, but the result is that such contours now appear with increased temporal frequency in the *same* places, and cause high degrees of satiation for this reason. In foveal parts of the cortex where much smaller retinal distances permit contours to remain separate, repeated appearance of contours and correspondingly repeated satiation in the same places will, of course, occur less frequently. Thus the very fact which Hebb regards as detrimental to our reasoning seems to have consequences which weaken his criticism. It still remains probable that, statistically, satiation is stronger in peripheral parts of the visual cortex, and thus tends to compensate for the small-scale representation of retinal sizes in these parts.

The present issue has been subjected to some experimental tests. Köhler and Wallach once compared a simple figural aftereffect fairly near the foveal region with the same effect in a more peripheral region and found that here the effect of the I-object extended much farther than it did in the neighborhood of the fovea.[23] More recently, Meyer, Sukemune, and Myers measured

[23] Köhler and Wallach, *op. cit.*, 302f.

the size of a figural aftereffect when the I- and the T-object were shown at varying distances from the fixation mark.[24] The aftereffect grew when the distance was increased although the centers of the objects (circles) were shown only at such short distances from the fixation mark as 2°, 4°, and 6° of visual angle. Earlier findings of, Heinemann and Marill also suggest that the range of figural aftereffects is increased in the periphery.[25]

I regard the present issue as fairly important because, according to histological evidence, geometrical discrepancies between retinal sizes (or shapes) and their cortical representations can be found in many parts of the field, while visual inspection shows no distortions of comparable size. What has just been said about the correction of the small-scale representation of the retinal periphery in the cortex also applies to such other geometrical irregularities in the striate area of the brain. If this is true, satiation does play an important role in normal vision. It does so even if we keep in mind Brown's observations.[26]

Statistical satiation may be highly persistent; but one would expect it to show symptoms of decay when, for a considerable period, its level has not been maintained by continued satiating action of cortical currents. This could happen when Ss are for days kept in situations in which they never see objects, that is, under conditions of visual deprivation. In some cases visual objects have afterwards shown slight distortions (and other abnormal characteristics).[27] One is tempted to assume that this happened because, after the period of deprivation, correction of cortical irregularities by statistical satiation was already less adequate.

[24] D. R. Meyer, S. Sukemune, and R. Myers, Local variations in the magnitude of a figural aftereffect. *Journal of Experimental Psychology*, 1960, 60, 314–317.

[25] E. G. Heinemann and T. Marill, Tilt adaptation and figural after-effects. *Journal of Experimental Psychology*, 1954, 48, 468–472.

[26] Brown, *op. cit.*

[27] B. K. Doane, W. Mahatoo, W. Heron, and T. H. Scott, Changes in perceptual function after isolation. *Canadian Journal of Psychology*, 1959, 13, 210–219. W. Heron, B. K. Doane, and T. H. Scott, Visual disturbances after prolonged perceptual isolation. *Canadian Journal of Psychology*, 1954, 8, 70–76.

At one point, the present remarks about persistent statistical satiation must be corrected. The simplifying assumption that contours are equally often projected on all parts of the retinae is not generally justified.[28] The environments of most people are such that objects and lines appear more often in lower parts of the visual field than in higher parts.[29] Consequently, we must expect that persistent satiation is stronger in cortical regions which correspond to the former parts. Wallach and I have mentioned several observations which agree with this expectation.

At this point, the discussion of arguments for and against our theory must now be briefly interrupted because, in earlier presentations of this theory, the meanings of some concepts have not been made sufficiently clear. This holds also for the presentation given in earlier pages of the present paper where I have still described the theory in oversimplified terms in order to facilitate the reader's task. I will now add the necessary clarifications and also suggest a change of our terminology. This change will help us to distinguish between two important facts in our field.

It remains correct to say that, when we try to explain figural aftereffects, we have to consider, first, the electrolytical polarization of cell surfaces by figure currents (physical electrotonus) and, secondly, the biological reaction of the surface layers of the cells to the passing of such currents through these layers (biological electrotonus).[30]

The accumulation of ions at cell surfaces (physical electrotonus) establishes forces opposed to those which maintain the current. The biological electrotonus caused by currents where they enter cells makes the surfaces of these cells less permeable to the ions and, therefore, accelerates and intensifies the polarization of these surfaces, that is, the physical electrotonus. In this

---

[28] Köhler and Wallach, op. cit., 281 and 346.

[29] E. Rubin, Visuell wahrgenommene Figuren. Copenhagen: Gyldendalske, 1921, 83.

[30] So far, the theory has only dealt with the effects which currents have where they enter cells, i.e., at anodic surfaces. In most cases with which we are now concerned this is a justified procedure. But there are other conditions, under which events that occur where the currents leave the cells (at cathodic surfaces) cannot be ignored.

sense, both effects of figure currents combine in causing the obstructions which weaken the currents, deflect them from their original distribution, and thus produce figural aftereffects. It is for this reason that, in the past, both effects have been subsumed under the common name "satiation." In the meantime, it has become obvious, however, that this simplifying terminology leads to serious misunderstandings. For, while both effects operate in the direction of growing figural aftereffects, they play different roles in doing so. In order to facilitate a better understanding of figural aftereffects, only the *physical* electrotonus, the polarization of cell surfaces, will now be called "satiation," while for the *biological* change of cell surfaces I will now use the old name "electrotonus." The main differences between the two effects of figural currents are as follows.

The polarization of cell surfaces by currents, their satiating action, *develops* very fast, in most instances probably within fractions of a second. It is then rapidly decelerated because it weakens the current by which it is being produced. When the current is now interrupted, say, by removal of the figure in question, the satiation (or polarization) also *disappears* very fast. Physicists would hardly expect it to survive for much more than a second.

The electrotonic change in the surface layers of cells may begin as soon as the current is established, but its further development is also soon decelerated, again because the satiation which occurs at the same time operates against further growth of the change. In one respect, satiation and electrotonus differ most strikingly: While satiation rapidly disappears when the current is interrupted, the electrotonic condition may persist for long periods without being maintained by a current, particularly when the level of the condition is high. In fact, it may persist for hours and probably even for much longer periods.

There is a further difference between satiation and electrotonus. Growing satiation, we have seen, limits not only its own development but also the growth of electrotonus by weakening the current which causes both. The electrotonic condition, on the other hand, enhances and accelerates the satiating effects of currents by making the affected cells less permeable, i.e., more polarizable. Consequently, when the tissue is in a highly developed electrotonic condition, a new current will establish extreme degrees of satiation at once. In other words, while satiation tends to limit the development of electrotonus, the electrotonic condition accentuates further satiation.

The preceding statements must have shown that, under many experimental conditions, figural aftereffects are observable only because the electrotonic condition established by figure currents is far more persistent than are their satiating effects. For, the actual satiation disappears almost immediately when the I-object is removed so that only the electrotonic condition is left. Even if the introduction of the T-object takes no more than, say, two seconds, the observed figural aftereffect is probably not caused by the satiation established during the exposure of the I-object but by the *new* satiation produced by the current of the T-object. This new satiation is accelerated and enhanced because it occurs in a medium which is still in the electrotonic condition produced by the current of the I-object.

A first consequence of the present explanations will be obvious. What we have called persistent statistical satiation is not satiation in the present sense at all; rather, it is a persistent electrotonic condition of the tissue in question, which has been established by numerous figure currents in the past. This condition then enhances the satiating action of new individual currents.

Once this has become clear, a second consequence immediately follows. In studying ordinary figural aftereffects, we rightly assume that the current of the I-object establishes a pattern of satiation and at the same time a similarly located and shaped pattern of the electrotonic condition. But when we study the effects of more persistent electrotonic conditions established in certain regions by many previous figure currents of all kinds, we deal with a different situation. The satiating action of *any* particular figure current which arises in such a region will be enhanced even if no currents which contributed to the persistent electrotonus of the region resembled the present particular current. This holds, for instance,-for the effects observed by Meyer,

Sukemune, and Myers.[31] They found, it will be remembered, that a randomly selected figural aftereffect was increased when it was tested in regions where the persistent statistical electrotonus could be supposed to be stronger. Our argument leads to the prediction that many other aftereffects produced in the same region would have been similarly enhanced.

In this sense, the effects of persistent statistically established electrotonus are far more general than those observed when the electrotonic condition involved is strictly localized and strictly patterned. For instance, when Gibson's curve is shown in a vertical orientation and Ss fixate its center, its lower parts begin to flatten more rapidly than its higher parts. This observation is probably related to the fact that statistically developed electrotonus is likely to be stronger in the lower half of the visual field. Obviously, no localized and specifically patterned electrotonic condition need be present in the tissue. The general state of high and persistent electrotonus in the lower half of the field would probably enhance the satiating effect of *any* pattern shown in the same region. It does not matter that, in such situations, the persistent electrotonic condition may be present in a much larger area. The acceleration of satiation caused by this condition occurs, of course, only where a satiating current flows. Outside this particular region the tissue remains passive in spite of its electrotonic state.

We can now apply our better defined concepts to the reduction of the Müller-Lyer illusion in repeated trials. Again, I must restrict my remarks to a few essential issues. Others, I hope, will readily be understood after the preceding explanations.

1. Few observations in this field have made so strong an impression as Moed's discovery that when the orientation of the Müller-Lyer pattern is reversed from trial to trial, the Müller-Lyer illusion is gradually reduced in both orientations.[32] So long as the term "satiation" is used in the usual ambiguous way, this finding

[31] Meyer, Sukemune, and Myers, *op. cit.*
[32] G. Moed, Satiation-theory and the Müller-Lyer illusion. *American Journal of Psychology*, 1959, 72, 609–611.

seems to contradict the theory offered by Köhler and Fishback.[33] For, according to this theory, the size of the illusion in a given orientation is reduced in repeated trials because "satiation" is particularly strong inside the angles of the figure and also between the angles on the side of the figure which at first looks shorter. It is the asymmetry of the resulting pattern of "satiation" which is thus supposed to reduce the size of the illusion. But Moed's procedure consistently operates against this asymmetry because, as trial follows trial and the two orientations of the figure regularly alternate, the resulting pattern of satiation must become more and more symmetrical. How can the illusion be gradually reduced under these conditions? The fact that it is so reduced appears particularly striking because Moed's Ss always fixated the apex of the middle angle so that the over-all geometrical symmetry of the experimental situation was well defined in cortical terms.

This theoretical puzzle disappears as soon as the general term "satiation" is replaced by the two specific terms "satiation" and "electrotonus" with their equally specific meanings. The way in which Moed changed the orientation of the figure from trial to trial shows that it must have taken him a few seconds to complete the change. This holds for the whole series of trials in which an S took part, and, as a result, only the local electrotonic condition established in a given trial (but no satiation) was left when the reversal was completed and the next trial could begin with the figure in the reversed orientation. Consequently, a more and more symmetrical distribution of the electrotonic state, mostly within the angles, had to develop and to grow as trial followed trial. Now, actual figural aftereffects in the visual field appear where local figure currents locally satiate the tissue; and, because of the growing electrotonic condition, this happened more and

[33] W. Köhler and J. Fishback, The destruction of the Müller-Lyer illusion in repeated trials: I. An examination of two theories. *Journal of Experimental Psychology*, 1950, 40, 267–281. W. Köhler and J. Fishback, The destruction of the Müller-Lyer illusion in repeated trials: II. Satiation patterns and memory traces. *Journal of Experimental Psychology*, 1950, 40, 398–410.

more rapidly and strongly in both orientations of the figure. Each time, of course, the satiating current was concentrated within the angles, and thus satiated mainly their interior. But this is the condition which, according to our theory, always weakens the illusion. It follows that, when experimentation was continued, and the electrotonic state grew symmetrically, the size of the illusion had to decrease in whichever orientation the figure was shown. It does make a difference whether one distinguishes between satiation and the electrotonic condition or hides the difference by using the same name for both.

2. Parker and Newbigging recently "pretrained" their Ss with a figure which resembled the usual M-L figure, namely, with a pattern in which the angles of the well-known figure were replaced by circles located where the angles are in this figure.[34] That such a pattern represents a variation of the M-L figure was indicated by the fact that it exhibited a weak illusion in the same direction as the M-L figure itself. This weak illusion tended to decrease when trials with the circle figure were repeated. Later, the M-L figure itself was presented in the same location and orientation. The illusion proved to be greatly reduced at the start, and then further declined when more measurements were done. The reduction was much stronger after forty than after merely eight pretraining trials. The authors believe that these findings mean transfer of what has been learned during the pretraining trials to the Ss' operations with the M-L figure. Actually, we cannot yet tell. It remains to be shown that their result is related to the particular characteristics of their pretraining pattern. We must also consider what effects satiation and electrotonus (as established during the pretraining trials) may be expected to have in such a situation. Now, the authors did not ask their Ss to fixate, and the theoretical assumptions made by Köhler and Fishback do not directly apply to experiments in which Ss can freely move their eyes; for these assumptions refer to experi-

[34] N. I. Parker and P. L. Newbigging, Magnitude and decrement of the Müller-Lyer illusion as a function of pre-training. *Canadian Journal of Psychology*, 1963, 17, 134–140.

ments meant to decide whether the gradual decrease of the illusion is a gradually growing figural aftereffect.[35] For this reason, fixation was prescribed just as it had been in the study of ordinary figural aftereffects. It is not easy to generalize, that is, to say precisely what patterns of satiation and electrotonus will be established in the situation used by Parker and Newbigging.

At this point, some thinking in terms of mere probabilities seems permissible. Occasionally, such a procedure may even be advisable, provided it leads to new questions which can be answered in simple experiments. This the following considerations will achieve. When, during repeated trials with the authors' pretraining pattern, Ss freely move their eyes, they probably do so mainly along the main dimension of this pattern. Satiation and the electrotonic condition will be established mainly by the cortical currents which flow through and around the circles of the pattern. But when the eyes move back and forth along the main dimension of the pattern, the circles and their currents move back and forth in the visual cortex. Consequently, the electrotonic condition will be established and gradually intensified in the cortical region covered by such movements. As a consequence, an approximately even belt of electrotonically affected tissue will develop in this region, although within the belt the level of the effect may vary slightly. We need not, at this point, refer to the satiation established under such conditions because this physical polarization will always rapidly disappear between trials. However, when after trials of this kind the M-L figure is shown with its asymmetrical arrangement of the angles, actual satiation within these angles will be strongly accelerated and intensified because of the electrotonus established in the whole belt during the pretraining trials, and this will happen wherever Ss fixate within the belt. It follows that, from the very beginning, the M-L illusion will now be reduced and will further decrease when measurements are repeated. Naturally, this effect of the pretrials will be stronger when the number of such trials has been great

[35] Köhler and Fishback, *op. cit.*

than when only a few have been given—a prediction which agrees with the authors' findings.

The present reasoning may not fit the facts in detail because one cannot tell precisely what eye movements the Ss perform in such situations. On the other hand, while nobody can be forced to accept the present argument, it does have the advantage of leading to experimental questions which can immediately be tested. For, the statement that, in the pretraining trials, an electrotonically affected belt is established in the tissue does not refer to any particular characteristics of the pattern used in these trials. It follows that virtually *any* patterns repeatedly shown during the pretraining may have similar effects. The only rule that would have to be followed throughout is that Ss are permitted to move their eyes. I am now planning to do such experiments; but for the reason already mentioned I am not prepared to predict what the outcome will be. Great caution is also indicated for a further reason. If the present considerations were accepted, they would lead to an unexpected conclusion. Since practically any pattern repeatedly inspected with freely moving eyes would establish a belt of electrotonically affected tissue, this would probably also be true when this pattern is the M-L figure itself. It would, therefore, seem to follow that (when eye movements are permitted) the size of the M-L illusion is gradually reduced mainly because during repeated trials an approximately even belt of electrotonically affected tissue is established. When shown within this belt, the pattern would then exhibit the change which actual satiation within the angles causes in the affected region, namely, a smaller illusion. One does hesitate to accept such a radical conclusion. Moreover, this conclusion could be accepted only if, when Ss are permitted to move their eyes, repeated pretrials with patterns quite unrelated to the M-L illusion actually reduce its size.

3. When Ss fixate a mark in the field, the theorist is confronted with a different situation. For, now the pattern of electrotonus that develops in repeated trials is a far more precise pattern. It is directly related to the M-L figure, and it is also localized.

It has recently been said[36] that, according to Day,[37] the illusion does not consistently decrease under these conditions, and it is true that in several of Day's experiments its size was not reduced at all. Since such findings are contradicted by those of Köhler and Fishback, of Moed, and of Mountjoy,[38] they have probably been caused by special experimental conditions. Now, in Day's experiments, the M-L figure was often shown in a small field surrounded by a black environment. The sharp contour seen in this situation must have established strong satiation and an intense electrotonic condition, which probably spread into the region of the M-L figure. When fixation is prescribed, decrease of the illusion depends upon a clearly defined and localized electrotonic condition. Obviously, therefore, no strong currents with correspondingly intense satiating and electrotonic effects should be permitted to interfere with the effects caused by and within the M-L figure itself. Hence, Day's experiments should be repeated under conditions in which the possibility of such an interference is avoided. As a matter of fact, Day himself did one experiment in which a considerable distance separated the figure from the next object, and precisely in this situation the illusion clearly decreased although fixation was prescribed.

4. It is nevertheless true that, when Ss fixate a mark in the field, an initial decrease of the illusion is often followed by a temporary change in the opposite direction. Köhler and Fishback found that this happened with many of their Ss.[39] In this respect,

[36] R. H. Pollack and M. R. Chaplin, Effects of prolonged stimulation by components of the Müller-Lyer illusion upon the magnitude of the illusion. *Perceptual and Motor Skills*, 1964, 18, 377–382.

[37] R. H. Day, The effects of repeated trials and prolonged fixation on error in the Müller-Lyer figure. *Psychological Monographs* 1962, 76 (14).

[38] Köhler and Fishback, *op. cit.* G. Moed, *op. cit.* P. T. Mountjoy, Fixation and decrement to the Müller-Lyer figure. *Psychological Record*, 1960, 10, 219–223. P. T. Mountjoy, Monocular regard and decrement to the Müller-Lyer illusion. *Psychological Record*, 1960, 10, 141–143.

[39] W. Köhler and J. Fishback, The destruction of the Müller-Lyer illusion in repeated trials: II. Satiation patterns and memory traces. *Journal of Experimental Psychology*, 1950, 40, 398–410.

the curves found by Mountjoy are most convincing.[40] There was no such development in the opposite direction when Ss were allowed to move their eyes; but the disturbance soon appeared when they had to fixate. Köhler and Fishback have given a simple explanation of this phenomenon. When Ss fixate, strong satiation and electrotonus are soon established within the angles of the figure, whereupon the distribution of the figure current must change. To repeat: According to elementary rules of physics, the current is now weakened within the angles and strengthened on their outside. Consequently, its satiating and electrotonic effect outside will also grow, a change which will make the size of the illusion grow in relation to its size just before "satiation in such wrong places" began. Such a change is not entirely impossible when Ss may move their eyes, but it is less likely to occur under such conditions, and also less likely to go as far as it often does when Ss have to fixate.

5. Köhler and Fishback have found that the disturbance tends to disappear when experiments are interrupted by long rest periods. In first tests after such interruptions, the illusion may even appear to be considerably reduced at once. This is not at all astonishing, because a major interruption permits the electrotonic condition established "in the wrong places" before the interruption to disappear again, whereupon new satiation in the next trial will immediately occur in the right places so that a weaker illusion is now seen.

In this connection, Mountjoy once did experiments in which the size of the intervals between trials was varied.[41] He did not find that, when these intervals were longer, the illusion decreased more rapidly. But since in these experiments Ss were not asked to fixate, no major disturbance of the kind just mentioned developed, and therefore the effect of longer rest periods could not appear. In Mountjoy's experiments with prescribed fix-

[40] Mountjoy, *op. cit.*
[41] P. T. Mountjoy, Effects of exposure time and intertrial interval upon decrement to the Müller-Lyer illusion. *Journal of Experimental Psychology,* 1958, 56, 97–102.

ation, the disturbance did appear and, when now a rest period of 24 hours was given, the illusion was in one case at once smaller after the interruption.[42]

Our theory has not yet been applied to all figural effects, for instance, not to the strong effects observed in the third dimension of visual space, to those in kinesthesis, and to those investigated by Held in which active movements of the Ss play an important role.[43] Sooner or later, attempts must be made to discover whether our assumptions may be used in explaining these phenomena. So far, this has not been possible because, in all these cases, the histological and physiological conditions involved are not yet known.

The same holds for several recent findings related to well-known aftereffects but also to facts which have previously not been considered in this connection.

Mountjoy has made the remarkable discovery that the M-L illusion is far more rapidly and strongly reduced when Ss inspect the figure monocularly than when both eyes are open.[44] Now, when Taylor and Henning studied the reversals and other transitions which occur in the Necker Cube and a simple hexagon during prolonged inspection, they found that the rate of the changes was generally higher under conditions of monocular than of binocular vision.[45] One feels inclined to believe that, functionally, these two facts are related to the same not yet known difference between monocular and binocular vision.

Rudel and Teuber report that, when the M-L illusion has been greatly reduced in the visual field, it is also considerably

[42] P. T. Mountjoy, Fixation and decrement to the Müller-Lyer figure. *Psychological Record*, 1960, 10, 219–223. P. T. Mountjoy, Monocular regard and decrement to the Müller-Lyer illusion. *Psychological Record*, 1960, 10, 141–143.

[43] Cf. J. Hochberg and R. Held, Nonvisual components in visual form perception. *Perceptual and Motor Skills*, 1964, 18, 559–560.

[44] P. T. Mountjoy, Monocular regard and decrement to the Müller-Lyer illusion. *Psychological Record*, 1960, 10, 141–143.

[45] M. M. Taylor and G. B. Henning, Transformations of perception with prolonged observation. *Canadian Journal of Psychology*, 1963, 17, 349–360.

weaker when the figure is afterwards haptically represented.[46] The transfer is even more striking when the haptic trials are given first, and the visual measurements follow.

We owe an equally important extension of our field to Spitz and Blackman who have found that a figural aftereffect is smaller in retarded Ss than it is in normal persons.[47]

To what degree such facts are related to the state called electrotonus and its variations remains to be seen. At the present time, however, the nature of this condition is not yet entirely known even to the physiologists. Variations of the condition from one individual to another and from one part of the cortex to another in a given person can, therefore, not yet be fully explained. Obviously, further work in physiology is needed at this point.

[46] R. G. Rudel and H. L. Teuber, Decrement of visual and haptic Müller-Lyer illusion on repeated trials: A study of crossmodal transfer. *Quarterly Journal of Experimental Psychology*, 1963, 15, 125–131.

[47] H. H. Spitz and L. S. Blackman, A comparison of mental retardates and normals on visual figural after-effects and reversible figures. *Journal of Abnormal and Social Psychology*, 1959, 58, 105–110.

five

NATURAL SCIENCE

15: *On the problem of regulation*

THE more we learn about regulation in the organic world, the more clearly biological theorizing approaches a decisive turning point. Only a relatively small number of investigators are concerned with problems of morphogenesis; therefore regulations, which have been observed after disturbance of normal embryonic development, and which lead by anomalous paths to the normal end result, have not had quite the theoretical impact that they deserve. But we are becoming more and more convinced that the functions of even the developed organism are capable of regulation to a much greater extent than could be recognized earlier, under the influence of a one-sided mode of thinking. Thus the experiments of Bethe show most clearly a new functional process in the remaining parts of an organism if a disturbance eliminates the functioning of individual organs; and again it is the result of such regulation that for the whole organism—in essentials and as far as possible—the same is achieved as under

Zum Problem der Regulation. *Wilhelm Roux' Archiv für Entwicklungsmechanik der Organismen*, 1927, 112, 315–332. Reprinted by permission of Springer-Verlag and translated by Mary Henle and Erich Goldmeier.

normal conditions.[1] But this is physiology and thus concerns a large region of human knowledge. It cannot fail to have consequences.

One thing will gradually have to be recognized: Such facts are no longer to be treated by special theories just for the case and the circumstances of particular regulations. In future we will, no doubt, have to conceive *normal* function too, in principle, in such a way that, under the conditions of a disturbance, the theory of it can simply go over into the theory of regulation. This means that we must seek new foundations for the theory of normal function in morphogenesis and in physiology.

Up until now, the one really clear picture in terms of which we could interpret normal morphogenesis and normal physiological function in its generally astonishing order and appropriateness has been the machine conception. And by this I refer very specifically to explanations which trace the order of events to the orderly laying down of fixed arrangements (in embryos and in the developed organism). Technology has accustomed us to systems that so limit and prescribe the dynamics of natural forces by means of fixed conditions, connections, paths, etc., that they compel a certain orderly course of events; and from the beginnings of European science, we have tried again and again to work with such ideas even in unconstrained nature, where a striking order of events was first observed. Even today, biology is full of such ideas, and they doubtless often contain some truth. But they can no longer be seen as *basic,* now that the capacity of organic events for regulation has proved so universal. If the mechanical arrangements are so rigid that they really guarantee the normal order of the function through their rigidity, then at the same time they exclude functional reorganization. And how should they be restructured so quickly when necessary, how should new arrangements be produced each time so that, by and large, the result is again just the right one?

Here the conflict between vitalism and the mechanistic way

[1] Cf., for example, A. Bethe, Altes und Neues über die Plastizität des Nervensystems. *Archiv für Psychiatrie und Nervenkrankheiten,* 1926, 76, 81ff.

of thinking had its beginning: The mechanists impatiently cite one or another special case of behavior of inorganic systems which act in some respect nearly like the behavior of organisms. This does not do anybody much good. For we are not interested in more or less chance similarities, but wish to understand fundamentally under what conditions, and by virtue of which of their basic characteristics, inorganic systems show, and must show, the kinds of behavior of organic systems—if that is the case. On the other hand, the vitalists are interested as a rule only in the general question of the autonomy of life. Thus it does not appeal to them either to undertake a dispassionate and impartial investigation of inorganic systems with respect to the different functions and types of behavior which are found in them and which, here and there, resemble organic behavior to various degrees. But only such a *theory of systems* seems to be capable of leading us out of the present situation in which the two sides struggle blindly with each other. Only if we know what aspects of natural events, in principle and in an understandable manner, constitute an approach to organic conditions, only then will we be able to judge whether there is an upper limit to such system characteristics in the inorganic world which necessarily excludes the transition to organic behavior. Such a theory of systems should thus be of the same interest to vitalists as to mechanists, although it does not look for life phenomena which must show autonomy but, on the contrary, from a survey of system behavior in the inorganic world, might discover its positive potentialities and thus its understandable limits. The need for this kind of investigation is very widely felt. Beginnings have indeed been made —e.g., by Roux and by Driesch—but nothing can show more clearly how much remains to be done than the present perplexity about physiological regulations, such as those in Bethe's experiments. These point to "a purposiveness for which an explanation compatible with the thinking of natural science still seems out of reach."[2] This is the situation: Machine conceptions are untenable here, and we are too little accustomed to consider the possible

[2] *Ibid.*, 83.

fundamental kinds of behavior of inorganic systems to know immediately what could replace them. What follows is an attempt to lay a foundation, at least at one point, for the theory of systems which, in time, will become increasingly necessary. From what has been said, it will not be a positive theory of organic regulation. Only the general principles of inorganic processes will be investigated which could come into consideration if we are to understand processes of regulation.[3]

THE problem of regulation concerns the *direction* of natural processes. A principle is to be sought according to which systems under very varied conditions follow just as varied courses which, on the whole and in the end, always converge to the same or essentially the same total states and total processes at which they would have arrived "without disturbance." In this formulation, a distinction between normal and regulatory processes is deliberately avoided, since the principle we are looking for must yield the normal case from normal conditions in the same way as it yields regulations from unusual conditions. For this reason also, we need no longer speak of "disturbances." For this concept, too, presupposes a starting process distinguished as normal, only after which the abnormal conditions of a disturbance are introduced. For the purposes of our discussion, the state after a disturbance (in the case of regulation) may simply be treated as one among many initial states, from which a system always changes in a remarkable way, so far as possible to one and the same final state.

What do we know in general about the direction which changes of systems take in inorganic nature? At the present time physics is inclined to consider only *one* principle within its domain as a statement about the direction of changes of systems, namely the second law of thermodynamics in its various forms. The most general form of this principle, which holds for pro-

[3] This task coincides in part with another, to describe the origin of time-independent states—which I have treated earlier because of their Gestalt properties.

cesses in regions of constant total energy, has the form of an inequality for two states of the system immediately following each other in time:

$$S_2 > S_1$$

(i.e., the entropy of the closed system as a whole increases during system changes). This shows that this is a statement about direction. If entropy cannot increase further under the given conditions, equilibrium must obviously be reached, and thus the Second Law at the same time defines distinguished final states of systems. But if this were really the only principle of direction that holds in inorganic nature, there would be little prospect of understanding the direction of organic processes in terms of physical principles. For the principle of increase of entropy means the direction toward "leveling," homogeneity, and appears therefore to lead away from specific structural differentiation rather than toward it. The statistical theory of the Second Law (Boltzmann) can only strengthen this impression.

Be that as it may, not everything has been said about the direction of system changes even in inorganic nature as long as we speak only of those factors on which the increase of entropy depends. Thus if we do not wish to work with concepts that are too narrow, we must consider what has been lacking so far.

It is correct that an equilibrium is reached in physical systems only if a maximal increase of entropy takes place in them. But the specific state of the system in which the equilibrium exists cannot be understood in terms of the Second Law alone if we are dealing with an equilibrium determined also by *dynamic* principles.[4] The equilibrium of electrical charges on a conductor is reached with the very specific distribution of charges in which each vector inside or tangential to the surface is balanced against all others. Thus this is an equilibrium of factors which are not even mentioned in the theory of purely statistical events. Pure statistics alone would never explain the distribution, improbable

[4] The distinction between dynamic and statistical lawfulness, as in M. Planck, *Neue Bahnen der Physikalischen Erkenntnis*. Leipzig: Johann Ambrosius Barth, 1914.

in itself, of all free electricity on the surface of the conductor. While the increase of entropy (Joule's heat, etc.) is a necessary condition for reaching and maintaining equilibrium, it can nevertheless not at all account for just the specific equilibrium distribution of vectors exactly balancing each other. And what is true in this case holds in general where dynamic factors are balanced in an equilibrium. The increase of entropy is *necessary* for the existence of a time-independent equilibrium, for without it, the currents flowing in the conductor, because of self-induction, would never reach a time-independent equilibrium state, but even with momentary cancellation of all dynamic vectors, the current distribution would continue to oscillate through this state of equilibrium. But the Second Law in and for itself has nothing whatever to say about the fact that just this distribution of charge and of dynamic vectors is maintained on the whole (if no macroscopic currents are still present). Nor can this law by itself make understandable the fact that, after all the distributions of charges and vectors which occur in the conductor initially, at the end surely that distribution appears in which the dynamic vectors cancel one another exactly. How does it happen that just such a state of the system always occurs and is stabilized because of increase of entropy, which constitutes an equilibrium in a sense different from that of the Second Law? This is no doubt a distinguished state, a very special distribution. In the dynamic processes, is there a direction toward such a distribution entirely apart from the Second Law?

These questions sound somewhat strange to the physicist since, as is well known, system changes which do not follow the Second Law, i.e., which show no increase of entropy, are called reversible. Assuming in any state, with any grouping of system parts, that the existing velocities are reversed: the further course of changes in the system would proceed in the opposite direction with the same necessity with which it would otherwise have maintained the original direction. Thus there actually seems to be nothing in purely dynamically determined behavior of systems that distinguishes one direction of processes even from its opposite.

Thus we find ourselves in a paradoxical situation: The fact that, in cases like the one discussed above, distributions of balanced dynamic vectors are always reached, and that the Second Law cannot account for such cases, demands recognition of a principle of direction for pure dynamics as well. The fact that purely dynamic events in general show the property of reversibility appears, on the other hand, to make it impossible to assign to them a particular direction.

This contradiction can be cleared up only if we first consider system changes wholly without increase of entropy, and if we consult the Second Law again only after it has become clear whether or not a principle of direction holds for processes without increase of entropy, in spite of their reversibility.

Something of this sort has been proposed. For example, it has been asserted that a heavy body always *falls* of itself, and does not rise, just as, according to the Second Law, two adjoining quantities of different gases diffuse into one another if left to themselves. In this manner the attempt was made to give a more general formulation to the Second Law, so as to include dynamic events and thus to assign to them too a natural direction. But if the body is, for example, the weight of a pendulum, it is seen that it can rise just as well as fall, and this without any influence foreign to the system. The analogy with diffusion, which always has a particular direction, is thus lacking; the Second Law remains limited to irreversible processes.[5]

Nevertheless there is an extremely simple and almost self-evident principle of direction even in the realm of so-called reversible processes, although admittedly in a somewhat concealed form. For example, we consider conservative mechanical systems, i.e., systems that are not only closed—that can always be achieved by sufficient extension of the region considered—but in which, besides, no transformation of mechanical energy into a different kind of energy (such as heat through friction) takes place. In such systems the effective forces have a potential, i.e., there is a function, the potential energy of the system, the nega-

[5] Cf. M. Planck, *Vorlesungen über Thermodynamik*, 7. Aufl., Berlin und Leipzig: W. DeGruyter, 1922, 84f.

tive derivative of which in any direction equals the force in that direction. If, now, we imagine the moving parts of such a system as initially at rest, and if they are then left to the existing forces, the following holds: "The forces seek to decrease the potential."[6] This principle may sound like an unimportant special theorem, but it is not, since it undoubtedly contains a principle of direction. Of course it will be useful for more general conclusions only when the limiting assumption which we have just made is dropped, i.e., that it concerns only the transition of the system from rest (as the initial state) to movement. This assumption *may* be dropped if we may assume that the forces which act in the system do not depend on the velocities of the parts of the system, but only on their *position*.[7] In this case, all the forces act on every moving particle exactly as if it were a particle at rest in this position. And for the totality of all forces and all parts of the system, therefore, at all times, and with arbitrarily chosen velocities of these parts, the statement must still hold: "The forces seek, on the whole and at all times, to decrease the potential."

We can give this statement a clearer formulation if we consider that how far the system departs from the equilibrium distribution, or whether it is in equilibrium, depends on the mechanical potential or the potential energy. For when the potential of a distribution has reached the smallest value possible under the given conditions, then in accordance with the known connection of potential and forces, it can do no more work, and we have the equilibrium distribution. Therefore, the smaller the potential, the closer is the position which the system has reached to the equilibrium distribution; and therefore our principle of direction may also be expressed in this way: "The forces seek, on the whole and at all times, to bring the system closer to the equilibrium distribution." Anyone who finds this formulation anthropomorphic may also say: "The effect of the forces is, on

---

[6] M. Planck, *Mechanik.*

[7] This assumption is valid for conservative mechanical systems. With electrodynamic systems a complication enters which, however, does not influence the main result of these reflections.

the whole and at all times, in the direction of the equilibrium distribution of the system."

It is not difficult to see how far this statement can serve as a principle of direction and yet not lead to contradiction of the reversibility of the systems under consideration. The decisive point is that the statement does not speak of the movements of parts of the system, but only of the direction in which the momentary forces of the system act on these parts and accelerate them. Obviously, a part of a system can *move* contrary to the sense of the statement, while at the same time, in accordance with the statement, the forces *accelerate* it in the opposite direction, as is the case, e.g., with a pendulum which has just passed its equilibrium position and now moves away from it, against the effective component of gravity. For this reason the principle of direction deserves to be called concealed. It does not, in general, hold for the movements in the system, but only for the actual total direction of the effective forces. Therefore, anyone who is interested only in the *motion* which occurs can correctly deny that a fixed direction of the events in the system is expressed *in it*. Theoretical physics has generally been interested in formulating laws of motion of the systems under consideration. No wonder that the general principle of direction just described is not usually presented. We find it mentioned only insofar as systems go from rest to motion (see above, p. 312) because for this transition the effects of the forces coincide with the directions of the motion. But there can be no doubt that we need the general formulation if we want to understand how a system subject to dynamic forces generally goes over to a state of balance of these forces, or reaches it at least under certain conditions, with which we will deal below.

For obviously it is due to the validity of this dynamic principle of direction that in systems whose changes also depend on the entropy principle, equilibria of the dynamic vectors are actually reached, a state of affairs that could not be understood in terms of the Second Law, because the conceptions underlying the Second Law had nothing at all to say about dynamic vectors. In what way the entropy principle leads to the *realization* of the equilibria, to which, according to the principle of direction, the dynamic forces always tend, remains to be considered. But one thing must be clear from the outset: This principle of direction itself has nothing at all to do with the ideas which underlie the Second Law; neither statistics nor the irreversibility connected with it play any role in the foundation of the principle of direction.

HOW, with the help of the entropy principle, a statement about direction of dynamic forces becomes a statement about direction of the actual system changes can be understood by first realizing why the *actual movements* in a purely dynamic system do not generally follow from the principle of dynamic direction. Indeed, it is not only in the case of a pendulum that the actual movements take place in the direction opposite to the forces as well as corresponding to them; the same holds, in general, for all purely dynamic systems. Motions which, on the whole, reduce the potential go over to motions which increase it, even with any arbitrarily chosen complication of the systems; hence the reversible character of such system changes which, in the customary physical treatment, indicates nothing about the direction of the events.

The laws of motion, e.g., for a conservative mechanical system, must be stated *generally*. This requires also that the parts of the system in the initial state, to which the laws apply, can have arbitrary velocities. For such a consideration, it is only a special case among an infinite number of possible ones if the directions of the initial velocities are just the same as those the forces of the system in the corresponding position would produce by themselves. The initial velocity of a pendulum, for example, may be opposite as well as corresponding to the effective component of gravity. If, then, the motion of the pendulum at first *remains* opposed to the force and to the principle of direction, this is due to inertia; in other words, the effect of a force is simply superimposed on an existing velocity and, as positive or negative acceleration, "respects" the existing velocity as such; this velocity, indifferent to the momentarily effective forces, tends to continue. But naturally, initial velocities, imposed from outside the system, are by no means necessary for inertia to cause the actual motion to take a course opposite to the principle of direction. For if the pendulum begins with zero velocity to follow gravity from any desired initial position (except that of equilibrium), the motion taking place at a given instant is not determined by the momentary forces of the system. A velocity produced by these very forces goes automatically and independently over into the next state of the system; and on this there is now superimposed the increase of velocity which the forces in this next state bring about, etc. In this way, in the course of falling, an even greater velocity is brought about, which is maximal at the moment of passing the equilibrium position and now tends to continue in the same direction, so that from the dynamics of the system itself a kind of motion follows which, beyond the equilibrium position, runs counter to the principle of the direction of forces. In this sense it thus depends on inertia that the principle of direction of the actually occurring processes does not correspond to the principle of direction of the forces, or—and on closer reflection this means the same thing—that such systems show the property of reversibility.

The familiar pendulum is to be treated as a system with *one* degree of freedom. Therefore every velocity possible for the pendulum lies on an arc which represents the path of the pendulum. Therefore the initial velocity also can only correspond to the effective force component of the direction or else be directed exactly opposite to it. Again, therefore, the pendulum certainly goes through the equilibrium position; other paths are impossible. In systems of more than one degree of freedom, this is not the case. There the initial velocities may lie oblique and crosswise to the effective direction of the forces, and since they enter independently in the form of the paths that arise, the initial velocities now even partly determine to what extent the system can ever lower its potential. The simplest examples show this; it will suffice if we consider the path of a planet around the sun. If it ever has a velocity which is not directed exactly away from the sun or directly toward it, then—assuming the absence of any friction—the planet can never reach the sun, although the force present is always directed to the sun and causes acceleration only in this direction. It is not the momentary force that determines the momentary direction of the orbit but, in accordance with the rule of the parallelogram of forces, the change of velocity due to the force is added geometrically to the velocity already present and continuing independently. Thus the planet does not come closer to the sun than its perihelion, where the minimal value of the potential is reached which this effect of the initial velocity permits. And since precisely here the planet has the greatest velocity, it immediately travels beyond this position into regions which again correspond to a higher potential.

The process remains the same if, instead of such simple cases, we consider cases of any arbitrary degree of complexity. *Everywhere,* not the actual forces alone, but these and the previously existing velocities, persisting through inertia, determine the actual movement. From this it invariably follows that the actually achieved configurations of relatively least potential energy may be far removed from those paths along which the system would move if it were a matter only of the direction of its forces. And even if no initial velocities are present, or only such as the forces of the system could themselves have produced, then the process will indeed run off in the beginning in accordance with the direction of the forces; but (as with the pendulum) because of inertia, it will travel beyond the equilibrium position (the potential minimum) and will then move against the direction of the forces.[8]

From this it follows that the independence of the existing velocities, their persistence without regard to the actual position of the system and the forces corresponding to this position of

[8] As long as we make the assumption that no factors of the nature of friction enter in, then everything that was said in the last two paragraphs is valid, also e.g. where the forces under consideration represent surface tension or the electrostatic field.

the system, in other words, the inertia effect, is the only reason why there is not a principle of direction for system motions to correspond to the principle of direction of the forces. Inertia is thus the reason why the events in such systems are reversible, i.e., can proceed in one or the other direction, why they behave indifferently in relation to the direction of time. Without inertia in this sense, they would follow the direction of the forces and end up directly in a permanent state of equilibrium, insofar as such a thing exists at all. When Planck refers to the fact that the reversibility of such processes follows from the mathematical nature of the laws of motion, insofar as these contain only the second derivative with respect to time, in the form of expressions for acceleration and force, time thus only to the second power, and therefore not affected by a change of sign of the time variable, this basically means much the same thing: namely, that the forces actually determine *accelerations* in the system and not velocities which are, on the contrary, independent of these because of inertia. This state of affairs is implicitly contained in all equations of analytical mechanics, and therefore we cannot derive a principle of direction from any of them.

But in view of what follows, we must once more remember that the direction principle described above is not in any way affected by this. In spite of all this, the effective direction of the forces always corresponds to it. The pendulum swings through the equilibrium position because of inertia, and thus its motion begins to go against the principle of direction; but at the same moment the effective force component also reverses its direction against the movement and consequently again points to the equilibrium position. If the direction of force and velocity, and therefore also the direction of acceleration and velocity, have agreed in the approach to the equilibrium position, then acceleration and velocity come into opposition as soon as the pendulum begins to recede from the distinguished position and acceleration becomes deceleration. In general, so long as the motion of any conservative system brings it closer to an equilibrium state, the forces on the whole cause acceleration; as soon as the motion leads away from equilibrium, the forces begin on the whole to cause deceleration. So, too, in the astronomical case; the planet will be accelerated by the sun until it comes as near to it as possible; but as soon as it has passed the perihelion, gravitation begins to reduce its velocity, etc. For any (conservative) mechanical systems, the same thing may be derived from the energy principle:

$$\text{Potential energy} + \text{Kinetic energy} = \text{constant}$$

As soon as the potential energy in any conservative mechanical system has reached the minimum that it can assume compatible with the given initial conditions and the given system properties, further motion must then take place with reduction of the kinetic energy, i.e., so that on the whole the velocities of the system are reduced. But this can only happen since from then on the forces act, on the whole, against the departure from the configuration of least potential energy, thus in the direction of negative acceleration.

SYSTEMS of the kind described so far show no obvious "capacity for regulation." The configurations of relatively least potential energy, which appear during the motion, depend, as we have seen, on the initial positions and the initial velocities. There is thus no unique final state toward which such a system moves, independent of the initial constellation. And this quite apart from the fact that, in every case, it immediately leaves the configuration of relatively least potential. On the other hand, the principle of direction of forces, according to which the forces act constantly in the direction of lowering the potential energy, holds for such systems; and this means an approach to conditions of equilibrium. It is easy to say what would happen if the actual changes of the system also followed this principle, i.e., if the above described inertial phenomena were in some way eliminated. In this case, the system in question, following the direction of the forces only, would constantly lose potential energy, and if, on the whole, a minimum of potential energy lies along

this path, then it will be reached, and thus the equilibrium configuration will be attained. Therefore we need only to consider
the equilibrium conditions in order to discover on what factors
the final equilibrium depends; from these it must follow whether
or not such systems possess "regulatory" properties after the hypothesized elimination of all inertia effects. As is well known,
that equilibrium condition (the principle of virtual displacements) implies that the system has come into equilibrium if its
forces in the aggregate can perform no work in the configuration
in question. This will be expressed by a homogeneous equation in
which only the forces enter (taken for the constellation in question) and certain small spatial shifts (the virtual displacements
for this constellation) consistent with the system conditions. In
this equation initial coordinates and initial velocities of the system thus play no part. Accordingly it could be concluded that
those systems for which an equilibrium exists at all, given a
particular set of system conditions, always reach the same final
configuration from any initial state and therefore, in general,
reach it by different paths. Thus they show "regulation." As we
will now see, this is correct with one single qualification.

In a conservative mechanical system there are always velocities which tend to continue without regard to the actual forces.
To this extent, a system in which such inertial effects have been
eliminated seems to represent a fiction. Nevertheless, the fiction
becomes reality as soon as the system under consideration shows
an increase in entropy (is subject to the Second Law) and is thus
no longer a conservative system. In contrast to the principle of
direction of dynamic forces, this persistence of velocities once
they exist or develop, independent of any forces, may be considered by itself; and so the question arises in what manner this
factor may be eliminated. If a system shows friction at all, which
is a major form of increase of entropy, then the amount of friction depends on the velocities of the parts of the system: the
greater the velocities, the more the friction. And now, since friction transforms macroscopic velocities of the system into un-
orderly microscopic heat motion, it tends to eliminate from the

macroscopic behavior of the system those velocity components which do not lie in the direction of forces and are not produced by these or maintained against friction.[9]

After the earlier discussion, it is clear that the processes in the system are thus fundamentally changed and, in general, go very different ways than before. It is likewise clear that this change of the processes which, with increasing friction, are ever more determined only by the forces and coincide with their direction, makes the behavior of the system conform increasingly with that principle according to which the *forces always* act. A planet which moves in a medium with friction would everywhere have less tangential velocity than in a frictionless medium. Consequently, the momentary velocity component produced by the effect of gravity would count relatively more strongly in the parallelogram of velocities, and the path of the planet would be curved more toward the sun. Since this would hold for every element of the path, instead of an ellipse, the planet would describe a spiral with ever closer approach to the sun.

Which forms of motion appear in an individual case will depend on how great the friction is, whether the friction coefficient is the same everywhere in the system, etc. It is not relevant to this general discussion to choose particular examples from the many possible ones, since we are in the fortunate position of being able to choose, for comparison with the most important organic cases, an extreme example which is especially simple. At least for the rather slow processes of which morphogenesis consists, it can be said with certainty that they take their course with the greatest friction, in such a way that directed velocities *without* corresponding force in the same direction practically never occur, just as, for example, in the theory of electric currents in liquid conductors, no directed movement of ions has to be assumed that could persist independently of forces. Therefore the *velocity* and not the acceleration is proportional to the force in such a case.

[9] The contrast between "macroscopic" and "microscopic" as in the writings of Planck. Cf., for example, M. Planck, *Acht Vorlesungen über theoretische Physik*, Leipzig: S. Hirzel, 1910, 46ff.

Let us assume such an amount of friction that all velocities vanish which are not produced and maintained specifically by the effective forces. Then, according to our earlier considerations, the principle of direction for the totality of *forces* must completely turn into a principle of direction for the actual *displacements,* because the latter are now completely determined by the former. The direction of such events must therefore be constantly toward the reduction of the potential energy, and if an equilibrium can thereby be reached at all, the transformation of the total system will certainly finally end in it. Initial velocities, arbitrarily chosen, can obviously now have no more influence on the final state eventually reached, since (macroscopic) velocities are possible only insofar as a force corresponds to them. But the initial positions of the parts of the system will be just as irrelevant, insofar as the potential—from any initial configuration on—must always decrease, and insofar as we can assume that with the given system properties, there is a *unique* constellation in which the forces are balanced, thus in which an equilibrium is reached.

As far as the above discussion goes, it is a general characteristic of such systems with maximal friction always to go over to the same end state from different beginning positions; they "regulate." It would be well to formulate this result somewhat more precisely. In every system there are properties which are not altered by the system events, on which, rather, as "system conditions," those events depend. Our discussion has now shown that a system *event* in general brings about one and the same final state by traversing different paths, from different initial positions, and thus also "after disturbances," i.e., it regulates. This end state is only determined by the totality of those fixed system properties which were called "system conditions" above, and of course also by the nature of the forces acting in the system. Accordingly, there is a regulation for the dynamically determined (i.e., process determined) system properties. If, on the other hand, a change takes place in the system *conditions* (which are not altogether dynamically maintained) then, in general, there is no regulation for such a disturbance. Consequently the system *events*, too, will then take a different course and lead to a different final state which corresponds to the changed conditions. With this we come to an observation which sets a necessary limitation to the validity of our reflections up to this point.

Organic systems, too, do not always show themselves capable of regulation, and so it would be suspect at the outset if the principle of direction in the inorganic world could do more than exists in the organic realm. A quite simple example shows at once how conditions can block complete regulation, by making the final result of a dynamic process dependent upon the initial conditions. If materials of different specific gravity are all mixed together in a cylindrical container, and do not dissolve in one another, and if the internal friction of the whole is great, eventually there will be a state in which the materials are arranged in horizontal layers according to their specific gravity. But if, for example, lead shot is placed in the container, and if a sieve is placed horizontally at some distance from the bottom, through which the shot cannot pass, then the final state will depend on whether all the shot was below the sieve at the beginning, or above it in some quantity. Such examples can be constructed in various forms. Common to all is the fact that a part of the fixed system conditions makes a particular path impassable and that, consequently, whether or not the optimal equilibrium is reached depends on the initial positions of the parts of the system. Even under these conditions, the system will always approach this equilibrium as far as possible, since it decreases its potential energy as much as possible. But the final state actually reached may fall short of the optimal equilibrium to various degrees, depending on the initial conditions. To be sure, in the comparison of inorganic with organic processes, we may not assume that obstacles of just this kind deserve special consideration. But it had to be mentioned that the earlier discussion did not include them; besides, they make more readily understandable the following impediment to regulations, important in a biological context.

Obstacles which do not themselves take part in the dynamics of the system, but codetermine these dynamics only as unchangeable conditions, can also occur through events within the system itself. Our argument up to now dealt mainly with mechanical systems in the narrower sense; but it can be extended and may be carried over without essential change, e.g., to the direction effect of surface tension, also to the distribution of electrostatic charges, etc. In the same way, we may consider the particularly important systems in which different kinds of forces are effective at the same time as, for example, surface tension, gravitation, and electrostatic forces, or still others besides. The "directed" energy of the system, which is constantly reduced with the transformation of the system and finally falls to a minimal value, is then only composed of the different kinds of energy together, and the equilibrium is then reached if the minimum condition is fulfilled for all of them *as a whole*. Even such systems will regulate, given sufficient friction, insofar as special preconditions do not favor some initial conditions over others, as in the above example (sieve). Meantime, we have to consider that, among the kinds of process which take part in the system events, there may also be those which represent very important examples of irreversible changes as, for example, chemical reactions which lead to the precipitation of certain compounds, perhaps in characteristic forms.[10] It is clear that once such a process has taken place, the forces acting in the system will not always be able to reverse it again, so that from now on an additional unchangeable system condition is present. If, now, a disturbance is created, i.e., if the system is diverted from its path, this fixed system condition which has meantime appeared is in the way of the dynamic restructuring in the direction of the equilibrium that would otherwise be reached, and it *remains* in the way. The system will still, to be sure, come as close as possible to the final state that it would otherwise reach, but it will not actually reach it. Then we have incomplete regulation. In principle, such a case is quite similar to the example of the sieve. The only difference is that, in

[10] There really should be a general discussion here about the relation to regulation of those (macroscopic) processes which come entirely under the entropy principle, i.e., heat conduction and diffusion. In the interest of brevity, I will omit this discussion. But even in such cases "regulation" occurs.

place of a given system condition, a condition has appeared which the system events themselves have formed. At any rate, the consideration of inorganic cases permits us, without difficulty, to discover principles according to which the capacity for regulation may be limited.

WITH this, we have a rough sketch of a solution of the problem set at the beginning. Insofar as inorganic systems follow their own forces and thus, through factors of the nature of friction, the persistence of macroscopic velocities without corresponding forces is prevented, they transform themselves in the direction of potential decrease. If the given system conditions permit a state of equilibrium to be reached, it is one and the same for quite different starting positions of the parts of the system, i.e., the systems "regulate"—insofar as the system conditions do not preclude certain paths and insofar as new fixed conditions of this kind are not produced by the process itself. Besides purely statistical laws (as those of diffusion, heat conduction, etc.), this is the only principle of direction that is to be discovered in the inorganic world. The increase of entropy plays a role in it only inasfar as it allows the system changes to follow the (entirely independent) principle of direction of forces by damping out unrelated macroscopic velocities. As a principle of direction of essentially dynamic nature, it is so general that there would be no place for a second principle. If, therefore, it is to be determined whether regulation phenomena in the organic world could be understood from the point of view of natural science, such an investigation must develop and test those possibilities which follow from this principle of direction (as well as from *purely* statistical laws). No other way is open.[11]

[11] In the nineteenth century, different philosophers have tried to lay down principles for the general direction of natural events, without specifically handling the question of regulation: thus Spencer, Fechner, Petzoldt, and others all speak of a "tendency to stability." As far as I can see, they proceed here either in a half speculative manner—as, for example, in Spencer's statements which leave Maxwell deeply dissatisfied—or they speak of this tendency on the basis of rough empirical impressions as to what happens, as a rule, on this earth and in space. The simple line of

The investigation up to now had one positive result: There are easily characterized inorganic systems of all possible degrees of complexity which show the basic property of regulatory behavior in an understandable manner, and must show it. From this in itself it does not follow that organic regulations depend on the same principles. For organic regulations have other peculiarities which we have not discussed, on whose account we could still perhaps be forced to have recourse to other principles than those of physics. Only the investigation of specific types of systems can show whether, for these peculiarities, too, an explanation from inorganic principles is possible. But in any case, such an investigation would have to start out from the principle of direction just described.

It is easy to enumerate several points where greater precision of the concepts employed so far must immediately carry us farther.

First, we have so far assumed that the time-independent final state to which the systems last discussed change is a static equilibrium. For the comparison with biological cases, steady states have much greater relevance as final states, as well as combinations of these with static equilibria. It is thus to be investigated whether; and in what way, the principle of direction leads to steady states, and what this has to do with regulation.

In the second place, the concept of a system which has been used up to now is perhaps not to be considered completely parallel to the concept of an organism. For that concept of a system refers to a region for which, as a whole, there is no question either of taking in or expending energy. Naturally this does not

---

thinking presented here I have, to my surprise, never been able to discover, not even any derivation of why, and in what form, a principle of direction exists also in pure dynamics. In J. Petzoldt (*Das allgemeinste Entwicklungsgesetz*, München, 1923) there is the error described above (p. 311), by which the relation of increase of entropy to dynamic direction becomes completely confused. (On this error, cf., for example, M. Planck, *Vorlesungen über Thermodynamik*, 7. Aufl., 85, n. 1.) The principle of LeChatelier and Braun might, on the other hand, have a close relation to the principle of direction discussed here; it is hardly only a form of the Second Law, as many believe. I hope to go into this matter in greater detail elsewhere.

hold, for example, for the organism during morphogenesis. What we have called system is, then, the organism together with its environment, which maintains an obvious energy exchange with it. A pressing task will then consist of the investigation of physicochemical cases where, as with the embryo in morphogenesis, an open system (with respect to energy exchange) is clearly segregated within the closed total system.

16: Direction of processes in living systems

OUR topic, "Organism and Machine," is clearly a short form of the following question: Can the functioning of organisms be explained in terms of the conditions and actions which are found in inanimate machines? It might at first appear that this question ought to be answered by experts in biology, namely, by anatomists, physiologists, and biochemists. Unfortunately, these experts are not inclined to deal with such general issues. If we were to ask a man who is now studying, say, the role of sodium ions in the transmission of nerve impulses, he would probably tell us to leave him, please, alone—that he has no time for speculation. Who would not sympathize with this scientist who likes to work on problems for which precise solutions can probably be found in the near future? On the other hand, specialists should not criticize us too severely if we are interested also in more general issues. For, if the behavior of sodium ions in the active nerve fiber were perfectly known, if we had discovered the last vitamin, and so forth, we should still have to ask why, taken

From *The Scientific Monthly*, 1955, 80 (1), 29–32. Reprinted by permission of the American Association for the Advancement of Science.

together and interrelated, the various operations of the organism tend to preserve its existence as well as they do. Can this achievement be explained in terms of machine conceptions?

Actually, the philosophers of science and the theoretical physicists may be at least as competent to clarify this issue as are the specialists in biology. I shall now try to indicate how these peoplé might approach our problem.

The tendency of organisms to maintain themselves by their own processes is too obvious to need illustrations. But how are we to decide whether this tendency can be explained in machine terms, if we are not sure what we mean by a machine? Is just any part of inanimate nature a machine? Sometimes we talk as though we used the concept in this extremely wide sense. Even the physical universe as a whole may occasionally have been called a machine. The trouble is that the same term has also a much more specific meaning, and that, when discussing the topic "Organism and Machine," we are for the most part not aware of this ambiguity. A machine in the more restricted sense is a physical system in which rigid arrangements or constraints compel events to take a certain course. In a well-constructed machine, this influence is one-sided. The constraints of the machine exclude all possibilities of action which would not be in line with the intended course; but, typically, the constraints cannot be altered by forces which action exerts on such solid conditions.

A simple example will make this clearer. One can easily compel an electric current to take a course which has the shape of a W. For this purpose, it will suffice to conduct the current through a rigid wire, part of which has this shape, and is kept in this shape by being firmly attached to a suitable support. There is nothing in a current as such that favors this particular shape. The form of a W is impressed upon the current only by the described arrangement. It is in this fashion that physical events are forced to follow prescribed ways in man-made machines.

We must next show that the form which a physical process assumes can also be determined in an entirely different manner. Take this example. A thoroughly flexible insulated wire which forms a closed curve is placed on a smooth and plane surface. At first, the curve may be given any arbitrarily chosen shape. This shape will at once be altered if now an electromotive force is induced in the wire so that a current is set up. The shape is changed by the magnetic field of this current, and the direction of the change is such that it enlarges the area surrounded by the conductor. Actually, the conductor may be transformed into a circle, the shape in which it circumscribes the greatest possible area.

The difference between this and the preceding example must be obvious. In the present situation, there are no particular constraints by which a special form of the conductor and the current is prescribed. Rather, it is the free dynamics of the system which brings about the change and determines its direction. Obviously, then, we have good reasons for distinguishing between these two factors on which the form of physical events in a system may depend; constraints, on the one hand, and directions inherent in the dynamics of the system, on the other hand. In a given instance, both factors may, of course, operate at the same time.

When trying to understand phenomena which exhibit a striking order or show a persistent direction, man thinks more readily in terms of constraints by which such facts might be explained than in dynamic terms. Thus the remarkable order of movements in the translunar world was once explained by crystal spheres to which the stars were supposed to be attached. In this fashion they had to perform prescribed movements. Again, when Descartes tried to explain the order of organic processes, he began at once to think in terms of anatomical arrangements which enforce this order. It never occurred to him that, quite apart from such arrangements, directions inherent in biological dynamics might play a major part in the self-maintenance of living systems. Even in our time, it seems sometimes to be felt that, when the dynamics of a system is allowed to operate on its own, the result is likely to be chaos.

In typical inanimate machines, operations are constrained to take courses which serve human purposes. But systems may have the characteristics of machines without having been built by man. The crystal spheres of Aristotelian astronomy, for instance, were assumed to be of divine origin; and Descartes probably believed that the anatomy of organisms had been chosen by the Lord, who in this fashion made it possible for them to maintain themselves. In our time, evolution has taken the place of such agents. Evolution has, of course, no interests and no purposes. Nonetheless, if we follow Darwin, living systems tend to change in a particular direction, the direction in which their chances of survival are increased; for, those that do not so change will soon succumb in the general competition inherent in living. But this does not explain the changes as such. What is their nature from the point of view of science? Darwin did not explain his theory in specific physical terms. In this respect, his work does not entirely satisfy the theorist of our time. However, his statements clearly imply that evolution changes mainly anatomical conditions; in other words, that it builds better and better arrangements by which organic events are forced to occur in biologically useful directions.

In this assumption, only one point seems to me open to criticism. Anatomical arrangements as such produce no action; they merely modify actions which occur for dynamic reasons. Consequently, the principles of dynamics cannot be ignored in a theory of evolution. But, actually, they are almost being ignored in this particular theory. Does the general principle of evolution contain any implications concerning the dynamics of organic processes? There is at least one such implication. In a strict theory of evolution, it must be assumed that evolution has changed no law of dynamics, and that it has introduced neither new forces nor new elementary processes. In this respect, the principle is therefore one of invariance rather than of change. Hence, in considering any *events* which occur in organisms, we have to think, first of all, of the laws of dynamics which are here involved. Presumably, these laws are still the same as they were before organisms appeared on this planet. Only as a second step can we then proceed to examine the particular conditions under which such laws now operate in given living systems.

Nobody will deny that, on the whole, histological facts serve to give organic events a useful form. The anatomy of the human eye, for instance, can hardly be described without referring to the use of this structure in clear visual perception. So numerous are examples of this kind that, without any doubt, organisms may to a large extent be regarded as machines in our more restricted sense of the term. Are we to conclude that living systems can be entirely explained in this fashion? Clearly, no such conclusion would be justified, because it can be shown that organisms maintain themselves, not only because of useful anatomical conditions in their interior, but also for reasons inherent in the principles of dynamics.

In the *first* place, we must remember a simple biological fact. It is true that certain anatomical arrangements force processes to take a course which helps the organism to survive. But what is the nature of such arrangements? Are they really comparable to the rigid constraints which we find in inanimate machines? In a most important sense, they are not. The very way in which they exist differs widely from the way in which constraints exist in machines. For the most part, such constraints consist of solid objects; they are composed of permanent materials which have been given one shape or another depending upon their particular purpose. On the other hand, no part of the anatomy of an organism is a permanent object. Rather, any such part must be regarded as a steady state, only the shape of which persists, while its material is all the time being removed and replaced by metabolic events. Surely, such steady states are fairly resistant and can, therefore, serve as constraining devices for more temporary functions. But from the point of view of our general topic, it is a most important fact that all organs, large or small, are processes rather than permanent objects. For it follows that any question concerning the useful course of those temporary functions must now be asked again with reference to the anatomical arrangements by which this course is enforced. If these arrangements are actually also processes, why is the form of *these* processes maintained for long periods, as it must be if the organism is to survive? It will hardly be suggested that the shape of the anatomical parts under consideration is maintained because there are further anatomical constraints which force metabolic events to operate in this fashion. For, what has just been said about the former anatomical arrangements would at once have to be repeated with regard to such hypothetical arrangements of a second order. They, too, would surely be steady forms of processes, rather than solid objects, and would therefore be subject to the same reasoning. Anybody who is familiar with the history of science will admit that, when theories take such a turn, something is probably wrong with basic premises.

At this point, some people take refuge in vitalism. I am not inclined to do so. It seems preferable now to consider a *second* reason which is opposed to an interpretation of organic events in machine terms alone. This reason is derived from physics. The organism would be a machine in the strict sense only if the behavior of *all* its parts were prescribed by special anatomical devices. Now this is clearly not the case. It will suffice if we mention one example. The distribution of the tissue fluid which pervades all parts of the body is not determined by particular devices. This continuum has, as the physicists would say, innumerable "degrees of freedom." To a large extent, its distribution is therefore a matter of dynamics. It follows that, if nevertheless this distribution tends to be favorable to survival, the self-maintaining conduct of the organism must be derived partly from a direction inherent in dynamics. Since the same consideration holds for other parts of the organism, principles of dynamics obviously play an important part in its self-maintenance.

This is my main point. From here, we should, of course, proceed to a thorough examination of dynamics in general, in order to discover what directions it takes in systems of one kind or another. Unfortunately, knowledge in this field is so restricted that only a few remarks can be made at the present time.

What we learn from the physicists in this respect may be formulated as follows. If, in a closed system, macroscopic velocities are constantly being destroyed by friction, transformations in the system will be such that the sum of all energies capable of producing further transformations decreases. When these energies have reached a minimal amount, the system will no longer change. Although this is a perfectly good principle, it cannot, in its present formulation, be applied to the organism. For the organism is obviously not a closed system; moreover, while the direction indicated by the principle may be called "downward," the direction of events in healthy organisms is on the whole surely not "downward" but, in a good sense, "upward." Thus the energy content of a young organism generally increases, and when at times it spends more than it gains, events soon take a turn by which the loss is balanced, if not overbalanced. Nevertheless no serious difficulty arises at this point, because the direction which events take in open systems need not be the same as that which they take in closed systems. In fact, events in some simple physical systems tend to develop "upward," just as does the energy content of a young organism. For instance, any fire which is locally started, and then grows or spreads, exhibits this behavior. It can do so because the first weak flame is in contact with combustible material and with the oxygen of the surrounding air, which together constitute a store of potential energy. In other words, the flame is an open system, and the closed system which must here be considered contains in addition this source of energy. For the closed system as a whole, it remains true that it must develop "downward." But it does not follow that the same must happen to the part of it in which we are interested, namely, the flame. For as soon as the fire is started, it begins to feed on the store of potential energy, so that its own energy grows.

It is quite possible that the same principle is involved when a young organism develops "upward." For, this organism is also an open system surrounded by stores of energy which it absorbs and spends in growing. Taken together, the food which it eats and the oxygen which it inhales constitute large amounts of energy. Only one point remains to be added. When a flame, say that of a candle, has developed to maximal size, it maintains itself at this level so far as it can. Need we be surprised if, once an organism is fully developed, it maintains its vigor so far as circumstances permit?

I must confess that, although this reasoning may point in

the right direction, it is, for my taste, too abstract and general. There are too many problems to which it does not refer at all. For instance, the fact that organisms are open systems does not protect them against illness or old age. In both situations their energy tends to decrease. Moreover, sooner or later organisms die, even if they are not injured by outside agents. This means, of course, that open systems *may* develop "upward," that they *may* maintain themselves in states of high vigor, but that they need not, and do not, do so under all circumstances. What, then, are the conditions under which the present principle works? When, on the other hand, will an open system deteriorate even though energy can be transferred to it from an outside store? So long as we cannot answer such questions, we are far from understanding the way in which living systems maintain themselves. As a further criticism, I should like to point out that between certain simple systems in physics, which develop "upward," and the organisms with their tremendous variety of operations there still remains an enormous gap. As a result, the behavior of the former does not help us very much when we try to clarify that of the latter.

Such shortcomings may, of course, be remedied in the future. Many physicists are now strongly interested in biological questions. It should not be difficult for them to discover under what circumstances open systems of the inanimate world show the "upward" trend, and under what others they do not. Moreover, such physicists might also investigate open systems which are not so simple as the flame of a candle. The most astounding characteristic of organisms is the fact that so many processes in their interior virtually seem to cooperate when, as a whole, they maintain the organism's existence. Let us hope that the problem which arises here can be solved with the conceptual tools of physics. But it must be admitted that at the present time the task still seems enormous. Even macroscopic physics is not yet a completed science. It has hardly begun to study the behavior of open systems.

six

SPECIAL PROBLEMS

17: The naturalistic interpretation
of man (the trojan horse)

IT must have been two years ago. The dean of men at Swarthmore and I were sitting together and talking. "Why is it," he was saying, "that nowadays so many of our boys are in an attitude of almost permanent apathy? Of apathy toward practically everything? I don't see, the boys tell me, why we should get excited about anything. Isn't this a depressing attitude?"

I admitted that it was depressing; but I could not tell the dean much that was new to him. He knew as well as I did that human beings are fundamentally all right as long as they have any goal or standard that invites and justifies action toward it. They work, they fight, they suffer, and sometimes they throw their lives away for a goal. Apathy, on the other hand, is the necessary consequence of any situation from which all goals have been removed. There have been times in which, to a young man, the world was so full of fascinating goals that he would

---

This is an informal talk which Professor Köhler gave at Swarthmore College, probably between 1942 and 1945. A few very minor editorial changes have been made. The American Philosophical Society is in possession of the original and has granted the privilege of publication.

not know to which to turn first. There have also been attempts to concentrate on certain goals because all others seemed to derive their power from those primary ones. In the seventeenth and eighteenth centuries the primary standard was, of course, reason; and to make things more rational appeared a great task. Others were not so sure about this. Mere reason, they said, impoverishes the world. Why live in an ice box? What about the sweet music of feeling, the daemonic power of passion, the unpredictable visions of genius? Thus the colorful clouds of romanticism began to trail across the landscape of history.

But to a degree all people reason, even inspired romantics, and some findings of reason simply remained, entirely unaffected by Sturm und Drang. Moreover, reason had taken a sturdy wife, empirical evidence by name, and from their union had sprung a number of healthy children, the sciences. The intoxication of extreme romanticism soon led to a next morning's headache, and when the headache was over, a chastened world began eagerly to take part in the sober games of those children. After a while nothing really counted but those games. The rules of the games became the rules of everything. It was quite clear that the more you played the games, the better everything would become. This was the great era of science; and the idol of the time was the positive fact. The sciences which played the game most successfully were the natural sciences; therefore, whoever wanted to play watched first of all these champions. Their scores filled the books, the papers, and after a while the very head of the common man. Thus grew up the religion which is called positivism because it believes in positive facts and in nothing else. But for the reason which I have just mentioned, this denomination may also be called naturalistic positivism. For it was not just any facts, but facts in the style of natural science which the new religion exhibited in murals along the walls of its laboratory churches. You will easily recognize that from this situation emerged the era in which we now live, the era of general gloom. The preceding ages, you will remember, had at least one great goal or another. We no longer commit such a primitive error. In polite society one no longer wears goals. Meeting a man who professes to have and to believe in a firm goal—it is like seeing a woman whose skirts sweep the ground.

The gloom is about man. Suppose we had with us tonight a representative of the church of gloom. What would he say if we were to ask him questions about his sad gospel? The other day I heard such a person talk to a student who had not yet fully absorbed the doctrine of disillusion.

"Young man," he said, "do you realize that one function of your organism after another is being satisfactorily explained by science? We now know about the secretions of your glands, about the nerve impulses in your neurons, and about the electric waves in your brain. Rapidly the time is approaching in which no hiding place will be left to any old superstitions about life. There is no special vital force in your body. In fact, no principle is involved in living which does not stem from ordinary nature. And do you know where you have come from? From a tiny bit of protoplasm, a cell—that's all. Reflect a moment. What does this mean? There is no evidence whatever that any mental function resided in that first cell. You don't believe in miracles, do you? Well, then, gradually many cells replaced the first cell; these cells gathered in organs; a nervous system developed. Presently you began to feel, to desire, and eventually to think. If no miracle suddenly added these mental facts to your bodily functions, does it not follow that all this mental life of yours is merely a by-product of purely natural processes? And this term I want you to take in a radical sense. The cell from which you developed was once a part of another cell, this again came from another cell, and so forth, back through millions of years, and through thousands of generations. We have, however, convincing reasons to believe that, as our thought wanders backwards and focuses on cell after cell, these cells differ from their modern offspring. They are simpler. Moreover, recent discoveries make us doubt whether, if we go farther back, there were any proper cells at all. Rather, the first cells seem to have developed from huge molecules, curious chemical compounds which had certain characteristics in common with cells, while on the other hand they were undoubtedly chemical molecules like others.

"We have just traced your ancestry to chemical particles. Miracles apart, therefore, all your mental life, your first love and your best thought, your admirations and your moral indignations, all spring from inanimate nature. Nor will this thought surprise anybody who considers present man in the sober spirit of science. The philosophers talk a bit too much about the dignity of thought and the insuperable strength of moral resolve. They ought to be more realistic about such matters. For any normal function, a human brain needs a constant oxygen supply. Reduce this supply below a certain level, and disorders will appear which no dignity of thought and no firmness of resolve can prevent. Reduce the supply still further, and the mental world of your subject will disappear entirely as he loses consciousness. Without a common inanimate gas, O_2, there can be neither high nor low mental processes. Moreover, if this condition is maintained for any length of time, those processes will never return to their normal form. Go a bit farther, and they will never return in any form, because your subject will now be dead."

So spoke the prophet. I found it difficult to keep a straight face. Personally, I find that there is something to be said for the message of gloom. If the gospel is preached consistently, it always makes me feel cheerful. Try it. Read Schopenhauer. I can never read much of this pessimistic author without feeling a curious exhilaration. The present prophet, too, had been very funny about the student's ancestor, who happened to be a big molecule. Obviously, from the point of view of the prophet, somebody who had molecules among his forefathers could not amount to very much. It was as though a Main Liner were sneering at another person merely because his grandfather was a truck driver. As I saw it, there was no reason for snobbery. On the contrary, I began to feel a great interest in molecules and more respect for these creatures than I had ever had before.

But the prophet had just presented an argument which seemed to impress the student. An imaginary subject had first lost consciousness and then had died because the prophet did not give him enough oxygen.

So I said: "Sorry. I must have missed your point. You said

that in the absence of oxygen a subject faints and dies? What about it?"

"Why do you ask?" answered the prophet. "Surely he dies."

"Well," I said, "if it is nothing else, why should we get excited? Death is an old experience of mankind. People have always fainted and died for a number of reasons. They were wounded in battle, fell from cliffs, were drowned in the sea, had heart failure or pneumonia; and sometimes they simply died from exhaustion or because they were too old to go on living. I do not see that the situation grows any worse if we learn that among other causes of death there is lack of oxygen. For thousands of years, it is true, people have dreaded death in all its particular forms. Nevertheless, when death was not exactly imminent, young people and people in good health have always found life a most worthwhile adventure and its goals distinctly attractive. What is changed in this respect if you now mention a particular form of death which for some reason seems to you more scientific than others?"

The prophet gave me an ugly look; he did not answer but addressed himself once more to the student. "One thing that follows from my argument is all important. Man is just a part of nature like other things. As such, he is subject to the same laws that hold everywhere in the world. There was a time when philosophers and religious people thought that man was more and that he was better. He was then supposed to have a special gift of reasoning which transcended anything found in nature. He was also believed to have a sense of duty which told him about right and wrong, an inner voice which he could follow, whatever happened to his lower and merely natural parts. Now, on closer inspection, it has been shown that such beliefs are utterly at variance with the findings of modern science. When it comes to positive facts, what is logic? The philosophers of science have recently shown that logic is no more than the grammar of a certain language and, like any other grammar, a kind of convention. We do like to stick to this language. And I will not deny that there are good reasons for doing so. But don't say that anything in this field transcends the competence of natural science. Never forget that man is a product of evolution. Evolution has given him eyes and ears, muscles and nerves. Evolution has likewise given him forms of mental processes which you call logic. What is their nature? In the course of evolution those individuals have survived longer, and therefore have had more children, whom accidental variations of the germ cells had gradually equipped with eyes and ears. Similarly those have survived longer and have had more offspring in whose brains evolution established certain mechanisms of thought. Man, as we now know him, is almost invariably endowed with the mechanisms that make for these particular thought processes. Again, being a social animal, man has developed such emotional responses to situations as make the social group, and with it the individual, better fit to survive in a dangerous world. This is the origin of logic and of ethics. But at the same time it is, of course, the explanation of their nature. For by no means did I say that in the course of evolution we have approached increasing insight into truth and duty. Such a statement would imply that things like truth and duty can be defined quite independently of evolution. Actually, these very terms have to be discarded. Right in a logical sense and good in the sense of ethics are concepts which do not fit into the scheme of science. Scientific concepts refer to facts and to actual events. Since ultimately everything has to be explained in the language of physics, and since no physical fact is either right or good, it is the very meaning of a scientific interpretation that it replaces right and good by purely factual terms. Therefore what I meant was that in the course of evolution individuals with certain responses were likely to die early, while those with certain other responses lived longer. At present, almost only people of the second type are left.

"To make quite sure that you understand what I wanted to show you, I will add this: I did not say that survival and having offspring are good things. I only said that this is what happens, and what had to happen, under the rules of evolution. In other words, I explained the natural causes which make uninformed people talk about right and good. Right and good as such? Ask yourself whether these terms can express more than misunderstandings. Such terms stem from a prescientific age and ought to disappear from the discourse of modern man. In no case do they express more than the way in which the human machine actually tends to work."

At this point the prophet stopped for a moment and then said: "I should perhaps correct my last statements. What I just said is perfectly all right so far as it concerns the concept of right in its cognitive sense. My scientific theory explains why we all accept the same rules of thought. But so far as the concept of good is concerned, I ought to have laid less stress upon evolution and given more emphasis to another cause of human behavior, namely habit formation. Read your textbooks of anthropology, of social and general psychology. Read about the great discoveries of psychoanalysis. And don't forget to read about the materialistic interpretation of history. There you will find overwhelming evidence for the thesis that, in the field of moral attitudes, evolution has left a great deal to the factor of habituation. Social environments vary a great deal from one tribe to another and from one historical period to the next. Under these circumstances it was conditioning processes in individual life, rather than hereditary arrangements, which had to provide the adaptation which leads to survival. As a consequence, we find the most varied sets of so-called moral convictions in the diverse parts of the globe; and as history changes conditions, even in a given spot, the people hold certain beliefs now and adopt different ones in the next period. Why is a certain set of rules accepted by a given individual? Because in his social environment these rules have been repeated so often that they are as firmly stamped in as the alphabet. Why do people believe that they have a moral conscience? Because, when they were children, father was always very angry on certain occasions. The aftereffects of his scolding are now preserved under the guise of so-called conscience. You see it is not wise to take any of these great words at their face value. All advanced thinkers now agree that the motives which actually lie behind a person's actions are only a few, and that they differ widely from that welter of great terms behind which the scientific truth is hidden. There is the economic motive, which represents a brutally egoistic principle, but which tends to masquerade in a hundred more attractive forms. Again, there is sex which, as you doubtless know, tends to be frustrated and then fabricates poetry or symphonies as substitutes, as ersatz. There is also jealousy or the urge to be on top. This motive, too, is so potent that, when all other ways are barred, it turns bitterly poet, composer, or scientist. Scratch any great achievement of man, and behind the varnish you will find some such crude force at work. Science is no longer deceived by fireworks."

So far the gospel of gloom. As to the poor student, my prognosis is not too favorable. I doubt whether he was convinced by one such tirade. But the poor fellow will read books of a similar trend; he will have courses in psychology or in anthropology. Naturally, no teacher will talk precisely as the prophet whom I have just quoted. Nevertheless almost all psychologists seem to believe that values are merely subjective phenomena which can easily be bent in any direction by social influences and by habits. There is simply no doubt about one thing: many college departments feed students plain agnosticism or, more often, strict relativism. This goes under the name of education. Is it any wonder that, a short time ago, we found students apathetic even in the face of utter impudence and terror?

BUT heaven forbid that I talk gloom like that prophet. What can we do about an evil that destroys young energies as surely as does tuberculosis? My friends among the philosophers tell me that nothing can help but an analysis of moral judgments on their own ground, a purely phenomenological analysis that derives validity of a conviction from the intrinsic nature of such a conviction itself. To a degree I share this opinion, and I am anxiously waiting for the outcome of that analysis. In the meantime we can perhaps do something else. This other thing may not be decisive. But if it is done properly, it should greatly contribute to the task of removing the atmosphere of disillusion and gloom in which we live. What is it?

Recently I was present when two philosophers of considerable reputation were discussing just this problem—the problem of the naturalistic interpretation of man. One philosopher emphasized certain characteristics of the mind to which, he said, no concepts of science could ever do justice. The other philosopher was a man of disillusion in the sense that he accepted the usual naturalistic view. But he was old enough to be cynical about it all. Why, he replied, should we attribute that much importance to man? Now, while I listened to the discussion, I felt more and more surprised by the fact that neither one nor the other ever raised what seemed to me to be the main issue. Obviously, in their dispute, both took it for granted that nature has certain not too valuable characteristics. Thus, for them, the only problem was whether man ought to be reduced to this low level or whether he should not be so lowered. Why did they never discuss the characteristics of nature? For, if the processes of nature are quite different from, and far inferior to, the acknowledged activity of human minds, then I should be very much inclined to be an antinaturalist. On the other hand, if it should be discovered that in certain respects nature proceeds along lines which are genuinely akin to those of the more important mental activities, why should I assume an antinaturalistic attitude?

In my belief that this is the basic issue, I have been strongly confirmed by a recent conversation. It happened entirely by chance. In a crowded restaurant a man approached my table because here he found the only empty chair. He was one of those individuals whose age it is extremely difficult to guess. Judged by his obvious vigor, he might have been about forty-five; but there was something about him which made me feel that he was much older. His face was unusually intelligent, perhaps a bit on the clever and sly side. He looked as though he had seen many strange things, many foreign lands, and also a great deal of the sea. You know that peculiar look in the eyes of old captains. His English had a strong accent. Actually it turned out that he was from Greece. Together we had a few drinks which helped us to become acquainted. After the second glass, I confessed that I was greatly bothered by certain philosophical problems, and first of all by naturalism. But such things, I supposed, were not exactly in his line. At that he just grunted, and soon he was started on a string of simply fantastic tales. I will report only the last one, which happened to refer to the topic of the present paper.

"The other day," he said, "because of gasoline rationing I was walking along a deserted country road, from which I could occasionally see the towers of a distant town. After a while I felt a bit tired, and since it was not a cold day, I decided to rest on a log which lay perhaps a hundred yards from the road, near some spruce trees. As the sun shown mildly on my face, I found myself dreaming of those old days when we used to have one adventure after another along the shores of the Mediterranean and on its islands. In this occupation I was presently interrupted by the sound of excited voices and of trampling on the road, as though a group of men were coming along in a great hurry, but at the same time laboriously. I looked out from among my trees and discovered a strange procession. Along the road a number of distinguished looking men were carrying a bulky something wrapped in blankets and tied with ropes. Clearly it was a heavy load. The sweat ran down their red faces, their strained breathing was audible from my distant seat, and when they talked their voices expressed intense anguish. I had the feeling that they expected the worst to happen at any moment, and that all their concern was about the thing in the blankets.

"I could not resist the temptation to step out into the road and to inquire about their trouble. Since they were simply tired out, they agreed that a short rest was just what they needed. Upon being assured that I meant no harm, they told me their story in disconnected, hasty sentences. They were philosophers. They were fleeing from a bunch of scientists who were after their most precious possession: the true picture of Man. That, I gathered, was the thing in the blankets, and they were trying to carry it to some hiding place where the scientists would never find it. To add to their troubles, however, dissension had broken out in their own ranks when the going grew hard and the burden too heavy for their shoulders. One, whom they called the Vitalist, had suggested that they throw away a part of the picture which belonged to common physics anyhow; why should they carry that? Not satisfied with this sacrifice, another had advised that they cut off what belonged to nature in any sense, throw it in the ditch, and hurry along with the lighter load of a purely mental picture. But a third man who called himself a disciple of Husserl had gone even farther and had proposed that everything factual, whether physical or not, should be dropped by the wayside. With nothing but pure essences on their shoulders, he had felt, they would be practically sure to reach the hiding place before the scientists could catch up with them. Unfortunately, in their preoccupation with this dispute, they had forgotten to throw anything away and had labored along with their full burden.

"To me the whole thing seemed preposterous and I asked: 'Just what do these scientists want your picture for?'

" 'They want to dismember it,' was the answer. 'And with the pieces they want to adorn a picture of their own which they call the true picture of Nature.'

"At that they jumped up, seized again by fright, and made ready to lift their load. Now, you know, I have been in the wars. In war time, I have learned how to deal with people in a panic. Just now I remember an incident that occurred when, in one war, we could not conquer a certain town in fully ten years; our troops were completely exhausted and our failure threatened to turn into a disaster. We did get that town, but we got it less by force than by a stratagem in which, I am proud to say, I played a certain role.

" 'Friends,' I addressed the philosophers, 'is it proper for philosophers to run away from danger? It is not proper; and, besides, in your exhausted condition it is a hopeless enterprise. In fact, if my ears do not deceive me, right now I hear your enemies coming along the road. In a few moments they will be here. You leave it to me. Don't worry. Let us just stay where we are. I promise that no harm will be done to your picture.' And at that moment the scientists actually appeared on the road, saw us, saw the picture in its blankets, and rushed toward our group like mad men. I did not like their looks at all. When I went to college in Athens, scientists used to look better. In fact, these fellows made the impression of impersonating scientists rather than of being genuine scientists themselves.

"Well, here they were. I stepped forward, raised a hand, and spoke: 'Gentlemen, I am afraid there must be some misunderstanding. The distinguished men whom you see before you are a committee of philosophers. They represent all their colleagues in philosophy and have been sent with me in order publicly to acknowledge the immortal merits and the insuperable power of science. No longer do the philosophers believe that there is any sense in fighting. They surrender. In token whereof they herewith deliver into your hands the true picture of Man for you to deal with according to the great principles of natural science. In fact, so completely have we changed our minds that we beg to be admitted to the ceremonies in which the picture of Man will now be made a part of the picture of Nature. Gentlemen, let us not postpone the great hour. Up and on our way!'

" 'Traitor!' I heard the philosophers behind me mutter in a rage. But the scientists were obviously glad that victory had been so easy, and soon we were on our way. We marched briskly, and after an hour or so we could deposit the load in the hall of science, right before the scientists' true picture of Nature. This picture looked more like a collection of graphs than what I would call a picture. I liked the philosophers' picture much better, when the blankets had been removed and it became possible to behold the shapely thing itself.

"Once more I addressed the scientists, who were ready to use their knives. 'Gentlemen,' I said, 'let us begin our glorious work. I have heard it stated that all conquests of science have assumed the form of explanations. Let us therefore proceed according to the time-honored principles of scientific conquest and carve each piece from this picture as soon as it has been explained. Incidentally, what is an explanation? In a true explanation, we all agree, there are two factors: on the one hand, there are certain characteristic facts and structures which are to be explained. They must, of course, qua facts, not be altered by the process. On the other hand, there are certain other facts, structures, and laws which we suppose to be independently and better known. These we use as the explaining data. We put them skillfully together in a new combination until the resulting frame of explaining data is congruent with the data which we wish to explain. It is, on a grand scale, a tailor's job. If we are successful, the suit of explanation will fit perfectly the body of the facts which we explain. I hope, gentlemen, that this appears to you a fair technique.' The scientists agreed.

" 'Under these circumstances,' I proceeded, 'what do we have? On the one hand, we have before us this pleasant picture of man, the thing which we want to explain. And on the other hand, we have a host of scientific data, facts, laws, and principles of nature. They are the material which we intend to use in building up an explanation of man. Now as you see nature, its principles are fundamentally those of inanimate events, while this thing that we want to explain looks to the layman as though it belonged to a somewhat different world. Just what principles, do you think, ought we to use in building a bridge from nature to man?' The answer came like a well-timed volley of shots: 'The principle of evolution.'

" 'Now, I am happy,' I said. 'That is just what I thought. I see we understand each other perfectly. Indeed, what else could it be? Let us, therefore, first of all apply the principle of evolution. Just what is brought about by evolution, at any of the stages which we attribute to this development? Not mere variety? What, for instance, about the laws of physics and chemistry—do they change as evolution builds up more and more complicated entities? No, I can see it in your faces, you will never admit that those fundamental laws can be affected by evolutionary changes. Throughout the whole development, you agree with me, the fundamental principles of nature run quite unaffected. Nor will evolutionary development ever alter the fundamental forces of nature. After all, the most important laws of nature are laws about natural forces. Laws and forces, then, are invariant all along the course of evolution. And it is just this imposing fact which makes the theory of evolution a unitary system of explanation. Laymen, we all know, tend to overlook this fact. They tend to see only what is on the surface. And on the surface, we will admit, evolution does appear as a principle of change. But to the trained thinker, evolution means equally clearly a principle of strict permanence, of unvarying necessity, of a necessity which remains the same whether we deal with electrons or with human beings.' There was general applause among the scientists. I continued: 'What, then, are the changes which evolution so obviously brings about? We need hardly formulate it, it is so obvious: the same forces, always springing from the same fundamental sources, may operate under one condition here and under another there. Clearly this is what evolution does: it changes the configurations of material, it builds new structures, new anatomies, and thereby creates new conditions under which the same dynamic actions, the universal forces of nature, always play their age-old game.

" 'Gentlemen,' I said, 'emotion almost disturbs my speech. We have hardly begun, and yet I already see a bright light shining on our path of explanation. Look at this picture of man which the philosophers say is a true picture. What is the most astonishing fact in this picture? What is the most central fact in it? What have the philosophers defended so long as its strictly unique characteristic? They admire its anatomy and they admire most other things. But much more, they admire in it the sense of an invariable ought and of right, of things that should be, whatever actually happens. Don't you see that an explanation of just this characteristic of man is almost within our grasp? Forces in nature point in fixed directions, undisturbed by any situations that deflect the actual course of natural events from those directions. Just so, in man the ought and the right spring from a given situation and there are cases in which he would rather die than sway from their direction. Gentlemen, I modestly suggest to you that we accept the theory of evolution and that in accordance with it, we distinguish between the variable conditions established by the evolutionary forces and the invariable forces or vectors which no evolution can alter, even in man. Again, accordingly, I propose that we incline our heads in respect for the forces of ought and of right. For, since they are *forces,* their origin lies in the unalterable depths of nature, and this makes them worthy of our respect. At the same time I congratulate you and myself. It does seem that unitary scientific principles are being extended to man at a rate which by far exceeds our most sanguine hopes. True to our purpose, we have not for a moment disturbed what we intended to explain. And also, with what fascination shall we from now on look upon the primary forces of nature! For, far from being by-products of the evolutionary process, ought and right appear to be their nearest relations. The primary forces of nature are brothers of ought and of right. Is everybody agreed that we now proceed to add right and ought to the true picture of Nature?'

"This time there was silence. The scientists recovered, however, and one of them said: 'Listen! You cannot do that kind of thing. In your explanation you have made use of certain notions which are no longer accepted in science. To be sure, we speak of forces; but we do so merely for the sake of brevity. Actually any formula in which a so-called force appears merely expresses the way in which one thing begins to move more quickly or more slowly when a certain other thing is in the neighborhood. We never use such a formula in that anthropomorphic sense which you have just taken for granted. Science deals with facts. And among the observable facts there are no forces. We observe, on the one hand, conditions, and on the other hand, changes which occur in the system under observation. Beyond that we refuse to go. If you talk about forces, you talk about nonobservables. And nonobservables are not admitted in the true picture of Nature. It is childish to ask for an active nexus which makes the state of a system grow out of given conditions.'

" 'Oh, I do apologize,' I answered. 'How stupid of me to overlook the disappearance of forces from science! Please ignore everything I have just said. You will, I hope, still allow me to take part in this great enterprise of ours. For at this very moment, another approach occurs to me which, I feel sure, will meet with your approval. Let us talk about brain processes. If there is any place in which nature is in close contact with the so-called world of the mind, is it not in the brain? Are you not convinced, as I am, that the explanation of brain processes in purely physical terms must, at the same time, give us a full explanation of mental life, among other things of ought and of right?'

"With this proposal the scientists were in hearty agreement, whereas the philosophers did not yet know what I was aiming at. Meanwhile the scientists and I reiterated our statements about the meaning of scientific explanation. In particular, I repeated several times that in an explanation we combine known data in a new fashion, until in this new combination they form a structure which coincides with the structure of the things to be explained. Hence, I said, the facts which we want to explain must remain exactly what they are apart from our explanations, because they are the standard against which we measure the value of the explanation. Also, for every characteristic of the facts to be explained there must be a strictly congruent trait in the explanatory structure. My insistence upon these points made the scientists slightly impatient; but they could not object, and so I started my second attempt to interpret the right and the ought in purely natural terms.

" 'In this picture of man,' I said, 'you can see without difficulty what we have to explain whenever man talks about ought and about right. Let us suppose that a situation is presented to a person. In many instances we can divide this situation into two parts. There is an object which has certain characteristics, and then another thing, an action, a treatment of that object, is added. From this combination of object and treatment of the object, there tends to spring in man a statement about right or wrong, about ought to be or ought not to be under any circumstances. Now, if we wish to explain this mental fact in terms of brain processes, what must we do? Obviously, as we understand the term explanation, we must construct a picture of brain processes which is in every respect congruent with the structure of the mental fact to be explained. Let us proceed.

" 'The object in question is an object as the subject is aware of it. If a man's awareness of the object is to be interpreted in terms of brain events we must, of course, assume that the object is represented by some process which occurs in the man's brain.

You will be willing to accept this proposal. Actually we must, however, go a bit farther. If the object as given to the subject has any structure at all, we must explain this structure. And any explanation of the object's structure must point to brain events which have exactly the same structural characteristics as the perceived object has. I trust you will find it easy to fulfill this condition. We can therefore turn to the second part of the situation, which is an action, a treatment which the object undergoes in that situation. This action or event is again to be interpreted in terms of particular brain events. Moreover, if the action has any structural properties, our explanation must point to such facts in the brain as have structural characteristics just like those of the perceived action.

   " 'Where are we now? We have one brain process which is structurally equivalent to the object. We have a second brain process which is structurally equivalent to the action or treatment. Have we anything else? Surely, as yet we have ignored the fact that what is called the action is felt to refer to the object in a most particular fashion. Let us take the most banal example: A baby wants to carry a stick through a gap in a wall. The gap is narrow, the stick is long. The child happens to hold the stick in a horizontal position, and as he approaches the gap, the ends of the stick strike against the obstructing wall. But an adult who is present takes the stick and approaches the gap. Before he reaches this place, he begins to turn the stick into a vertical position. At this moment the child rushes toward the adult. He is given the stick in any arbitrary position. Now, however, the stick is immediately turned into the right position and thus passes through the gap without any difficulty. What has happened? While the adult turned the stick, the child saw the spatial relation between stick and gap change in such a way as to make it obvious that now the stick must pass; in other words, that this was the right relation of stick and gap under the circumstances of the given situation.

   " 'What does this mean? The child is aware of an objective situation which has certain structural properties. Gap and stick are experienced as being in a certain relationship. Now this situation undergoes a treatment; the stick is turned until a new relation is established. And this new relation is immediately apprehended as being the right one. Given the purpose of the child, it follows from the structural characteristics of stick and gap in their mutual relation that this action fits the situation. And the fact of fitting is felt to grow from the intrinsic characteristics of the situation and of the action.

" 'Gentlemen, in this case of a particularly simple mental situation, with its immediately perceived right and fitting, please help me to give a true explanation in terms of brain events. Here is the wall with the gap. This part of the situation, we remember, is represented by a structurally congruent set of brain processes. Here also is the stick, which again is represented in the brain by a structurally equivalent process. But there is more. The gap and the stick are perceived as being in a certain structural relation. You will agree with me that this particularity, too, must be given a congruent interpretation in terms of brain events. Moreover, as the stick turns, it is seen to approach one particular position with regard to the gap which fits and is, in this sense, right. Surely, since you know so much about the brain, you will be able to suggest to me how this perceived relationship of fitting is represented in the brain. For clearly, fitting, like any other structural characteristic of this mental experience, must find its congruent representation in the brain. In experience, this fact of fitting is felt to grow from the nature of stick and gap. Consequently, if we wish to give a congruent explanation in terms of brain events, there must be certain functional relations among brain processes which also grow directly from the nature of the related brain facts.

" 'I see that you are hesitating. You just told me that nowhere in your picture of nature are there any connections or actual functional relations among things. And if there are no such connections in nature, it is of course also impossible that in nature any functional connection grows from the nature of the related things. But don't despair; I know a way out. Before I mention it, however, let me tell you that our little example is, of course, only a particular instance of a whole class to which the most important mental facts belong. Thus in human thinking, a conclusion is felt to grow from the very nature of its premises. And if I feel that a certain situation demands a certain action on my part, I have not merely a situation and, in addition, a possible action; rather, the demand for just this action is felt to grow from the nature of the situation and also of the action. As soon as such intrinsic requiredness, the emergence of right things from a given situation, is strictly represented in congruent brain events, we can give you the whole picture of man, that you may add it to your picture of nature. And now, gentlemen, it is easily done.' With these words I took a large pencil from the table, went to the true picture of Nature and began to draw with quick strokes the outlines of intrinsic requiredness just in those places in which scientists had nothing but facts of regular sequence and concomitance, and no nexus whatever.

"At this, a wild cry arose from the scientists. They rushed toward their picture of Nature, they threw the blanket around it, and the very next moment saw them carrying their precious possession away through the door. Then, afterward, they were seen fleeing along the road to a hiding place in which no philosopher could find it."

18: Value and fact

THE problem which is implied in the title has two sides, because we use the term "value" in two different meanings. From R. B. Perry we have learned that when we deal with value we must clearly distinguish between two levels of discourse. To start with the lower level: In a general sense the death of a competitor will be a value to *some* persons, and so will revenge or undeserved praise. Also, some individuals tend to like blond individuals of the other sex, some find the taste of buttermilk very pleasant, and some are repelled by the smell of tobacco. So long as we remain on this first level of value, there is no reason why we should not continue the list with instances like these: I must keep my promise; it is bad to deceive one's friend in order to

From *The Journal of Philosophy*, 1944, 41 (8), 197–212. Reprinted by permission of the publisher.

The author wishes to remark that the present version of this paper differs at several points from the original which he read on November 28, 1943, for the Symposium on "Value in a World of Fact," at the Conference on Methods in Philosophy and the Sciences, New School for Social Research. In this corrected version free use has been made of the criticism which members of the audience, particularly Professor E. Nagel and Professor C. G. Hempel, raised in the discussion.

356

gain some personal advantage. Value in a generic sense, i.e., value mainly defined by its contrast with neutral facts, is an ingredient which the latter examples have in common with the former. But many philosophers feel that, nevertheless, two issues must here be sharply separated. On the lower level of value theory, they would say, there is no reference to validity or to obligation. Value experience itself, however, forces us to rise to a higher level, and to segregate from values in general a more specific group whose values claim to be binding. Once we are on this level, a secondary evaluation of values in general becomes necessary in terms of binding value. Many values are positive on both levels. On the higher level it remains, for instance, a good thing if we like nice people. But some values which have prima facie a positive sign, assume a negative sign from the higher point of view. It seems to be generally acknowledged that revenge is in this class. Again, other values appear now as neutral. Gentlemen are under no obligation to prefer blondes; on the other hand, they cannot be blamed if they do so.

In the following, I propose to concentrate on value in the general sense of the word. The problem of valid value will only be discussed so far as seems necessary to prevent a fairly common misunderstanding. There are two reasons for the restriction. In the first place, it has become customary to ignore certain difficulties which concern value in its modest general sense. In the second place, certain errors which disturb our thought on the higher level are not peculiar to this level but only persist because they are first committed on the lower level. Both reasons make it advisable for one to refrain from an immediate discussion of valid value.

According to the scientists, no object and no event in nature has value characteristics. It does not matter whether we refer to value in general or to binding value; the whole genus is excluded from the description of nature. Physical objects merely exist, and physical events merely occur; such is the verdict of natural science. On the other hand, every bit of human conduct, from trifles up to the present war, involves value as its most important content. This constitutes our problem.

A few hundred years ago there was no such problem. Everybody knows that in Aristotelian physics value concepts were freely applied to nature, and that remnants of this attitude are clearly discernible in the statements of great scientists as late as the seventeenth century. It is nevertheless true that at the present time a physicist would risk his reputation if he were to use value concepts in relation to his subject matter. At the same time the dualism to which I just referred is nowhere more striking than in the case of the scientist himself. He will scorn as ridiculous any suggestion that value might reside in physical facts. But his conduct as a scientist implies firm belief in a whole set of values. Quite apart from practical applications, knowledge and research are to him matters of tremendous value. The objectivity of science, clearness of reasoning, and honesty in the treatment of observational data are all values about which he has stern convictions. Paradoxically enough, even the absence of value from the subject matter of science impresses him as a great value which he will defend at all costs.

We would not have to be particularly disturbed by this attitude if it had no further consequences. But during the past three hundred years science has, for good reasons, gained a prestige with which few other human enterprises can compete. As a result large sections of civilized mankind have learned to look at things with the eyes of science. They have also adopted the values of science, for instance, the conviction that a keen mind with strong theoretical interests is best applied if it is applied to science. Thus the most intelligent men of generations went into science, and consequently forgot about the problems of value. They *had* value; but apart from its absence in nature they were not concerned with the topic. Under the same influence philosophers, who actually kept outside, did far more penetrating work about our access to the outside world and related problems than they did about questions of value. Is it astonishing that in a period which had this orientation the study of value degenerated? After all, value was not merely ignored in science. Rather, complete absence of value from any scientific material was now a fact of which all scientists were firmly convinced. Therefore, when new disciplines developed which proudly adopted the ways of science, not only scientific techniques in a positive sense spread far and wide, but also the scientists' dislike of value as a component of any subject matter. This happened in biology, in psychology, but to a degree also in social science. Thus during the nineteenth century value tended to become a matter of contempt, i.e., a negative value, among the intellectuals. I remember distinctly that as a young student of science I once expressed my condescending sympathy with an historian of art because in his field the poor fellow had to put up with value. It is obvious that this sophomoric behavior merely reflected a view which was then widely held. No less a man than Professor Titchener excluded value from serious consideration in scientific psychology. According to him this science deals with strictly neutral facts, just as does physics. It is quite possible that future generations will look back upon this period in utter perplexity.

One feels inclined to assume that in the minds of some scientists the situation caused uneasiness. If it did, such misgivings were soon dissipated by a remarkable doctrine which claimed that value could be explained on the basis of assumptions which never left the field of science. This achievement appeared possible in the framework of Darwin's theory of evolution. According to Darwin, characteristics of organic life which look as though they implied value can nevertheless be accounted for in terms of neutral facts. Presently an interpretation of values was proposed, and widely accepted, which applied the form of Darwin's reasoning to this further subject.

In Darwin's theory a species develops and improves its organs by accidental variations of germ cells, and by the early elimination of individuals who stem from cells with less fortunate variations. The elimination is brought about by the environment, in which the less fit individuals die earlier. An extension of this principle to the case of value will take more or less this form: The equipment of man as to mental tendencies is just as much a function of the germ cells as his anatomical characteristics are, and his equipment in this respect will vary when certain chance variations occur in those cells. Now, man is a social animal, and he will survive longer if he has mental tendencies which make him fit for life in a group. Thus in the remote past those individuals had the best chances who came from cells in which such tendencies were strongly preformed. The others died earlier and had fewer offspring. Nowadays, therefore, most people come from the better equipped stock. But what do we mean if we say that a man's mental tendencies favor his living and surviving in the group? Obviously we mean what are otherwise known as his moral attitudes with regard to others. They preserve the group, and through the group, the individual himself.

We need not investigate whether the authors of the evolutionary theory of value believed that in this fashion value was actually deduced from categories of natural science. There is little doubt that the theory was generally understood in this sense, and that it still owes its great popularity among scientists to that claim. In actual fact, of course, the claim represents a remarkable instance of self-deception. Plainly, Darwin's theory derives biological phenomena from neutral facts only inasmuch as the conditions which accidentally vary in germ cells are, and refer to, such neutral facts. It may be that Darwin's strictly biological reasoning fulfills this prerequisite. But, surely, the same prerequisite is not fulfilled in the evolutionary theory of value. For if here dispositions for moral attitudes in group life emerge in germ cells, such curious newcomers have certainly no ancestry among the neutral facts which make up nature according to natural science. Dispositions of this kind may vary from one germ cell to another; but, if so, it is dispositions *for value* which vary; instead of being deduced from neutral facts, value per se is tacitly taken for granted and, without an explanation, simply added to such facts. Or does natural science give us any hint of how a neutral fact can become a disposition for value? In other words, merely the form of Darwin's reasoning is here preserved. This form causes the erroneous impression that the theoretical achievement is also the same, namely, the reduction of a puzzling phenomenon to principles of natural science.

This ought to have been clear almost a priori. In the scientific thesis that no value attribute applies to any facts of nature, it is clearly implied that neutral facts and values are two sharply distinguishable genera. If this is right, how can any sequence of neutral facts, be it ever so long and complicated, have value as its end product? A theory which holds that this happens in evolution *must* somewhere commit an error. To be sure, evolutionary theorizing may be able to explain that human conduct shows certain regularities, i.e., that under given conditions one activity rather than another is likely to follow. But as soon as human action implies "good," "bad," or "ought," we are dealing not with additional regularities of mere occurrences but with a new class of facts. Moreover, far from being influenced by philosophical prejudice, we make this sharp distinction because it is made so sharply in science. In fact, therefore, the scientists themselves ought to have been the first to object to the confusion of neutral fact and value which characterizes the evolutionary theory. Actually, the criticism which the theory so much deserves has come from philosophy. During the past forty years there has been a renaissance in the field of ethics, and more than one philosopher has made it clear that, wherever the error lies, if the evolutionary theory is accepted, value is necessarily denaturalized. Evolution conceived as a sequence of changes in the hereditary make-up of our ancestors will never explain value. I wish to add that this statement holds quite generally. Although both the evolutionary theory and its critics have been principally interested in moral value, our argument against the theory holds for value in any sense, including its most modest specimen. And we may generalize still further. Quite apart from evolutionary theory, so long as the present strictly negative view of natural science with regard to value is maintained, no datum concerning the physical world, among others no fact of neurology or nerve physiology, can have any bearing upon the nature and the problems of value as such.

In the meantime it has proved impossible to exclude value from the investigations of at least one empirical discipline, namely, psychology. Many psychologists may never use the term. Value is none the less implicitly accepted inasmuch as, after the gradual collapse of pure connectionism and conditionism, *motivation* has been generally recognized as the central issue of psychological inquiry. Few will deny that in human subjects the goal of motivated behavior has value characteristics. Now, in our

present argument this acceptance of value as an empirical subject appears little short of baffling. For if natural science acts as
though the attribution of value to anything in nature would be
almost a crime against the spirit of factual research, how can
one form of empirical investigation ignore this view, and yet
proceed with a considerable measure of success? It is quite true
that psychology has long followed the orders of natural science;
on the other hand, at the present time psychologists may not be
fully aware of the fact that with their study of motivation they
are out of bounds so far as natural science is concerned. But it
seems surprising that the transgression has no evil consequences.
Neither law and order on the objective side nor exact procedure
on the side of method appear endangered when motivation, and
with it value, are freely included in empirical research.

To be sure, psychology has not yet shaken off the old fetters
entirely. For the most part psychologists hold a view of value
which is at odds with value experience, and must be caused by
a prejudice. The prejudice, it appears, still has its roots in the
unwillingness of science to admit value as an ingredient of objective situations. The now prevailing theories of motivation are
subjectivistic, which implies that the interpretation of value in
psychology is equally subjectivistic. It is widely taken for granted
that all motivation originates in the self, and, as a result, value
is generally said to be valuation, i.e., to spring from the self's
subjective attitudes. Perry, for instance, whose theory is primarily a psychological theory, makes great efforts to prove that
value is wrongly localized when it appears within objects.

I have often asked philosophers and psychologists who defend this subjectivistic view just why they are so insistent about
this point. So far I have never received a satisfactory answer.
Least of all do answers point to direct observations of value
experiences. Behind the answers there always seems to lie some
deep conviction which is never openly formulated. I am afraid
the objective parts of human experience, more particularly, our
percepts, are for most of us so closely related to the world of
natural science that the verdict against value in nature is inadvertently extended to the percepts. Even in their theoretical
thought, few people can keep percepts and physical objects

sharply separate. Consequently, since physics is regarded as a realm of purely neutral facts, percepts, which in a numerical sense tend to be identified with physical entities, can also never have value attributes. If percepts are not actually identified with physical objects, they are at least interpreted as almost literal translations of patterns of physical stimuli into patterns of corresponding sensations. Nerve physiology seems to give an adequate account of the genesis of such sensations in terms of natural science, and thus it once more follows that in percepts there is no place for value. Apart from these and closely related arguments, I can find no reason for the persistence with which the subjectivistic interpretation of value is still being defended. That part of our experience which we call the self—with its moods, efforts, emotions, and so forth—is not so closely related to nature as investigated by physicists and chemists. Therefore it does not seem to matter if this entity is made responsible for value as merely one strange function among many others.

A time will probably come in psychology and philosophy in which it will be a principle of method that the obvious characteristics of primary observational data are to be respected at their face value, whatever their relation to general preconceptions may be. It will then be acknowledged that we are not allowed to interpret black as really white, and here as actually elsewhere, unless we are forced to do so by further convincing observations. The time in which this rule will be generally accepted is likely to be remote. But it can be brought nearer only by one attempt after another to do precisely what the rule demands. The rule asks for phenomenology.[1]

How, then, does value appear in common experience?

1. It seems to be a fairly general fact that value appears as an attribute of things and events themselves rather than as

[1] To avoid misunderstanding it will here be necessary to add that phenomenology in the present sense differs from Husserl's technique. I do not believe that we are justified in putting certain phases of experience in brackets. A first account of experience ought to be given and carefully studied without selections of any kind. It is otherwise to be expected that even if the brackets are introduced as mere methodological tools, they will sooner or later turn out to be weapons of an ontological prejudice. In fact, I am not sure whether Husserl himself has not used them as such weapons.

an activity of the self or as the result of such an activity. We should therefore falsify our primary observational data if we were to say that the essence of value is valuation. Phenomenologically, value is located in objects and occurrences; it is not an action to which they are subjected. Value may reside in the most varied classes of things. A dress may look elegant or sloppy, a face hard or weak, a street cheerful or dismal, and in a tune there may be morose unrest or quiet power. I admit, one's own self is among the entities in which values may reside. Such is the case when we feel fit or, at another time, moody. But the thesis that it is always valuation as an act which imbues its object with value as a pseudoattribute is perhaps nowhere more artificial than precisely in this instance. Here the self would have to equip itself with value attributes such as fitness or utter fatigue. The idea seems slightly fantastic. And if in this instance a thing per se manages to have value characteristics, why should we deny this possibility where other percepts are concerned?[2]

To repeat: For what reason are we to accept the thesis that value in objects can only be understood as an illusion, and that the truth of the matter consists in acts of the self which we wrongly objectify? There are instances in which the thesis would ask us to believe what is clearly impossible. Men sometimes succumb to what they would call the irresistible womanly charm of certain persons. Now, this is a value attribute on which women have a monopoly. It would be absurd to maintain that when the intensely male interests of such men impinge upon the actually neutral appearance of the women, female charm develops in these objects as an illusory projection of the males' conations. Female charm is not a component of such male conations. How, then, can it be projected? It has been said that in pure description value characteristics do reside in objects; that to this extent the objective location of those characteristics is not an illusion; but that they are nevertheless *caused* by cona

[2] It will not be necessary to explain that the self, taken in the simple sense in which fitness or fatigue may temporarily become its attributes, *is* a particular percept; in other words, that it is neither the physical organism nor the epistemological ego of certain philosophies.

tions of the self. This theory still rests on the tacit premise that it is more natural for value to spring from the self than to reside in things. And we can only ask again: Whence that premise? Moreover, even in this form, the act theory of value negates phenomenological evidence, particularly in the case of certain negative values. When suddenly an object looms dangerous and threatening, it is not felt to have that appearance because there is first fear and a tendency to escape in the self. On the contrary, fear with that tendency is felt to be a consequence of the danger that threatens from the object. The theory is therefore at variance with experience.

It is merely a construction even in those instances in which value within the object actually varies with the intensity of the corresponding subjective need. It may well be that female charm is greatly enhanced when the sex need in a male has grown particularly strong. Does it follow that the sexual conation of the male self is responsible for that intensified perceptual value? If we say so we ignore another possibility. Glandular action (which is physiological action and not sexual conation as a psychological attitude) may have two parallel effects upon the nervous system. Those parts of the tissue whose states are correlated with phenomenal states of the self may become ready for processes that go with sexual conation. But in other parts which contain the correlates of perceptual objects, such processes may at the same time be intensified as are the somatic counterparts of certain tertiary qualities. From this point of view the latter change would not be established *by* the conation but *together with* increased readiness for such conation. If it is asked why, say, in the case of sex that glandular action should emphasize just those *particular* characteristics of certain percepts, the obvious answer is the other question: Why does the same physiological cause make the self ready for sexual conation rather than for any other conation? The former connection is not a bit more problematic than is the latter.[3]

[3] If for a moment we have here left the phenomenological realm, we have done so because the view under discussion is itself a hypothetical construction.

It might be argued that a theory of value should not be concerned with mere percepts and their characteristics, since ultimately value must be referred to objective reality. But this argument seems to me mistaken. In the first place, if objective reality is meant as a synonym of the physical world, the scientific view which is at present generally held excludes any such consideration. According to this view there can be no value in objective reality. In the second place, we do not actually refer our moral obligations (or values in general) to the physical world. For all practical purposes we are naïve realists, and percepts are our real objects. It is quite true that in referring to the values of such objects we often go beyond perceptual fact. For everybody's percepts are equipped with characteristics which are matters of indirect knowledge rather than of sensory experience. This "thought content" of percepts, however, just like the content of other knowledge, is phenomenally objective. It is located within the percepts, and if it has value characteristics these, too, have an objective location. Incidentally, when images have value characteristics, their value is also phenomenally objective. Images are not part of the self.

In concluding, I should like to suggest that further interpretations of value in terms of valuating acts be accompanied by a statement of the premises which make the author prefer that interpretation to the testimony of value experience. It may be that once these premises become clear, the preference itself will be greatly weakened.

2. So far our phenomenology of value agrees with the descriptive accounts given by several philosophers in England although, on the whole, their accounts refer to specifically moral and valid value rather than to value in the generic sense. But if the same authors regard value *merely* as a quality which resides in objects, they seem to me to ignore an important phase of their subject. To the extent to which value characteristics are located in things and events themselves, and need for their existence no activity of the self, a relational interpretation of value would be misleading. But if the independence of value is admitted to this degree, we have not yet touched upon an-

other side of value experience which we cannot omit without unjustified abstraction. Even though value does not depend upon acts of the self, it is often clearly referred to certain facts within the object which exhibits the value. Moreover, these facts are for the most part *relational* facts. Anybody who perceives a graceful object or gesture will on reflection admit that this is obviously true. Actually, the observation holds for most instances of value; a situation or an object is felt to be valuable with reference to certain structural characteristics of the situation or the object. In this sense Professor Ross appears to be right not only when he regards value as a "consequential" quality but also when he accepts Professor Urban's thesis that as a rule value adheres to a *Sachverhalt*. In this German term it is implied that the factual datum to which the value characteristic of a situation refers tends to be a structural or relational trait of this situation.

I find it difficult to decide whether the preceding statements concern merely frequent or actually necessary characteristics of value. But with regard to a further trait I have no such doubts. Professor Urban holds that value is not adequately described unless we mention what may be called a *demand* character that belongs to its very nature. The plus and the minus signs which are characteristic of all value do not solely indicate that value qualities as such lie in one direction or the opposite with regard to a neutral point. Rather the plus and minus also mean "to be accepted, reached, maintained, supported" and "to be avoided, eliminated, changed in the positive direction." I am not acquainted with values of which this is not true. No value attribute seems to deserve its name if it has no such demand character. Moreover, while natural science would hardly worry about any other qualities with which phenomenology chooses to deal, it is precisely this demand character of value, in a wide sense the "ought" or the "requiredness" in it, which science wants to exclude when it refuses to use any value terms in reference to its subject matter. It is in contrast with any "ought" that facts of science are called *neutral* facts.

While, therefore, value cannot simply be interpreted in relational terms, it nevertheless contains a reference beyond its existence as a quality and beyond the object in which it resides. This reference is dynamic. Now the act theory which we discussed in earlier paragraphs emphasizes such a dynamic ingredient in value. But while this theory tends to identify value with a "vector" which issues from the *self*, in actual experience it is first of all value in an *object* which goes with a demand. In other words, the vector issues from the object qua valuable. The dangerous object threatens, the cool drink is tempting, the problematic situation invites closer inspection, and so forth. Here again, therefore, we have to reverse the account which the act theory gives of value. It shall not be denied that the demand which issues from a value object is mostly, though perhaps not necessarily, directed toward the self, and that as a consequence the self is likely to become active toward, or away from, that object. In this case, it may rightly be said, vectors actually arise of which the self is the center. But as a rule this happens because, in the first place, there is a positive or negative demand in the object.

3. We have just used the expression "Value in an object goes with a demand." This expression is not quite adequate. Between the value as such and the demand there is more than a factual connection, as though the demand merely accompanied the value characteristic. For, generally the attraction (or the negative vector) which issues from the object is felt to spring from the very nature of that value attribute. So far as I know it was W. Dilthey who first introduced the concept of understandable relationships. The eighteenth century was very fond of the term "reason." Reason was then considered a mental faculty. At the present time we prefer to speak of rational or understandable relationships which are experienced within actual mental situations. By this we mean that a given content may be felt to be required by others. But there is one further point at which the rationalism of that period must be corrected. We often apprehend that one thing follows from another as its natural consequence not only in the strictly intellectual field but also in motivation, emotion, and value experience. An understandable relationship in thought may not in every respect be

comparable with such a relation as experienced in those other instances. But, surely, the relation between anger and its object, or joy and the situation from which it springs, is also understandable in the sense that, as a rule, such emotions appear adequate with reference to the facts from which they derive. We should, for instance, feel it to be both against the nature of the emotions and their objects if the object of my joy were all at once, without a change of its character, to cause the emotion of anger. A relationship of precisely this type is meant if we say that demands which issue from value objects are felt to spring from the nature of those objects and their values. In other words, we understand it as sensible that we are attracted by objects which have certain characteristics, and that we are disgusted by others. These are not mere sequences; at least prima facie it is felt to be adequate that just such vectors issue from such objects. The limitation which is contained in the term "prima facie" refers, of course, to the possibility that on the level of valid value it may become an obligation to resist such perfectly understandable demands. If this happens, the relation between the value objects and their demands may nevertheless remain understandable in the present sense.

It is at this point that a remark about the problem of valid value obtrudes itself. Plainly, this problem is whether the demand which issues from a situation may be experienced not only as understandable but also as binding. If there are instances of this kind, two further questions follow immediately: First, under what specific circumstances do understandable demands appear as binding? And, secondly, what in this connection is the meaning of the term "binding"? It is a serious blunder when in relativistic arguments such phenomenological questions are replaced by questions of inductive generality, as though any problem of validity could be solved by counting how many people or tribes agree, or disagree, with certain judgments. Validity of a demand is quite compatible with factual dissension concerning the same demand. We see this every day in the purely cognitive field; but in this field of thought we draw no relativistic conclusions concerning the validity of logical demands. Even if it is to be granted that validity in thought is not throughout equivalent to validity, say, in ethics, the comparison shows that as a form of reasoning the relativistic arguments confuse two entirely different issues.

After this exploration of generic value as such, we can now return to our main problem, the dualism of value and the neutral facts of natural science. So far it has been our impression that no bridge can span the gap between these two concepts. If this were actually true, value in any sense of the word would have jumped into our world from nowhere when the development of living organisms had reached a certain stage, namely, when percepts had for the first time inviting or forbidding value characters. In a period which is as eagerly concerned with unity of knowledge as ours is, this must appear as a disturbing thought. Nor does it help us if we are told that, after all, values are also facts, and that therefore we need not bother about the relation of facts and values. This is not a question of mere terms. If values are facts, they are none the less facts of a peculiar kind. Otherwise why should natural science exclude this kind from its domain? Thus, if the scientists are right, the dualism as such remains in full force whether or not we subsume values under the category of facts.

We should, perhaps, be less disturbed by the dualism if value were only a quality of a particular kind. Quite apart from value attributes, a great many qualities of human experience are strangers in the world of natural science. Everybody seems to be resigned to the fact that, even if these qualities may once gain a better place in the scheme of science than they now have, present thought appears utterly unable to imagine what that place could be. In this respect value characteristics qua qualities are hardly more enigmatic than sensory qualities such as green or gray. We will therefore not attempt to relate our first characteristic of value to the world of science. It should, however, be remarked that if value characteristics were interpreted as projections of valuating acts, the qualitative differences among these acts would be just as puzzling to natural science as value qualities which reside in objects and events themselves.

The second and the third points of our description concern

natural science more directly. For these points refer to structural characteristics of value rather than to mere qualities. If a demand issues from a thing and affects another, this is a structural fact; and if this demand is experienced as springing from the nature of its substratum, this is once more a matter of functional structure. Here science finds itself in a curious position. While it excludes value from nature, it postulates at the same time that the structural characteristics of all functions in the world be interpretable in terms of physical facts. This will become clear if we once more return to the principle of evolution. Evolution has two sides. It is commonly regarded as a principle of *change*, because evolution has established one new anatomical condition after another. Much less clearly do we realize that evolution is just as much a principle of *invariance*. Not only are those new anatomical conditions supposed to have originated according to the old laws of nature in general; it is also nothing but the primordial basic processes of the physical world which, according to the principle of evolution, are still operating under the new conditions. It follows that no elementary functional structure can appear in organisms that is not derivable from the fundamental concepts of science. And this applies also to the structure of value. Now, so long as science declares that nature before evolution was devoid of value in any sense, no amount of new organs can give us an understanding of value in terms of natural science. So much we have seen in a preceding discussion. Therefore, since the structural characteristics of value are said to have been absent from nature to begin with, and since, with this premise, evolution as a principle of change cannot be made responsible for those characteristics, we here find natural science contradicting itself. It adheres to evolution, i.e., to continuity and uniformity of all functions in the world. But it also denies any possibility of applying this principle in the case of value. We will next consider how science could extricate itself from this inconsistency.

It would, of course, be possible to sacrifice the principle of evolution. Then all difficulties would disappear excepting the one that the resulting dualism between neutral facts and value would destroy all hope that the unity of knowledge, of which modern philosophers of science are so rightly fond, will ever be achieved. I cannot believe that those philosophers or any scientists will be prepared to make such a sacrifice. But under these circumstances there is only one way out. Since, as a typical experience, value with its characteristic structure cannot be eliminated, and since science postulates the unity of all functional structures, science will have to deliberate whether its own concepts do not admit of certain modifications. For if science discarded the thesis that the functional characteristics of value are absent from nature, the inconsistency would disappear, the unity of knowledge would potentially be established, and evolution would become a principle which makes sense.

It is surprising to see how little such a step would affect science. There are two ways in which the necessary change can be discovered. We can either compare value situations with physical situations in general; or we can apply the same procedure to value situations and such particular situations in nature as are directly related to value experiences, namely, the somatic correlates of value situations in the brain of man. I prefer the second alternative. It will no longer be denied that any perceptual object is somatically represented by a cortical process, and that in each case this process is located in some particular part of the tissue. Similarly, the self in the sense in which we have used the term is represented by a complex of processes. We have every reason to assume that the location of this latter complex differs from that of a process which corresponds to an object. Now, in the case of a value situation, the percept in question has qualities which make it valuable. These qualities as such we have decided not to discuss. But we have found that no such quality alone constitutes actual value, because all objects which are valuable are sources of positive or negative demands. For the most part these are demands upon the self, which they either attract or repel. If we ask ourselves what somatic facts in the tissue could be the correlates of such demands, we are at once reminded of the physical concept "field." The field between two physical objects or processes extends from one to the other, and tends either to reduce or to widen their distance. The parallel is obvious. It is true, physicists vacillate between two interpretations of fields. Before Faraday fields were regarded as mere mathematical constructions; according to Faraday and Maxwell fields were the most important entities in nature; but at the present time there seems to be a certain reaction against this view, probably because the concept of field can hardly be divorced from that of causation, which is now unpopular. If we wish to give the demands of valuable percepts physical counterparts in the brain, we need do no more than adopt Faraday's view. Not only does a field attract an entity toward, or repel it from, the source of the field—just as the self is affected by the demand of a value. That attraction or repulsion in a field is also independent of further conditions which, apart from the field, may be operating in the given situation. It has sometimes been said that we find nowhere in nature an analogue of the difference between "happens" and "is," on the one hand, and "ought," on the other hand. This is incorrect since any object in nature that is subjected to a field remains thereby directed toward, or away from, the source of the field, even when, because of further conditions, it may actually move in another direction.

We have still to decide what the somatic counterpart of another characteristic of value is: the demand of a value object is felt to *follow from* the nature of the object. Now we have just seen that it depends merely upon our choice between several, otherwise equally acceptable, interpretations of the concept field whether or not a value demand can be referred to a somatic correlate. Our situation is precisely the same when we turn to the understandable relation between the nature of value objects and their demands. According to natural science the relation between objects and their fields is a relation of mere fact. But this proves only that the procedures of science have access to no more than such a factual connection. Whether the relation is actually of this nondescript type, or whether, if more were known, the nature of the field would in each case prove to follow from the nature of the objects involved—this is a question which natural science alone cannot answer. The issue simply lies beyond the possibilities of observation in physics. And, instead of excluding the latter alternative, science ought merely to say: I am unable to decide. We are therefore again at liberty to choose the interpretation which appears on the whole more satisfactory. In doing so we can never come into conflict with scientific data, because these data are not affected by our decision. Obviously, our choice will be such as to do justice to the nature of value, to establish the unity of knowledge, and to abolish the inconsistency in which science is now caught. This means that, on the evidence of phenomenology, we shall interpret the relation of objects and their fields as one of *following from*. With this choice, value situations as experienced and corresponding functional situations in the brain of man become structurally congruent.

It takes some courage to suggest that phenomenological observation be here accepted as evidence in matters of nature. But once the principle of evolution is taken for granted, such an attitude appears perfectly natural when we deal with problems of functional structure. We readily admit that, as to quantitative exactness and in the establishment of strict factual laws, the observational techniques of science achieve incomparably more than can be gained from phenomenology. But when we ask to precisely what relations these laws refer, then natural science is at the end of its resources, and restricts itself to noncommittal terms which just cover its own data. This is our starting point. We try to relate the phenomenology of value situations with corresponding somatic situations, and find that a demand extends from a value object to the self, just as a field in the brain would issue from an object process and affect the somatic correlate of the self. So far natural science can have no cause for objections. If, then, science assumes an agnostic attitude with regard to the particular relation between objects and their fields, any other evidence which fills the empty space must be welcomed. It happens that phenomenology sees more of that relation than is implied in the terms of least content which science likes to use. Under these circumstances, why should one further insist on an agnostic attitude?

Not even the parsimonious tendency of science offers an excuse. For it is not an important parsimony that tries to keep the number of data in the limited realm of natural science at a minimum. The clear, unitary system of knowledge as a whole is far more essential, and any schism in this respect must be regarded as a most undesirable expense. There is, moreover, one expense which this systematic parsimony of human thought simply cannot afford, and that is self-contradiction. Only the present suggestion seems to be capable of avoiding that expense where the relation of fact and value is concerned.

19: Psychological remarks on some questions of anthropology

IN his investigation of primitive mentality Lévy-Bruhl is led to the conclusion that in primitive man mental operations are essentially different from those with which we are familiar. *"Les représentations collectives,"* all the notions with which, during childhood and adolescence, an individual is imbued by the surrounding group, are *"mystiques"* in the case of primitive tribes. Where we apply the laws of logic, *"la mentalité prélogique"* applies *"la loi de participation."* The author seems to conclude that in many cases the anthropologist's attempt really to understand and to explain primitive behavior will necessarily end in failure. We even have difficulties in defining the term *"mystique."* Again, who can formulate clearly what is implied in the *"loi de participation"*? Still, when we find that one more primitive belief or custom is mystical and that it follows the law of participation this is, according to the French sociologist, perhaps all that we can do about the case in question.

From *The American Journal of Psychology*, 1937, 50, 271–288. Reprinted by permission of the University of Illinois Press.

Often, I am afraid, Lévy-Bruhl's skepticism is justified in practice, though perhaps not for the reasons which he indicates. The origin of some tribal beliefs and institutions may be so complicated historically that there simply is no unitary sense in the phenomena themselves. To that extent, of course, we cannot fully "understand" their nature, whether or not primitive mentality differs essentially from our own. Besides, several primitive cultures are known only from reports in which the white observer's preconceived notions seem to be hopelessly intermingled with the ethnological material as such. Not a few of these cultures disintegrate quickly, if they have not actually disappeared. Since the opportunity for more objective investigation is gone, in such cases the available data themselves will remain ambiguous. Much of their obscurity may be due to serious misunderstandings rather than to an alleged impermeable nature of primitive mentality.

Though some anthropologists do not like to admit it, psychological principles play an important role in the interpretation of anthropological facts. Theoretical difficulties may, therefore, arise quite as easily from inadequate psychological notions as from the strange ways of primitive mentality. As Lévy-Bruhl has pointed out, the psychology which Tylor and his school applied to anthropological problems can hardly be regarded as an adequate tool in this field. In the meantime, however, psychology has again changed a great deal. Perhaps some of the facts in anthropology which, to the French author, seem to be outside the white man's understanding will prove more approachable if we apply to them recently developed psychological ideas. In the following pages a modest and hesitant attempt will be made in this direction. It must be hesitant because, for the two reasons given in the previous paragraph, we should not try to find more psychological sense in our material than it can be expected really to contain. Our attempt must be modest since no outsider can hope to have a sufficient survey of anthropological data for a more comprehensive interpretation of primitive cultures. It ought to be modest in another sense, too, because some of the ideas which I shall bring forward have, at least implicitly, been used before by experts. I should be pleased, however, if psychologists would give some attention to the following discussion. In our desire to be thoroughly exact, we are in the present phase of psychology apt to concentrate our efforts on a few special problems. In consequence of this we begin to lose sight of most questions for which the social sciences expect answers from psychology. If we do not answer because our outlook is too narrow, discontent, of which there are some signs already, will doubtless grow steadily. It may be that the following discussion will satisfy neither psychologists nor anthropologists. In this case it might still have some value, if it induces other psychologists to do better work in the same field.

Many examples may be given in which the behavior of primitive man certainly looks incomprehensible at first. May I select two at random.

Moffat reports from South Africa that once a woman came to him in order to get the medicine which he had prepared for her sick husband. When he made it clear to her that half of the potion should be taken at once and the rest several hours later, she asked whether it would not be possible to drink all of it at once. Upon his assent the woman suddenly swallowed the medicine herself. To the missionary's protest she answered by asking whether it would not cure her husband if she drank the medicine.[1] Many Africans, it is true, like to take our drugs because of their "power." It would, however, hardly be fair to assume that this factor suffices as an explanation. Anthropology knows of too many cases in which what we might call medical treatment or measures of hygiene applies to the family group almost as much as to an individual member upon whom our physicians would concentrate their efforts. Neither is it satisfactory to say that among primitives the individual is less a separate entity than in our society; or that, for them, the individual's boundaries are not the same as for us. Both statements may be true. But in such matters our own point of view seems to us so obvious and neces-

[1] R. Moffat, *Missionary Labours and Scenes in Southern Africa.* London: J. Snow, 1842, 591f.

sary that we fail to understand on what basis other views could ever develop.

I have the following report from a missionary who is working in East Africa. While sleeping in his hut a man dreams that he is in another village and that there he commits a crime which, according to the convictions of the tribe, deserves death punishment. Frightened, he tells his people about the dream. Unfortunately something of the kind really happens in that other village and approximately at the same time. The man is indicted, he confesses and is killed, although he was miles away from that other village when the crime was committed. Such things will occur less often the more European officials and European schools begin to influence the natives, but my informant, a perfectly calm and sober man, told me that he has direct knowledge of more such cases. Primitive mentality does move in strange ways; it does not seem to mind contradiction. According to our thinking the man could not be in another village while he was sleeping in his hut. This is exactly, however, what the natives believe and what the poor victim of such logic apparently believes himself.

I have gradually become convinced that in many such cases our difficulties are due to a special coordinate system of our own, no less than to peculiarities of primitive mentality. In a way, scientifically trained people of our time may be particularly unfit for the understanding of less intellectual cultures. What are the objective facts of nature? What is the best access to objective knowledge in this sense? What influences, on the other hand, are apt to hamper our progress in this field? Since the seventeenth century such questions have gradually introduced a definite set of values which is now so dominant that, far beyond the circle of scientists proper, the outlook of civilized people is thoroughly governed by these particular ideals. A sober attitude toward a real world is instilled in children of our civilization by the words and actions of their parents. Long ago the most basic convictions of scientific culture lost the character of theoretically formulated sentences. Gradually they have become aspects of the world as we *perceive* it; the world *looks* today what our forefathers learned to say about it; we act and we speak accordingly. In this form the consequences of a few centuries of science are present in the remotest corners of the civilized world.

The ideals which I mentioned, the special interest which they represent, and the particular aspect which they have given to the world, are doubtless very apt to further quick progress of natural science and practical behavior in contact with reality. I wonder whether to some degree they do not disturb the advance of anthropology. Physicists have gradually separated their real world from the realm of mere percepts. In doing this they have also learned to distinguish between phenomena which tell the truth about the real world and others which are illusory. On this basis percepts and their traits are good or valueless according to this distinction. Similarly, properties of percepts which are easily understood in their relation to physical stimulation will be readily accepted in sense physiology. Whatever does not fit into this scheme will be neglected and despised because of its "subjective" nature. Under the influence of scientific culture the very appearance of the world around us is being transformed. It will not only be "intellectualized." Such characteristics of the world will become less conspicuous, they will gradually recede into the background, for which the physicist and the sense physiologist have definitely no use. Those aspects, on the other hand, are made outstanding which we regard as representatives of reality.

For natural science, I repeat, this development may mean strict progress. I shall not deny that the modern aspect of the world around us agrees better with our picture of physical reality than older views did. But I insist upon the fact that, before the era of scientific culture, the perceptual world could not have looked as it appears to us now. Psychologically speaking our view of the "given" world is the product of complicated historical processes. Judged from a merely psychological standpoint and without any reference to physical reality, this aspect of the world is therefore no more genuine than any previous appearance of man's perceived environment. To some extent even more "natural" traits of perception will be found where science has not exerted its modifying influence. They would be most prominent in the primitive's world.

Their study, however, is difficult. The psychologist no less than other people has learned to see the world through the eyeglasses of natural science. What he beholds in this manner seems to him so obvious, he is so little aware of his eyeglasses, that any other view will appear to him as a distortion of the genuine aspect of the world. If primitives have such another view, their mystical thinking will be made responsible for it. They have changed the genuine appearance of the world which is, of course, originally the same everywhere and identical with our own view.

It seems to me that the opposite judgment would be at least as correct. Primitive perception, to be sure, contains a great deal of intellectual elaboration. It is improbable, however, that such influences should ever have been more systematic and intense than have been the effects of scientific learning in our own case. It would therefore be of great advantage if, in studying the appearance which the world has for primitives, we could overcome the tendency to use our own view as a norm. Anthropologists have generally been at pains to follow this principle. More might be done, however, if even in the application of psychological thought to primitive perception the white man's customary outlook were recognized as a disturbing factor. Recently we learned that a definite type of scientific analysis had nearly made us unable to apprehend most common sides of perception and of mental life in general. We shall try to apply this lesson to anthropological questions.

Almost fifty years ago von Ehrenfels pointed out that percepts have properties which cannot be derived from so-called sensations. A sensation has a good physiological standing. It is the phenomenal correlate of a well-defined stimulus. The properties of percepts which von Ehrenfels had in mind seem, however, to occur only where groups of stimuli cooperate in causing one phenomenal datum. The stimuli in question may be spatially or temporally distributed. Correspondingly, von Ehrenfels' qualities are the attributes of percepts which extend through areas in space or through stretches of time. They are not popular in sense physiology, which likes to study the reactions of single receptor cells to single stimuli. Properties which are character-istic of larger entities—and only of these—will evidently not fit into this scheme. A well-known example is the major or the minor character of a melody or of a chord. No single tone has minor character, whereas it is an essential trait of many tunes and chords. Although quite familiar to musicians, among psy-chologists such traits of auditory percepts had never before found the attention which they deserve. After what has been said above we need not discuss the reasons for such aloofness.

It would not be difficult to show that all percepts have such qualities. When things are called "tall" or "bulky," persons "slender" or "stout," movements "clumsy" or "graceful," reference is made to definite von Ehrenfels qualities. When we describe events as "sud-den" or "smooth," "jerky" or "continuous," we refer to the same class. Esthetically they are doubtless of paramount importance, but they are hardly less so, I think, in biological contexts. The color of the hair, the pitch of the voice may have much to do with the strong impression which specific persons of one sex make upon specific persons of the other. Still, properties of shape, of gesture, and of general movement are generally found to be at least as dangerous—and these are von Ehrenfels quali-ties.

In a certain sense such qualities of percepts are subjective. As we perceive them, they are functions of nervous processes; but this is true of all properties of all percepts. They seem more subjective than "green" or "blue" because no simple physical stimuli are responsible for their occurrence. It may be doubted whether, despite this serious disadvantage, they are not often particularly important as witnesses of objective reality.[2] Beyond any doubt they appear quite as much properties of the world around us as, for instance, colors and smells. Phenomenally, they are *objective*.

If I am present when two cars crash at a crossing, and if then I speak about the vehement or violent impact of one upon the other, one might say that in this description I attribute to

[2] W. Köhler, *Gestalt Psychology*. New York: Liveright, 1929, 174ff.

what I see traits that are borrowed from my own muscular or other subjective experiences. My answer would be that this is not the point which we are discussing at present. Whether the explanation by empathy is right or wrong, we have to distinguish between the functional genesis of phenomenal characters and their phenomenal appearance and localization as such. Supposing even that von Ehrenfels qualities like "vehement" have a subjective origin, from a descriptive point of view they are therefore no less objectively localized, are no less aspects of events themselves. Clumsy dancing looks clumsy there, outside, in a man or woman whom I see moving before me. It is again Fred Astaire, not I, who performs unheard of von Ehrenfels qualities in dancing; it is on the screen that I perceive them, not in my muscles. If genetically I should be responsible for all this, I am at least in simple experience unaware of my authorship. After all, it is a theory, not an observed fact, that such traits of percepts are always due to subjective sources. For unsophisticated perception vast numbers of von Ehrenfels qualities appear precisely where colors and other attributes appear with which customary thinking is better acquainted: in and on things, persons, and events. It follows that the less sophisticated people are, the more will they accept such properties of percepts at their face value.

Primitives are, of course, naïve realists. They cannot possibly distinguish between "mere percepts" and independent physical realities. A thing percept is for them the very prototype of reality, although they believe in further realities besides. In fact, percepts are for them—as for children—so real that they would hesitate to accept the name, if they could clearly understand its meaning. Why should they call a tree a "percept"? There simply *is* a tree before them to which, it is true, more or less attention may be given. That this tree which we call a percept remains unaltered in its place even when nobody is present who might have the percept, this is, for a naïve view of the world, the most natural thing. When before us, the tree certainly shows no striking symptoms of depending upon any subjects for its existence. One has to be far along in physics, physiology, or philosophy before anything like a problem can be discovered in this connection.

It is again well known that without such sophistication no

doubt will ever arise about the independent reality of all the sensory qualities which the tree or any other object may possess. We have seen, however, that the von Ehrenfels qualities of percepts are localized in and on these percepts. Primitives have no physics, no physiology, and no epistemology which could throw any shadow of suspicion upon these qualities. Consequently their naïve realism will apply to such characteristics of the world as it applies to any others. For them, things and events will have these properties independently and objectively. Thus their environment will have many aspects to which they attribute full objective value, while our scientific civilization denies such value and accordingly tends to impoverish our perception.

Many of these qualities are distinctly *dynamic*. What is "sudden" may, with increasing intensity, become "startling," "frightening," and "threatening." Such terms imply the subject's emotional reaction. But they also imply that in certain events or things there is a perceptual basis for the reaction. Here, as so often, much phenomenological truth is contained in language.

Not always is the "threatening" a high degree of the "sudden." While climbing once in the Alps I beheld, on stepping cautiously around a corner of the rocks, a big dark cloud which moved slowly and silently toward me along the slope. Nothing could look more sinister and more threatening. Genetically this might have been a case of empathy; but for my awareness the menace was certainly in the cloud. I could perhaps persuade myself that a cloud as such is an indifferent percept. If, however, I had been a primitive, no reason whatsoever could have given me such sober consolation. The threatening character of the cloud itself would have remained just as objective as its ugly dark color. Similarly the ocean itself is "wild" in a gale; and a mountain which appears high above the other tops in strange illumination is itself "majestic" or "forbidding." Primitives have no science of physics in our sense of the word, but those opinions about the world which they develop instead will necessarily differ widely from our own views. If the expression is admissible, it must be a curious "physics" in which the menacing character of a cloud, the wildness of a gale, the majesty of a mountain percept have at least the same rank and objectivity as, with us, measured distances, velocities, and weights. It is in the nature of such "physics" that it can never be a calm and critical survey of facts, as our science likes to be. The primitive's reality is apt to be too exciting for sober appreciation, since not only its effect on the subject, but also its own appearance is so often emotional. Awe and respect are more likely to characterize the primitive's attitude in such matters than is a spirit of critical investigation. Whatever else may follow, from this starting point ways may even lead to religion.

> In passing, a remark should be made on an old philosophical controversy. David Hume denies that any of our 'impressions' contain the quality of power or force. His opinion can only be held so long as, in a quiet environment, we discuss phenomenological questions in abstracto. At his writing desk the philosopher is apt to see the world as static and tranquil. It is, however, the sailor in a small ocean-going vessel, the airplane pilot, the tramp left to his own resources in any weather, who can tell us best whether there are any experiences of power, force, or dynamic traits in general. For us it is, of course, another question whether such dynamic traits of experience have any physical counterparts; but on the level of naïve realism this question has no sense. Here the objective world exhibits forces directly and not at all infrequently.

Not all dynamic qualities of things are startling. There is heaviness in a middle-sized stone, hardness in the same object, elasticity—not as a property defined by the physicist but as a perceived quality—in a young tree which my arm bends. Everyday physics of the layman deals with such properties of things as he is directly aware of them. This is true in Central Africa, but also in civilized countries, whenever people do not actually use the more sophisticated concepts of physical science—which is of course only done by a few. Regularly and with many objects this procedure is quite safe, because in many respects such simple von Ehrenfels qualities correspond fairly well with certain concepts of physics. So long as this is the case nobody objects and nobody would speak of mystical ideas.

Now and again, however, the situation acquires a slightly different character; namely, where the dynamic side of things and events grows beyond our feeling of control. Instead of a young sapling, a primitive may have bent an older and stronger tree. If he had any physics, he would look upon the situation with some knowledge of objective danger, otherwise with a sober and calm mind—but he has no physics in our meaning of the word. Instead, there is now in the tree a perceived power beyond the limits of what the man is able to handle safely. He will respect such power. It may be actually frightening when suddenly the tall stem breaks its bonds and jumps fiercely up into space. There is an awe-inspiring quality in the thing, just as there is in the sudden rush of high wind which often precedes a thunderstorm, or in the lightning which accompanies it.

Even when enhanced beyond the common, and concentrated to fearful intensity, such characteristics will for naïve realism still remain objective properties of things and events themselves. There is no reason why primitive man should not behave correspondingly. From the more trivial power qualities a nearly continuous series will extend for him through more striking cases to those where he is overwhelmed by fear. It is only natural that in his environment nothing should appear to him more important and impressive than unusual power in this sense, particularly since he knows so little of its rules and whims.

Here, it seems to me, we have the perceptual foundation of what some Melanesians call *mana*, the Crow Indians of North America *maxpé*, and some tribes in West Africa *njomm*.[3] Mana at least is a notion in which the thinking of widely differing peoples seems to agree. When Codrington first mentioned it, it appeared as a rather enigmatic term. If the phenomenological side of psychology had then been further developed the notion would have seemed less puzzling. In earlier phases of anthropology, before mana became better known, the notion was probably often misunderstood to mean a deity, a spirit, or a soul in things. Though it seems possible that on a certain level the con-

---

[3] R. H. Lowie, *Primitive Religion*. New York: Liveright, 1924, 75f.

cept of a soul develops as a special case of the general class mana, this term and its synonyms cannot originally and generally have had the special meaning of our word "soul." Tribes in many parts of the world find mana in certain things and events; but among these tribes there are some in which not even the human person himself has a soul comparable in meaning with the soul of Christian doctrine or Descartes' philosophy.[4] Few factors in our civilization make the anthropologist's work so difficult as our popularized mind-body dualism.

I should also hesitate to interpret mana as though it meant "supernatural." Where a thing, a person, or an event has mana, it remains for primitive man on the same general level of existence as other parts of his environment, although it is more conspicuous by its peculiar appearance or inherent power. Using our word "supernatural" in this connection, we are apt to lose sight of those obvious phenomenal facts upon which, if I am right, the notion of mana is ultimately founded. To some extent all things may have their mana. Innocent enough as simple heaviness of a stone, it may still be the same in principle where its intensity or particular behavior arouses respect and fear.

I mentioned above that in ordinary life our own treatment of many things refers to their power qualities as we perceive them naïvely. This attitude, however, is rather strictly limited by the scientific atmosphere in which we live. We have learned that most mana is merely a "subjective" phenomenon. No such restraint disturbs the naïve realism of primitive man. He remains consistent in handling things according to their inherent dynamic qualities. Consequently some of his activities will seem to us quite natural and sober, others altogether strange because they are contrary to the lessons of science. Here we begin to speak about *mystical* thinking and about *magic*. Westermann, however, denies that for the Kpelle themselves there is any sharp dividing line between "normal" activities and everyday magic. This may not apply to the Indians of North America; but among Africanists the same opinion seems to win more and more ad-

[4] D. Westermann, *Die Kpelle: Ein Negerstamm in Liberia*. Göttingen: Vandenhoeck, 1921, 174ff.

herents. Take the special case of medical practices. "The word
musamo . . . connotes . . . not only various medicinal remedies
proper, but also, and much more, many things whose power we
should call magical. The difficulty is to separate the two. From
the native point of view there is no difference."[5] When the African takes a hearty meal and thereby "fills himself with power,"
we are not surprised. If he is convinced, however, that by eating
the meat of a courageous animal he will himself acquire more
courage, we speak about superstition. As a matter of fact, we
have no evidence that for the native there is any essential difference between these cases.

With this example, it is true, we have touched upon a new
aspect of power qualities. Even where for us their functional sub-
jectivity seems altogether obvious, people without any science
will still remain naïve realists. For an object to have mana it is
by no means necessary that its peculiar characteristic appear
under all circumstances. The *new* thing, an event which does
not usually happen, is for this extraneous reason apt to be mana.
Certainly, the unexpected looks different; it has its peculiar appearance even for us; surprise, as other emotions, has its phenomenally objective counterpart. But we subtract easily from
"the real facts" what, for our critical attitude, reveals its subjective genesis so easily. Not so the native. Objects may have
for him the very highest degrees of mana which are for us as
trivial as possible. He does not yet realize clearly that the "striking"
in the new thing is due to its newness only. Strangeness is a
property of the thing itself; awe is the consequence, and action
will be taken correspondingly.

On the other hand, if an object has once exhibited power,
such experience has an aftereffect. It will look its power or have
the flavor of it, even under conditions where, without such previous experience, nobody would find its mana aspect very impressive. If in our own psychology we had no examples of "sign-
gestalt," as Tolman calls it, we could hardly understand much
primitive behavior. It is this principle which imbues thousands

[5] E. W. Smith and A. M. Dale, *The Ila-speaking Peoples of Northern
Rhodesia.* London: Macmillan, 1920. Vol. I, 222.

of objects with power which for the neutral observer may seem quite incapable of having any particular mana. When the courageous animal has been killed, its meat certainly does not look courageous to those who do not know from what it has been taken. But as the living animal will be regarded as courageous even at times when it is peacefully at rest, so its meat will still contain the valuable power. We add skeptically: for those whose apprehension of the object is distorted under the influence of previous experience. Yet the natives are not so sophisticated. So long as naïve realism is quite undisturbed the effect of previous experience prevails, while little attention is given to its psychological history. After all, it can happen here. The place where yesterday a cruel murder was committed would have today a strange look for most of us, even if no visible trace of the crime were left; many would feel uneasy in such a locality, and few would choose it as their living place.

For the native, mana qualities do not only *exist* in his environment, they also have definite forms of *behavior*. At least one of these is easily understood, if only we begin with examples where our own judgment agrees with that of primitive man. What is a smell? Very few people, those who have studied this special part of sense physiology, can give a clear answer. On the level of naïve realism on which to some degree we all remain in everyday life, a smell is a quality that tends to spread from one object and one place to others, as though it had the properties of an intangible light liquid. We do not put kerosene near butter or bread, lest the kerosene smell penetrate into the food. With onions the same precaution has to be taken, although here it is another quality which spreads to surrounding objects.

Smell is by no means the only entity that shows this behavior. From a fire the quality of heat migrates in all directions. The rain, the fog, and the thunderstorm spread from one place to the other. Most important of all, many a sickness creeps through the community from hut to hut; and an uncanny change which has just come over one man is soon discernible in others. Qualities of all kinds seem thus to travel through space, even though we cannot trace their ways in every detail. Should we object to this description of facts? One hundred years ago heat was an unweighable stuff even in orthodox physics; and its behavior was akin to that of smells and of infectious diseases. In a more general formulation: Qualities are transmitted from one object to another; and for primitive thinking such *transmission* seems to be the basic form of *causation*.

The same idea lingers still in our thought. It may also be entitled to more attention than it receives in modern epistemology. Even now our theorists are under the spell of David Hume's powerful work. Transmission of qualities has no place in our positivistic concept of causality. For our present purpose this concept may be sufficiently characterized as follows: An object has the property x, while in the same object and in its immediate environment we have the conditions a, b, c . . . . When a, b, c . . . change into a^1, b^1, c^1 . . . , instead of x the object assumes the property y. It is, since Hume, customary to say that no internal relation connects the nature of the change $x \rightarrow y$ with the nature of the change a, b, c . . . $\rightarrow a^1, b^1, c^1$. . . . Facts of coexistence and of sequence are *mere* facts, which means that a priori any datum might coexist with or follow any other. In principle, we do not get more out of nature than incomprehensible rules.

One sees at once that between this idea of causation and causation by transmission there is a striking difference. According to the positivistic notion, no matter how long we consider causes, we can never derive from this inspection any prediction as to the nature of the effect. Contrariwise, if causation is transmission of an identical quality, state, or entity from one locality, it follows necessarily that the effect, the appearance of that entity in the second place, must be similar to the cause which is the same entity as it appeared in its first place. *Causa aequat effectum.*

> It seems appropriate at this point to say one more word about a famous period in the history of European philosophy. Why should Descartes' school be so uneasy about the idea that mind and body interact? The reason seems to be simple. In his time causation was still widely conceived of as transmission of some quality from one thing to another. This primitive but rather

plausible idea had much power on the best minds as late as 1650. Two incomparable substances, they say, cannot influence each other. A modern positivist might ask: Where is the difficulty? But for the older view the problem is doubtless serious. If mind and body are really incomparable substances, nothing can be transmitted from one to the other. Otherwise the second would, by the fact of transmission, become similar to the first, which is impossible, since they are supposed to be incomparable forever. Thus neither can exert an influence upon the other. "Influence" is just the right word. No other term could express more characteristically what causation normally meant before the concept was so utterly changed by Hume.

Primitive people could point to many examples in which observation agrees well with the concept of causation by transmission. Effects are so often similar to causes that modern epistemology would do well to give the fact at least some attention. Take any of the cases which I have mentioned above. What is first in one place soon appears as something similar in the neighborhood. Some qualities do travel like thin fluids. But primitive man never formulates a definite notion of causality. It is probably not by a great number of confirming experiences that he is induced implicitly to favor just this particular notion. Rather its intrinsic plausibility seems to make it dominant—so dominant in fact that where the primitive is definitely wrong, the white man's appeal to contradictory experience is generally of no avail.

Very often the primitive *is* wrong. Unacquainted with any of our critical procedures, he extends his naïve realism to all possible qualities of things. Quite as uncritically, he applies to all these qualities his unformulated principle of causation by transmission. We accept some of the qualities and neglect many in our practical behavior; for we are trained by science. We are not very clear about causality; but our tacit acknowledgment of causation by transmission is definitely checked, again by the scientific attitude of our culture. Superadded criticism distinguishes our view of the world from that of primitive man, not mental traits of his which we could not understand at all. Once more: It seems a misconception to say that in some domains primitive man acts soberly, as we do, while in others he relies on peculiar mystical practices which constitute the sphere of magic. So long as no scientific criticism is possible, the practices of magic are probably as natural as any activities of which we approve. Both spring from the same sources: naïve realism and causation by transmission.

The fundamental rule of magic follows from these premises. If you wish to produce a definite effect in an object or in a person, you have to bring near him or, better, into him such things as are conspicuous by the quality in question. When we are cold we approach the fire or take a hot drink. This is not regarded as magic. Apply the principle generally, and civilized people will say that you perform magical practices. The primitive's child is slow in acquiring speech. The child's tongue lacks the necessary agility. Where do the parents find agility? In the lizard's tongue. Consequently the child will be fed lizard's tongues. The white critic might say that agility is not like calories which can really be transmitted from one object to another. Why not? The strange power of fire can thus be transmitted. We light a match, hold it near the cigarette, and at once the burning quality is transferred to the cigarette. For people who have no science there is no essential difference between one case and the other. Among the Thonga in Southeast Africa a mother who has not enough milk for her baby will eat euphorbia plants. These contain the necessary milkiness.[6] Without any chemistry people will rely on perceptual characteristics as they are directly given. Among the Spaniards of Tenerife, men who are losing their hair will eat the hairy stems of certain plants. The "hairiness" of these will make the hair grow. Primitive mentality need certainly not be essentially different from our own in order to develop such ideas. It has only to remain naïve and, in its basic primitive conceptions, thoroughly consistent.

Where power qualities are not absorbed in the form of food, but supposed to spread through space, magic seems to us more strangely magic. Still, the underlying principle remains the same

[6] H. Junod, *The Life of a South African Tribe* (2nd ed.). London: Macmillan, 1927, 47ff.

and agrees with our experience in the case of smell and heat. Instead of eating the strongest parts of a strong animal, a person may wear them somewhere on his body. From this *amulet* the power quality will permeate the owner. Since there are many capacities which a rich man will wish to possess, he may be forced to carry along a bundle of different power substances, one for each purpose—as he really does in West Africa. Contact is, of course, better than mere neighborhood. A few years ago the first national sweepstake was held in a country of Western Europe. A sailor won the big prize. When he came to the capital in order to get his money, the girls in the office crowded around the man and touched his body with their fingers. Apparently they felt that some of his luck-power might be conducted to themselves.

For reasons which I have mentioned above, considerable power may be contained in an object which, to European eyes, does not look conspicuous. This is generally true of those substances which are the main parts of so-called fetishes in West Africa. It is widely recognized at present that as a rule these objects are not idols or images of gods, but mana batteries like our storage cells. Their preparation by special experts involves the same principle of causation by transmission. In a special hut, protected against disturbing influences, the prospective new fetish is put near an old powerful battery and thus gradually charged.[7] It is in line with such ideas that, when wrongly treated, even the best fetish may lose much of its power. If that happens it is recharged or sold at a lower rate.

Even imitative magic, at first one of the more surprising activities of primitive man, seems to follow from the same principles: naïve realism in an extreme form and causation by transmission. At the time when rain should fall certain Mexican Indians carry a baby around the fields. The child is known to contain the power of nearly inexhaustible wetness. Apparently this quality will spread and soon it will begin to rain. I hope I do not exaggerate if I say that most monographs on primitive

[7] E. Pechüel-Loesche, *Volkskunde von Loango*. Stuttgart: Strecker, 1907, 366.

peoples contain reports about analogous practices. Often imitative magic produces the characteristics of an event rather than of any object. We know of several tribes where lightning or thunder is imitated as representative of thunderstorms and heavy rains.

I am not overlooking the fact that definite formulae and chants are generally quite as essential for magical purposes as powerful objects and performances. What can mere language have to do with mana? The obvious answer is that for naïve perception language may contain at least as much mana as any objects; and certainly it spreads. Once more our lack of understanding is self-produced. We know about sound waves, we have learned that in language indifferent auditory phenomena are merely associated with meanings. Such knowledge makes us unfit to realize what language is for the unsophisticated mind: a stream of often forceful content that issues from the mouth of man, full of hatred in one case, of love in another, of despair in a third. How could primitive people come upon the theory that language consists of sounds to which the hearer adds a subjective interpretation? Whatever may be true functionally, from a phenomenological point of view even we must acknowledge that this is not a correct description of language, that for naïve apprehension meanings are *in* the words and sentences of common speech. Small wonder that the native's naïve realism remains consistent in this case.

May I take an example from one of Malinowski's books. When among the Trobriand people a woman expects a baby, much has to be done for the child's health and beauty. One practice is this: Other women prepare a special skirt or coat for the mother. During their work definite formulae, sweet words about beauty, are spoken literally into the coat. Carefully folded, so that the wind cannot reach the inside and thus remove the charm, the cloth is carried to the mother who, with the coat, covers herself with the mana of those words.

In anthropological literature similar ideas are even applied to questions of human personality. Phenomenologically this seems a sound procedure. Some persons have a strikingly powerful appearance; and many people are conspicuous for their particular varieties of perceptible personality mana. When we think of unusual people, perhaps for a moment only, of Mussolini, of Lloyd George, of Greta Garbo, there is before us, often with a visual image, a characteristic and distinctive quality of being or living in each case. We cannot define it, yet it is obvious enough; it has the earmarks of a von Ehrenfels quality, comparable with the Mozart-character of some music and the Brahms-quality of another.

Since even common people talk and act in their individual manner, in all of them there is *some* mana which gives them or, perhaps, *is* their particular kind of aliveness. At certain times, however, this power does not show so clearly; apparently.it is absent. This would not be more surprising than that heat or a smell are here now and elsewhere later. Take the case of the man who is sleeping in his hut. Compared with what he is in daytime, he seems to be completely lacking in his distinctive personal essence. In the morning when he awakens it will be evident again. Where, then, has it been in the meantime? The man had a dream in which he was in another village. Thus we see where his personal power roamed while his body lay inert in the hut. When temporarily outside the body, that power will of course behave as human persons do. The dream tells us about its concrete activities. If these were of a criminal nature, punishment will seem to be fully justified. Lévy-Bruhl assumes that for native belief a man may be in two places at the same time, and that we can do no more than accept such an extraordinary contention. I hesitate to adopt this skeptical attitude so long as, in the manner just indicated, a more plausible interpretation is available.

IS THIS one more attempt to offer a standard solution for all anthropological enigmas? It is not meant to be. Criticizing another thesis, Lowie has once said, "that its very simplicity should militate against its acceptance."[8] I admit that the principles

---

[8] Lowie, *op. cit.*, 259.

which I have tried to apply to primitive behavior are simple. But then, only the very simplest forms of such behavior have been given an interpretation; and the discussion ends at a point where both problems and possible explanations begin to assume a higher degree of complexity. Hardly a word has been said about primitive religion, none about primitive art, again none about social life with all its institutions and ramifications. I am convinced that in these fields, too, psychology can be of more help to anthropology now than, say, thirty or even twenty years ago. But for such help other principles besides those of the present essay will have to be introduced. Even the problems which have been treated present certain aspects which can hardly be understood on such a narrow psychological basis. Causation by transmission, for example, is doubtless an essential factor in primitive thinking. But we know many primitive beliefs which, although somewhat similar to those discussed above, can nevertheless not be reduced to this principle. Lévy-Bruhl is right, I believe, in his assumption that typical cases of "participation" do not involve what we should call causation in any of its forms.

A more serious objection might be raised precisely on the ground that primitive society as such and its overwhelming influence on the individual have not been mentioned at all. No special form of magic, for instance, to which I have referred should, according to this criticism, be interpreted in terms of general psychology. Only in the group, as products of its creative faculty, can such practices ever arise; to the group the individual owes his magical beliefs; and as the nature of group life varies from one part of the world to another, the importance of magic and its special forms vary correspondingly.

This objection, it seems to me, is partly justified insofar as no attempt has really been made to explain any differences which, in such matters, are found among the various peoples of the globe. These differences are remarkable and of the greatest interest for anthropology. The reason why they have not been discussed is quite simple. One cannot do it without at once becoming involved in all the major disputes of present anthropology. On the other hand such a discussion was not strictly necessary. To some extent magic exists in practically every society. If my interpretation is right, at least some of its major premises are not peculiar to a few specific tribes but are the common property of all mankind below a certain high level of sophistication. From this common stock, which general developmental psychology is entitled to study and to explain, different societies, with their different environments and histories, have in fact derived different varieties of actual practices. I do not believe that we can fully understand the origin of such varieties before we know on what ground magic in general grows. That this ground is the group as such, and that the individual is no more than an empty container for the products of group mentality, seems to me an unacceptable thesis. If the individual were intrinsically incapable of such attitudes as fear, respect, aversion, love, and joy, of such functions as perception, learning, and memory, no influences of the group, however strong, could ever produce in him these mental events. It is my contention that the same applies to the psychological sources of magic. What springs from these sources is codetermined by the particular tradition of the group. Much magic also applies to group relationships as such, but the group contains no ultimate source of magic which is not also found in the individual.

20: *The obsessions of normal people*

I HAVE been asked to speak about some topic which concerns the frontier of knowledge in the social sciences. In trying to do so, I will first describe a curious phenomenon in the recent history of Western culture, which I will call the Smog. This phenomenon is worth our attention under all circumstances because it is still with us and is likely to disturb the work of the social scientists just as it disturbs other cultural activities of our time. But, from the psychological point of view, the Smog is only a special instance of a large class of psychological facts, the sentiments and obsessions of individuals and social groups. In virtually all social life, these facts, some good but others fairly dangerous, play an important role. In the second part of my paper, I will therefore discuss the functional characteristics of the whole class. It is my hope that, once these characteristics are better known, the social scientists will find it easier to deal with such phenomena in gen-

A paper read at the inauguration of the Graduate School of Arts and Sciences of Brandeis University, 1958. Reprinted by permission of Brandeis University.

eral, and with the Smog in particular. If this should happen, our knowledge of many social issues might be considerably improved.

I

When this country became independent, its leaders expressed their political convictions in most powerful statements. Seldom in the history of the species have men held quite so optimistic views; once the people were free to follow their natural virtues, they would, of course, advance toward ever higher levels of private and political conduct.

At the time, similar opinions were accepted also in parts of Europe—but there they were not accepted for long. Soon the first whiff of the Smog made itself felt, for now Schopenhauer began to fill chapter after chapter with lamentations about the sad lot of man. Must we not admit, he would say, that almost all our knowledge is made of purely subjective fabric? And is it not the only objective truth that irrational urge constitutes the very essence of being? Presently Schopenhauer's pessimistic philosophy was being discussed in many an elegant salon, and *Weltschmerz* became the fashion of the day. When Richard Wagner took over and made his tenors sing Schopenhauer and doom for hours, even the comfortable bourgeois was gradually converted to the case of enjoyable despair. In our days, the semi-intellectual Hitler still lived in this atmosphere, and we have it from Goebbels himself that scenes of utter destruction filled him with a strange glow of satisfaction.

But I have just skipped long stretches of history and more than one phase in the development of the Smog. Once it had arisen in one place, namely, in metaphysics, further clouds began to form in others, for instance, in social philosophy and in the history of culture. At this point, Marx's theory of economic facts and of related issues must be mentioned, because radical conclusions which Marx himself would not have accepted were soon developed from his theory by others. These distorted views became extremely popular—and their content was Smog at its worst. We remember the main argument. Since man must eat,

drink, and find shelter, the production of the material necessities
of living and, therefore, the economic motive are basic to all his
social and cultural achievements, including his legal systems, his
arts, and even his religious ideas. Hence, the explanation of all
these achievements must be given in terms of the economic motive. But a powerful economic class knows how to hide its preoccupation with profit behind an impressive façade of other, and
seemingly independent, values. Thus, less privileged people are
deceived, believe in the facade, and submit, for its sake, to the
rule of the class on top.

Now, it is a truism that in the lives of many people economic factors actually play a powerful part. Nevertheless, the
strange picture of human affairs to which I have just referred
cannot be accepted by any unbiased observer. There is no factual
evidence that all major actions of human beings spring from
the economic motive, or that their other motivations can be derived from this one source. It is true that people must eat, drink,
and find shelter. But then, they must also breathe. Who would
conclude from this fact that the nature of their cultural activities
expresses no more than their need of oxygen? And as to the
façade, how can the underdog be impressed by it, if all his own
needs, too, are merely versions of the economic motive?

There is something immature about the thinking which
could produce or accept such views, and there is also quite a
bit of spite behind it. Apparently, those who invented such interpretations of culture liked to destroy. In fact, they went so far
as to jeopardize man's conviction that, on the whole, he knows
the meaning of his own actions. For instance, those who, according to this doctrine, erect and embellish the façade, the philosophers, artists, and so forth, clearly fail to recognize what they
are doing, and what their own motives are, for, as they see it,
their work is mainly directed by demands inherent in their various tasks. Actually, however, they are now said to serve no
greater causes than their own wish to earn the material necessities of living and, indirectly, the paying capitalists' wish to
obtain a deceptive façade. If people know so little about the nature of their own actions, then they can hardly be regarded as

responsible agents. This is the most destructive implication of the doctrine. It does not matter whether such views have consistently been defended by this or that known author. At times, they have undoubtedly been held by many young intellectuals— who felt superior when they had just accepted the view that culture is not what it seems to be.

I need hardly discuss the efforts of some philosophers and scientists to invent so-called naturalistic explanations of man's thinking and his sense of moral obligation. Once the theory of evolution had become widely known, many attempts of this kind were made. Their authors always tried to show that the most outstanding mental facts derive from quite different, and far more primitive, sources. The implication is, of course, that these activities are outstanding only in appearance. All arguments of this kind involve the mistake which philosophers of our time call the "genetic fallacy." No explanation of the origin of given mental facts can be allowed to alter the characteristics of these facts as such. But this is precisely what happened in such speculations. Naturally, those who accepted them had henceforth a much lower opinion of man than they had had before—and so the Smog thickened.

I now turn to psychoanalysis, the source of more, and of darker, Smog than any other doctrine has produced. It takes some courage to speak of analysis in such terms, for nobody likes to be regarded as a reactionary, and at the present time acceptance of the tenets of psychoanalysis is taken for granted among those who must, under all circumstances, have so-called advanced views. One also hesitates to criticize psychoanalysis for better reasons. In the first place, Freud did reform psychology by placing motivation, which was then badly neglected, into its very center. Moreover, some analysts are obviously wise men in a general human sense, quite apart from their theories, and, with their wisdom, they seem to be capable of helping many a troubled mind. What, then, is to be criticized in psychoanalysis? The original thesis that sex lurks behind all our actions and thoughts can no longer disturb us seriously. It has been repeated too often and now begins to sound stale. Actually, there is danger that Eros himself, the boy with the bow and the arrows, who is not, of course, a god of sex alone, might eventually seem to be a bore. If this were to happen, we should have a very good reason for criticizing psychoanalysis. But we have a far more serious reason: according to the analysts, we seldom know why we act as we do, because our real motives are hidden in the unconscious. Psychoanalysis and certain forms of Marxism have two things in common: first, the thesis that one motive alone is of paramount importance—although the two views differ as to what this motive is; and, secondly, the claim that, over and over again, we are utterly unaware of the fact that this one power is at work—whichever it may actually be. How is a person to feel responsible for his actions once he has accepted such statements? According to the analysts, can he trust what seem to him to be the most convincing demands of his conscience? No, conscience has been unmasked. The voice of conscience, we are told, is only that of the censor, and the censor is a mere coward. He always insists on behavior of which the Joneses approve. But, then, what other guide are we to follow? There is only one left. We have to go to the analyst. He will hold our weak little hand; he will probe deeper and deeper into regions inaccessible to observation, but readily accessible to analytical theory; and he will finally talk us into decisions—which, under the circumstances, are bound to be the analyst's decisions. They may be good; they may be bad. The main point is that, in this fashion, the right way of living becomes a matter of which a specialist has to take care for us. Could any doctrine be more disheartening? And yet, few people seem to be disturbed by it, for, by now, we have learned to regard almost any Smog as part of our natural environment. In fact, there are now schools in which students are actually advised to rush to the analyst whenever the slightest problems arise in their lives. What will such young people do in situations in which they have to make their own decisions? But other consequences are just as bad. When we are teaching, we never tire of emphasizing that factual evidence, reliable method, and strict proof must be our students' guiding lights. But all this is suddenly forgotten when we invite the young people to be analyzed, for, in analysis, one just knows without such lights, and almost any theory invented by a facile imagination has chances of being accepted as truth. What is evidence? When I dream of "white," "white" is accepted as such if its occurrence in my dream fits the analyst's theory. But the same "white" may be interpreted as meaning "black" if this color fits the theory better. In the latter case, the censor has simply replaced the evil "black" by the more innocent looking "white." Trust the analyst to decide. Under the circumstances, it is by no means impossible that considerable parts of analytical doctrine will eventually prove to be mere inventions. And yet, we encourage our students to seek advice which is based on such dubious procedures. Why, then, do we talk so much about evidence, method, and proof in our classes?

The Smog produces a curious symptom. Soon, those who are strongly affected become unable to distinguish clearly between one intellectual food and another—provided the food fulfills this main condition: it must taste bad. In fact, the affected people fairly search the markets for food that would be rejected by others. After a while, sex in a less attractive sense no longer fully satisfied their appetite, and so they added the death instinct to their program. In the twenties, they even discovered that actually other motives may be more important than sex. To the outsider, this discovery proved that even their most confidently advertised dishes must be regarded with considerable caution. But, apparently, the proof was ignored. At any rate, analysis now offered a new food, which also had a bitter taste, namely anxiety. Whether we know it or not, we are never really safe, and what we do, or how we feel, tends to spring from this source. Thus the real invariant of the Smog, which is pessimism, was still preserved, and people could still feel as nicely despondent as they had done before. After all, earlier theories in which sex was replaced by other motives had also been eagerly accepted because they, too, fulfilled the necessary condition that man be shown to be a pathetic figure. Thus, according to some, it was the wish to succeed in society which makes man run. We are all climbers; and, since we cannot all climb as high as we wish, we constantly

404   *Special problems*

try to invent excuses for our failures, to avoid further tests so that we do not fail again, and to find substitutes for our real goals. What, after all, is greatness in the arts? Let us not be deceived. A painter may attain tremendous success in his efforts to overcompensate for a weakness of his eyes. But this is not good for him. And so we discover to our satisfaction that greatness correlates with a neurotic condition.

By now, all this has filtered into millions of minds by way of innumerable channels. I regret to say that it has also affected the minds of quite a few psychologists. If it is not anxiety about which these people write, then it is frustration; and, when it is neither, then it is likely to be aggression. Death instinct, anxiety, inferiority complex, frustration, aggression—what a vocabulary! Surely, we need not analyze the analysts and such psychologists. It suffices to hear them talk, or to read their books and papers. Never will they mention cheer, joy, happiness, hope, or fortitude. It is as though, among the chemists of our time, there were a fashion to talk endlessly about sulphur and arsenic, but never about iron and nickel, silver and gold. Incidentally, is it only the analysts and some psychologists who are no longer able to recognize the brighter parts of human life? Far from it. Nowadays, many writers are extremely well-informed people. We cannot be astonished if, after reading Smog abundantly in the experts' books, they soon write in the same vein. Entirely convincing examples may be found, for instance, in literary criticism. Quite recently, I read in an essay that artists are distinguished from other people by being able to shape the pain from which we all suffer. Is there nothing else they might occasionally be tempted to shape?

It will hardly be necessary to continue. Once a person has learned to recognize the Smog, he will discover its presence also in quarters to which I have not referred. But what can we do about this unfortunate predilection for the more dismal aspects of human life? It cannot, of course, be cured by a forced optimism. Clearly, the overbright view of human nature which was widely held toward the end of the eighteenth century must seem to all of us to be in need of some corrections. Evidence against this simple view is fairly strong. At least, it cannot be right for all human beings. This the last twenty-five years of history have clearly demonstrated. Hence, even though the sad picture of man that has developed in the years of Smog is seriously misleading, some fairly dark spots will also be left in a more adequate picture.

Now, if we take this for granted, but at the same time object to mere Smog, how are we to handle the present situation in which so much of this nuisance is still left? I sometimes wonder whether any particular measures are actually needed, for I have reasons to suspect that the big cloud will soon disperse spontaneously. In our colleges, for example, quite a few students begin to show a certain restlessness when Smog doctrines are explained to them at some length. On such occasions, their faces often look as though they wanted to say: "By now, we are a bit tired of this kind of thing. Why not talk about something else for a change?" Or take the following sentences which I have found in Jarrell's *Pictures from an Institution* (1954).

> Gertrude hated for anything to be latent or tacit or implicit: if there was an inexpressible secret to the world—or one unexpressed because taken for granted by everybody—she would express it or die. So her books analyzed (besides the sun, the moon, the starry heavens, and the moral order) the dew on the cobweb and the iridescence of Titania's wings; and they did not murder to dissect, but dissected to murder.

> Of any thousand pigs, or cats, or white rats, there are some who eat their litters and some, a good many more, who do not. Gertrude understood the first, the others she did not understand; she explained everything in terms of the first. They would all have behaved like the first except for—this, that, the other. She saw the worst: it was, indeed, her only principle of explanation. Consequently, she seemed to most people a writer of extraordinary penetration.[1]

[1] Quoted with the permission of both the author and his publisher (A. A. Knopf). Two sentences have been omitted at the end of the first paragraph, and a few words at the end of the second. The meaning of the original text is not changed by these omissions.

Can there be any doubt that the author of these remarks is fully aware of the Smog? It does seem that we need no longer worry. In fact, as a scientist, I almost fear that this ailment of our time may disappear too rapidly, for, as I said in the beginning, there is a large group of psychological facts, the obsessions of normal people, of which the Smog must be regarded as a special example. If we are to understand the psychology of individuals and of social groups, this whole class must be thoroughly studied; and since, from the point of view of social science, the Smog is a particularly striking specimen, it ought to be studied very soon—before it disappears. But what exactly do I mean when I refer to the obsessions of normal people? I will now explain.

II

In 1822, the novelist Stendhal published a remarkable book to which he gave the name *De L'Amour*. In this book, he described how love for a person of the other sex first comes into existence, and how it then develops into a persisting part of the individual's life. Love in Stendhal's sense is not, of course, a temporary feeling which arises only when the other person happens to be present, or when the first person actually thinks of the second. Rather, it has the characteristics of an enduring disposition which tends to give a person's thoughts, feelings, and actions a particular orientation. In fact, one is tempted to call it a most lively *thing*. Human beings develop various dispositions of this kind which, while differing widely in other respects, seem all to be formed and maintained according to more or less the same general principles. In modern psychology, the importance of such dispositions was first emphasized by British authors such as Shand, Stout, and McDougall—who called them *sentiments*. In America, it was mainly G. Allport who insisted on the importance of this concept. The term *sentiments* is probably not well chosen, and the word *attitudes,* which is often used in this country, seems to me equally inadequate. Both names sound as though they referred to fairly tame dispositions. Actually, while some may rightly be called tame, the more conspicuous members of the class tend to be rather wild creatures. Stendhal was mainly interested in the more powerful specimens; he therefore used the term *passions*. I prefer to talk of *obsessions*. This concept need not, of course, refer to pathological phenomena; in fact, we sometimes speak of an obsession when people merely exhibit a persistent preoccupation with their garden—or with the order of papers in their files. The term *obsessions* has a further advantage. It does not imply that all members of the class are characterized by strong accompanying emotions. Obsessions in the present sense may be intense and unyielding, and yet rarely operate at a high emotional temperature. I regret the fact that there is more than a hint of criticism in the meaning of the suggested name, for, while some obsessions are nuisances, and others actually dangerous entities, quite a few may be regarded as harmless, and many are simply necessary for coherent human living. The study of the obsessions as such must therefore be undertaken in a spirit of strict neutrality—whatever we may later say about individual instances. Hostility to the whole class would be a foolish attitude under all circumstances, for it is invariably obsessions which enable man to do creative work of one kind or another. No great novel, no major work of art, and no important investigation in science can ever have been completed without a sustaining obsession.

When discussing such facts, one is sometimes tempted to use expressions which are more commonly used in biology. For this there is a very good reason: an obsession tends to behave as though it were an organism which operates within the living organism as a whole. However it may first have come into existence, a vigorous youngster of the class often acts in a way which promotes its own growth. For instance, watch a person whom certain experiences make feel that his security is seriously threatened. Is his incipient obsession concerned only with these particular facts? Not at all, for soon his cognitive field begins to change in a remarkable fashion. Events which others would regard with perfect equanimity may now look dangerous to him; individuals who could possibly cause further insecurity are almost sure to become his enemies, and eventually he may even find it hard to open his letters—because each could announce a new threat. When you try to tranquilize the man by pointing to rather promising factors in his situation, what will he do? Most probably, he will refuse to accept your arguments, for, as he sees it, what seems to you promising is either irrelevant or favorable only in appearance. He just knows. Take him along for a walk, in the hope that exercise and the view of a pleasant countryside will dissipate his worries. Chances are that you will be disappointed. Why doesn't he quietly walk, but suddenly rushes so? You inquire, and to your amazement you hear him pouring out a veritable torrent of new misfortunes—clearly all of them his own creations.[2]

Obsessions are perfectionists, and once their intensity is considerable, they often manage to perfect themselves without the slightest help from the outside. It is well known that the "positive" obsessions act in this fashion. We are all acquainted with the fact that love may cover even a mediocre object with extraordinary charms. Stendhal called this process *La cristallisation* because he compared it with the formation of scintillating crystals on a meager twig which has been dipped in a concentrated solution of salt. Once he remarked that love is the only passion which thus "pays itself with money of its own fabrication." At this one point, it seems, Stendhal was wrong. We have just seen that fear which has become an obsession does exactly the same thing. Any student of the major obsessions will discover that the crystallization occurs in "negative" obsessions just as it does in the "positive" specimens. In the former, the process only takes a different direction; and, surely, nothing scintillates when the product is ready. In one case and the other, the final outcome, plus or minus, is conspicuous by its uniformity. But, unlike the generalization which can be observed after any ordinary process of conditioning, the uniformity established by obsessions is both caused and maintained by most intense psychological vectors.

[2] At this point, and also in the following, the present discussion obviously resembles statements which Krech and Crutchfield have made in the sixth chapter of their *Theory and Problems of Social Psychology* (McGraw-Hill, 1948). I refer particularly to a paragraph on page 104.

So far, only one aspect of the life of the obsessions has been considered. But an equally important aspect of this life can simply be derived from the first. When an obsession has begun to perfect its own object, this object becomes a better object from the point of view of the obsession itself. Hence, the motivational power of the obsession is now intensified. But as soon as this power is thus increased, its pressure on the cognitive field must once more grow, and thus make it even more uniformly fitting—whereupon the power grows again, and so forth. To use a now fashionable term, this is an excellent example of positive feedback. Clearly, unless radical measures are taken from the outside, major obsessions will tend to grow toward maximal uniformity of their objects, and at the same time toward maximal intensity of their driving vectors. Gestalt psychologists have often called attention to the fact that the products of perceptual organization tend to be most clearly structured. This is the main content of what the school has called the *Law of Prägnanz*. Actually, a more striking *Prägnanz* may be attained in the development of an obsession than has ever been found in mere perception.

Obsessions, we have just seen, tend to develop *upward* in the sense that their power grows to a maximum. From the point of view of natural science, this may at first appear to be a strange phenomenon. But, actually, we need not be surprised by this tendency. Any healthy young organism—I now use the term in the customary sense—exhibits the same development toward greater power. It is obviously enabled to do so by the fact that, all the time, it absorbs energy contained in its environment. The organism is an *open* system. Apparently, this principle is also involved when an obsession grows to ever greater strength, for it seems to grow at the expense of other motivational energies and of the valences contained in *their* objects. Stendhal reports that, when a person in love begins to despair of success, he will often try to fall back upon life's other attractions; but, he dryly adds, under the circumstances there just aren't any. How many other interests may have been left in Michelangelo while he furiously painted the frescoes of the Sistine Chapel? Anybody really caught by a major task will find that, at the time, the valence of most other occupations is reduced; and those who have to live with such a person will emphatically, and often bitterly, agree with his observation. To be sure, some authors object to this interpretation, according to which the growth of an obsession is, in a sense, a parasitic growth. There is no constant amount of mental energy, they would say, from which an obsession could extract portions to further its own growth. But this is hardly a convincing argument. Why should an obsession be capable of borrowing energy from other interests only if the total energy of this kind had a constant value? Moreover, how do the critics explain the simple facts which have just been mentioned? Major obsessions do tend to reduce the intensity of motivations which have other directions.

III

I began with a description of the Smog and then claimed that this phenomenon has the characteristics of an obsession, the strong obsession to discover more and more dismal facts in human life, and to distort others until they also fit this program. The claim that the Smog belongs in this category need hardly be justified in detail. We remember the vocabulary used by psychologists who have this disposition. No term in this vocabulary could make one suspect that, at times, living may be sheer joy, that a great enterprise may become more important to a person than his precious little ego, and that at least some human actions spring from plain decency. The uniformity in our picture of man which is achieved by such omissions, and by actual distortions, is obviously a product of what Stendhal called crystallization—although one hesitates to use this term when the final result looks so muddy.

Once more I suggest that we study this particular obsession before it passes away. It must particularly interest the student of social life because it has appeared not only in this or that individual, but in wide strata of society, and, historically, in one generation after another. Several periods of history have been characterized by obsessions of their own. The Renaissance, for instance, rebelled against the formalism of the Schools and against traditional rigidity in the arts. This period wanted to go back to what is regarded as Nature, and, in trying to do so, it chose as its teachers ancient Greece and Rome. What then happened exhibits all the symptoms of a grand obsession. With a different principal content and with a different tone of feeling, the great Era of Reason exhibited another powerful obsession. Both periods ought to be examined from the present point of view, precisely because we can now see them from a distance. But great historical distance also causes difficulties, which will not arise if we study the Smog, for the Smog is still fairly strong. Hence, if we invite the right people, we can actually observe its curious symptoms in our own living room.

Could it be said that, in describing the behavior of the obsessions, I, myself, have contributed to the Smog? I do not think so. To be sure, I have stated that an obsession tends to transform a person's cognitive field, that as a consequence, its power grows, that it can do much further transforming, and so forth. Moreover, I have added that coherent human living is possible only if it is sustained by obsessions of one kind or another. But does it follow that, for such reasons, all human conduct is a pitiful affair? By no means. First of all, while no example of a valuable obsession has here been discussed—I barely mentioned the great obsessions of two historical periods—there actually are a great many such instances. For example, it is the main characteristic of some obsessions that, while they also transform the cognitive field, they generally do so by making it clearer, and by revealing new facts which nobody has seen before. When an obsession affects its own subject matter, it does not always do so by altering the characteristics of given facts, or by simply inventing new facts, for there may also be actual evidence which, once it is discovered, will support the obsession. Highly sensitive to this possibility as it is, the obsession will, of course, make such discoveries with particular ease. Hence, any obsessions, including those which we do not like, may change the cognitive field not only by distorting its content but also by adding new objective knowledge. To be sure, in some instances this new knowledge will interest only the person whose obsession has led to the discovery. In others, we may feel that the facts in question would better have remained undiscovered. But there is one obsession in which the attempt to discover new facts is always meant to serve a purpose of which we all approve. This is the obsession of a scientist (or a historian) who does research of considerable scope. He transforms his cognitive field by finding new facts which may presently make it both clearer and more coherent. It is the very object of his obsession that this happen. This applies, of course, also to the obsession of a great physician who tries to find out what lies behind the curious combination of symptoms in certain patients—and to that of the man from Scotland Yard who is in charge of an investigation in the field of crime.

Not all obsessions which we accept, or admire, operate in this fashion. Is it really the business of all human activities to deal with objectively established facts or to find some more? The poet, the novelist, the painter, the sculptor and, of course, the composer, all add to existing facts new creations of their own. When these have been completed, there simply are more real facts in the world than there were before, and from the point of view of value, some such facts can readily compete with most real facts in the usual sense of the word. Obviously, it does not matter whether the new specimens have counterparts among the old. To be sure, certain obsessions are necessary for their production, and there is no doubt that these obsessions do a lot of forming in the artist's cognitive field. But this is precisely what they must do if the new facts are to be worth the efforts of their authors and the attention of other people.

21: *The scientists from europe*
and their new environment

I HAVE been invited to speak about the immigration of European scientists in general. Unfortunately, this is too big a task for me. I propose to make only a few remarks about developments which, twenty years ago, followed the immigration of outstanding men in natural science, and will then turn to an entirely different immigration, which occurred in psychology, and began much earlier.

The influence of the immigration in natural science was immediate, and obviously all to the good. Since both among the Europeans and their American colleagues standards of experimentation and reasoning were extremely high, no serious disputes could ever arise between the two parties. Actually, among the newcomers many were well known in this country long before they immigrated. Most American scientists will nevertheless admit that closer personal relations soon increased the rate at which new discoveries were now made.

The men from Europe had not been here for many years when a situation arose in which some could show their intellectual power in a most frightening application of physics to public affairs. It was a mathematical physicist from Germany who, in a letter written in the fall of 1939, called President Roosevelt's attention to discoveries in subatomic physics which had recently been made by investigators in various countries. According to the physicist, so powerful a weapon might be constructed on the basis of these discoveries that even the strongest explosives so far produced in munition factories would look obsolete in comparison. The United States did not want to remain behind a potential enemy with regard to any weapon which human ingenuity could build at the time, and so the Manhattan Project came step by step into existence. Several European scientists played a leading part in the actual construction of what is now called the atomic bomb. When the first of these terrific devices had just destroyed large parts of a Japanese city, both Mr. Truman and Mr. Churchill found it necessary to explain to the world what had happened, and why they had believed that it must happen. Ever since, we have lived in a new era of political and military thought, torn between the hope that, after this extraordinary demonstration of man's ability to destroy, nations simply must learn to live together in peace—and a suspicion that even this lesson might not have been enough.

It is my impression that, on the whole, both the Americans and the Europeans who participated in this work intensely dislike their own creation. They probably hope never to see it used again in an attack on people, least of all on civilians. Science has never made a greater impact on mankind than it did by this sinister product of collaboration between physicists from abroad and Americans. To my regret, the great revelations about the nature of the physical world, which made the bomb possible, have left most of us pretty cold. That fascinating achievement of the human mind which we call physics is in this country adequately known only to small groups. But we tremble when thinking of the fearsome consequences which would follow if it should next be our turn.

In the meantime, collaboration between the men from Europe and the American physicists has become so intimate that their descent from different cultural stocks is half forgotten when they work together, excepting that the two parties may sometimes tease each other. Thus a European might make a friendly joke about the American tendency to emphasize so-called know-how, for instance, in building ever bigger and better cyclotrons; and an American might retaliate by asking how the Europeans manage to build a new universe every few years in mere thought—not to mention their articles about the new models, which read like modern poetry, and are equally hard to understand.

THERE has also been an immigration of excellent biologists, and the work of some has clearly added new ways of studying living systems to the methods previously familiar in America. One of the most important advances in biology has, however, been brought about by physicists, in fact precisely by the work of those who constructed the atomic bomb. The "piles" which are used for this purpose yield not only the substances which explode in atomic bombs but also less harmful materials. While the atoms of these materials are chemically equivalent to ordinary atoms, such as those of carbon or phosphorus, they differ from their common relatives by being radioactive. This means that they announce their presence by electrical disturbances in their environment, which can readily be detected. Now, until recently, physiologists had considerable difficulties in tracing the course of various chemical substances within the organism. At present these difficulties are gradually being overcome, because when the new radioactive atoms are substituted for their ordinary counterparts they form the same chemical compounds as these and are, in such compounds, transported to the same places. There is no serious interference with normal processes within the organism while, nevertheless, the distribution of important chemicals in these processes can now be followed by means of sensitive electrical devices. For this reason the new elements are called "tracers." A whole literature is rapidly growing up in biology and medicine which is exclusively concerned with the paths of radioactive atoms in the body. It stands to reason that not only the physiology of normal organic processes but also the study of certain diseases must greatly profit from this excellent method. Physicists from abroad and their American colleagues are likely to feel considerably relieved when realizing that, in the long run, far more human lives may be saved in this fashion than have so far been destroyed by bombs which came from the same piles.

In this instance, the physicists' contribution to biology was only a by-product of work which originally had another purpose. But in recent times some physicists have turned to biological investigations quite deliberately. This is a new development which some time ago began in Europe, and is now spreading in America mostly under the influence of physicists from abroad. In more than one direction, physics has now advanced so far that, within the boundaries of this science, further progress in the same directions is hardly possible. But it seems that one cannot stop a good physicist. When he reaches a boundary, he finds it natural to look beyond. If what he sees appears to him interesting, he will presently trespass, and begin work on the other side. Now, beyond physics lies biology. The result is that some of the best physicists and chemists are now investigating fundamental problems in this science. For instance, such men are now making great progress in the study of viruses. What could be more fascinating than the behavior of these curious agents, which can in certain respects be compared with that of living matter, while in others it is that of enormous molecules? Most probably, such studies will also prove to have important consequences in medicine. For we all know that several dangerous diseases originate when viruses rather than germs invade the organism.

Another fundamental problem in biology which is now being studied by physicists and chemists from Europe is that of photosynthesis. Most plants have the gift of combining simple chemical substances into organic compounds with the help of light. Without photosynthesis, there would be no human beings. We cannot live without food, and our food consists of organic substances which are formed either in plants or in animals. In the former case, the substances in question derive from simpler organic compounds which owe their existence to photosynthesis. But this is the ultimate origin of our food also in the latter case. For, in the last analysis, animal life is possible only because so many animals eat plants, and thus assimilate chemical compounds, the first origin of which is photosynthesis. Obviously, when we eat parts of carnivorous animals, the original source of our food is still the same. Thus, photosynthesis occupies a key position in general biology. If, therefore, exact science could fully clarify this particular process, our understanding of life in terms of more general principles would be greatly advanced.

I WILL now turn to my own field, which is psychology. But let us distinguish. Much psychological wisdom may be found in Cervantes, in Shakespeare, and in the great novelists of the nineteenth century. Psychology in this sense, I must say with regret, has never played an important role in the psychology with which I shall now deal, the psychology which claims to be a science. The former must therefore be excluded from my report. For another reason, I cannot discuss a certain field in which a mixture of psychoanalysis and social psychology is now rife. Let me mention only two discoveries in this field. The education of Japanese boys is very strict; therefore the adult Japanese is aggressive, and starts wars. Or, Russian babies have to wear their diapers extremely tight; therefore Russian grown-ups are not nice to the people of other countries. What particular fashion in diapers, long since discarded, must we blame for the fact that the now grown-up discoverers of such causal connections never feel the slightest need of proving that their assertions are right? This need is so strongly felt in what we call science that the discoveries themselves must here be ignored. In the following, I will mainly deal with those parts of psychology in which a solid core of knowledge is gradually being established.

It would be quite misleading to say that American psychology has merely been influenced by an immigration from Europe. In this respect, developments in psychology have differed entirely from those in the natural sciences. For, sixty or seventy years ago, American psychology as a whole was virtually created by the immigration of men and ideas from Europe. Moreover, one European psychologist after another then came to this country, and somehow affected the ways of American psychology long before Mussolini and Hitler came to power. The arrival of a few more European psychologists in the thirties could therefore no longer have a decisive influence upon further developments. Under these circumstances, I cannot restrict my remarks to the post-Hitler period. I must look farther back, and must describe how psychology as a science was first imported, how America reacted at the time, and how she reacted again when more and more psychologists arrived from abroad. Technical matters I cannot, of course, explain here. Rather, what I have to say will be related to issues in which many are likely to be interested. For my main theme is the way in which particular trends in the history of American psychology have sprung from far more general convictions held by individuals or groups, both American and European.

When, late in the nineteenth century and early in the twentieth, the student population of America began to grow in the most extraordinary fashion, and young people heard for the first time about the achievements of science, the effect on some must have been almost intoxicating. But, if natural science could make such an impression, how utterly fascinating must have been the news that, just a short time ago, the Germans had succeeded in establishing a rigorous science also of the mind. Obviously the new discipline could best be studied at its source. Thus American psychology came into being when a number of young people first went to Germany to study experimental psychology under Wundt in Leipzig, and then returned to America, where they promptly founded psychological laboratories in the

German style. As a result, early American psychology had an unmistakable European flavor. It also happened that presently a few Europeans came over, who were equally enthusiastic about the new science, who knew it even better, and among whom at least one, the Englishman Titchener, was not only an expert in Wundt's psychology but also a most powerful person. At the time, the Germans used two procedures: one consisted of experimentation and measurement, preferably in the fields of sensation and memory; in the other, simple human experiences were established in trained observers, and then critically inspected, until their true nature, no longer discolored by any impurities, was finally revealed. It was these procedures which Titchener and others recommended to their American students.

Neither one technique nor the other appealed to William James of Harvard. His eyes were open to anything that passes through human minds, and he had just gathered into a great treatise what he had found there. One can hardly say that his contempt for the new psychology was only an American reaction. Rather, it was the reaction of a man who felt life more strongly than most others, who was intensely interested in philosophical problems, and who had an unfailing sense of proportion. The new endeavor seemed to him unbelievably pretentious with its scientific trimmings, pathetically narrow in scope, and therefore boring almost beyond endurance. Why did the new psychologists measure at all, if what they measured were unimportant nuances of sensation and the like? He strongly felt that when people begin to measure for the sake of measuring, and thus to deal with small things which alone can be so treated, the existence of all greater things will eventually be ignored. While little harm would be done in this fashion if the mistake were made in some corner of natural science, results were bound to be deplorable when the subject matter in question was the most important of all, the nature of man himself. This part of the world, James felt, should not be so distorted under any circumstances, not even in the name of science. We remember that it was William James who once, embittered by the one-track mentality of certain scientists, ascribed to them the slogan:

Fiat scientia, pereat mundus, which may loosely be translated as "Science comes first. If meanwhile the world goes to pieces, we do not care."

The new psychologists, on the other hand, paid little attention to William James. For, with his need for a wider visual field, he did not spend untold days in a laboratory; he refused to measure, because he was not interested in what was being measured; and the full drama of mental life remained to him incomparably more important than the fact that, in detail, something had now become possible in psychology that resembled science. Apparently he was not a scientist at all. To a degree, the contrast between James's view and that of the experimentalists-at-all-costs still exists, and it will not entirely disappear until scientific psychology has become great enough for its tremendous task.

I mentioned two procedures which were initially recommended in the new science: the various techniques of experimentation and the patient observation of certain mental data as such. The latter procedure was not accepted for long in America. Impatient young Americans would soon ask: "Is the study of psychological events to be postponed until the last static element of human experience has been sufficiently inspected? Why not start at once with the investigation of what actually happens, that is, of mental function?" They had hardly spoken when much louder voices were raised which demanded that the second procedure, the inspection of mental data as such, be given up entirely. The voices were those of the early American behaviorists. "What is this," they would say, "a science, or one more version of old-fashioned philosophical speculation? We are invited to inspect what is happening in our own minds? As scientists, we strongly object to this advice. So-called mental facts do not constitute a material with which a real science can deal with any confidence. In science, one observes only what is accessible to everybody. No other observation can be called objective. But in the alleged inspection of mental data a person is concerned with purely subjective phenomena to which nobody but he has any access. To make things worse, no second person can ever be sure that in a first person there are any mental facts at all. Psychologists should therefore study only a subject's vocalizations, which are physical sounds, or the movements of his face, or those of other parts of his body. In other words, so long as psychological procedures claim to be scientific they must be restricted to the study of behavior."

I wonder whether the word "science" has ever been written in bigger capitals than it was by the behaviorists. Epistemologically, of course, their argument was rather naïve. It could easily be turned upside down on the ground that no physicist, and also no behaviorist, can ever directly observe the objective facts of which the behaviorists were so fond. Such facts become known only by perception, that is, by one of the subjective phenomena with which the behaviorists did not want to deal. At the present time we no longer get excited about such errors. They go with being very young. It takes some time to become mature, and history seems to have no treatment by which the process can be greatly accelerated. Also, it is only fair to add that during the past forty years behaviorism has changed considerably; there is far more sophistication in its present attitude than could be discovered in its early statements. Actually, however, precisely these early statements were a tremendous success. The part of the imported science which dealt with the inspection of mental data collapsed in a surprisingly short time; even former students of Titchener were gradually converted to the new religion, and when I first came to this country a young psychologist would hesitate to confess that he was not yet entirely convinced. Whichever way he turned, all around him the Joneses in psychology were now talking Behaviorese.

What all this amounted to was, of course, that experimental psychology, which had come from Germany as a pretty narrow enterprise, became for a while narrower still in this country. The behaviorists, forever suspicious of mental facts, seemed to be afraid even of the vehicle by which such facts are in a way transmitted from one person to another, that is, of language. At any rate, many members of the new school turned away from man, who can talk, and preferred to work with animals, who cannot. But if in this fashion the scope of psychology was seriously reduced in one direction, the young science rapidly expanded in the new direction. Animal psychologists invented one technique of investigation after another, and at the present time their methods belong to the best we have. Another, and equally propitious, development soon followed. Dealing with animals as they were, some behaviorists learned to combine psychological experimentation with physiological procedures, and the result was what we now call physiological psychology. From its very beginning, physiological psychology has been mainly an American enterprise, and in other parts of the world there is little that can be compared with the work of Professor Lashley and his students. Strange things happen in the history of intellectual culture. When, in a certain period, some mistake is made by practically everybody, this very mistake has sometimes fortunate consequences.

One cannot deny, however, that the opposite also happens. The very virtues of an historical period often give birth to little affiliated vices. Who would now object to the behaviorists' admiration of science? But, unfortunately, this admiration soon went so far that concepts and techniques of natural science, which are meant to be man's tools, soon threatened to become the psychologists' masters. When no longer able to move along the rails laid down by the older sciences, the new scientists would feel seriously disturbed; and when asked to deal with facts, the like of which seem never to be found in physical nature, they would become both frightened and indignant. It will be my next task to illustrate these remarks by specific examples.

Some European psychologists had in the meantime recovered from that extreme devotion to experimental science which, during the early years of scientific psychology, must sometimes have been almost like a fever. One of these men, William McDougall, immigrated from Oxford just when the behaviorists were running a higher temperature than had ever been observed in Europe. Upon his arrival, and being confronted with behaviorism, he made statements more or less as follows:

> The commandments of natural science must, of course, be obeyed. But the behaviorists forget to mention one such commandment, in fact, the one which should be given first rank. If in a given field we make certain observations, and particu-

larly if we make them all the time, such observations must be accepted under all circumstances, whatever may happen elsewhere. Otherwise, why should activities in this field be honored by the name of empirical science? The behaviorists, however, not only fail to mention this commandment, they disobey it consistently. What is the reason for this strange conduct? There can be only one reason: In this fashion they are enabled to choose such facts as fit their particular philosophy, and to ignore all those which do not fit. Now there is something that clearly does not fit. Watch a rat in a maze. The most outstanding characteristic of his behavior is *striving*. Always the creature is after something, or tries to get away from something else. It is, of course, the same with man, including the behaviorist who, for a certain purpose, selects some empirical data, and refuses to recognize others. Striving is the very essence of mental life. Really, behaviorists ought to learn about the more elementary facts of life before they advertise their junior-size science.

So the immigrant from England, in spirit if not literally. It is to be regretted that, in his own later work, McDougall did not always follow the other commandments of science, those which the behaviorists rightly respected. Nothing weakened his influence upon American psychology so much as did this fact. But there is no question that he was an uncommonly courageous man. Not all scientists are willing to swim against the current which carries most of their colleagues in the opposite direction. Moreover, his main thesis, William James all over again, was undoubtedly right.

The uproar which followed McDougall's statements was terrific. The banners of strictly scientific psychology raised high, the behaviorists counterattacked at once. Not only was McDougall obviously an armchair psychologist; far worse, he was a philosopher who had just slipped back into medieval speculation. For had not science begun its modern development when she discarded the notion that there are goals or purposes in nature? How could psychology hope to prosper if such concepts were admitted in the new science? Unperturbed, McDougall answered that, as a help in thinking and making certain observations, the armchair was probably a better instrument than many gadgets used by the experimentalists. Perhaps more armchairs and correspondingly intensified thinking were just the remedies which the behaviorists needed.

The behaviorists did not like this remark; and they indignantly rejected the suggestion that McDougall's observations, unsupported by any experimentation as they were, should be seriously considered in psychology. In the new science everything had to be just as it was in natural science, including the methods of observation and the basic characteristics of facts. It does seem that love can make people blind, even a certain love of science. In 1925, soon after my first arrival in this country, I had a curious experience. When once talking with a graduate student of psychology who was, of course, a behaviorist, I remarked that McDougall's psychology of striving seemed to me to be associated with certain philosophical theses which I found it hard to accept; but that he might nevertheless be right in insisting that, as a matter of simple observation, people do this or that in order to reach certain goals. Did not the student himself sometimes go to a post office in order to buy stamps? And did he not just now prepare himself for certain examinations to be held next Thursday? The answer was prompt: "I never do such things," said the student. There is nothing like a solid scientific conviction.

Once more we realize that the impact of European psychology upon developments in America occurred under conditions entirely different from those under which the immigration, say, of European physicists occurred in the thirties. When these physicists arrived, there was no longer any doubt what the fundamental facts, the main procedures, and the essential tasks of physics are. Irrespective of where individual physicists were born, they would therefore give any new discovery about the same place in a well-established system. Psychology, on the other hand, was almost an infant when Europeans, such as McDougall, tried to make themselves heard in America. In a science which is so young, premises of individual or national origin are bound to have a strong influence upon scientific conduct. Physicists, of course, also work with a background of convictions which is not, strictly speaking, derived from scientific evidence alone. But in physics such convictions are at least largely under the control of vast amounts of knowledge which all physicists share, and thus their convictions show great uniformity. Psychologists had no such common background at the time of McDougall's criticism. Even now, coherent bodies of knowledge develop only slowly in this young discipline, and therefore background convictions may still vary tremendously from one psychologist to another. Psychologists who love a particular form of science are, of course, also swayed by convictions which are by no means results of science. It may not have been particular scientific findings in the usual sense which made James and McDougall so strongly aware of certain phases of mental life. But surely it was not empirical evidence of any kind which caused the behaviorists' refusal to deal with these facts at all. They just knew, or believed that they knew, what can happen in the world, including its mental division; and they knew even better what cannot possibly happen in this realm. In such matters, the situation in psychology will not change until, as a consequence of the work of many, with many different backgrounds, actual knowledge forces common convictions upon all of us.

Scientific psychology is not only a creation of human beings; it also mainly deals with human beings. While, therefore, in natural science, which is supposed to study neutral facts, general convictions tend to be fairly calm, trends in psychology often depend upon convictions of a much more powerful sort. In many, these convictions refer to the very nature of man, and to what one is permitted, or not permitted, to do about him. Such people are not likely to remain entirely calm when they feel that other psychologists distort mental life into a caricature, the outlines of which are prescribed by a narrow conception of science. On the other hand, the psychologists who are so criticized will not only feel offended by this critique, which accuses them of a certain blindness, but will also be indignant when their opponents refuse to regard experimental science as the final arbiter in all matters.

In clinical psychology much use is made of so-called projective techniques. A patient is shown ink blots, or pictures of certain scenes, and is invited to interpret what he has before him. His interpretation is supposed to contain much information about his personality and his mental troubles. When we want to know what kind of people the various psychologists are, and what they believe in, we do not need such tests. Psychologists are quite eager to give us the necessary information in their articles and books—if not in so many words, at least implicitly. An understanding reader will soon know what background convictions lie behind a psychologist's work, not only because in a given instance certain topics are strongly emphasized and certain explanations consistently preferred to others, but also because some topics and possible explanations are never mentioned. Testimony of this kind is just as eloquent as any interpretations of ink blots can ever be. But why do convictions vary so much from one psychologist to another? Partly, the variations may derive from congenital differences in the make-up of individual personalities. Far more obvious, however, is the influence of the cultural climates in which the various psychologists have grown up. McDougall came to America with convictions about the nature of mental life which were inspired by the cultural tradition not only of his country but also of Europe in general. Aristotle, St. Augustine, Pascal, and Spinoza had as much to do with these convictions as had Hume and Stuart Mill. The behaviorists, too, held convictions which had arrived from Europe; but these convictions had far less illustrious sources.

At this point I should like to make a more general remark about contacts between people whose cultural traditions differ. Many take it for granted that cultural traditions constitute, without exception, subjective facts, even if the subjectivisms in question are trends of thought and feeling which history has established in whole populations. If this were right, it would, of course, be futile to argue about such traditions. As a matter of fact, well-meaning persons sometimes assure us that, if we merely made it a rule never to mention such differences among peoples as stem from the cultural histories of their various countries, the world would be a far more peaceful place. This, I believe, is dangerous advice. For how long would peace be safe if it were based on a cultural skepticism which itself is not defensible? Surely, not all effects of cultural traditions lie beyond the scope of reasonable argument. For it is also an effect of such traditions if the great importance of certain issues is clearly realized somewhere, and hardly recognized elsewhere. Suppose that, as a consequence of certain traditions, some nations have many good schools, while others have no more than a few. How can we possibly maintain that in such a case only two different national prejudices have been at work? To be sure, the various beliefs and attitudes which we find in one part of the world or another are results of historical developments. But this holds also for mathematical knowledge, a product of history which, as we all know, grew up earlier in some countries than in others. Nobody concludes that mathematics is merely an expression of national predilections. Hence, why should we assert that all other products of particular cultures are subjective in this sense? Some aspects of cultural traditions cannot, of course, be matters of serious debate, just as individuals rightly refrain from arguing about certain personal preferences. I need not give examples. But now take an Englishman who has been trained to temper political conviction with a feeling of responsibility for practical consequences. If such a man were to tell a Frenchman that traditional forms of parliamentary conduct in France might sooner or later wreck his country, would his remark express no more than a British prejudice? Again, if after studying life in the United States a Frenchman were to say that many Americans seem to work too hard for their own good, his judgment would, of course, be in line with certain traditions of his country, just as the criticized American behavior agrees with an American tradition, possibly that of Puritanism. But would it follow that the Frenchman is wrong? Most probably, national traditions represent mixtures of harmless local subjectivisms, of local shortcomings, but also of national virtues. In the cultural pattern of almost all countries there may be virtues which others have not developed to the same degree. If this is true, one country ought to be willing to be another's pupil as well as teacher. Obviously, I am now supposing that those who, on a given occasion, happen to be teachers proceed with utmost tact, and that they always remain prepared to assume the role of pupils on the next occasion.

This applies to the contact between psychologists from Europe and their American colleagues just as it applies to more general issues. To my knowledge, no disputes between American and European psychologists have ever degenerated into antagonisms of a nationalistic kind in the usual sense of this term. But if we say this with approval, we must also repeat that not all differences of opinion in psychology which spring from different cultural traditions should, because of this origin, simply be ignored. On the contrary, some such differences are clearly proper subjects of discussion, and ways of looking at mental life which now are mainly found in a certain local tradition may very much deserve the attention of psychologists with a different tradition. The same holds, even more obviously, for local differences as to scientific procedure. As a simple example, I should like to mention that probably all European psychologists who came to this country learned from their American colleagues to be much stricter about experimental proof than they had been before. In this respect, the American tradition had been superior. But Americans were also willing to learn from those who came from Europe. The great question whether scientific psychology should be concerned with striving and purpose did not for long remain related to the difference between one kind of passport and another. Actually it was a behaviorist, Professor Tolman of California, who first admitted that purpose must be given a central position among the concepts of psychology. He also convinced other behaviorists by showing that purpose can be subjected to exact experimental investigations.

For a while, we remember, purpose had not appeared to be acceptable in psychology because it had no counterpart in natural science. We remarked, however, that there was a further difficulty. As the master of young psychology, the spirit of traditional science objected not only to certain subject matters; it also restricted observation to particular forms of investigation. On what evidence did McDougall maintain that the study of purpose is a major task of psychology? He offered no results of experimentation, and no statistics. Under the circumstances, why should a psychologist listen to him?

Although, in the present instance, this argument has fortunately not prevailed, it is very much worth our attention, because at times it still determines a psychologist's attitude toward new facts. The very excellence of the procedures now generally used in experimental psychology tends to limit the scope of its investigations; for simpler forms of observation, which are less impressive and in a sense less precise but nevertheless altogether indispensable, have gradually become quite unpopular. Let me say a few words in defense of such observations.

In the first place, experimentation need not be a quantitative procedure. First attempts at clarification in a new field will often be greatly facilitated if the investigator observes in a qualitative way what happens under one condition and another. Outstanding work of this kind has sometimes been done even in modern physics. Secondly, observations of the very greatest significance may also be made without experimentation in any sense. Naturally, psychologists from Europe are more likely to admit that this is true than are their American colleagues, because psychological observations of a very simple kind had been part of the cultural tradition in Europe long before psychology learned to use experimental methods. Aristotle knew about the association of ideas. Both he and the Arabs were familiar with the moon illusion. Leonardo studied the curious system formed by the various colors. Contrast, afterimages, and dark adaptation were matters of fairly general interest around 1800. When McDougall pointed to the virtual omnipresence of purpose in mental life he also simply reported what seemed to him a plain fact. As such a fact, it then became a matter of experimentation. Let us not forget that other subjects of present technical investigation in psychology have come to us from the same humble source. When Ebbinghaus invented methods by which certain forms of memory could be studied with great precision, his first questions in this field were clearly derived from a knowledge of memory which was acquired without the help of any experimentation. Everybody can gain similar knowledge in one part of psychology or another. No more is needed for this purpose than that he be interested in facts, and that he watch. Since in this fashion so much has been gained for psychology in the past, contempt for equally direct observation now and in the future would clearly be a dangerous attitude. Is further evidence to be accepted only if it is already polished with the special tools of science? I cannot believe that anybody will seriously recommend such a policy. It would deprive us of our best chances to extend our work beyond its present scope.

With these remarks in mind, we will now consider what happened when another psychological concept was imported from Europe. This concept was *insight*. It was brought over by the Gestalt psychologists. Since clouds of misunderstanding still seem to hide its meaning, I had better give a brief explanation. When a physicist wants to discover how a given system reacts to certain conditions, he observes two facts: the conditions to which the system is subjected, and the behavior of the system itself. Conditions are then varied, and if there are corresponding changes in the system, both the new conditions and the new states of the system are registered. Eventually, results are gathered in a table with two columns. In one column the various conditions which have been applied are enumerated; in the other, the corresponding states of the system are given. With considerable caution, which expresses itself in certain additional tests, it is then assumed that, when again exposed to the same conditions, the system will once more show the same reactions, and that therefore the relation between the data in the two columns represents a causal law. The physicist does not claim that causal connections as such can be observed; on the contrary, he maintains that, in his field, no such observation is possible. How, then, does the physicist protect himself against the possibility that chance rather than an actual causal connection is responsible for the relation of the data in his two columns? Since he has no means of deciding by direct observation he relies on certain indirect criteria. His whole procedure in this situation is called induction. It works to everybody's satisfaction. Curiously enough, no philosopher of science has so far been able to tell us precisely why it can be used with so much confidence.

When the first Gestalt psychologists came to this country they tried to convince their American friends that, in this respect, observation in psychology is often superior to observation in natural science. Mental facts, they said, are by no means always experienced as separate events. Rather, when we are aware of certain mental facts, we may at the same time be aware of causal relations between these facts. Actually, the immigrants maintained, instances of this kind occur in practically every moment of mental life, and among the most commonplace experiences. Suppose, for instance, that somebody lifts in succession a fountain pen and an ink pot, and that he then says, "The inkpot is heavier." Does this statement merely follow his actions as a separate further event? If we ask him, he will surely deny that this is a matter of a mere sequence in time. "When I talk," he will perhaps say, "I generally talk sense. In this particular case, for example, I knew that I talked about a relation which I had just perceived, and that the direction expressed in my statement was clearly caused by the direction found when I compared the two objects. Moreover, the latter direction, that involved in the relation as such, followed from the nature of the impressions which I had of these objects. In other words, not only were specific references of certain things to others given with these things themselves; the why of their sequence was also obvious throughout."

Another example: When a young man sees a lovely figure with a lovely face on top, and then finds himself moving in the direction of so much perfection, does he need the indirect techniques of induction for discovering that those lovely conditions and the displacement of himself as a system are causally related? Few will maintain that he does. Psychological causation may, of course, also be felt to operate in the opposite direction. Every year, before the fifteenth of April, some people make detours around their writing desks on which certain forms are spread, and find one excuse or another for being occupied elsewhere. This is called an avoidance response. In most responses of this kind those who do the avoiding know perfectly well what they avoid. Also, in our present example, the nature of the avoided objects appears to them as a most natural cause of their avoiding. Imagine somebody having to discover by induction that it is Form 1040 rather than the shape of some book on his desk which fills him with horror.

All these are instances of what the Gestalt psychologists call "insight." Some time before them, a philosopher, Wilhelm Dilthey, had the same facts in mind when he referred to *verständliche Zusammenhänge*—in English, "connections which are understood." Elementary connections in physics are not understandable for the simple reason that, as we have just seen, the physicist cannot observe such connections at all. He observes only facts of concomitance and of sequence, and can therefore never tell us what a causal connection actually is. But in psychology we have both: connections which we experience and understand, and others of which we know no more than physicists know of connections in their field. It was precisely this contrast which convinced the Gestalt psychologists that their term "insight" referred to an unmistakable characteristic of many mental situations. They did not mean, however, that insight is merely a further item which must be mentioned when so-called contents of human experience are enumerated. Rather, it was their suggestion that awareness of causal relations among mental facts largely contributes to the way in which mental activities take their course. For instance, thinking in any serious sense of the word would, from their point of view, be impossible in the absence of insight.

So far, psychologists in this country have not shown much interest in the observations to which I have just referred. And yet the very make-up of the mental world is here involved. If our awareness of a mental situation gave us only the same kind of evidence as the physicist obtains from his observations, such a situation would have to appear to us as an array of functionally unrelated facts—until the scene was studied with the techniques of induction; and the same would hold for our awareness of mental sequences. Since we actually experience that certain parts of the scene are causally related to others, any treatment of mental processes which ignores this insight is, of course, utterly misleading.

The American tradition is averse to nonexperimental forms of observation. It would therefore have been advisable not to insist too much on the simple kind of evidence from which the concept of insight had been derived. The conditions under which insight arises, and the consequences which it may have, can surely be investigated in perfectly orthodox experimentation. If a few American psychologists who did work of this kind had been more strongly supported, insight itself might gradually have been accepted by all in spite of the way in which it was first observed. Clearly it must be possible to combine the American insistence upon precise procedures with the European tendency first of all to get a good view of the phenomena which are to be investigated with so much precision. Both trends have their good points and their weaknesses. As always in the contact of two cultural traditions, optimal achievements may be expected if the weaknesses of both cancel each other, while their virtues are strengthened by cooperation.

There is no reason why we should be pessimists in psychology. We already know many things in this science, and if William James could see what we are now doing, his judgment would surely be far more favorable. He might criticize the fact that there is still less coherence among our findings than would seem desirable. But while at present this criticism would probably be justified, we need not feel discouraged on this ground. Facts in science have a way of coming together, and becoming coherent, almost on their own account. Recently I put my ear to the ground in psychology and listened. Underneath, the findings of psychology were stored just as wines are stored in French cellars. In these cellars, the wines ripen, and then taste so much better and stronger. The improvement is probably brought about by a slow chemical reaction. It seems to me that, as the result of a similar fermentation, the products of psychology are now also gaining more power. At least, while I listened, something obviously stirred in our cellar. We ought to be prepared for the time when our drink is ready. But do we all prepare ourselves? To drop my alcoholic metaphor, occasionally a psychologist makes the impression of being somewhat tired by the debates of the past, and of not being interested in major issues for this reason. In this mood he will still do one experimental investigation after another; but he will prefer to stay within a circumscribed area in which he feels safe. It would be most unfortunate if, as a result, a certain conservatism were to develop in psychology. Actually, even outstanding men have sometimes encouraged such an attitude. For instance, it has been said with approval that psychology now tends to be eclectic. Again, we have been told that in psychology we had better stay in the middle of the road. I cannot agree with these prescriptions because, if they were followed, psychologists would have to look first of all backward. In an eclectic attitude, they would be too much concerned with ideas which are already available; and, in attempting to find the middle of the road in psychology, they would have to give too much attention to the tracks along which others have moved before them. Such attitudes could perhaps be recommended if, in research, security were an important issue. Actually there is no place for it in this field. In research, we have to look forward, and to take risks.

It is interesting to see how our great ancestors in science felt about such matters. At least in this respect, a look backward ought to be instructive. Some time ago, I therefore turned to the history of physics. The first man I saw there was Galileo. Apparently he was not at all in an eclectic mood; for he was just writing the last sentences of a devastating attack on Aristotelian physics and astronomy, his *Dialogue on the Two Chief Systems of the World, that of Ptolemy and that of Copernicus*. His face was firm and grim, and made me fear that he might actually hurl the book at the Aristotelians. My next information came to me when I was sleeping. I dreamed that I met Faraday. "What are you now investigating?" I asked him. "Unfortunately," the great man answered, "I have no time for conversation. I am much too busy reversing figure and ground all over physics. The result will be called field physics." Clearly, Faraday had not even heard of a middle-of-the-road in natural science.

The attitudes which people assume in a science are, of course, largely determined by the situation in which this science finds itself at a given time. Some years ago, the situation in psychology may actually have been such as to make a certain amount of caution desirable. I do not believe that we need hesitate quite so much at present. In fact, the situation in psychology may soon change to such a degree that fairly long steps can be taken without fear.

Bibliography of the writings of
Wolfgang Köhler   compiled by
Edwin B. Newman

Akustische Untersuchungen. I. *Zeitschrift für Psychologie,* 1909, 54, 241–289. (Doctoral dissertation also published separately as *Akustische Untersuchungen. I.* Leipzig: Johann Ambrosius Barth, 1909.)

Akustische Untersuchungen. II. *Zeitschrift für Psychologie,* 1910, 58, 59–140.

Physiologisch-psychologische Untersuchungen über den Tonsinn. *Verhandlungen der Deutschen Otologischen Gesellschaft auf der zwanzigsten Versammlung in Frankfurt a. M., 2 und 3 Juni, 1911.* Jena: Verlag von Gustav Fischer, 1911, 412–417.

Bibliographie der deutschen und ausländischen Literatur des Jahres 1910 über Psychologie, ihre Hilfswissenschaften und Grenzgebiete. *Zeitschrift für Psychologie,* 1911, 59, 331–473.

Über akustische Prinzipalqualitäten. *Bericht über den 4. Kongress für Experimentelle Psychologie, Innsbruck, 1910.* Leipzig: Johann Ambrosius Barth, 1911, 229–233.

Bibliographie der deutschen und ausländischen Literatur des Jahres 1911 über Psychologie, ihre Hilfswissenschaften und Grenzgebiete. *Zeitschrift für Psychologie,* 1912, 62, 321–496.

Bemerkungen zu G. Zimmermann's Aufsatz: "Zur Physik und Physiologie der Schallbewegung." *Pflüger's Archiv für die gesamte Physiologie,* 1912, 146, 147–150.

Akustische Untersuchungen. *Bericht über den 5. Kongress für experimentelle Psychologie, Berlin, 1912.* Leipzig: Johann Ambrosius Barth, 1912, 151–156.

Akustische Untersuchungen. III und IV (Vorläufige Mitteilung). *Zeitschrift für Psychologie,* 1913, 64, 92–105.

Psychologische Beiträge zur Phonetik. *Archiv für experimentelle und klinische Phonetik,* 1913, 1, 11–26.

Zur Funktionsprüfung bei Aphasischen. *Münchener Medizinische Wochenschrift,* 1913, 60, 2651. (Summary of talk given at the 1658th regular session of Aerztlicher Verein, Frankfurt a. M., on October 20, 1913, and summary of subsequent discussion.)

Über unbemerkte Empfindungen und Urteilstäuschungen. *Zeitschrift für Psychologie,* 1913, 66, 51–80.

Akustische Untersuchungen. III. *Zeitschrift für Psychologie,* 1915, 72, 1–192.

Optische Untersuchungen am Schimpansen und am Haushuhn. *Abhandlungen der Königlich Preussischen Akademie der Wissenschaften* (Berlin), physikalisch-mathematische Klasse, 1915 (Whole No. 3).

Die Farbe der Sehdinge beim Schimpansen und beim Haushuhn. *Zeitschrift für Psychologie,* 1917, 77, 248–255.

Intelligenzprüfungen an Anthropoiden. I. *Abhandlungen der Königlich Preussischen Akademie der Wissenschaften* (Berlin), physikalisch-mathematische Klasse, 1917 (Whole No. 1).

Nachweis einfacher Strukturfunktionen beim Schimpansen und beim Haushuhn. Über eine neue Methode zur Untersuchung des bunten Farbensystems. *Abhandlungen der Königlich Preussischen Akademie der Wissenschaften* (Berlin), physikalisch-mathematische Klasse, 1918 (Whole No. 2).

Sinnesphysiologie der höheren Tiere (mit Ausschluss des Menschen). *Jahresbericht über die gesamte Physiologie*, 1920, 70–77.

Die physischen Gestalten in Ruhe und im stationären Zustand: Eine naturphilosophische Untersuchung. Braunschweig: Friedr. Vieweg & Sohn, 1920. (Republished: Erlangen: Verlag der Philosophischen Akademie, 1924.)

Intelligenzprüfungen an Menschenaffen. Zweite durchgesehene Auflage. Berlin: Julius Springer, 1921. (Reprinted: Springer Verlag, Berlin und Heidelberg, 1963.)

Die Methoden der psychologischen Forschung an Affen. In Emil Abderhalden (Hrsg.), *Handbuch der biologischen Arbeitsmethoden.* Berlin: Urban & Schwarzenberg, 1921 (Abt. 6, Teil D), 69–120.

Forschungen an Menschenaffen. *Zeitschrift für Ethnologie*, 1921, 52, 461–465. (This is not a paper by Wolfgang Köhler, but a report on a paper read by him.)

Zur Psychologie des Schimpansen. *Psychologische Forschung*, 1922, 1, 2–46.

Über eine neue Methode zur psychologischen Untersuchung von Menschenaffen. *Psychologische Forschung*, 1922, 1, 390–397.

Zur Theorie der stroboskopischen Bewegung (Im Anschluss an die Untersuchung Hartmanns). *Psychologische Forschung*, 1923, 3, 397–406.

Zur Theorie des Sukzessivvergleichs und der Zeitfehler. *Psychologische Forschung*, 1923, 4, 115–175.

Tonpsychologie. In G. Alexander und O. Marburg (Hrsg.), *Handbuch der Neurologie des Ohres.* Berlin, Wien: Urban & Schwarzenberg, Band 1, 1. Hälfte, 1923–1924, 419–464.

Bemerkungen zum Leib-Seele-Problem. *Deutsche medizinische Wochenschrift*, 1924, 50, 1269–1270.

The problem of form in perception. In *Proceedings of the 7th International Congress of Psychology.* Cambridge: Cambridge University Press, 1924, 22–28.

The problem of form in perception. *British Journal of Psychology*, 1924, 14, 262–268.

Gestaltprobleme und Anfänge einer Gestalttheorie. *Jahresbericht über die gesamte Physiologie und experimentelle Pharmakologie.* Band 3. Bericht über das Jahr 1922 (published in 1924), 512–539.

The Mentality of Apes. Translated from the 2nd revised edition by Ella Winter. New York: Harcourt, Brace & World, Inc., 1925. (Also London: Kegan Paul, Trench, Trubner & Co., Ltd., 1924.)

Intelligence of apes. In C. Murchison (Ed.), *Psychologies of 1925.* Worcester, Mass.: Clark University Press; London: Oxford University Press, 1926, 145–161. Also in *The Pedagogical Seminary and Journal of Genetic Psychology,* 1925, 32, 674–690.

An aspect of Gestalt psychology. In C. Murchison (Ed.), *Psychologies of 1925.* Worcester, Mass.: Clark University Press; London: Oxford University Press, 1926, 163–195. Also in *The Pedagogical Seminary and Journal of Genetic Psychology,* 1925, 32, 691–723.

Komplextheorie und Gestalttheorie. Antwort auf G. E. Müllers Schrift gleichen Namens. *Psychologische Forschung,* 1925, 6, 358–416.

Zur Komplextheorie. *Psychologische Forschung,* 1926, 8, 236–243.

L'intelligence des singes supérieurs. Traduit sur la deuxième édition allemande par P. Guillaume. Paris: Librairie Félix Alcan, 1927.

Zum Problem der Regulation. *Wilhelm Roux' Archiv für Entwicklungsmechanik der Organismen,* 1927, 112, 315–332.

Carl Stumpf zum 21. April, 1928. *Kant-Studien,* 1928, 33, 1–3.

Zur Gestalttheorie. Antwort auf Herrn Rignanos Kritik. *Scientia,* 1928, 43, 309–322. (This is reprinted with minor changes as the first part of a longer discussion in *Psychologische Forschung,* 1928, 11, 188–202. Pages 202–234 of the article in the *Psychologische Forschung* are in answer to the reply of Rignano in *Scientia,* 1928, 43, 323–356, to *Scientia,* 1928, 43, 309–322 by Köhler. The original article by Eugenio Rignano was published in *Scientia* in 1927. There is an abbreviated translation of Rignano's critique in *Psychologische Forschung,* 1928, 11, 172–187, entitled Die Gestalttheorie.)

Bemerkungen zur Gestalttheorie. Im Anschluss an Rignanos Kritik. *Psychologische Forschung*, 1928, 11, 188–234. (Cf. previous item for comment.)

Gestalt Psychology. New York: Liveright Publishing Corp., 1929; London: Bell, 1930.

Ein altes Scheinproblem. *Die Naturwissenschaften*, 1929, 17, 395–401.

Concepto de asociación. *Archivos de la Sociedad de Biología de Montevideo, Suplemento: Actas del Congreso Internacional de Biología de Montevideo* (7–12 Octubre, 1930) (Fascículo 1, Sección "Biología General"), 1930, 19–24.

La perception humaine. *Journal de Psychologie normale et pathologique*, 1930, 27, 5–30.

Les forces motrices du comportement. *Journal de Psychologie normale et pathologique*, 1930, 27, 367–390.

Some tasks of Gestalt psychology. In C. Murchison (Ed.), *Psychologies of 1930*. Worcester, Mass.: Clark University Press; London: Oxford University Press, 1930, 143–160.

The development of physiological hypothesis as basic for experimentation. In *Proceedings of the 9th International Congress of Psychology*. Princeton: Psychological Review Co., 1930, 268–270.

Über einige Gestaltprobleme. In *Proceedings of the 9th International Congress of Psychology*. Princeton: Psychological Review Co., 1930, 270–272.

Das Wesen der Intelligenz. In A. Keller (Hrsg.), *Kind und Umwelt, Anlage und Erziehung*. Leipzig und Wien: Franz Deuticke, 1930, 132–146.

El problema de la psicologia de la forma. *Anales de la Sección de Orientación Profesional de la Escuela del Trabajo* (Año III, núm. 3), March 1930, 57–103. (Lectures, presumably four, in Barcelona in 1927.)

The new psychology and physics. *Yale Review*, 1930, 19, 560–576.

Some notes on Gestalt psychology. *The International Forum* (new series), June 1931, 1, 16–20.

Zur Boltzmannschen Theorie des zweiten Hauptsatzes. *Erkenntnis*, 1932, 2, 336–353 (*Annalen der Philosophie*, 1932, 10).

Wesen und Tatsachen. *Forschungen und Fortschritte*, 20 April, 1932, 8 (12), 152.

Carl Stumpf zum 85. Geburtstage, *Forschungen und Fortschritte*, 20 April, 1933, 9 (12), 179.

Zur Psychophysik des Vergleichs und des Raumes. *Psychologische Forschung*, 1933, 18, 343–360.

Psychologische Probleme. Berlin: Julius Springer, 1933. (Translation of *Gestalt Psychology*, revised and enlarged.)

Über die gegenwärtige Lage der Psychophysik. *Forschungen und Fortschritte*, 1 Mai, 1934, 10 (13), 168–169.

Über eine Wirkung von Bereichsbildungen im Spurenfeld. *Bericht über den 13. Kongress der Deutschen Gesellschaft für Psychologie, Leipzig, 1933.* Jena: Gustav Fischer, 1934, 144–145.

(With Hedwig von Restorff.) Analyse von Vorgängen im Spurenfeld. II. Zur Theorie der Reproduktion. *Psychologische Forschung*, 1935, 21, 56–112.

Psychological remarks on some questions of anthropology. *American Journal of Psychology*, 1937, 50, 271–288.

The Place of Value in a World of Facts. New York: Liveright Publishing Corp., 1938.

Dynamics in Psychology. New York: Liveright Publishing Corp., 1940. Also Grove Press, 1960 (Evergreen E–242).

The nature of associations. *Science*, 1941, 93, 466. (Abstract.)

On the nature of associations. *Proceedings of the American Philosophical Society*, 1941, 84, 489–502.

(Reports from Recipients of Grants from the Research Funds, Grant No. 528, 1941, $600.) Experimental schemes to demonstrate and to clarify the nature of the Höffding function in animals. *Year Book of the American Philosophical Society*, 1941, 170–172.

Kurt Koffka: 1886–1941. *Psychological Review*, 1942, 49, 97–101.

(With H. Wallach and D. Cartwright.) Two theories of visual speed. *Journal of General Psychology*, 1942, 27, 93–109.

A perspective on American psychology. *Psychological Review*, 1943, 50, 77–79.

New facts in visual perception. *Transactions of the New York Academy of Sciences*, 1944, 7, 39–42.

Max Wertheimer: 1880–1943. *Psychological Review*, 1944, 51, 143–146.

(With Hans Wallach.) Figural after-effects: an investigation of visual processes. *Proceedings of the American Philosophical Society*, 1944, 88, 269–357.

Value and fact. *Journal of Philosophy*, 1944, 41, 197–212.

Gestalt Psychology: An Introduction to New Concepts in Modern Psychology (Rev. ed.). New York: Liveright Publishing Corp., 1947.

(With Dorothy Dinnerstein.) Figural after-effects in kinesthesis. In *Miscellanea Psychologica Albert Michotte*. Louvain: Éditions de l'Institut Supérieur de Philosophie, 1947, 196–220.

(With David A. Emery.) Figural after-effects in the third dimension of visual space. *American Journal of Psychology*, 1947, 60, 159–201.

The humanists' sin of omission. *American Scholar*, 1948, 17, 97–98.

(With Richard Held.) The cortical correlate of pattern vision. *Science*, 1949, 110, 414–419.

Psychology and evolution. *Acta Psychologica*, 1950, 7, 288–297.

(With Julia Fishback.) The destruction of the Müller-Lyer illusion in repeated trials: I. An examination of two theories. *Journal of Experimental Psychology*, 1950, 40, 267–281.

(With Julia Fishback.) The destruction of the Müller-Lyer illusion in repeated trials: II. Satiation patterns and memory traces. *Journal of Experimental Psychology*, 1950, 40, 398–410.

Relational determination in perception. In L. A. Jeffress (Ed.), *Cerebral Mechanisms in Behavior: The Hixon Symposium*. New York: John Wiley and Sons, Inc.; London: Chapman & Hall, 1951, 200–243.

Direct currents of the brain. *Science*, 1951, 113, 478. (Abstract.)

(With Richard Held and Donald Neil O'Connell.) An investigation of cortical currents. *Proceedings of the American Philosophical Society*, 1952, 96, 290–330.

The scientists from Europe and their new environment. In F. L. Neumann et al., *The Cultural Migration: The European Scholar in America*. Philadelphia: University of Pennsylvania Press, 1953, 112–137.

Direction of processes in living systems. *Scientific Monthly*, 1955, 80, 29–32.

(With William D. Neff and Jonathan Wegener.) Currents of the auditory cortex in the cat. *Journal of Cellular and Comparative Physiology*, 1955, 45 (Suppl. 1), 1–24.

(With Jonathan Wegener.) Currents of the human auditory cortex. *Journal of Cellular and Comparative Physiology*, 1955, 45 (Suppl. 1), 25–54.

(With Donald Neil O'Connell.) Currents of the visual cortex in the cat. *Journal of Cellular and Comparative Physiology*, 1957, 49 (Suppl. 2), 1–43.

Perceptual organization and learning. *American Journal of Psychology*, 1958, 71, 311–315.

(With Pauline Austin Adams.) Perception and attention. *American Journal of Psychology*, 1958, 71, 489–503.

The present situation in brain physiology. *American Psychologist*, 1958, 13, 150–154.

The obsessions of normal people. Waltham, Mass.: Brandeis University, 1958. (A paper read at the inauguration of the Graduate School of Arts and Sciences of Brandeis University.)

Dynamische Zusammenhänge in der Psychologie. Bern und Stuttgart: Verlag Hans Huber, 1958. (Translation of *Dynamics in Psychology* by Gertrud Meili-Dworetzki.)

Estado actual de la fisiología del cerebro. *Revista de Psicologia General y Aplicada*, 1959, 14, 255–267. (Translation of The present situation in brain physiology, *American Psychologist*, 1958, 13, 150–154.)

Gestalt psychology today. *American Psychologist*, 1959, 14, 727–734.

Psychologie und Naturwissenschaft. *Proceedings of the 15th International Congress of Psychology, Brussels, 1957.* Amsterdam: North-Holland Publishing Company, 1959, 37–50.

The mind-body problem. In Sidney Hook (Ed.), *Dimensions of Mind: A Symposium.* New York: New York University Press, 1960, 3–23.

Gestalt psychology in 1962. *Psychologia*, 1963, 6, 3–6.

Movement aftereffects and figural aftereffects. *Perceptual and Motor Skills*, 1965, 20, 591–592.

Unsolved problems in the field of figural after-effects. *Psychological Record*, 1965, 15, 63–83.

A task for philosophers. In P. K. Feyerabend and G. Maxwell (Eds.), *Mind, Matter, and Method: Essays in Philosophy and Science in Honor of Herbert Feigl*. Minneapolis: University of Minnesota Press, 1966, 70–91.

Gestalt psychology. *Psychologische Forschung*, 1967, 31, xviii–xxx.

Werte und Tatsachen. Berlin und Heidelberg: Springer Verlag, 1968. (Translation of *The Place of Value in a World of Facts*.)

The Task of Gestalt Psychology. Princeton: Princeton University Press, 1969.

Il Posto del Valore in un Mondo di Fatti. Firenze: C/E Giunti—G. Barbèra, 1969. (Translation of *The Place of Value in a World of Facts*.)

REVIEWS

Lord Rayleigh, On the perception of sound, *Proceedings of the Royal Society London*, 1909. *Zeitschrift für Psychologie*, 1911, 58, 407.

J. Katzenstein, Über Probleme und Fortschritte in der Erkenntnis der Vorgänge bei der menschlichen Lautgebung, nebst Mitteilung einer Untersuchung über den Stimmlippenton und die Beteiligung der verschiedenen Räume des Ansatzrohres an dem Aufbau der Vokalklänge, *Passows u. Schaefers Beiträge z. Anat. usw. des Ohres usw.*, 1909. *Zeitschrift für Psychologie*, 1911, 58, 409.

Hermann Gutzmann, Zur Messung der relativen Intensität der menschlichen Stimme, *Passows u. Schaefers Beiträge z. Anat. usw. des Ohres usw.*, 1909. *Zeitschrift für Psychologie*, 1911, 59, 408–409.

F. Bezold u. Th. Edelmann, Ein bewegliches Modell des Schalleitungsapparates zur Demonstration seiner Mechanik, *Beitr. z. Anat. usw. des Ohres usw.*, 1909. *Zeitschrift für Psychologie*, 1912–1913, 63, 142.

W. Wojatschek, Über verschiedene Formen des sog. Trommelfelltonus, *Beitr. z. Anat. usw. des Ohres usw.*, 1909. *Zeitschrift für Psychologie*, 1912–1913, 63, 142–143.

K. L. Schaefer, Über eine Erweiterung der Anwendbarkeit des Struckenschen Monochords, *Beitr. z. Anat. usw. des Ohres usw.*, 1911. *Zeitschrift für Psychologie*, 1912–1913, 63, 143.

K. L. Schaefer, Über eine neue Methode der Schwingungszahlenbestimmung, *Verhdlgn. d. Deutschen otol. Ges.*, 20. Vers. in Frankfurt a.M. *Zeitschrift für Psychologie*, 1912–1913, 63, 143.

M. Bourdon, Un nouvel acoumètre, *Bulletin de la Société Scientifique et Méd. de l'ouest*, 1910. *Zeitschrift für Psychologie*, 1912–1913, 63, 143–144.

G. E. Shambaugh, Die Membrana tectoria und die Theorie der Tonempfindung, *Zeitschr. f. Ohrenheilk.*, 1909. *Zeitschrift für Psychologie*, 1912–1913, 63, 144.

V. Urbantschitsch, Über den Einfluss von Schallempfindungen auf die Sprache. *Arch. f. d. ges. Physiol.*, 1911. *Zeitschrift für Psychologie*, 1912–1913, 63, 144–145.

H. Marx, Methode zur Entlarvung der Simulation einseitiger Taubheit, *Zeitschr. f. Ohrenheilk.*, 1909. *Zeitschrift für Psychologie*, 1912–1913, 63, 145.

O. Voss. Ein neues Verfahren zur Feststellung einseitiger Taubheit, *Beitr. z. Anat. usw. des Ohres usw.*, 1909. *Zeitschrift für Psychologie*, 1912–1913, 63, 145.

Wittmaack, Zur Frage der Schädigung des Gehörorgans durch Schalleinwirkung, *Zeitschr. f. Ohrenheilk.*, 1909. *Zeitschrift für Psychologie*, 1912–1913, 63, 145.

C. Stumpf (Hrsg.), *Beiträge zur Akustik und Musikwissenschaft*, Heft 4, Heft 5. Leipzig: Barth, 1909, 1910. *Zeitschrift für Psychologie*, 1912–1913, 63, 146.

E. Waetzmann, Kritisches zur Theorie der Kombinationstöne, *Annal. d. Physik*, 1909. *Zeitschrift für Psychologie*, 1912–1913, 63, 146.

E. M. von Hornbostel, Über vergleichende akustische und musikpsychologische Untersuchungen, *Zeitschr. f. angew. Psychol.*, 1910. *Zeitschrift für Psychologie*, 1912–1913, 63, 146–149.

H. Schmotin, Untersuchungen über den Einfluss der Anämie und Hyperämie auf die Empfindungen der Hautsinne, *Zeitschr. f. Biologie*, 1909. *Zeitschrift für Psychologie*, 1912–1913, 63, 150.

E. Becher, Einige Bemerkungen über die Sensibilität der inneren Organe, *Arch. f. d. ges. Psychol.*, 1909. *Zeitschrift für Psychologie*, 1912–1913, 63, 150–151.

T. Sano, Zur Frage von der Sensibilität des Herzens und anderer innerer Organe, *Arch. f. d. ges. Physiol.*, 1909. *Zeitschrift für Psychologie*, 1912–1913, 63, 151.

C. Ritter, Experimentelle Untersuchungen über die Sensibilität der Bauchhöhle, *Arch. f. klin. Chirurgie*, 1909. *Zeitschrift für Psychologie*, 1912–1913, 63, 151–152.

W. Wojatschek, Einige neue Erwägungen über das Wesen der Seekrankheit, *Beitr. z. Anat. usw. des Ohres usw.*, 1909. *Zeitschrift für Psychologie*, 1912–1913, 63, 152.

M. Katz, Die Schilderung des musikalischen Eindrucks bei Schumann, Hoffmann und Tieck, *Zeitschr. f. angew. Psychol.*, 1911. *Zeitschrift für Psychologie*, 1912–1913, 63, 466.

Felix Auerbach, *Die Grundlagen der Musik (Wissen und Können, v. 18)*, Leipzig: Barth, 1911. *Zeitschrift für Psychologie*, 1913, 66, 283–284.

Karl L. Schaefer, *Musikalische Akustik*, 2. neubearb. Aufl. Berlin: Göschen, 1912. *Zeitschrift für Psychologie*, 1913, 66, 284–285.

C. Stumpf (Hrsg.), *Beiträge zur Akustik und Musikwissenschaft*, Heft 6. Leipzig: Barth, 1911. *Zeitschrift für Psychologie*, 1913, 66, 285–287.

Carl Stumpf, *Die Anfänge der Musik*. Leipzig: Barth, 1911. *Zeitschrift für Psychologie*, 1913, 66, 287–290.

Karl L. Schaefer, Über die Wahrnehmbarkeit von Kombinationstönen bei partiellem oder totalem Defekt des Trommelfelles, *Beitr. z. Anat. usw. des Ohres usw.*, 1913. *Zeitschrift für Psychologie*, 1913, 66, 292–293.

T. H. Pear, The experimental examination of some differences between the major and the minor chords, *Brit. J. Psychol.*, 1911. *Zeitschrift für Psychologie*, 1913, 66, 293–294.

T. H. Pear, The classification of observers as "musical" and "unmusical," *Brit. J. Psychol.*, 1911. *Zeitschrift für Psychologie*, 1913, 66, 294–295.

G. Anschütz, Tendenzen im psychologischen Empirismus der Gegenwart. Eine Erwiderung auf O. Külpes Ausführungen "Psychologie und Medizin" und "Über die Bedeutung der modernen Denkpsychologie." *Arch. f. d. ges. Psychol.*, 1912. *Zeitschrift für Psychologie*, 1913, 64, 441. (G. Anschütz's reply is in *Zeitschrift für Psychologie*, 1913, 66, 155–160.)

Zu den Bemerkungen von G. Anschütz, *Zeitschrift für Psychologie*, 1913, 66, 319–320. (G. Anschütz again replies, *Zeitschrift für Psychologie*, 1913, 67, 506. This is followed by Köhler's Schlussbemerkung, *Zeitschrift für Psychologie*, 1913, 67, 506.)

Ernst Kretschmer, *Körperbau und Charakter*. Berlin: Julius Springer, 1921. *Psychologische Forschung*, 1922, 2, 156–158.

Eugen Bleuler, Naturgeschichte der Seele und ihres Bewusstwerdens. Berlin: Julius Springer, 1921. *Psychologische Forschung*, 1923, 3, 170–171.

J. von Uexküll, *Umwelt und Innenwelt der Tiere*, 2. vermehrte und verbesserte Aufl. Berlin: Julius Springer, 1921. *Psychologische Forschung*, 1924, 5, 196–197.

J. S. Szymanski, Allgemeine Methodik zur vergleichenden Psychologie, In Abderhalden (Hrsg.), *Handb. d. biol. Arbeitsmeth.*, Teil D, Heft 1. Berlin u. Wien: Urban und Schwarzenberg, 1921. *Psychologische Forschung*, 1924, 5, 198–201. (Here Köhler also discusses his own article that appeared in the same volume, "Methoden der psychologischen Forschung an Affen.")

Gustav Kafka, Tierpsychologie. In G. Kafka (Hrsg.), *Handbuch der vergleichenden Psychologie*, 3 vols. München: Ernst Reinhardt, 1922, vol. 1: Die Entwicklungsstufen des Seelenlebens. *Psychologische Forschung*, 1924, 5, 206–207.

Karl Wessely, *Goethes und Schopenhauers Stellung in der Geschichte der Lehre von den Gesichtsempfindungen*. Berlin: Julius Springer, 1922. *Psychologische Forschung*, 1925, 6, 200.

George Humphrey, The theory of Einstein and the Gestaltpsychologie: A parallel, *Amer. J. Psychol.*, 1924. *Psychologische Forschung*, 1925, 6, 201.

Hermann Kranichfeld, Die Geltung der von W. Roux und seiner Schule für die ontogenetische Entwicklung nachgewiesenen Gesetzmässigkeiten auf dem Gebiete der phylogenetischen Entwicklung. In W. Roux (Hrsg.), *Vortr. u. Aufs. üb. Entwicklungsmechanik d. Organismen*, Heft 31. Berlin:

Julius Springer, 1922. *Psychologische Forschung*, 1925, 6, 202–204.

Valentin Haecker, Über umkehrbare Prozesse in der organischen Welt. In Schaxel (Hrsg.), *Abh. z. theor. Biol.*, Heft 15. Berlin: Gebr. Borntraeger, 1922. *Psychologische Forschung*, 1925, 6, 204.

Hermann Hoffmann, *Vererbung und Seelenleben: Einführung in die psychiatrische Konstitutions- und Vererbungslehre.* Berlin: Julius Springer, 1922. *Psychologische Forschung*, 1925, 6, 206–207.

Hermann Hoffmann, *Die individuelle Entwicklungskurve des Menschen: Ein Problem der medizinischen Konstitutions- und Vererbungslehre.* Berlin: Julius Springer, 1922. *Psychologische Forschung*, 1925, 6, 208.

Joseph Fröbes, *Lehrbuch der experimentellen Psychologie*, 2. und 3. umgearb. Aufl., Bd. 1. Freiburg i. Br.: Herder u. Co., 1923. *Psychologische Forschung*, 1926, 8, 398–399.

Johannes von Kries, *Allgemeine Sinnesphysiologie.* Leipzig: F. C. W. Vogel, 1923. *Psychologische Forschung*, 1926, 8, 399–405.

K. Fodor und L. Happisch, Die Bedeutung der Zeit zwischen zwei Vergleichsreizen bei Bestimmung von Unterschieds-schwellen; Untersuchungen am Gesichtsorgan. *Pflügers Archiv f. d. ges. Physiol.*, 201. *Psychologische Forschung*, 1926, 8, 409–410.

Nadie Kohts, *Untersuchungen über die Erkenntnisfähigkeiten des Schimpansen.* Moskau-Petrograd, 1923. *Psychologische Forschung*, 1926, 8, 410–411.

John A. McGeoch, *The Psychology of Human Learning.* New York: Longmans, Green & Co., 1942. *American Journal of Psychology*, 1943, 56, 455–460.

Norbert Wiener, *Cybernetics or Control and Communication in the Animal and the Machine.* New York: John Wiley & Sons, Inc., 1948. *Social Research*, 1951, 125–130.

INDEXES

Names

Adrian, E. D., 278
Allesch, G. J. von, 37 n.38
Allport, Gordon W., 406
Aristotle, 426, 429
Arnheim, Rudolf, 117
Asch, Solomon E., 108 n, 117
Augustine, Saint, 426
Avenarius, Richard, 125

Barron, D. H., 272, 278, 280 n.9
Benussi, Vittorio, 30 n.30, 111
Bergson, Henri, 37 n.38, 159, 160
Bethe, A., 305
Beyle, Marie Henri. See Stendhal
Blackman, L. S., 302
Bohr, Niels, 251
Bremer, F., 256
Brentano, Franz, 33
Brown, K. T., 288, 290

Cornelius, Hans, 14 n.2
Crutchfield, Richard S., 408 n

Darwin, Charles, 172, 330, 359, 360

Day, R. H., 299
Descartes, René, 329, 330, 387, 390
Dilthey, Wilhelm, 68, 368, 432
Driesch, Hans, 307
duBois-Reymond, Emil, 277
Duncker, Karl, 93, 117, 140

Ebbinghaus, Hermann, 108, 429
Eccles, John C., 272
Eddington, A. S., 113, 167, 250, 251
Ehrenfels, Christian von, 110, 164, 165, 381, 382, 383, 384, 385, 395

Faraday, Michael, 434, 435
Fechner, Gustav Theodor, 108, 324 n
Fehrer, Elizabeth, 285, 286 n.18
Feigl, Herbert, 77, 81, 82, 83, 84, 88, 89, 94
Fishback, Julia, 120, 295, 296, 299, 300
Fogelsonger, H. M., 174 n
Fox, B. H., 283
Freud, Sigmund, 401

Subjects